10872438

Radical Paradoxes

PETER CLECAK

Radical

DILEMMAS OF THE AMERICAN LEFT: 1945–1970

Paradoxes

HARPER & ROW, PUBLISHERS

New York, Evanston,
San Francisco, London

For Hazel Peter

Portions of this book originally appeared in *The Massachusetts Review, Modern Occasions,* and *The Nation.*

Excerpt from *Monopoly Capital* by Paul Baran and Paul Sweezy (New York: Monthly Review Press) copyright © 1966 by Monthly Review Press. Reprinted by permission.

Excerpt from "To Posterity," in *Selected Poems of Bertolt Brecht,* translated by H. R. Hays, copyright 1947 by Bertolt Brecht and H. R. Hays. Reprinted by permission of Harcourt Brace Jovanovich, Inc.

FIRST EDITION

Designed by Dorothy Schmiderer

Library of Congress Cataloging in Publication Data

Clecak, Peter.
    Radical paradoxes.
    Includes bibliographical references.
    1. Radicalism—United States—Addresses, essays, lectures. 2. Right and left (Political science)—Addresses, essays, lectures. I. Title.
HN90.R3C55 1973   322.4'4'0973   73-4072
ISBN 0-06-010819-3

Contents

Perhaps the only prophetic oracular utterance we should pay attention to is one that tells us things will be worse than we hope, and possibly not as bad as we fear.

—D. W. Brogan

Socialism in our time is undergoing a crisis. It is not a crisis of existence, for our age has seen the arrival of socialism on a scale that surpasses the fondest hopes of socialists of the past generation. . . . Nevertheless, when we look not to its outward manifestations of success but to its inward state of mind, there is no doubt that socialism is in crisis.

—Robert L. Heilbroner, "Roots of the Socialist Dilemma"

Preface

I began this study in the middle 1960s with the simple intention of clarifying my own inner doubts about the nature and relevance of contemporary socialisms. At the outset I concentrated on the radical paradox of powerlessness, the seemingly permanent separation of power and goodness in America. Yet the clear absence of a political bridge from the present social organization to a new one raised more fundamental doubts about the value of radical visions, not only in the United States but elsewhere. In search of clarification I turned to a group of politically independent old Left critics—C. Wright Mills, Paul Baran, Paul Sweezy, and Herbert Marcuse. In their postwar writings, each of these men developed, explored, and attempted to resolve their own doubts about the radical enterprise. Of course I could have focused on any number of illuminating social critics on the Left—Paul Goodman, Irving Howe, Carey McWilliams, Eugene Genovese, William Appleman Williams, I. F. Stone, Noam Chomsky, Michael Harrington. But I chose to concentrate on these four figures for personal reasons as well as for the intellectual considerations outlined in Chapter 1.

Mills was the first American radical critic I encountered as an undergraduate in the late fifties. I read *The Power Elite* with enormous enthusiasm. As a graduate student at Stanford, I met Baran in his last years and studied political economy with him informally. After Baran's death, Paul Sweezy helped me in countless ways, offering generous criticism of my work and providing constant encouragement. My interest in Marcuse developed initially out of student demand in the middle sixties. Since the critics represented in Part I of this study were among my most important teachers, I suppose there is some attempt to settle accounts with them. But this motive is as minor as it is presumptuous, for I cannot hope to repay them, especially with a study that has turned out to be far more critical than I originally intended it to be. Throughout, I have attempted to trace their separate radical odysseys as a way of illuminating my own. In the process of completing this eccentric design, the larger intention of making a contribution toward clarifying the inner crisis of American and Western socialism emerged. I hope this volume will contribute to that important collective venture.

A note on terms. Since I follow more or less conventional usage, the context should generally delimit the meaning of such terms as "radical," "old Left," "new Left," "socialism," and "communism." There are nevertheless unavoidable ambiguities (not to mention implicit ideological choices) in any lexicon of the Left. "Radical" is perhaps the vaguest and most inclusive member of this cluster of concepts. Without denying its possible usefulness in describing phenomena on the Right, I use it first of all to refer to individuals and groups who espouse critical analyses and alternative visions of social organization (which in North America range from the mildest sort of socialism to utopian variants of anarchism and communism). Second, "radical" designates styles of personal and social action that may include but are not confined to traditional modes of electoral politics—protest, demonstration, confrontation, and long-range programs of public education.

In this broad sense, old Leftists and new Leftists are considered "radicals." The old Left includes those shifting theoretical positions and political organizations which were dominant, say, from the end of World War I until the late fifties. The primary reference points are the Marxist and ex-Marxist sectors whose members defined themselves within or against changing Stalinist (Communist Party), Trotskyist, and social democratic views of capitalism, socialism, communism, and the politics of transition. In a sense, the chapters in Part I constitute extended definitions of several independent old Left intellectuals whose political imaginations were partially forged within the caldron of these debates. The "new Left," as I use the term, refers to the resurgence of radicalism in the 1960s, especially the organizational structures, moods, and ideological currents that culminated in proposals for political and cultural revolution toward the end of the decade. Its subsequent history—if it does not disappear without a political trace—is yet to be created.

I employ "Communist" (or "socialist" in some contexts) to designate parties and nations which consider themselves socialist, or at least in the theoretical and political forefront of the transition to socialism and communism. The specification of these latter terms generally conforms to my own reading of the classical Marxian pattern of a two-stage modulation from capitalist (or neocolonial) social orders. Chapter 2 provides fuller definitions and refinements of these terms, and Chapter 8 includes a discussion of the main principles of democratic socialism.

Many friends, colleagues, and students have helped to shape the ideas developed in this study. My greatest obligations are to Donna Boyan, G. William Domhoff, Corky Fikes, Eugene Genovese, Richard Gillam, Kay Voegelin, and Rick Voegelin. I also owe a special debt to Cynthia Merman, a patient, generous, and skilled editor. And I wish to thank the following people who have read all or parts of the manuscript at various stages of its growth: Gar Alperovitz, Angus Cameron, Emile Capouya, Michael DePorte, John Diggins, Frank Donner, Raul Fernandez, Jim Flink, Henry Gutierrez, Jerry Graff, Robert Heilbroner, Irving Howe, Abby Israel,

Diranne Kelekyan, Christopher Lasch, Alan Lelchuk, Frank Lentricchia, Ralph Miliband, Stanley Moore, Carlos Muñoz, Loren Okroi, Spence Olin, Howard Sherman, William A. Williams, and Albert Wlecke.

Vivian Clecak has taken time from her own career to participate in every stage of this book's development. As my most concerned critic and editor, and my closest friend, she has contributed in ways that cannot be measured.

Through their warm encouragement and frequently heated criticism, each of these people counterbalanced solitary hours of research and writing, proving once more that the preparation of a book is ultimately a social act. Whatever merit this study may possess in its final form is due largely to their patient commentaries on the several drafts. The faults, of course, must remain my responsibility.

Parts of this book have been published elsewhere, in somewhat different form. The chapter on Mills first appeared in *Modern Occasions* (Winter 1972). The chapter on the new Left, along with brief portions of the concluding chapter, was published in *The Massachusetts Review* (Summer 1971). Preliminary versions of the chapters on Marcuse and Baran appeared in *The Nation* (June 16, 1969, and February 22, 1971). Permission of the editors of these periodicals is gratefully acknowledged.

P.C.

History as a way of learning . . . can offer examples of how other men faced up to the difficulties and opportunities of their eras. Even if the circumstances are noticeably different, it is illuminating, and productive of humility as well, to watch other men make their decisions, and to consider the consequences of their values and methods.

—William Appleman Williams, *The Contours of American History*

1

Radical Paradoxes

Americans, in the main, do not cultivate what Nietzsche called "the sixth sense," the sense of history. We create history for others to study, and we re-create the past to strengthen optimistic myths about the present and the future. Recently, in a national atmosphere of pessimism, many people have come to suspect that history is being made behind their backs. Yet beneath these divergent colorations of mood lies the implicit assumption that we *ought* to fashion our own personal and social destinies, if necessary, against stubborn outside forces. It was therefore quite in character for young American radicals to renounce the feeble old Left in the early 1960s, and soon after to ransack the past for romantic figures and heroic movements of opposition. By resurrecting ghosts from the tomb of American radicalism—Eugene Debs, Big Bill Haywood and the Wobblies, Woody Guthrie—young Leftists created myths for their movement. What they could not risk, however, was a steady exercise of the sixth sense, because a clear understanding of the old Left between the end of World War I and the Eisenhower era would have prefigured the severe

1

political and historical constraints on their own emerging ambitions.[1]

The modulation from social analysis to myth was therefore an inescapable consequence of the search for a new radicalism that would avoid the obvious failures of the old. For by 1960 the ideologies and organizations of the old Left had virtually collapsed. The essential outlines of the story are familiar:[2] in the early twenties, many American radicals looked to the Soviet Union as the incarnation of socialism in history, a dream turning into reality if not directly before their eyes, then no more than an ocean away. Lincoln Steffens's celebrated remark, "I have been over into the future and it works," conveys the buoyancy that permeated much of the American Left immediately after the October Revolution.[3] That future did work, though not toward the fulfillment of early hopes. To many radicals who neither made nor betrayed the Russian Revolution, forty years of Soviet reality—most of it gray, some of it bloody—constituted a record of persistent failure. Yet the Soviet Revolution and its aftermath remained at the center of their political imaginations, an old vision turned into nightmare. The history of the old Left before 1960 is largely a record of men who, at one point or another, shattered their revolutionary illusions by measuring various socialist and communist ideals against Soviet realities. From the suppression of the rebellious sailors at the Kronstadt naval base in 1921 to Khrushchev's 1956 revelations about the reign of Stalin, a succession of historical moments tried and broke the faith of American Leftists.[4]

The Marxist sectors of the old Left concentrated on the international fortunes of socialism primarily because of their domestic political isolation and frustration. After the First World War, the fragmented groups never amounted to a politically significant force.[5] In fact, "by the middle twenties," as Christopher Lasch observes, "American radicalism had acquired the characteristics it has retained until the present day: sectarianism, marginality, and alienation from American life."[6] Though formed in the luxury of historical retrospect, Lasch's conclusion, in my view, accurately summarizes the political fate of the old Left, a fate sealed before the resurgence of radicalism in the 1930s and its subsequent decline in the forties and fifties.[7] During the initial fifteen years of cold war, the political far Left survived only as a collection of antique sects—the American Communist Party, several Trotskyist splinters (which divided with the compulsion of cells), and an assortment of other marginal groups. Beyond these organizations was a scattering of intellectuals with neither party nor program. The political irrelevance of the sects and the isolation of independent figures brought the vital "two-way intellectual traffic between criticism and protest" to a halt.[8] Without a mass movement, radical theory in America was stripped of its primary rationale: the consummation of thought in political action.

Thus, by the early 1960s, when Daniel Bell proclaimed the end of ideology, young radicals found most independent intellectuals on the Left nearly as antiquated as the insular sects. Though unaffiliated with any political party or group, such critics as C. Wright Mills, Paul Baran, Paul Sweezy, and Herbert Marcuse were nevertheless tied to their own radical pasts. What could such men—over forty, removed from politics, bound to obsolete visions, and inhibited by memories of old debates over Stalinism—contribute to a new radicalism? Very little, it was commonly supposed, beyond the example of their political failure.

This answer, as the sixties demonstrated, was both incomplete and premature, perhaps fatally so. Many of the charges against the old Left (especially the early analyses by such critics as Staughton Lynd, Tom Hayden, James Weinstein, and Howard Zinn) do strike me as essentially justified. But the intellectual odysseys of independent critics still retain much of their interest, if only because they "offer examples of how other men faced up to the difficulties and opportunities of their eras." In a slightly different time, under somewhat different circumstances, these men tried to define and resolve what I call "radical paradoxes." Each is an intrinsically interesting figure, a social critic educated primarily in one academic discipline, yet not constrained by the usual borders:

Mills was a sociologist; Baran and Sweezy, economists; Marcuse, a philosopher. Despite international reputations, they have generally been confined to the margins of American academic and intellectual life through various combinations of ignorance and abuse.[9] In Part I, I attempt to redress this critical imbalance by drawing intellectual portraits of these figures.

But this study is more than an effort at restoration. For the independent intellectuals whom I consider also bridge both phases of the Left. They all experienced a part of the sixties, reacting to those eventful years in both similar and idiosyncratic ways. Moreover, the new Left, especially those sectors which turned to militant schemes for political and cultural revolution, repeated what Richard Hofstadter has termed the "tragic rhythm of American radicalism," imitating rather than avoiding the central errors of their predecessors. In Part II, I contend that Mills, Baran, Sweezy, and Marcuse each illuminate a phase in the progress (or regress) of the new Left during the sixties: Mills was influential in the early stages when political issues concerned the extension of democracy and civil rights; Baran and Sweezy came into play in the "revolutionary" and third-world phase (after 1964); and Marcuse importantly prefigured themes of the cultural revolution beginning in the latter part of the decade. Taken together, then, these critics (in the order of their appearance) recapitulate the main course of American radicalism in the sixties.[10] Beneath what now appears as stale rhetoric, inflexible positions, mistaken assumptions, and false hopes lies the substance of their personal search, which has taken the form of an extended examination of the nature and historical fate of socialism, the most crucial public question of this century.

Though the ideological and organizational shapes of the Left in America have changed considerably during the first quarter century of cold war, the paradoxes confronting every sector retain their general forms. This amorphous collection of theoretical positions, moods, and organizations ranging from the fringe of the Democratic Party to the revolutionary sects may be larger than at any time in the postwar years. But it remains at roughly the same political impasse in the early seventies as it was after the collapse of the Progressive Party in the late forties. Various individuals and groups agree generally about their opposition to advanced capitalism, and in less precise ways on the need for a less repressive or even nonrepressive socialist society.[11]

Apart from a fluid core of similar assumptions, however, there is no consensus about the current organization of social reality, the vision of a just society, or a politics of transition. The return to a crude Marxism in the middle sixties only reactivated old diseases of the Left: anti-intellectualism, sectarianism, isolation from the main currents of American life, and, in the end, organizational collapse. Both the disintegration of Students for a Democratic Society and the subsequent failure of the emerging adult Left to form effective groups leave a political vacuum only partially disguised by the proliferation of radical sentiments. As the energy of opposition multiplies—among young people, workers, ethnic and racial minorities, the poor, women, and disillusioned professionals —it generally disappears into politically ineffective channels. While revolutionary splinter groups organize tiny vanguards for a hopeless showdown with "the imperialist monster," a majority of those on the Left continue to be isolated, demoralized, and politically inconsequential.

We are a divided nation, apparently unable to resolve our multiple social crises, yet powerful enough to threaten the very survival of mankind in the quest to preserve the essential features of the current social order. And we have a relatively small, divided Left, thus far politically powerless to alter substantially either the domestic or the international course of the country. This, in the starkest terms, constitutes the ideological and historical framework of "radical paradoxes."[12] As Mills remarked, "the intellectual who remains free may continue to learn more and more about modern society, but he finds the centers of political initiative less and less accessible. . . . In the world of today the more his knowledge of affairs grows, the less impact his thinking seems to have. If he grows more frustrated as his knowledge increases, it seems that knowledge leads to powerlessness."[13] More often than not, it appears that there is no political "ground on which theory and practice, thought and action meet."[14]

The gap between radical social theories and the narrow contexts of radical politics in postwar America seems unbridgeable. Whether imagined as peaceful or violent, dramatic or gradual, revolutionary change from capitalism to socialism remains politically impossible, however desirable it may be in theory. It is by now a tedious script: throughout the twentieth century, the developing capitalist order has simply deflected those diverse radical challenges it did not absorb.[15] Like the many spokes of an endlessly turning wheel, conflicting radical analyses and proposed courses of action meet at the still center of powerlessness—so much motion without appreciable movement. Powerlessness (or, at best, partial power within the current system) still engulfs the Left from one side of the spectrum to the other, affecting desperate conspiratorial groups willing to launch a violent revolution without a supporting chorus of the masses, no less than the cautious democratic socialists working for medium-range structural reforms.

This situation may change, perhaps even rapidly, though its directions cannot be predicted with assurance, as I suggest in the closing chapter. A more modest assumption underlies the main body of this study: in the quarter century following World War II, the overwhelming powerlessness to achieve intermediate or long-range socialist ends has made every theoretical resolution of the general form of radical paradoxes politically unsatisfactory; and this disparity between social aims and social realities, rather than admittedly important lapses in theory, defective visions, and fratricidal "politics," largely accounts for the marginal impact of the Left on American life. *Viewed from every serious radical perspective, the historical situation itself has enforced the paradox of powerlessness on Leftists of every ideological cast.*

Although this aerial view of the entire postwar American Left obscures important differences in theory, vision, and politics, it does bring the unifying condition of powerlessness into sharp relief. But this is not the only facet of the problem, and in the longer view perhaps not the most important. Another set of factors arising from conflicts between personal and public values adds a complicating dimension. What can the intellectual do if he is "strongly opposed to the current drift of American society, yet equally strongly committed to certain liberal values, such as rational inquiry, intellectual freedom, tolerance, and civilized discourse . . ."?[16] Cutting across the entire Left, this dilemma defines and exacerbates divisions among groups and within individuals. In the most elemental terms, ethical paradoxes of radical intellectuals arise from conflicts between liberal, humanistic values and neo-Marxist analyses of the dominant forces of modern history. Even from the social and political vantage points of liberals, the issue assumes disturbing proportions, since their basic personal values have been ineffective guides to the formation of public policy throughout the long season of cold war. The defense of democracy abroad has turned out to be the defense of a series of regimes, ranging from the openly despotic to the minimally democratic, united mainly in their opposition to genuine, desperately needed social revolutions and in their willingness to provide attractive investment opportunities for American multinational corporations.[17]

And in the pursuit of democracy, personal freedom, and social justice at home, liberals have lost enough ground to cast serious doubt on the political adequacy of their leading intellectual and moral assumptions. Even the *idea* of pluralistic democracy barely survives the realities of government by plain deception, packaged public figures, frequently repressive law enforcement, and increasingly visible imbalances of economic power that distort the democratic intent of political and judicial institutions. As rational, skeptical men of intelligence, the best liberal intellectuals fully expect wide disparities between their aspirations and the complexities of industrial and postindustrial societies. But for those who continue to envision roughly coherent mediations between ethics and politics, the depth and intensity of the cleavages bring on moods of despair. Understandably so. In a tortured polemic, Harry Ashmore concedes that what survives of liberalism "can best be described as a cast of mind and a code of personal conduct." The liberal, he maintains, does not know what to do, only "what not to do—what indeed he cannot do without abandoning the values he lives by."[18]

Left intellectuals who accept humanistic values and democratic norms confront an even more painful dilemma arising from their rejection of an economic and social order that most liberals ultimately defend. Few would deny that the American system preserves important values in some of its institutions: "It should not be necessary," Eugene Genovese reminds us, "even in these crazy times, to defend the genuine achievements of our national culture, among which we may find a profound commitment to personal freedom, political participation and social justice."[19] But this recognition turns liberal problems into radical paradoxes, for these norms apparently remain tied to a corrupt and irrational system which largely vitiates them. As Christopher Lasch observes, liberal values "have come to be embodied in a social order resting on imperialism, elitism, racism, and inhuman acts of technological destruction."[20] Viewed from various radical perspectives, historical systems exist as dynamic wholes whose economic, social, political, and cultural parts, though of mixed weight and value, are inextricably bound together. How, then, does an opponent of the general drift of society address himself to those parts he wishes to aid in preserving? What stands are both politically and ethically viable—immediately and over the long haul?

During the 1960s, the main tendency of political and cultural revolutionaries in America, and more generally in the West, seemed to shift away from the ethical dilemmas I have sketched out. Various groups and mass-media figures regarded them as hangovers from a defeated radical past that persisted because of a continuing dependence on "bourgeois" modes of thought, feeling, and moral response. In diverse syntheses of theory, vision, and politics, they sought power and moral purity through total repudiation of Western society and culture, of its institutions and ideologies no less than its leading intellectual and moral assumptions. The euphoric and desperate atmosphere of those years made it possible to dismiss ethical paradoxes, at a price some have not yet calculated. Like their predecessors, however, new Leftists could not long fail to recognize their powerlessness. And after the collapse of illusions, old problems reasserted themselves.

Put simply, how can the perennial dilemma of revolution versus reform be adequately redefined and morally resolved under the contemporary cloud of political powerlessness? Neither the old Left nor the new could solve this puzzle. In making the difficult decision to suspend personal values in the name of future social ends, revolutionaries frequently lost sight of both, if only because of their frustrating powerlessness against larger social forces. Their total opposition to advanced capitalist society resulted in total failure. But the impossibility of revolution as a mode of transition to socialism only underscores the inadequacies of reform. Although they may raise new demands for reform while probing pressure points of the system, radicals have not yet seriously endangered the operation of the whole, and in many instances have actually strengthened it. Helping to secure a modicum of social justice for themselves and others, radicals who engage in a politics of reform simultaneously lend indirect support to the antihumanist values imposed by the American social order, especially at the peripheries of its informal empire. Nor have transitional strategies of change, combining selected, politically feasible measures with longer-range socialist aims, made very convincing headway. The American working class, the pivot of various Marxian theories of transition, simply declined its "historic mission." Rather than embarking on either major road to socialism, it divided into at least two sectors—a blue-collar segment (the modern equivalent of Marx's proletariat) and a diverse collection of white-collar groups (clerks, teachers, professionals, technicians, middle-level managers and bureaucrats) that has been provisionally subsumed under the heading of the new working class, a fuzzy theoretical category in search of a politics.

Radical paradoxes take on added complexity when examined in

relation to the badly fragmented socialist world. The Soviet Union and the Communist countries of Eastern Europe, as well as the relatively underdeveloped countries (such as China, North Korea, parts of Southeast Asia, and Cuba), have obviously distorted socialist ideals in their quite different attempts to enact them. Indeed, the Soviet experience suggests the massive difficulties, perhaps even the impossibility, of constructing a genuine socialist society against the obstacles of economic backwardness, hostile foreign powers, and the lack of a well-organized, democratic working class. Nor is it yet clear whether the political and moral costs of modernization under authoritarian regimes permanently distort their futures, precluding a transition to democracy even at advanced stages of socialist development.

The overriding question, then, that haunted many independent old Left intellectuals, remains unanswered, however significantly the terms have changed: does either major bloc of nations—Communist in name, protosocialist in form, socialist and communist in professed intention—embody the material and institutional *potentialities* to evolve toward decent human environments that eliminate the gross inequalities and injustices associated with Western capitalisms? If so, what forms of opposition and cooperation might intellectuals in socialist nations pursue? This is, of course, a delicate matter that outsiders immune to the personal and political consequences of their speculations must approach tentatively. Political as well as moral considerations nevertheless compel American Leftists to examine the forms that radical paradoxes assume in Communist societies. For specific characterizations of these dilemmas elsewhere in the world must influence perceptions of their changing forms in the United States.

The political and ethical dimensions of radical paradoxes seem complete, especially to those in the West who wish to preserve humanistic values as personal guides to public action and as social—indeed, socialist—ends. The paradoxes may induce paralysis, tempting the intellectual on the Left to renonunce "social action" because it always "requires him to pass through that customs office of political realism which deprives him of all those values he holds most dear."[21] But radicals of every vintage resist this species of purity because it subverts their commitment to participate in change through various combinations of analysis and political action.

Defined in its broadest sense, the imperative of action remains in full force, even when ethical norms stand in a paradoxical relation to current political and social options. Thus radical intellectuals who did not deliberately seek patterns of flight into metapolitical regions have had to resolve the dilemmas through uneasy syntheses of theory, vision, and politics. Changes in social structures and political options, as well as the cumulative weight of the critics' own experience, have made for an interesting spectrum of responses over the past quarter century. Those who resisted political sects tended to devise distinctive compromises between ideals and social realities. But the persistence of dominant configurations of power has also limited their range of alternatives. Hence in addition to commenting on radical paradoxes—an obvious, often fruitful way of managing double binds—independent intellectuals have often very subtly modulated from social analysis to utopian myth, a pattern most blatantly exhibited by elements of the new Left in the sixties. The nature of their compromises and the progress toward myth form a major center of interest throughout this book.

Of course the new Left of the sixties was not simply a mirror image of the old. Yet the striking resemblances are unmistakable even if many of the participants refused to recognize one another. It may be argued that the question is dead, a matter for historians. That is partly true: the sixties, as I suggest in Part II, did bring a period of American radicalism to a close—perhaps two periods. But to forget what happened by consigning it to the category of the past, however recent, seems a dangerous concession to the cultural spirit of incessant innovation. Politically unaffiliated Leftists must still work out, perhaps eventually out of, the perspective of radical paradoxes, for there is as yet no general formula for resolving them without abandoning or seriously compromising one of the essential elements: neo-Marxist analysis or socialist ends, humanistic values or a commitment to immediate political action.

Every serious person on the Left has confronted and defined radical paradoxes in the postwar era. Many, perhaps even a majority, have held more than one view. For clear reasons: "consistent" resolutions, as I shall argue, lack sustained plausibility since they impose an arbitrary order on rapidly changing situations. They also require rigid moral illusions that only symbolically attenuate harsh human realities and disappointing social trends. But full acceptance of the paradoxes entails the experience of ambiguity, which has limited psychological appeal. Thus any temporary "solution" is highly elusive and, to one degree or another, unsatisfactory. It is also a personal matter, though one hopes it has public implications. Rooted in differing structures of temperament and diverse experiences, conflicting orientations to radical paradoxes are not beyond argument, though they may lie beyond resolution through analysis. No one on the Left has been able to solve these puzzles. No one could have solved them. But each of the critics I shall consider defines the issues in different and I think partially valid ways. The interplay between the personal and public aspects of their distinctive odysseys should serve to illuminate our own.

Part I

THE PLAIN MARXISTS

How do socialists act when they have enough power to influence, but not to basically change, capitalism? Must they either righteously, and ineffectively, abstain from exerting this influence, or should they use it and thus strengthen the system they hate by making its exploitation more rational and tolerable?

—Michael Harrington, *Socialism*

2

The Argument

Although not primarily a depiction of the postwar Left, the intellectual portraits of C. Wright Mills, Paul Baran, Paul Sweezy, and Herbert Marcuse in the chapters ahead do characterize the common themes of radical paradoxes; together, they illustrate one important direction of the search for tolerable resolutions during the quarter century following World War II. Radical paradoxes haunted Left intellectuals of every theoretical cast. However strongly they disagreed about political opportunities in the long run, these critics shared a general awareness of the massive power and essential stability of the American social order. This is one source of the deep undercurrent of pessimism running through their work of the fifties and after. The other derives from the suspicion that world history, having either destroyed or endlessly deferred their socialist hopes, had also passed them by. Forced by the conditions of their age to be men without a party, these critical rationalists nevertheless wanted their ideas to matter, to have public impact. The desire for historical relevance, along with the persistence of socialist visions, distinguished them from other

15

American scholars and critics. These seemingly incompatible aspirations also narrowed their moral and political alternatives.

In the first phase of the cold war, intellectuals who sought historical resonance for their hopes and ideas lived in the magnetic field of the principal antagonists. Wanting to connect their visions with a living social system that might develop into a genuine socialist society, many flirted with one side or the other. The ablest critics generally resisted full identification with either the United States or the Soviet Union, since neither was immediately attractive from socialist points of view. America remained belligerently antisocialist and anti-Communist after the defeat of the Axis powers, accelerating the cold war while consolidating a new kind of sprawling empire without colonies.[1] During the McCarthy period, when Left politics had collapsed, independent intellectuals who stayed within the Marxian tradition were intimidated, isolated, often unable to find work; those identified with the American Communist Party faced prison and exile. With the sad exception of Julius and Ethel Rosenberg, however, most dissenters were not forced into silence by the threat of execution: to be a character in opposition during those years demanded a measure of courage and stoicism, but generally not heroism. In fact, the preservation of a comparatively wide scope of personal and political freedom sustained the slim hopes for a new politics of the Left.

On the other side, the economic structure of the Soviet Union was nominally socialist, or at least protosocialist.[2] And apart from the virtual occupation of bordering European countries after the war, it did not launch a program of neoimperialist expansion comparable to the American enterprise that drained the wealth and prolonged the misdevelopment of African, Asian, and Latin-American nations. For some intellectuals, especially Baran and Sweezy, the chief historical questions concerned the probable future of socialism in the Soviet Union and Eastern Europe: was Stalinism essentially a transitional phenomenon that would result in full industrialization of the U.S.S.R., despite heavy damage inflicted by the Nazis and military encirclement by Western powers? More important, would the economic and social achievements of Stalinism cancel its totalitarian premises and permit gradual democratization? The immediate ethical dilemma was whether intellectuals in the West could support regimes that, for whatever extenuating reasons, prevented free inquiry, suppressed political opposition, and often precluded the exercise of simple personal decency.

In such circumstances, any coherent, historically relevant outlook required attenuation or abandonment of at least one major element of radical paradoxes: neo-Marxist theory, socialist and communist visions, or the insistence on tolerable connections between personal values and democratic public norms. The interests of consistency and the demands of sanity required unhappy compromises. A majority of those who did not defect from the Left or wholly cast aside Marxian perspectives suppressed the paradoxes by remaining uncritically pro-Stalinist or anti-Communist.[3] Though now and then attracted by the consistency of these polar positions, independent intellectuals could never completely exorcise the dilemmas. In retrospect, then, their theoretical odysseys and moral quandaries remain more interesting if not always more personally agonizing than those of men fully identified either with the State Department or with a Marxist party.

Apart from the sects, there were two principal clusters of independent Left intellectuals: the anti-Stalinist (or democratic) socialists gathered around the journal *Dissent,* and the "plain Marxists."[4] Democratic socialists such as Irving Howe, Lewis Coser, Bernard Rosenberg, and more recently Michael Harrington, confronted radical paradoxes in similar ways without ever forming a consciously unified political force. For these critics, liberal democratic norms became the overriding criteria of political action and historical evaluation. Howe regards this emphasis as "the greatest lesson of contemporary history: the unity of socialism and democracy. To preserve democracy as a political mode without extending it into every crevice of social and economic life is to make it increasingly sterile, formal, ceremonial. To nationalize an economy without enlarging democratic freedoms is to create a new kind of social exploitation. Radicals may properly and fraternally disagree about many other things; but upon this single axiom, this conviction wrung from the tragedy of our age, politics must rest."[5]

This attitude softened certain elements of radical paradoxes. Democratic socialists categorically opposed every postwar society that did not guarantee extensive personal freedom and political liberty. For them, the socialism of Communist countries was permanently authoritarian, a cruel caricature and full negation of original ideals. But they simultaneously rescued their images of socialism from its contemporary manifestations: living moderately well though "in the shadow" of political and ideological "defeat," Howe and Coser could still declare in the middle fifties that *"socialism is the name of our desire.* And not merely in the sense that it is a vision which, for many people throughout the world, provides moral sustenance, but also in the sense that it is a vision which objectifies and gives urgency to their criticism of the human condition in our time."[6] Believing that socialism had failed everywhere, these intellectuals could, in clear conscience, refrain from entering another round of sectarian politics; many had been there once before during brief encounters with Trotskyist groups in the late thirties and early forties. Reduced to a slim domestic base of operations, democratic socialists defended America's defensible institutions and values while remaining critical of its dominant social structures. And they criticized aspects of United States foreign policy while supporting its overriding aim, the containment of Communism.[7]

Their mode of resolution had serious defects beyond political marginality and isolation from larger historical trends. While claiming a moral monopoly on the Left, democratic socialists tailored their ideals—even the ideal of liberty—to grim historical and political imperatives. In the last analysis they blunted the ethical dimensions of radical paradoxes by adopting a double standard, a posture at once rigorously, even rigidly, applied to authoritarian socialisms in the East and indulgently used to evaluate capitalist democracies in the West. But only in the last analysis. Whereas the weakest of these figures engaged in tedious moralizing, the best (including Howe and Harrington at their best) have respected the paradoxical and problematic implications of their analyses of contemporary affairs. Their complex attitudes toward America enabled them to attain a small measure of historical relevance (or at least a mode of intellectual survival) in the fifties, and the bare beginnings of a democratic socialist program in the late sixties.[8]

As a leading proponent of democratic socialism, Howe has also led an aggressive critique of "plain Marxists," characterizing them as "authoritarian Leftists." In 1965 he observed that "Sweezy's *Monthly Review* is the main spokesman in this country for the view that authoritarianism is inherent or necessary in the so-called socialist countries; that what makes them 'socialist' is simply the nationalization of the means of production; that democracy, while perhaps desirable in some long-range calculation, is not crucial for judging the socialist character of a society; that the claim that workers must be in a position to exercise political power if the state can in any sense be called 'theirs,' is a utopian fallacy,"[9] Though partially valid, Howe's intemperate judgment vulgarizes the shifting positions of able critics. It is both ungenerous and wrong to dismiss "plain Marxists" as immoralists who abandoned the complexities of their world in favor of rigid, deterministic ideologies. Their theoretical efforts, as I shall demonstrate, involved a clear if not always consistent and sophisticated recognition of the changing nature and historical implications of radical paradoxes.

The later Mills, Baran, Sweezy, and Marcuse are all "plain Marxists." Their similarities set them off from democratic socialists; their differences set them off from one another. Generally undogmatic and politically independent, these men use classical Marxism as a methodology rather than as a body of sacred texts.

According to Mills, "plain Marxists (whether in agreement or disagreement) work in Marx's own tradition. . . . They treat Marx like any great nineteenth-century figure, in a scholarly way; they treat each later phase of Marxism as historically specific. They are generally agreed that Marx's work bears the trademarks of the nineteenth-century society, but that his general model and his ways of thinking are central to their own intellectual history and remain relevant to their attempts to grasp present-day social worlds."[10] The plain Marxists do not solely address the common themes of radical paradoxes. Despite important differences in background, outlook, temperament, and style, they also illustrate a discernible pattern of adjustment to endless deferments of the socialist promise in America, and to betrayals and defeats elsewhere. Taken together, the chapters ahead on Mills, Baran, Sweezy, and Marcuse trace the main intellectual development of old Left critics who confronted the bewildering postwar world with the hope of balancing all the elements of radical paradoxes, if not immediately in the United States, then on a global scale. Whereas democratic socialists typically attenuated the dilemmas by insisting upon the unity of socialism and democracy, "plain Marxists" came to insist on the unity of socialism (or, more precisely, communism) and community. This difference proved to be decisive.

The pattern of resolution embodied by the plain Marxists as a group rests on a major theoretical ambiguity—ultimately, I think, a serious confusion—which Stanley Moore delineates in a remarkable essay on "Utopian Themes in Marx and Mao." Moore suggests that the current worldwide debate among Marxists remains opaque because the participants consistently refuse to distinguish the fundamental aims of revolution in the twentieth century. The proletarian revolution projects two goals: "Negatively, it must abolish exploitation by establishing a classless economy. Positively, it must construct a new community to replace the old society."[11] The elimination of exploitation, in the precise Marxian sense,[12] requires at least the substitution of socialist for capitalist forms of economic organization, whereas alienation can be ended only by a rebirth of community. As Moore puts it: "The socialist principle of distribution—to each according to his contribution—marks accomplishment of the first task, the transition from class to classless society. The communist principle of distribution—to each according to his needs—marks accomplishment of the second task, the transition from society to community. Transition to socialism is inaugurated by establishing proletarian dictatorship; transition to communism, by withering away of the state."[13]

Marx was deliberately vague about the specific character of these revolutionary aims, and he took more than one view of the mode, timing, and circumstances of the transition to postcapitalist societies.[14] In his mature writings, however, the two tasks of proletarian revolution are serially defined. Briefly describing the separate stages of socialism and communism in the *Critique of the Gotha Programme* (1875), Marx observes that the broad outline of a communist society[15] cannot be projected as if it would develop "on its own foundations," but rather as it *"emerges* from capitalist society; which is thus in every respect, economically, morally and intellectually, still stamped with the birth-marks of the old society from whose womb it emerges."[16] Socialism not only intervenes between capitalism and communism; its specific contours depend on the presocialist society from which it evolves, the moment of its birth, and the character of the human agents and the class agency of revolution.

Marx then sketches in the essential continuities and differences between bourgeois and socialist societies. As long as the majority of men live under the domination of material scarcity, he argues, the fundamental bourgeois form of *quid pro quo* (the principle of equivalent exchange) must loosely govern individual behavior as well as social production and distribution. In fact, this is the most civilized principle, the signal moral achievement of presocialist society. Capitalism, however, applies the concept primarily to "commodity exchange," and hence only on "the average." Dominant classes still control the mechanisms for extracting huge portions of the surplus. But socialism extends the principle of equivalent exchange to the "individual case," because each man can contribute nothing except his labor and can receive only "individual means of consumption."[17] Under socialism, then, the individual acquires a purchasing power roughly equivalent to his work: "the individual producer receives back from society—after the deductions have been made—exactly what he gives to it."[18] The bourgeois principle of *quid pro quo* is thereby transformed from an essentially ideological notion that conceals an exploitative reality into the working principle of the transitional society: "from each according to his ability, to each according to his work."

In contrast to exploitative, multiclass societies of the past, socialism was to have been essentially a single-class society, a democratic dictatorship of the proletariat.[19] This seemingly contradictory notion makes sense only in the context of Marx's leading assumptions concerning the nature and circumstances of the transition. He anticipated that by the time political power changed hands, the proletariat would constitute the decisive majority in technologically advanced capitalist nations. And since it had to develop democratic habits and ideas in the course of the struggle against the old order, the proletariat would also be a democratic majority. Until the surviving bourgeois elements disappeared, however, democratic methods of rule could not be extended to the whole of society. But this limitation presented no major theoretical problem, because Marx conceived of socialism as a brief interlude between a highly developed capitalism and communism.

Having criticized bourgeois society for perpetuating a grotesque disparity between democratic pretensions and practices, Marx goes on to illuminate the historical limitations of socialism, arguing that full realization of the principle of equivalent exchange is no more than a step toward genuine equality, liberty, and fraternity. Enactment of the principle of equal rights—economic, social, and political—cannot eliminate individual inequities, because "equality" in this case consists primarily in a uniform external standard of measurement (in Marx's example, "labour").[20] Just as an equal distribution of a limited supply of goods excludes the variable of differing individual needs, the *quid pro quo* criterion of measuring productive performance excludes variations in individual abilities such as intelligence, levels of physical energy, and temperament. Hence an equal right under capitalism and socialism remains fundamentally a right of *"inequality in its content."*[21]

Genuine equality requires rights that are unequal instead of equal.[22] This communist conception cannot be fully translated into social practice, however, until a society establishes general material abundance and virtually abolishes work as an externally imposed, instrumental activity. These achievements remove the social necessity for measuring either individual performance (ability) or individual need against external standards. Under communism, all men could realize their differing capacities through creative activity—through labor as opposed to work—while satisfying their unequal needs by appropriating goods from an abundant storehouse. "Only then," Marx declares, "can the narrow horizon of bourgeois right be fully left behind and society inscribe on its banners: from each according to his ability, to each according to his needs."[23] A wholly new outer world would reflect and reinforce man's changing consciousness and moral vision. Alienation, which in Marx's view arises from scarcity and the division of labor, disappears. As the repressive functions of the state become superfluous, it gradually turns into a mechanism for administering things, not men. Democracy, the preferred method for resolving conflicts among alienated men, also becomes obsolete, though its essence—liberty, social justice, and tranquillity—is preserved in a harmonious social whole. Socialist society evolves into a vast communist community.

According to this paradigm, then, socialism signifies the end of economic exploitation and the full realization of bourgeois democratic rights (excluding, of course, most property rights). But a democratic socialism does not, it should be emphasized, establish community, or what Marx called "a voluntary association in which the free development of each is the condition of the free development of all." And since it does not include the creation of a

Gemeinschaft community, socialism cannot fully overcome alienation.[24] This is the promise of communism, a later and fundamentally higher stage beyond capitalism and socialism.

Moore traces contemporary confusions of the distinct goals of revolution to a central tension in classical Marxism: "On the one hand . . . [Marx's] theory of history is a *sociology of change,* focused on analyzing the interaction of technology and institutions. On the other hand, it is a *dialectic of liberation,* focused on exposing the sham freedoms of capitalist culture." The account of the transition to socialism is "very largely based upon his sociology of change." It consists of a series of projections of historically possible changes—changes in consciousness, institutions, and relations of power that were both materially feasible and at least politically plausible in the latter part of the nineteenth century. But Marx's "account of the transition from socialism to communism is almost entirely based on his dialectic of liberation." It is a utopian fantasy whose realization would require a quantum leap out of history. The dominant tension between historical and utopian strains persists in various combinations throughout classical Marxism, connecting the early manuscripts with the later works of political economy.[25]

Versions of this same tension also characterize the entire course of Marxian theory and politics in the twentieth century. In what follows, I assume that since no country has eliminated scarcity or work—or even promised to do so—the idea of communism remains utopian in theory and impossible in practice. Even the tendency to regard socialism as a "prelude to communism" has often "proved a serious hindrance to facing, rationally and empirically, the problems of improving existing socialist societies."[26] Among orthodox Marxists, communism has all too frequently functioned as an ideology concealing the failures and limitations of socialism. As Moore contends, "the experience of half a century dictates rejecting—as romantic and utopian in theory, oppressive and reactionary in practice—the Marxian call for a new birth of *Gemeinschaft.*"[27]

The problems of contemporary socialism, as well as its prospects, are more ambiguous. Though the primary goals of ending exploitation and establishing democracy as a means of widening the scope of human freedom survived the nineteenth century, the conditions of success outlined by Marx never fully materialized. In no case did a politically self-conscious proletariat become a democratic majority in a relatively advanced capitalist nation with a sophisticated technological capacity and a systemic inability to avert crisis and collapse. As a conditional perspective, then, the paradigm has been cruelly vindicated: democratic socialism repeatedly failed to make its way into history because a widespread belief in the main aims never coexisted with the social conditions for its political success.[28] The fundamental paradox of powerlessness, or at best partial power, has therefore plagued everyone in the Marxian tradition—in the U.S.S.R., in Western Europe and North America, and throughout the underdeveloped world. Socialism, in this view, is either a discredited illusion of the past or a future possibility.

Yet the classical goals of Marxian socialism, often mingled with utopian elements, survived as powerful ideologies that affected the course of twentieth-century history. Instead of replacing centers of capitalism and spreading to underdeveloped areas, as Marx predicted, a new kind of socialism was born in conditions of backwardness.[29] It was not introduced by a democratic proletarian majority but rather by surrogate historical agents and agencies— parties acting in the name of small urban proletariats and large peasantries. Having come into history through an unexpected entrance, it did not successfully proceed to Western Europe and North America. Backward or authoritarian socialism took root in undemocratic soil, first in the Soviet Union and later in Eastern Europe, China, and parts of the third world. The democratic dictatorship of the proletariat, which Marx hoped for, became a dictatorship over the proletariat and other elements of these societies. And if the old classes gradually disappeared, new mechanisms of limited exploitation emerged.[30]

But despite the horrors of Stalinism—despotic rule, denial of basic freedoms, abrogation of elementary legal guarantees, and severe restrictions on consumption—the Soviet Union managed to fulfill the first installment of the socialist promise. Against the internal impediments of backwardness and the external menaces of Western capitalism and fascism, it established the basic preconditions of a socialist society: food, clothing, housing, medical care, education, useful work, and moderate amounts of leisure. Though in an earlier stage of a different pattern of development, China too has made spectacular beginnings. And considering the narrow historical options of perpetual misdevelopment or revolution, a majority of the poor nations of the world increasingly look to some form of socialism, often reluctantly, as their only way out of endless misery.[31]

I accept, in a general way, neo-Marxist analyses of the dominant historical trends of this century—away from capitalism and toward varieties of socialism. But I do not share the very different utopian illusions of orthodox Communists and Maoists. Authoritarian socialism, often achieved by prolonged and brutal revolutions, seems the chief historical option for most men in our time. And yet it would be foolish to minimize the pain associated with ambiguous progress. As Isaac Deutscher observed, "The impossibility of disentangling progress from backwardness is the price that not only Russia and China but mankind as a whole is paying for the confinement of the revolution to the underdeveloped countries. But this is the way history has turned; and now nothing can force its pace."[32]

At most, then, authoritarian socialist societies may yet achieve full socialism; they may abolish or vastly reduce exploitation and develop democratic institutions, while altering the kinds and lowering the degrees of alienation. This remains a goal within history: existing communist nations may become democratic, just as capitalist nations of the West may find their distinctive ways to new forms of democratic socialism. The importance of democracy as a goal cannot be overstressed, for as long as *Gesellschaft* societies based on the division of labor and scarcity remain historically necessary—under advanced capitalism and varieties of socialism —individual rights need to be protected by and from the whole society. Democracy is a fragile historical potentiality that must be repeatedly won and defended, for it is the only humane alternative to dictatorship and hence a necessary constituent of a just society.[33] To abandon it in the name of a chimerical community without alienation entails the sacrifice of individuals to larger and inevitably more repressive collectivities. Though such a course may be prerequisite to overcoming economic backwardness in some parts of the world, ideologies of development should nevertheless be analyzed bluntly rather than celebrated uncritically as shortcuts to a communist utopia. Especially in the West, where hunger, disease, and illiteracy are not the main impediments to a just society, the utopian cure of community, imagined as a substitute for democratic socialism, may well be worse than the disease of alienation. In short, then, I assume that socialism, including modes of democracy and alienation, is possible and desirable in history, and that communism, going beyond conventional democracy and alienation, is not.

Using these basic assumptions about the transition to postcapitalist societies, I attempt to describe, analyze, and evaluate the distinctive intellectual odyssey of each plain Marxist, and to define the overriding pattern these critics illustrate during the postwar years. Baran and Sweezy's initial characterizations of radical paradoxes were based on essentially Leninist versions of the Marxian paradigm, adapted to backward nations: they believed that the movement to communism would entail a far longer detour through authoritarian and democratic phases of socialism than Marx imagined.[34] By the middle fifties, this theory was being severely tested in the arena of history, since socialism, defined narrowly as a classless society, should have begun to realize its democratic potentialities in nations where backwardness had been largely conquered. Baran and Sweezy worked within this perspective, whereas Mills and Marcuse played with it skeptically. Considering the slim historical and political options open to socialists, the prospect of an eventual transition to communism seemed remote. Like their anti-Stalinist counterparts on the Left, most plain Marxists looked for partial resolutions to radical paradoxes within history, and for the beginnings of complete resolutions in their own time. They used the ideal of communism as a critical concept to expose the inadequacies of present social structures, and on occasion to rationalize the ugly aspects of authoritarian socialisms. Displacing their visions of full social justice well into the communist future, these thinkers retained a tenuous contemporary relevance without wholly sacrificing their claims to ethical respectability.

By the end of the fifties, however, they shared deep anxieties about the tortuous progress of socialist countries in shaking off the authoritarian legacy of their pasts. Tolerance for dictatorships that neither widened democratic rights appreciably nor reduced alienation at an acceptable rate approached the breaking point. And the old paradigms of Marx and Lenin, which most Western intellectuals had discarded long before, rapidly lost their plausibility as rational vehicles of radical faith. At the same time, the emergence of a new stage of Maoism, the accelerated revolutionary activity throughout the third world, along with the rise of a semianarchistic, semiexistentialist new Left in the Western countries, created new prospects and new problems. Latent tensions between the historical and utopian strains of Marxism reappeared in exaggerated forms. Once the received paradigms of transition were shelved, critics had to confront the old problem of the role and timing of consciousness in social change. For it could no longer be supposed that consciousness would evolve along with the institutional transformations from capitalism to socialism to communism. Without new men, any revolution remained in permanent danger of betrayal. Rather than growing out of present social formations and structures of consciousness, the transition to communism would have to be insinuated into history by collective acts of will. Only a heroic new breed of men could hope to remake old societies.

Thus the failures of socialism—its defeat in the West and its reversals elsewhere—made utopian perspectives all the more inviting as the sixties wore on. Each of the plain Marxists contributes something to this transition from plausible visions of socialism within history to impossible visions of communism based on the dialectic of liberation. Mills, who did not begin with a vaguely pro-Soviet commitment or with utopian illusions about a communist future, worked out of an eclectic sociology of change, attempting to forge a radical theory and politics that would contain the best features of traditional Marxism and liberalism. Rejecting myths of the communist hero, he reached back to the nineteenth century for images of the free and rational man, the human key to his most hopeful visions of the future. He died in 1962 before having to confront the hard choices that the others were forced into later in the decade.

Baran and Sweezy initially saw the socialist countries as historically progressive efforts to lay the economic and social foundations of a more rational order that would eventually develop into communism. Baran died in 1964, struggling to preserve this illusion. Sweezy cast off his earlier sociology of change, arguing that the creation of a new communist man must begin in the first stages of the revolutionary process. He placed his hopes in Maoism as the only authentic way of resolving moral paradoxes in the Communist world (and as a *deus ex machina* that might destroy imperialism). And Marcuse, after a bout with the darkest sort of pessimism, contended that a new man must come into existence before any genuine political revolution could occur in the West: to create a truly communist—or "liberated"—society, small groups must initially internalize a postindustrial, postrational sensibility and morality.

The basic pattern thus exhibits a certain symmetry. Taken together, plain Marxists of the postwar period reversed older priorities of social change in order to save their long-range moral

and social visions; they moved away from awkward characterizations of radical paradoxes within history toward projected resolutions beyond history, exchanging the broken promises of socialism
for illusions of communism. Though each made some contribution,
the reversal culminates in the later work of Sweezy and Marcuse.
Instead of insisting on a democratic socialism whose arrival
seemed endlessly delayed, they made more ambitious, utopian
claims on the historical present, confusing the struggle for democracy with the abolition of alienation. It is not surprising to find
that mythic modes of thought appeal powerfully to the very young
and to those who have spent the better part of their lives exploring
and refining their radical commitment in the shadow of defeat. Yet
despite their submission to utopian mirages, the plain Marxists'
collective failure to resolve radical paradoxes remains a respectable and illuminating one that deserves a fairer examination than it
has yet received.

Nowadays men everywhere seek to know where they stand, where they may be going, and what—if anything—they can do about the present as history and the future as responsibility.

—The Sociological Imagination

3

C. Wright Mills:

The Lone Rebel

For C. Wright Mills, the sociological imagination represented the most comprehensive mode of social vision in the twentieth century. It does not focus exclusively on what he calls "the personal troubles of milieu," which "occur within the character of the individual and within the range of his immediate relations with others." Nor does it merely illuminate "the public issues of social structure," which "have to do with the organization of many . . . milieux into the institutions of an historical society as a whole." Rather, the sociological imagination entails a comprehensive effort to "grasp history and biography and the relations between the two within society."[1] Beyond this, it is a form of self-consciousness, a way of defining oneself both as a character and as an actor in the historical present. Mills's generally optimistic perspective suggests the possibility of breaking out of the confining round of ignorance and confusion enforced by merely personal and local points of view. But when it leads to the conclusion that there is nothing to do about "the present as history and the future as responsibility," this critical mode of vision may also generate its own kind of

31

despair: fear and bitter knowledge take the place of anxiety and ignorance.

Mills's main theoretical investigations of American society led him toward despair as the sociological imagination brought the grim realities of the 1950s into focus. Rather than succumb to the mood, however, he continued to search for ways out of the national and international impasse. A man without a party, a movement, or a received ideology, he worked alone, cutting against the grain of the smug "American celebration" that devitalized the intellectual life of his time. He was thrown back on the formidable strengths of his personality—moral vision, courage, and determination—and the tools of his craft: reason and historical analysis. As Ralph Miliband observed, Mills was "a man on his own, with both the strength and also the weakness which go with that solitude. He was on the Left, but not of the Left, a deliberately lone guerrilla, not a regular soldier. He was highly organized, but unwilling to *be* organized, with self-discipline the only discipline he could tolerate."[2]

Because of his restless energy and compelling presence, Mills was easily turned into a hero, a man larger than life. But if he possessed heroic marks, he also shared the defects of representative men of his time. Though his faults and merits have been discussed publicly since his death in 1962, no clear portrait emerges, in part because friends and enemies saw him differently, in part also because he was a tissue of contradictions, a complex man. As Harvey Swados remarked, Mills was "egomaniacal and brooding, hearty and homeless, driven by a demon of discontent and ambition, with faith only in the therapy of creative work, whether intellectual or physical. . . . In all of his writing, as in his lecturing and his public stance, and indeed in his private existence, it was the blending of these forces that gave his work and life its ineluctable impact, its sense of a powerful mind and a forceful personality at grips not with the petty and the ephemeral but with the profoundly important questions."[3]

In the welter of conflicting recollections, Mills's intellectual seriousness stands out. Replying to critics of *The Power Elite,* he describes his conscious attitude toward the subtle interplay of public truth and private mood with a characteristic simplification that sacrifices nuance and detail to boldness and clarity: "the world I'm trying to understand does not make me politically hopeful and morally complacent, which is to say, I find it difficult to play the cheerful idiot. . . . I'm a very cheerful type, but I must say that I've never been able to make up my mind whether something is so or not in terms of whether or not it leads to good cheer. First you try to get it straight, to make an adequate statement. If it's gloomy, too bad; if it's cheerful, well fine."[4]

His major intellectual thrust in the late forties and the fifties reflects a continuing, systematic attempt to make an "adequate statement" about the separation of knowledge and moral vision from power in America. In the process of this enterprise, Mills worked his way into the impasse of radical paradoxes, earning by a steady effort whatever pessimism marked his later years. After *The Power Elite,* he tried to exorcise doubts about the future in his usual way, through a therapy of work. During the final years of a career ended abruptly in midflight, Mills divided his energies, launching an ambitious search for new theoretical perspectives and frenetically publicizing his concerns about the rapid drift toward global catastrophe. These major movements—the extended definitions of radical paradoxes and the attempted resolutions—deserve separate consideration.[5]

American Dilemmas

The chief elements of radical paradoxes are clearly, often painfully, registered in Mills's postwar writings. His studies of the major echelons of American society—*The New Men of Power* (1948), *White Collar* (1951), and *The Power Elite* (1956)— form parts of an overall effort to understand the American "present as history and the future as responsibility." Adopting the scope and methods of classical social thinkers, chiefly Max Weber,

Marx, and Veblen, Mills also assumed the traditional values of Western humanism, pursuing historical, political, and moral problems in the light of a central goal, "the presumptuous control by reason of man's fate." Aware of the unique possibilities of reason and freedom in the twentieth century, he was nevertheless compelled by the realities of his time to define their declining relevance to power, and hence to constructive social change. It should be remembered that his principal theoretical contributions appeared in the Eisenhower period, which is to say in a kind of moral, political, and cultural vacuum: "It is not," he observes, "that we have explicitly rejected our received codes; it is rather that to many of us they have become hollow. No moral terms of acceptance are any longer available, but neither are any moral terms of rejection. As individuals, many of us are morally defenseless; as groups, politically indifferent."[6]

In all of his intellectual work, Mills employed a set of moral norms summarized in his nostalgic image of the free and rational man. For him, these qualities were inseparable: "Freedom is not merely the chance to do as one pleases; neither is it merely the opportunity to choose between set alternatives. Freedom is, first of all, the chance to formulate the available choices, to argue over them— and then, the opportunity to choose. That is why freedom cannot exist without an enlarged role of human reason in human affairs. Within an individual's biography and within a society's history, the social task of reason is to formulate choices, to enlarge the scope of human decisions in the making of history."[7] Mills's devotion to reason and his practical outlook prevented him from concentrating on a dialectic of liberation, a leap, in Marxist terms, from socialism to communism, and more generally from a *Gesellschaft* society to a community beyond alienation and beyond history. Utopian speculations about life in a setting of general abundance were simply foreign to his temperament. He was, rather, committed to developing a sociology of change, an understanding of how men might yet shape their fate according to humane values. Though occasionally driven toward utopian fantasies, Mills would generally have preferred Barrington Moore's less ambitious conception of a "decent society," which "means no more than the elimination of that portion of human misery caused by the workings of social institutions."[8]

Committed to moral and political ends, Mills nevertheless regarded objectivity as the primary imperative of his intellectual craft. Applying his criteria of reason and freedom to an analysis of contemporary history, he saw cheerful robots inhabiting a semifree state, not free men in a free society. In *The Sociological Imagination* (1961), a summary statement of the main themes and conclusions of his criticism in the 1950s, Mills argues that increasing centralization of economic production in private corporations and concentration of power in bureaucraticized military and political centers creates unique historical opportunities: "consider now, the major clue to our condition: Is it not, in a word, the enormous enlargement and the decisive centralization of all the means of power and decision, which is to say—all the means of history-making?"[9] These emerging configurations of power transformed the making of history into a more conscious political process, permitting greater rational control of man's fate.

But in fact, these new possibilities were being perverted: most people in America felt powerless, and justifiably so. Rather than argue that men ceased to create history, Mills concluded that major powers of decision had been absorbed by small groups, elites of power. Ironically, then, as history turned into a more conscious and therefore potentially more manageable process, it also became far less democratic. Power in postwar America was increasingly separated from knowledge and morality—that is, from reason. In his delineation of the American social structure, Mills pursued the consequences of this separation: he studied power in order to discover the reasons for his own powerlessness as a representative man on the Left; he studied irrationality in order to discern the possibilities of coordinating reason and power; and he examined the split between liberalism and Marxism with the intention of constructing an alternative theory, vision, and politics that would bring together the best features of both. These motifs provide moral and intellectual coherence to his studies of various American social configurations in the fifties.[10]

Mills explores the theme of powerlessness in his changing analyses of labor, the traditional agency of progressive social change in industrial societies. In *The New Men of Power* (1948), a study of American labor in the emerging cold-war society, he argues that growing concentrations of wealth and power in the unions could form the basis of a Left-liberal coalition with intellectuals and white-collar workers. "Inside this country today, the labor leaders are the strategic actors: they lead the only organizations capable of stopping the main drift toward war and slump." Their potential power also entailed international consequences: "What the U.S. does, or fails to do, may be the key to what will happen in the world. What the labor leader does, or fails to do, may be the key to what will happen in the U.S."[11] But as it became more apparent that big labor and big business were bound together in an informal though quite effective alliance, Mills's cautious optimism faded.

By the middle 1950s he qualified his earlier estimates, arguing that labor leaders had failed to articulate the needs and aspirations of the working class, even though they remained influential figures. Rather than resisting the "main drift in American society," men at the top of unions had become a dependent part of the structure of power, an interest group within the major political parties and a junior partner in the corporate world. Far from opposing the cold war, most trade-union leaders participated in it. By 1960 Mills had put aside all faith in the traditional working class: "I cannot avoid the view that in both cases [parliamentary democracy and the working class] the historic agency . . . has either collapsed or become most ambiguous; so far as structural change is concerned, *these* don't seem to be at once available and effective as *our* agency any more."[12]

Mills's analysis of labor rested on the assumption that American capitalism had evolved into a relatively stable system. Like other independent intellectuals of the 1950s, he was awed by its seeming permanence and malleability, having accepted the proposition that the new warfare/welfare economics guaranteed indefinite life. Through a combination of military and civilian outlays, the intervening hand of the state would continue to rescue the private sector from severe crises. In such circumstances, the traditional Marxian conception of the working class was more clearly than ever a romantic illusion, a "labor metaphysic" without historical substance or political relevance. Moreover, the structural prerequisites for *any* enlightened mass politics no longer existed. Anticipating Marcuse, Mills concluded that the American working class had become an essentially conservative force, hostile both to revolution and substantial reform.

Turning his attention in the early 1950s to the middle levels of society, Mills examined the diverse white-collar worlds, projecting the dominant images of society as "a great salesroom, an enormous file, an incorporated brain, a new universe of management and manipulation."[13] Everywhere he looked in the realms of salaried employees, Mills perceived an increasingly common social type, "the cheerful robot" shaped by large, centralized bureaucratic institutions. Deprived of his sense of participation and power in major decisions, this "New Little Man" was forced into a dull round of enervating work and leisure. His job was usually routine and meaningless, and his leisure only a specious variation on work. Those in the white-collar world—salespeople, clerks, and the enormous army of brain workers—had to cope with traditional problems of capitalist society, enduring the adverse effects of recession, war, and even of boom. Plagued by high taxes, inflation, and declining public services in prosperous periods, they also provided the bulk of the material for war, and the personnel as well. Moreover, the white-collar strata confronted contemporary situations with meager individual and collective resources: "The New Little Man seems to have no firm roots, no sure loyalties to sustain his life and give it a center. He is not aware of having any history, his past being as brief as it is unheroic; he has lived through no golden age he can recall in time of trouble."[14]

If this alienated figure has no sense of a past, if he is a victim of the present, he also remains innocent of the future: "Perhaps because he does not know where he is going, he is in a frantic hurry; perhaps because he does not know what frightens him, he is paralyzed with fear. This is especially a feature of his political life, where the paralysis results in the most profound apathy of modern times."[15] Mills remained gloomy about the political future of the amorphous middle layers of American society. Apathetic, divided, and driven into private life, the new middle classes, he believed, were up for grabs. *White Collar* concludes with a bitter, sardonic portrait—in fact, a caricature—of these middling groups:

> Since they have no public position, their private positions as individuals determine in what direction each of them goes; but, as individuals, they do not know where to go. So now they waver. They hesitate, confused and vacillating in their opinions, unfocused and discontinuous in their actions. They are worried and distrustful but, like so many others, they have no targets on which to focus their worry and distrust. They may be politically irritable, but they have no political passion. They are a chorus, too afraid to grumble, too hysterical in their applause. They are rearguarders. In the shorter run, they will follow the panicky ways of prestige; in the longer run, they will follow the ways of power, for, in the end, prestige is determined by power.[16]

The intensity of this portrait results, I think, mainly from Mills's anger and frustration over not being able to identify a social force capable of reversing national and international trends of the fifties. It derives part of its energy from a recognition of himself in the bureaucratic trap. For *White Collar* is implicitly the self-portrait of a fierce individualist, a nineteenth-century type caught in a social setting that curbed the full exercise of his values and aspirations. It is a preliminary evaluation of Mills's own kind—the intellectuals—who, like every other major group, were participating as powerless technicians and salesmen in the "American celebration": the "intellectual who remains free may continue to learn more and more about modern society, but he finds the centers of political initiative less and less accessible. This generates a malady that is particularly acute in the intellectual who believed his thinking would make a difference. In the world of today the more his knowledge of affairs grows, the less impact his thinking seems to have. If he grows more frustrated as his knowledge increases, it seems that knowledge leads to powerlessness." In the end, "He comes to feel helpless in the fundamental sense that he cannot control what he is able to foresee."[17] It would be hard to find a more succinct characterization of powerlessness, the principal dimension of radical paradoxes, in American social criticism of the 1950s.

But Mills did not opt for the fashionable tragic vision, a detached perspective on man's fate beyond history and politics. "Having examined it carefully, I have rejected it as a political blind alley, as sociologically unreal, and as morally irresponsible. . . . It is a way of saying to oneself: 'We're all in this together, the butcher and the general and the ditch digger and the Secretary of the Treasury and the cook and the President of the United States. So let's all feel sad about one another, or if we're up to it, let's just see it all as one great comedy.' But 'we' are *not* all in this together. . . . Only if all men everywhere were actors of equal power in an absolute democracy of power could we seriously hold 'the tragic view' of responsibility."[18] Generally avoiding both a metaphysics and politics of self-indulgence, he set out to define actual agents of change, or rather of conservation: the upper circles of American society.

Mills's search for the sources of decisive power no less than the perception of his own powerlessness provided the impetus for studying dominant institutions: the corporations, the military establishment, and the political directorate. The principal themes of *The Power Elite* are too well known (and too thoroughly criticized) to require elaborate treatment here. In general, Mills argued that structural trends toward centralization and concentration of power in major institutions leave decisions of national and international consequence in the hands of small, self-perpetuating elites whose members usually act irresponsibly, without a genuine political mandate from the vast majority of Americans: "the power elite is composed of men whose positions enable them to transcend the ordinary environments of ordinary men and women; they are in positions to make decisions having major consequences . . . they are in command of the major hierarchies and organizations of modern society. They rule the big corporations. They run the machinery of the state and claim its prerogatives. They direct the military establishment. They occupy the strategic command posts of the social structure, in which are now centered the effective means of the power and the wealth and the celebrity which they enjoy."[19] If Mills did not precisely characterize and demonstrate his hypotheses about the sources and structures of power in mid-century America, he unquestionably focused critical attention in the right direction: toward the higher circles. Rather than offering an alternative program or politics, however, *The Power Elite* suggested the enormous obstacles to a radical turn. It identified the gigantic centers of power as conservative, thus complementing earlier conclusions about the powerlessness of the drifting middle echelons of labor, white-collar workers, and intellectuals.

Mills's radical pessimism during this period is even more evident in his conception of a mass society developing at the bottom of the American social structure: "the classic community of publics," he declares, "is being transformed into a society of masses."[20] Whereas well-defined publics formerly ensured a measure of democracy in the formation of opinion and the formulation of policy, the emergence of impotent masses negated liberal democratic norms. This growing political fragmentation and personal alienation from larger structures of power and meaning provided ominous clues to a future without freedom. Using stark, abstract categories, Mills projected a society of powerful elites and impotent masses, separated by inocuous middle layers.

By 1956, then, the most ambitious social portrait of postwar America was virtually complete. Mills had found the main loci of national power. He had described the morphology of powerlessness. And he had shown that growing imbalances of power expanded the social role of irrationality while reducing the scope of genuine freedom. But these conclusions only compounded the larger problems of how new modes of power could be redistributed rationally and democratically. To explain the widespread public acceptance of irrational structural trends, Mills offered a preliminary analysis of the thick ideological atmosphere that functioned both as a cause and as an effect of increasingly atomized masses and scattered publics. The "cultural apparatus," he writes, "is composed of all the organizations and *milieux* in which artistic, intellectual, and scientific work goes on, and of the means by which such work is made available to circles, publics, and masses. In the cultural apparatus art, science, and learning, entertainment, malarkey, and information are produced and distributed." Without attempting to show the operation of this apparatus in detail, Mills suggests that its sheer size, pervasiveness, and complexity are sufficient to create an irrational secondary world of images, slogans, and ideologies that distort actual relations between individuals and their social environments: "taken as a whole, the cultural apparatus is the lens of mankind through which men see; the medium by which they interpret and report what they see. It is the semi-organized source of their very identities and of their aspirations. . . . With such means, each nation tends to offer a selected, closed-up and official version of world reality."[21]

Locked into their local worlds, intellectually disoriented by the cultural apparatus, individuals find it increasingly difficult to "reason about the great structures—rational and irrational—of which their milieux are subordinate parts."[22] The decline of reason, Mills argues, is a function of the growing separation of private troubles from public issues: "It is not too much to say that in the extreme development, the chance to reason of most men is destroyed, as rationality increases and its locus, its control, is moved from the individual to the big-scale organization. There is then rationality without reason."[23] As a partial consequence of these distortions of knowledge and power, the moral dimensions of reason disappear into a calculating rationality with related public and personal dimensions. In its public aspect, this mutilated rationality reduces reason to a set of strategies for perpetuating the economic, social, political, and cultural status quo. Transposed into individual terms, it helps men pursue separate aims within narrow worlds. For example, if huge military expenditures are integral components of the "national interest," an engineer may decide to work for Hughes Aircraft instead of, say, Boeing or Lockheed, because Hughes offers him a better salary and more attractive working conditions. Similiarly, if it is in the national interest to kill livestock, the farmer will bury his pigs in exchange for a government subsidy. But when the national interest dictates a 5 percent rate of unemployment, the personal dimensions of calculating rationality must yield to public considerations: deprived of even meaningless work, the unemployed victim has to settle for a meager handout. Of course the dominant (and frequently unarticulated) public rationality has as little connection with Mills's concept of reason as the private rationality of those who take the status quo as the only framework of reality. "Such rationality," as Mills observes, "is not commensurate with freedom but the destroyer of it."[24] Military planners, corporate executives, political leaders, "obfuscating liberals," labor moguls, and conformist academics all promoted "crackpot" definitions of reality to preserve the power of the few at the heavy price of submitting to irrational trends, and perhaps in the long run, to national and international disaster.

Powerless to act beyond the narrow scope of private affairs, social critics on the Left, according to Mills, may even be thinking about the historical present in moribund categories. Reason reveals personal and social irrationalities without implying rational political alternatives. Mills argued in passing that the major political orientations in the West—Marxism and liberalism—"have virtually collapsed as adequate explanations of the world and ourselves," since both depend upon Enlightenment presuppositions: reason as the principal condition of freedom; the identification of reason with progress; faith in science as unambiguously progressive; the belief in mass education as the key to political democracy.[25] But the contemporary social world turns these basic assumptions inside out: a calculating rationality restricts freedom, science is used in the creation of enormous instruments of violence and repression, and mass education produces political imbeciles. Mills thus focuses on the typical dilemma of people on the Left. As radicals, they adopt a Marxian (or Millsian) analysis of American society. As intellectuals, they assume liberal, humanist values as codes of personal conduct. Accepting both, they become men with personal moral visions in conflict with the realities of politics. In this social environment, then, liberal values cease to be dependable guides to public action.

But liberalism survived, Mills shrewdly observes, in petrified forms, as the official rhetoric of American society. That it had become the common denominator of political and moral rhetoric suggests the power of its ideals: "it also testifies to the fact that these ideals have been increasingly divorced from any historical agencies by which they might have been realized."[26] In fact, liberal rhetoric concealed a conservative mood which Mills presciently saw as "quite appropriate to men living in a material boom, a nationalist celebration, a political vacuum. At its heart there is a knowledge of powerlessness without poignancy, and a feeling of pseudo-power based on mere smugness. By its softening of the political will, this mood enables men to accept public depravity without any private sense of outrage, and to give up the central goal of western humanism, so strongly felt in nineteenth-century American experience: the presumptuous control by reason of man's fate."[27]

In his critical work of the early and middle fifties, then, Mills identified the development of the power elite and the parallel growth of mass society as the primary structural causes of the collapse of liberalism in America. At the top, the main national problems were defined and resolved by elites. At middle levels of power, a balance of publics neutralized each other. And at the bottom, a passive mass society ideologically molded by the "cultural apparatus" was taking on an ill-defined shape: powerful but immoral elites, declining publics, and impotent masses summarized the condition and direction of America at midcentury.

The structural changes and trends that devitalized liberalism also led to the "collapse of socialist hopes." The working class in America had failed its projected mission. And the perversion of socialist ideals in Communist countries during the Stalin era struck Mills as convincing evidence of the obsolescence of orthodox Marxist theories of transition. Neither the liberalism of the West nor the official Marxism of the East could adequately explain contemporary events and trends. Both failed to suggest a politics of progressive change, even though they survived as ways of rationalizing existing social systems, and as compelling if ambiguous ideals.

Toward Global Vision

Through his studies of American society in the fifties, Mills encountered the crucial elements of radical paradoxes: the impotence of potentially progressive agents and agencies of change, and ethical dilemmas arising from the disparity between private values and narrowing public options. Yet his distinctive approaches to these paradoxes may at first seem to constitute grounds for exclusion from the independent Left critics I have grouped together under Mills's own rubric of "plain Marxists." He was, after all, neither an orthodox Marxist nor an old Leftist by birth, background, or training, having grown up in Texas rather than New York, Frankfurt, or Paris.[28] He had little emotional investment in prewar ideological disputes and hence no intellectually imprisoning radical past to overcome: "he never belonged to any socialist group, faction, or party and . . . he does not appear to have been sufficiently in sympathy with any socialist tendency in America to identify specifically with any of them."[29] Granted, Mills was a lone rebel, a man who made a point of not fitting easily into any theoretical or political tradition. That he so clearly defined radical paradoxes by using a theory of elites rather than the traditional Marxian categories of social class only suggests their pervasiveness: any intellectual of the 1950s who observed postwar American society historically, comprehensively, and in the light of the central values and aspirations of Western humanism would have come upon the same dilemmas.[30]

In his definitions and explorations of radical paradoxes, then, Mills's own blend of classical social theories functioned as a very rough equivalent of the Marxism of, say, Baran and Sweezy. And it led him to a similar impasse during the late fifties. As a sociologist he sought to identify the largest structural trends of his time; as a committed intellectual he sought to evaluate these changes, and then to go beyond the role of disinterested spectator toward a new program and a new politics. The deeply held conviction that intellectual work should be a serious undertaking with public consequences rather than a sophisticated game played in academic isolation placed Mills in the tradition of radical social critics, despite his frequent disclaimers. He was moved—perhaps driven —by the ideal of an interplay between theory and politics, yet his social analyses in the early and middle fifties revealed only broken connections. Mills's preoccupation with "the present as history" thus guaranteed his discovery and refinement of radical paradoxes; his belief in progress moved him to seek a way out; and the intensity of the two commitments—to truth and to progressive change —usually prevented him from accepting easy pseudosolutions.

From about 1956 to his death in 1962, Mills sought fresh perspectives on radical paradoxes, moving in several directions with striking speed and characteristic determination. On the domestic front (and generally in the West), he continued the search for new levers of change that would combine knowledge and moral vision with power in order to enlarge the scope of human freedom. Having given up on traditional agencies, he turned to intellectuals and to the young. At the same time he broadened the scope of his study, exchanging an earlier preoccupation with American themes for a concern with the major historical drifts of the epoch: socialism in advanced Communist nations, and revolutionary upheavals in the "third world."

Mills also operated in more than one intellectual theater during this period. His expanding interests required extensive travel and reading in new fields. And his sense of urgency, based on the accelerating tempo of historical change, its global dimensions, and the threat of nuclear catastrophe, persuaded him to communicate his developing outlook immediately—and impatiently—to a wide audience. Hence his public image during these last years is of a free-swinging polemicist, the author of *The Causes of World War III* and *Listen, Yankee!* Simultaneously, however, he was undertaking an ambitious venture in theory, a " 'six to nine volume comparative study of the world range of present-day social structures.' "[31] The many facets of these activities converge upon a single point: the extended definition of radical paradoxes and their possible resolution.

Predictably, Mills turned to his own kind, the intellectuals, as a social agency that might resist what he regarded as "the drift toward catastrophe." Though subject to dominant social trends— the concentration and centralization of power, and the decline of democracy—intellectuals retain a capacity for reason, which is, after all, an intrinsic part of their commitment to understanding man and society within history. "All social scientists," Mills observes, "by the fact of their existence, are involved in the struggle between enlightenment and obscurantism."[32] And because intellectuals, according to this definition, play a significant part in the creation of political philosophy (ideology in the broadest sense), their ideas can become a historical force—indeed, a powerful force in the latter half of the twentieth century, since the structural changes Mills imagined enlarged the role of political philosophy in the shaping of history. His bleak analyses of actual historical trends thus had a potentially positive side. "Surely this is the paradox of our immediate situation: The facts about the new means of history-making are a signal that men are not necessarily in the grip of fate, that men *can* now make history. But this fact is made ironic by the further fact that just now those ideologies which offer men the hope of making history have declined and are collapsing in the Western societies."[33]

Of course Mills was perfectly aware of another crucial flaw in this position: instead of pursuing the wider opportunities in the late 1950s and early 1960s, American intellectuals in the main had made a separate peace with the status quo. Because their presumed capacity greatly exceeded their will, the dubious hypothesis that ideas could "make a difference" remained untestable until intellectuals reclaimed their vocation by shaking off the bureaucratization of mind characteristic of the postwar years; to gain a measure of power, they first had to regain reason. This remained an off chance, but one that Mills felt able to pursue with his own personal and intellectual resources. And so he confronted the American intellectual community as a prophetic witness to the default, exposing failures of nerve, charting important tasks, and outlining what he termed "the politics of truth."

That Mills's aggressive critique of the social-science industry has by now become routine if not very widely heeded should not detract from its original force and its continuing importance. In *The Sociological Imagination* and in other essays, he repeated what needed to be said: that intellectuals, especially social scientists, had withdrawn from modern (or, if you will, postmodern) life by rejecting their commitment to reason. He attacked those who were obsessed by formal considerations, the "Grand Theorists" in general and Talcott Parsons in particular: "The basic cause of grand theory is the initial choice of a level of thinking so general that its practitioners cannot logically get down to observation. They never, as grand theorists, get down from the higher generalities to problems in their historical and structural contexts. This absence of a firm sense of genuine problems, in turn, makes for the unreality so noticeable in their pages." Restricting themselves to the higher regions of sociological abstraction, these thinkers spin out "a seemingly arbitrary and certainly endless elaboration of distinctions which neither enlarge our understanding nor make our experience more sensible. This in turn is revealed as a partially organized abdication of the effort to describe and explain human conduct and society plainly."[34]

If grand theorists are paralyzed by an arid formalism, those at the other end of the spectrum, the "abstracted empiricists," study problems without any conceptual framework. This category includes a diverse collection of social scientists who amass data and develop sophisticated modes of statistical analysis but rarely produce interesting results because their obsession with narrow methods confines them to the study of trivial problems. Technique rather than any well-articulated theory determines the kinds of issues abstracted empiricists take up; their "methodological inhibition stands parallel to" the grand theorists' "fetishism of the Concept." And both, according to Mills, "are withdrawals from the tasks of the social sciences."[35] Grand theory and the "statistical ritual" amount to abdications of the intellectuals' overriding responsibility to exercise the sociological imagination, to comprehend seminal problems and chart emerging possibilities in the long-range human project of controlling history.

Toward the end of the fifties, Mills's advocacy of the sociological imagination also brought him into direct conflict with end-of-ideology theorists such as Daniel Bell, Irving Kristol, and Seymour Martin Lipset. He recognized the split-level character of the main thesis, which was at once an abstract apology for their own radical pasts and a rationalization of current social arrangements. "Ultimately," he asserts, "the end-of-ideology is based upon a disillusionment with any real commitment to socialism in any recognizable form. *That* is the only 'ideology' that has really ended for these writers. But with its ending, *all* ideology, they think, has ended. *That* ideology they talk about; their own ideological assumptions, they do not."[36] The end-of-ideology thesis, then, was largely a pseudoresolution, by critical fiat, of radical paradoxes fashioned by ex-Left intellectuals who renounced earlier Stalinist or anti-Stalinist affiliations and their images of socialism as well. Their thesis also justified self-conscious participation in "the American celebration," since it presupposed the end of major political issues in the West. "The mixed economy plus the welfare state prosperity—that is the formula," Mills declares. "US capitalism will continue to be workable; the welfare state will continue along the road to ever greater justice. In the meantime, things everywhere are very complex, let us not be careless, there are great risks. . . ."[37] Mills knew that this outlook was nonsensical. From a global point of view, it was provincial though not, as he implies, unmanly nonsense, "a slogan of complacency, circulating among the prematurely middle-aged, centered in the present, and in the rich Western societies."[38] Moreover, the end-of-ideology is itself a fragmentary ideology "of an ending: the ending of political reflection itself as a public fact. It is a weary know-it-all justification—by tone of voice rather than by explicit argument—of the cultural and political default of the NATO intellectuals."[39]

The impatient criticism of intellectuals in the late fifties reflected Mills's growing preoccupation with the heart of radical paradoxes, namely the matter of political program and action. Having spent more than twenty years analyzing the changing forms of American society, charting its growing potentialities and declining performance, he had to face up to the question of what to do, a dilemma that so many of his contemporaries assiduously evaded. Though candid enough to admit that he did "not know the answer to the question of political irresponsibility in our time," Mills was nevertheless temperamentally incapable of abandoning it: the significance of his entire intellectual venture depended upon a workable answer.[40] Mills knew that the problem of action contained two related parts: "To ask and to answer the question, 'What is to be done?' is not enough. We must also specify who is to do it."[41] And he saw that the prevailing strategy of evasion adopted by the end-of-ideologists and others depended on collapsing the two questions into one: presupposing the disappearance of agencies of qualitative change, postwar American intellectuals tended, by a sleight of hand, to finesse the problem of what *ought* to be done. If a tiny group of moralists such as Paul Goodman offered social prescriptions without bothering to show how they might become public facts, a majority of critics merely acquiesced in current structures of power, refusing to offer judgments or to sketch out political alternatives.

According to Mills, then, "the reason . . . why so many have abandoned the making of programmes is that they see in the United States no real public for such programmes."[42] A politically effective public, he argues, would "have to be part of an organization, a movement, a party with a chance to influence the decisions now being made and the defaults now being committed."[43] Moreover, it would "have to contain people who are at least attentive to ideas and ideals; people among whom one has a chance to get a hearing."[44] When these two conditions are met, intellectuals can be "programmatic in a 'politically realistic' way."[45] Like other critics of his time, however, Mills also believed that no such political opportunities existed on the American social landscape. What then? The intellectual has two options. He may "modify the ideas, or at least . . . file them away; and then, temporarily at least . . . take up new allegiances and expendiencies for which . . . [he] might work in a 'realistic' way. This is the way that is called 'practical politics.' " Or he may "retain the ideals, and hence by definition . . . hold them in a utopian way, while waiting. This is the way that is called impractical and unrealistic."[46]

Mills advocated the second way. To put ideas and ideals aside in the contemporary American context amounted to an "abdication of any possible role of reason, indeed of sanity, in human affairs."[47] Moreover, it constituted a "surrender of any power we might possibly have to those now in charge of the decisions that make history and the decisions not made which might well turn history in other directions."[48] Intellectuals must therefore continue to engage in "the politics of truth," exercising the sociological imagination and offering programs based on their analyses. This "resolution" to radical paradoxes was not conceived as a permanent position outside history, but rather as a transitional strategy designed to help intellectuals comprehend emerging social forces and to become an influential public in their own right. In the topsy-turvy social world of the late fifties, Mills's dominant perspective was simultaneously realistic and utopian. In fact, he argued that the only truly realistic positions were utopian: "What the powerful call utopia is now in fact the condition for human survival."[49]

This familiar plea for yet another politics of exposure in America was about as close as Mills ever came to a specific set of programs and a constituency that might enact them. He did, of course, elaborate a principal implication of his extended critique of the intellectual default: that the work of intellectuals, of those who withdrew as well as of those who assumed the sociological imagination, had public, indeed political, consequences. He therefore urged others to create programs, debate them, and "make of these programmes *divisive* and *partisan* political issues within the U.S.A."[50] Intellectuals should also engage in public ideological combat, using the "cultural apparatus" to expose the power elite and to speak to whatever small publics may be around.[51] In the course of debating and publicizing their work, he predicted, intellectuals would have to express their commitment to civil rights and liberties: "The thing to do within a formal democracy is to act within it and so to give it content. If we do not do so, then we ought to stop 'defending' democracy and say outright that we do not take it seriously."[52] And as a first step toward a new foreign policy, Mills advised American intellectuals to end their complicity in the cold war by making a separate peace with their counterparts in the socialist countries.

Though Mills pleaded with his colleagues to enter the public sphere, he stopped short of advocating a traditional far Left politics in America, concluding that it would be foolish to abdicate "our roles as intellectuals to become working-class agitators or machine politicians, or by play-acting at any other direct political action."[53] Avoiding futile sects on the Left, Mills also counseled against the complacency of democratic socialists as he gradually severed his loose affiliation with the *Dissent* group: "Intellectuals accept without scrutiny official definitions of world reality. Some of the best of them allow themselves to be trapped by the politics of anti-Stalinism, which has been a main passageway from the political thirties to the intellectual default of the apolitical fifties. . . . They use the liberal rhetoric to cover the conservative default."[54] Mills's ill-tempered reply to Irving Howe's review of *The Causes of World War III* reveals the depth of the split. Though the angry exchange fails to delineate theoretical issues in a very sophisticated way, it does underline his growing dissatisfaction with Howe's stance: "we differ, I suppose, in two evaluations: You do not take as seriously as I do the new beginnings in the Soviet Bloc since the death of Stalin. You no longer take as seriously as I do the lack of new beginnings and the disuse of formal freedom in the USA since World War II."[55] The bitterness of the break, I think, results largely from Mills's increasing frustration at being caught in the trap of radical paradoxes, and his sense that *Dissent* intellectuals had accepted defeat far too calmly. In a fit of bad taste, he suggests that Howe needs a "big dose of new fact" if he is to break out of old political sets. As in so many other instances, Mills was speaking to himself—in this case to a former political self—through his criticism of others, arguing that additional knowledge of world affairs might significantly change the terms of radical paradoxes and open the way to new resolutions.

For the end-of-ideologists, socialism ceased to be an ideal; for those in the tradition of *Dissent,* it became "the name of their desire," a rhetorical cover for a moderate social democratic politics that Mills considered futile. Abandoning all sectors of the old Left and the ex-Left, he went his own way, hoping to discover new modes of resolving old problems. The "joint political-cultural struggle" to which he called his colleagues was to be waged "in intellectual and moral ways rather than in a more direct political way."[56] On the bleak domestic front, intellectuals should act as if there were a "two-way traffic between criticism and protest" in order to forge one; or failing that, to retain their dignity in a time of narrowing political options. Mills sums up this perspective bluntly: "If this—the politics of truth—is merely a holding action, so be it. If it is also a politics of desperation, so be it. But in this time and in America, it is the only realistic politics of possible consequence that is readily open to intellectuals. It is the guideline and the next step. It is an affirmation of one's self as a moral and intellectual center of responsible decision; the act of a free man who rejects 'fate'; for it reveals his resolution to take his *own* fate, at least, into his own hands."[57] The rhetorically defiant surface of this characterization of radical paradoxes finally failed to disguise Mill's sense of despair—and outrage—over his own isolation from American politics and power. As an outsider disillusioned with the traditional Left, he resisted the national drift toward irrationality with the strength of his personality and often with a kind of rhetorical bluff aimed partly at his audience but mainly at himself.

Reiterating this intensely personal approach to radical paradoxes in his "Letter to the New Left" (1960), Mills added another public dimension: the worldwide upsurge of the young. Here, finally, was a new historical agency of change that might hold answers to the main dilemma of radical powerlessness. "Who is it," Mills asks rhetorically, "that is thinking and acting in radical ways? All over the world—in the bloc, outside the bloc and in between—the answer's the same: it is the young intelligentsia."[58] He then marshals a series of disparate events in support of this contention:

In the spring and early summer of 1960—more of the returns from the American decision and default are coming in. In Turkey, after student riots, a military junta takes over the state, of late run by Communist-Container Menderes. In South Korea, too, students and others knock over the corrupt America-puppet regime of Syngman Rhee. In Cuba, a genuinely left-wing revolution begins full-scale economic reorganization—without the domination of US corporations. Average age of its leaders: about 30—and certainly a revolution without any Labor As Agency. . . . And even in our own pleasant Southland, Negro and white students are—but let us keep that quiet: it really *is* disgraceful.[59]

After acknowledging obvious reservations about the meaning and direction of the rise of youth, Mills turns the caveats into opportunities for intellectuals to practice the politics of truth: "wait a bit," he advises; "in the meantime, *help* them to focus their moral upsurge in less ambiguous political ways; work out with them the ideologies, the strategies, the theories that will help them to consolidate their efforts: new theories of structural changes of and by human societies in our epoch."[60] And yet Mills remained ambivalent about the prospects for the actual emergence of a new political force in the West. Discussing his projected volume on this topic with Saul Landau, Mills was asked, " 'What's missing?' " He sat back "with a grin on his face" and replied: " 'The New Left, that's what's missing.' "[61] In his more cautious moments, then, Mills used the concept of a new Left as a theoretical construct, an idea that would break the hold of radical paradoxes—if only it could become a political reality.

The turn toward youth as a possible substitute proletariat, or at least a promising new public, formed only one strand of Mills's overall design to break the impasse of radical paradoxes in the late 1950s and early 1960s. But it was an important one; for by providing historical resonance to the programs of intellectuals and by giving an international dimension to the paradoxes, the rebellion of youth permitted Mills to shift his focus away from America, which, apart from the fledgling civil-rights and student movements, appeared closed to significant social change. A global canvass, however, required global vision. Widening the geographical scope of his study convinced Mills of the need to deepen his theoretical comprehension of the historical present. To add substance to the vague guidelines of the sociological imagination, he reexamined Marxism, analyzing its earlier forms and searching out its contemporary meanings.

Mills's reconsideration of Marxism is at once an extension of his previous critique of American society and a response to new theoretical, historical, and political directions precipitated by the disintegration of the Stalinist monolith after 1956. In analyzing and evaluating political philosophies, Mills used four interrelated categories. First, a political philosophy is an *"ideology* in terms of which certain institutions and practices are justified and others attacked." Second, it is "an articulation of *ideals"* used with varying degrees of sophistication to judge "men, events, and movements, and as goals and guidelines for aspirations and policies." Third, any political philosophy "designates *agencies* of action, of the means of reform, revolution or conservation." And finally, it contains, implicitly or explicitly, *"theories* of man, society, and history."[62] Using these indexes, Mills reiterated his earlier critique of liberalism, arguing that it remains compelling "as an articulation of ideals," whereas "on each of the other three aspects . . . as ideology, as designation of historical agencies, and as a set of theories about man, society and history—its relevance is now largely historical only."[63] Contemporary Marxisms proved to be a more complex matter, however, since several versions of the outlook survived as combinations of ideologies, ideals, agencies, and ideas (theories)—that is, as living political philosophies.

The Marxists, Mills's last completed work, constitutes a preliminary effort to sort out and assess varieties of Marxism in the light of these indexes. After summarizing his previous critique of classical Marxism, he elaborates its theoretical deficiencies and the failure of its central nineteenth-century projection: the working class as the historically determined agency of revolutionary change. Despite past failures and grotesque distortions, however, Marxism retains the tremendous advantage of being the source of comprehensive though flawed political philosophies that incorporate the "secular humanism of the West . . . as deep and pervasive moral assumptions."[64] Mills's attitude toward Marxism in the early 1960s rests chiefly on his distinction between a model and a theory: "A *model* is a more or less systematic inventory of the elements to which we must pay attention if we are to understand something. It is not true or false; it is useful and adequate to varying degrees. A *theory,* in contrast, is a statement which can be proved true or false, about the causal weight and the relations of the elements of a model."[65] However wrong Marx's theories may have been, his model remains enormously valuable. This, Mills argues, "is what is alive in marxism"; it presents a "classic machinery for thinking about man, society, and history." It describes a "total social structure, but also . . . that structure in historical motion."[66]

By adopting this basic approach to Marxism, Mills was in a position to examine and assess its various twentieth-century forms: he understood the Marxism of Marx as a historically specific model of inquiry that generated a variety of theories about different periods in history. But the refutation of a particular Marxist theory by subsequent events and trends did not by itself invalidate the model. From this position, Mills was able to inquire into the contemporary status of Marxism considered as a set of frequently conflicting theories, ideals, ideologies, and agencies of change. In a word, he was able to examine the historical present as a plain Marxist. This perspective freed him from the simplifications of anti-Stalinist intellectuals who found contemporary forms of socialism wanting by measuring every historical manifestation against the ideals of Victorian Marxism. And it largely freed him from the illusions of intellectuals who desperately wanted to see Marx's ideals imminent in the operations of one socialist country or another.

Though remaining highly critical of European socialist countries, Mills began to view them as historically changing phenomena that ought to be assessed not only against the ideals of Marx but also against the historical limitations and options confronting each of them. He thus recognized that "The ideals which Marx expected to be realized in post-capitalist society have not been realized in the Soviet Union. Their use has clearly been utopian and optative. . . ."[67] At the same time, however, he grasped the central historical reasons for the flawed reality: ". . . the Soviet Union has not been the fully industrialized society envisaged by Marx as *the* condition for a successful marxist revolution. It *is* approaching that condition. However brutal the means have been, stalinism has done the work of industrialization and modernization that was done by capitalism in other societies."[68]

But Mills remained steadily ambivalent about the problems and prospects of advanced socialist countries. On his second visit to the Soviet Union in 1961, he conveyed his mixed feelings to Saul Landau, his traveling companion and research assistant. "On the one hand," Landau recalls, "he would say: 'they're hicks.' And then: 'My God, these people are going to make it.' "[69] Mills could not evade his perception of the disparity between the provinciality and stifling conformity of Soviet intellectual life, the absence of genuine democracy on the one side and the impressive "transformation of society" on the other. According to Landau, he believed that the Soviets were slowly building a "classless society." But when asked about his own reactions, Mills replied: "As with everything here I feel ambivalent. They have done away with some of the state machinery and replaced it by perhaps even more rigid societal controls, an old technique. You have read Tönnies. You know what the essential difference between *gemeinschaft* and *gesellschaft* is. Well, that is essentially it. They have started to organize an industrially advanced, technologically based society, and returned to a primitive level of law and control."[70]

Mills's ambivalent feeling is the emotional correlative of a theoretical confusion between the historical and utopian strains of Marxism, a confusion that, as we shall see, Baran wrestled with and Sweezy and Marcuse finessed by choosing utopian resolutions. Mills, however, did not attempt to resolve the dilemma by working out a theoretical account of the transition from authoritarian to democratic socialism and finally to communism. He rather registered his confusion by recording his contradictory impressions of authoritarian socialism in the U.S.S.R. and the tiny shoots of what he hoped were the seeds of communism. These recollections suggest that Mills did not join the Soviet camp, as some democratic socialists have charged. " 'Buddy,' " he remarked to Landau as they entered the Soviet Union, " 'you wouldn't like to live here.' "[71] Mills did not, indeed could not, join *any* camp. After impulsively taking off for Cuba in 1960, he asked his guide and translator, Juan Archucha, " 'What the hell am I doing here? I was very quietly writing a book in New York and thinking about the next one. All of a sudden I decided to leave everything and come here to write the truth about Cuba. . . . Can you explain to me why I came here?' "[72] If Mills belonged anywhere, it was in America, where, during the last years of his life, he did not want to be. Repelled by the international course of his own country, he tried to become an exile, but finally returned to die of a second heart attack in 1962, a spiritual outcast in a culture he could not shake off.

Disenchanted with America, ambivalent about the socialism of the European nations, Mills looked to the third world, especially Cuba, as a promising context for new societies unencumbered by the legacy of Stalinism. In his assessment of these nations, he sketched the problems and prospects of socialism historically, in the contexts of underdevelopment. Though he studied these problems only briefly, Mills defined the main issues clearly. ". . . industrialization requires: (1) an increase in agricultural productivity; (2) an investment of the surplus thus achieved in capital goods for industry; while (3) holding consumption levels down. I do not think you can get away from these simple hard facts. . . ."[73]

Appraising the Cuban Revolution, he outlined its achievements and problems candidly, arguing that it promised important gains in securing the first prerequisites of a just society: food, clothing, shelter, medical care, education, work, and a modest amount of leisure. But he respected the ethical paradox: approving of the long-range social goals of the revolution, he also criticized the immediately authoritarian, undemocratic characteristics of the regime. But as a partisan Mills declared: "*I am for the Cuban revolution, I do not worry about it, I worry for it and with it.*"[74] He hoped that Cuba and other third-world nations would escape the political forms of Stalinism, though he recognized that each country had to work through similar conditions of backwardness and underdevelopment.[75] Wanting to be optimistic, Mills nevertheless had growing doubts about the chances of a third way between capitalism and bureaucratic socialism. According to Landau, he agreed with Sartre in the spring of 1961 that the chances of avoiding a repetition of the authoritarian socialist past in Cuba were slim. But he held onto his hopes: "I think there's a chance that it will keep on its unique course if the original men keep leadership."[76] Six months later, Fidel delivered the famous speech in which he proclaimed himself a "Marxist-Leninist." Thus Cuba, too, betrayed Mills's hopes for a new way out of radical paradoxes.

In his brief reassessment of Marxist theory and socialist realities, Mills posed more questions than he had time to answer. He did not develop a comprehensive theory based on Marx's model of inquiry, though his insights into the problems of social change in advanced and undeveloped socialist countries are often interesting, if rudimentary. Nor did he develop a convincing theory of imperialism. Still, in my view, he asked the most fruitful questions about the very different potentialities of socialisms throughout the world. Consider, as an example, the last one he posed in print. "Is it merely wishful thinking to ask . . . : Might not a society conforming to the ideals of classic marxism be approximated, *via* the tortuous road of stalinism, in the Soviet world of Khrushchev and of those who will follow him?"[77] It is clear that, had he lived, Mills would have joined other plain Marxists in asking, and tentatively answering, similar questions about other societies that have officially proclaimed the intention of creating socialism and communism under conditions Marx never imagined.

Mills as Critic and Mythmaker

How, then, *did* Mills "face up to the difficulties and opportunities" of his era? And how would he have reacted to the radical opportunities and defeats of the 1960s? His premature death at forty-five precludes definitive answers to these intriguing questions. He did not live to carry out his grand opus designed "to account for man in society by accounting for man in history."[78] Nor was he able to work through the elements of radical paradoxes as a plain Marxist in the context of national and international upheavals of the sixties. Any evaluation of his postwar critical performance must therefore be partial and provisional.

The studies of American society in the 1950s are eminently susceptible to critical assessment, since they represent a more or less completed body of intellectual work. Mills almost single-handedly reopened the debate over the sources and distribution of power in America. *White Collar* and *The Power Elite* provoked angry criticism from several quarters. Pluralists like Robert Dahl argued that Mills simplified and distorted the structures of American power beyond recognition by deemphasizing the importance of various groups and voluntary associations interposed between individuals and the national government. On the other side, Marxist critics attacked his conceptual apparatus, especially his use of elites in place of the broader conception of a ruling class. In *The Power Elite,* the Marxian concept of ruling class is brushed aside with a simplistic footnote: " 'Class' is an economic term; 'rule' a political one. The phrase, 'ruling class,' thus contains the theory that an economic class rules politically. . . . We hold that such a simple view of 'economic determinism' must be elaborated by 'political determinism' and 'military determinism'; that the higher agents of each of these three domains now often have a noticeable degree of autonomy; and that only in the often intricate ways of coalition do they make up and carry through the most important decisions."[79] Paul Sweezy, representing the Marxists, suggests that Mills weakens his theoretical effort by employing the concepts of social class and elites indiscriminately.[80] In particular, Sweezy contends that Mills mistakenly regards the military as a semi-autonomous sphere formally equivalent to corporate power, rather than examining it as a dependent part of the American ruling class. As a result of this theoretical error, Mills misunderstands the reasons for "the increased militarization of American life," attributing it to such spurious "external" causes as the "military ascendancy" and the danger of Soviet aggression. " 'Elitist' thinking," Sweezy concludes, *inevitably* diverts attention from problems of social structure and process and leads to a search for external causes of social phenomena."[81] Moreover, in Mills's case it precluded an understanding of the dynamics of neoimperialism.

Aided by critiques from the Left and the Center, others in the tradition of Mills—principally G. William Domhoff—have amplified his work, clarifying theoretical confusions and updating empirical studies of the "higher circles." Domhoff has shown, convincingly I think, that a useful version of Mills's general sociological matrix can be worked out with the assistance of the insights of pluralists and Marxists. He suggests that Mills does not sufficiently allow for the "considerable political diversity on the American scene," especially at state and local levels.[82] But if Mills overemphasizes concentrations of power at the top, Domhoff points out, pluralists generalize too recklessly about its dispersion throughout society. In fact, both are partially right: diversity exists at local levels, whereas decisions of national and international scope and consequence are generally made in, by, and for the higher circles.

Similarly, Domhoff arranges a compromise between Mills and the Marxists on the troublesome question of social class: ". . . contrary to Mills, we wish to suggest that the corporate elite, who, according to recent research, control those institutions considered 'major' by Mills, form the controlling core of the power elite. The interests and unity of the power elite are thus determined primarily by the interests of the corporate rich, with the factors mentioned by Mills contributing in a secondary fashion."[83] Domhoff thus defines the power elite "more explicitly as 'politically, economically, and culturally active members of the social upper class and high-level employees in institutions controlled by members of the upper class.' "[84] Though differing formally from Mills's definition, Domhoff's characterization leads empirically to identification of the "same persons as members of the power elite."[85] But his definition bridges Marxist and pluralist positions, compensating for Mills's theoretical fuzziness: "On the one hand, [the power elite] is a necessary concept because not all national leaders are members of the upper class. In this sense, it is a modification and extension of the concept of a 'ruling class.' On the other hand, empirical studies on community power, viewed in the light of this redefinition, suggest that Mills was right to say that the power elite is directly involved mainly in decisions of national and international consequence."[86]

The controversy since Mills's death over the precise character and structure of the American governing class illuminates, in microcosm, his major strengths and weaknesses as a sociologist and social critic. That he undertook *White Collar* and *The Power Elite* in the 1950s testifies to his intellectual courage and independence. That these books precipitated a serious and fruitful controversy reveals his intellectual boldness: a master of the broad stroke, the sweeping generality, Mills accomplished more than most of us, not only because he worked harder but also because he was able to cut to the center of massive problems swiftly, generally without undue simplification. The controversy also illuminates Mills's corresponding defects, chiefly an inability to sketch out qualifying assumptions and details, which in turn marred his more abstract generalizations. The interrelated strengths and weaknesses of Mills's intellectual character and craftsmanship permeate his work of the early and middle fifties. The deficiencies, especially his theoretical carelessness, also contribute to the most pervasive fault that runs through all his postwar work: a tendency to transform social criticism into a myth of personal consolation.

The confusion between elites and social classes identified by Sweezy illuminates the larger tension that Mills acknowledged from time to time but never carefully worked out. He recognized that the main structural tendencies in American society of the 1950s ran counter to his own values and hopes: power was divorced from knowledge and moral vision; powers of individual rationality and purposeful action beyond the personal sphere had been largely arrogated by major institutions. Thus, without the concept of elites at the top, Mills would have been unable to account for the conscious role of men—even the wrong men—in the making of postwar history. Both Sweezy's notion of a ruling class and Domhoff's conception of a power elite primarily dependent on the economic system reduce the element of will in the making and remaking of history. Or they implicitly relocate the capacity for radical change in some combination of individuals and classes that Mills considered powerless. But the partially accurate concept of elites enabled Mills to explain the powerlessness of most men and the irrational direction of society without submitting wholly to the mood of despair.

By preserving the power elite as an essentially anthropomorphic category of explanation, Mills retained the hope that history was not necessarily at a dead end. Though currently under the direction of the irrational few, it could theoretically be made democratically by the many: reason and freedom might be linked up with power. As a matter of historical fact, Mills argued, concentration and centralization of power were causally associated with the decline of democracy and freedom in America; this was the historical "drift," the reason for despair. The corollary potentialities for rational, democratic control of man's fate constituted the slim hope, the myth of consolation. Rather than implying a political way out of the historical impasse, however, these theoretical potentialities only preserved the hope that one might be found through a transfer of power from elites to publics. Moreover, Mills's supreme faith in the history-making power of one public, the radical intelligentsia, created a serious moral tension in his developing political philosophy. Substituting a myth of elites for the discarded Marxian notion of the masses as creators of history, he came perilously close to subverting his belief in democracy. " 'Every man,' " Mills frequently remarked, quoting his grandfather, " 'should have one gun, one vote—and one woman at a time.' "[87] Yet it is as a pragmatic elitist who also believed in participatory democracy, rather than as an unyielding democrat, that Mills admired Lenin, Trotsky, and Castro: in contrast to the old Left groups in the West, these men successfully pursued power —and shaped history—at least for a time.

Although social critics should not be expected to "solve" the theoretical puzzle of the ratios of freedom (chance and choice) and determinism in history, they can be expected to offer lucid statements concerning the mixture as a preliminary context for detailed discussions of concrete situations. In turn, specific analyses should reveal ways of qualifying initial abstractions. By muddling the first task in the fifties, Mills ensured failure at the second. It is not that he was unaware of tensions between the apparently irreconcilable facts of power and the unrealized potentialities of democracy and freedom. He articulated them at the highest level of abstraction. By mingling the concepts of elites and classes, however, he placed both elements—reason and irrationality, power and powerlessness, fate and will, freedom and determinism—in a larger and politically paralyzing construct of hope and despair. At this level, Mills represented the actual elements of "drift" as reasons for pessimism, and the potential "thrust" of publics as the cause for hope. The only problem was that the wrong people monopolized power, adding their thrust to the historical drift toward oblivion.

In his desire to perceive the making of history as an increasingly conscious activity, Mills probably assigned too much weight to the elites at the top. Having done this, he was committed to over-explaining the powerlessness of other groups. The myth of consolation appealed to powerless individuals, but it implicitly subverted the creation of a new politics. Convinced of this stark version of radical paradoxes—a version bordering on myth—Mills was often unable to write convincingly about domestic politics or about international problems. For example, he holds forth on the causes of World War III without examining the structure and dynamics of the American social order in depth, arguing that

It is out of . . . elite default and incompetence that theories of historical inevitability are now constructed; it is upon such defaults that feelings of fatalistic resignation rest. But the truth . . . is that it is the rigidity of those who have access to the new means of history-making that has created and is creating the "inevitability" of World War III. Increasingly now it becomes clear that not "fate" but doctrinaire incompetence is leading mankind into the great trap. Ours is not so much a time of big decisions as a time for big decisions that are not being made. A lot of bad little decisions are crippling the chances for the appropriate big ones.[88]

This perspective, in short, allows Mills to fix guilt and responsibility on the power elite, for sins committed and omitted. But it slights, without altogether ignoring, the class and institutional contexts that define the options and mold the psychology of the men at the top of the several hierarchies. The theoretical ambiguity symbolically releases the frustrations of powerless intellectuals and serves the personal need for optimism, but it also partially subverts Mills's conscious aim of "making an adequate statement."

The confusion and emptiness of the abstractions becomes increasingly evident as Mills assigns more specific causes for World War III. Consider the list he presents:

I. The immediate cause of World War III is the military preparation of it. . . .

II. The immediate causes of the arms race are the official definitions of world reality clung to by the elites of the U.S.A. and of the U.S.S.R. These nationalist definitions and ideologies now serve as the mask behind which elite irresponsibility and incompetence are hidden. . . .

III. The official theory of war—the military metaphysic—is itself among the causes of the thrust toward war. . . .

IV. It is the continual preparation for war that the power elite now finds the major basis for the furthering of the several and the coinciding interests of its members. . . .

V. For the politicians, the military metaphysic provides a cover under which they can abdicate the perils of innovative leadership. . . .

VI. For the corporation executives, the military metaphysic often coincides with their interest in a stable and planned flow of profit. . . .[89]

The glaring inadequacies of this summary list of causes are obvious: it does not carefully define, structure, and weight the various causes of World War III. "Military definitions of reality" come *before* the economic considerations. No mention is made of neoimperialism and the American potential for counterrevolution-ary activity throughout the undeveloped world. The amorphous conclusions result mainly, I believe, from the failure to add qualifying assumptions to the most general initial approximations of history as some combination of fate and will, drift and thrust. But the cloudy and unconvincing analysis prepares the reader, and perhaps Mills himself, to accept the hopeful corollary of the pessimistic predictions: the military metaphysic, the military ascendancy, and "the private incorporation of the economy and its capitalist mechanics," he contends, *are* causes; but they are able to operate as causes largely because of civilian hesitations and political vacillation. Military and corporate elites have been able to come together and share higher decisions, as well as to make them separately, because of the fact of the political vacuum."[90]

Despite the potential safety valves that Mills built into his analyses of the American present, he remained unable to show how sane forces might fill the political void. In fact, he was unable to invest the mythic dimension of his criticism with political credibility, if only because the implied advocates of a new turn no longer existed in significant numbers. In his criticism of the fifties, the nostalgic image of the rational and free man served mainly as a rhetorical device to illuminate ominous social trends. It was also an ideal self that Mills projected into his work, making him alter-nately the hero and victim of his own symbolic world. At this mythic level, the conflict between elitist and democratic selves takes on a kind of inner consistency. He believes that rational and free men—men like himself—ought to shape history democrati-cally. But he also considers himself part of a small minority, a moral elite that might yet achieve power. Like those of other plain Marxists, Mills's response to the ethical dimensions of radical paradoxes contains an authoritarian undercurrent: in order for history to be made democratic, it cannot be made democratically.

As he became increasingly absorbed with the problems of action, Mills was bound by the mythic dimensions of his social vision to project this old image of a new man as the human agent of progressive change. Ironically, then, the fragmentary and contradictory political philosophy toward which he was groping in his last years depended upon the very social type which, according to his earlier work, had become nearly extinct in contemporary American society. As with other plain Marxists, Mills's concrete hope for a viable Left finally rested on a symbolic construct, a "new" man who, were he not politically lifeless, might enact a genuinely radical program. In the end, the less ambitious personal myth of consolation—the abstract hope that men could still shape history rationally and democratically—allowed Mills to continue his own work: that and no more.

No judgment of Mills's work after *The Power Elite* can be adequate, since he did not have the chance to flesh out his reassessment of Marxism or to absorb the results into his own projected multivolume treatise on historical sociology. When considering a figure of Mills's stature, however, it is tempting to speculate on the ways he might have confronted radical paradoxes in the 1960s. The preliminary revaluation of Marxism, as I have indicated, revealed him at his best: the bold thinker charting new territory, the voracious reader making preliminary generalizations, the powerful mind formulating essential and leading questions. Had Mills spent more time on Marx, however, he would have had to propose concrete answers to his own hard questions. Specifically, what are the precise characteristics and mechanisms of neoimperialism? Can countries in the "third world" develop within the umbrella of the "free world"? Are harsh, Stalinistic patterns of development the only practical courses open to backward nations choosing socialism? To what extent are socialist countries in the Soviet sphere of influence capable of exchanging authoritarian norms and institutions for democratic ones? Mills formulated these questions sensibly at the most general level of abstraction: he wanted to assess prospects for decent societies *within* history rather than to imagine utopian contexts beyond human reach. And like other plain Marxists, he acknowledged "the unresolved ten-

sion in Marx's work—and in history itself: the tension of humanism and determinism, of human freedom and historical necessity."[91]

It is impossible to tell whether the weaknesses that ramified
throughout his work of the fifties would have marred the later
stages of his study of Marxism and the present as history. In the
late 1950s and early 1960s, he was able to suspend domestic and
international versions of radical paradoxes in midair by advocating
"the politics of truth" for intellectuals. But the domestic pressures
of the decade—the radicalization of the young Left, the conservative turn in American politics, the effects of the war in Vietnam—
would probably have pushed him, as it did others, toward more
definite and "consistent" formulations and resolutions of radical
paradoxes. Though his "Letter to the New Left" (1960) suggests
that nothing less than a new historical force could loosen the
political logjam in the West, the designation of intellectuals and
youth as the main lever of change had a forced hopefulness about
it. This untested, overly optimistic resolution was apparently dictated by his characterization of the principal radical dilemmas, his
desire for historical relevance, and his isolation from power.
Rejecting "the old futilitarians of the dead American Left," he
often mistook young men for the new men who might build a
viable radicalism.

Mills might have continued to dismiss all intellectual and political activity not consciously in opposition to national and international policies of the power elite. Even in that event, however,
nothing in his past indicates that he would have sought the kind of
schematic consistency offered by "revolutionary" groups, although
he might have been drawn into the more chic if scarcely less
sectarian fashion of the later sixties: the romanticization of youth
as an international revolutionary force. The opening stages of the
rebellion of the young did fit Mills's characterization of radical
paradoxes at the end of the fifties and seemed to offer a possible
way out. In the beginning, the amorphous movement was vaguely
democratic, bold, and hopeful. But what would Mills have done
when large sectors of the young Left slid into metapolitics, reject-

ing in the process the legitimacy of the social role of intellectuals?

The course of the new Left in the 1960s would surely have intensified the conflict between his candor and his optimism, between his desire to "make an adequate statement" and his need to be a part, however removed, of an organized solution to the drift—and thrust—toward disaster. His theoretical blind spots and his tenuous hopes for a decent society might have concealed the sharpening dilemmas for a time; his continued involvement with the young Left would not. Sooner or later, he would have been forced to reexamine the concepts of alienation and community, of democracy and freedom in complex, centralized societies—capitalist and socialist alike. The resulting choices and compromises would have tested Mills's rational and emotional limits. He would have continued to pose the hard questions that young Leftists airily dismissed in their pursuit of a dialectic of liberation: What kinds and degrees of freedom and social rationality are possible in the last third of the twentieth century? What kinds and degrees of alienation and separation are necessary (even desirable) in various social configurations?

Though Mills did not write extensively on alienation, from time to time he did express the view that it was a secondary concern that fitted into a larger design for social change. At the personal level, intellectuals could convert alienation into productive activity; at the social level, alienation could be reduced only by far-reaching structural changes. Thus, efforts to reduce alienation required political action by individuals and groups capable of combating the affliction personally through acts of pure will. Consider, for example, this passage from *White Collar:* "Today there are many forms of escape for the free intellectuals from the essential facts of defeat and powerlessness, among them the cult of alienation and the fetish of objectivity. Both hide the fact of powerlessness and at the same time attempt to make that fact more palatable." Moreover, " 'Alienation,' as used in middle-brow circles, is not the old detachment of the intellectual from the popular tone of life and its structure of domination; it does not mean estrangement from the ruling powers; nor is it a phase necessary to the pursuit of truth. It is a lament and a form of collapse into self-indulgence. It is a personal excuse for lack of political will. It is a fashionable way of being overwhelmed."[92] In the 1960s, the middlebrow alienation of many young revolutionaries took the somewhat different form of a "cultural revolution," a flamboyant set of quasi-political, quasi-religious demands for total liberation. Mills would doubtless have pointed out the continuity of these forms of alienation and sharply criticized the strong component of self-indulgence that marked fashions in the pop psychology of these two decades.

In the end, I should like to believe, Mills's sense of candor, his commitment to reason and freedom as ideals and as flawed historical realities, would have turned him into a critic—perhaps sympathetic but I think not—of political and cultural "revolutionaries" in America, of the figures and movements that abandoned the search for a sociology of change in favor of pursuing a dialectic of liberation. Though his own later criticism implicitly tends toward myth, Mills would not consciously have abandoned politics and history for religion and metaphysics. As a response to disenchantment, he might have devoted his main effort to critical theory, since he was finally his own man. Political isolation, even after a brief period of notoriety, would have been preferable to manipulation by the Left and by the media.

Such projections may be as unfair as they are presumptuous. Since Mills was something of a popular hero to many of us in the late fifties, however, it is impossible to reread his books without imagining him as a man—alive and at the same time remote to those of us who knew him only through his work. His death removed a powerful presence from the American scene. And since the man and his work were inseparable, the public legend quickly faded. Social scientists found it convenient to forget him, or to bury his legacy with routine tributes. Those New York intellectuals who could not forgive Mills his growing interest in the problems and prospects of socialist countries also let his image fade, after tarnishing it in a series of tasteless personal reminiscences. And the more seasoned young revolutionaries whose political memories reached back as far as the Eisenhower era soon transcended the theoretical and moral dilemmas that engaged Mills, exchanging the facts of radical paradoxes for visions of apocalypse.

As Andy Warhol facetiously remarked, "Everyone in America will be famous for fifteen minutes." Mills had his hour, and it came none too soon. Had he lived, the remaining years of the sixties might have been painful. Young Leftists, unable to tolerate any political or intellectual leader for more than a few months, would surely have abandoned Mills. Yet this would not have troubled him nearly so much as their growing intolerance of reason and democracy. There was finally no way out of radical paradoxes, no way for Mills to throw off what he poignantly called " 'this moral anguish which is crushing me.' "[93]

You, who shall emerge from the flood
In which we are sinking,
Think—
When you speak of our weaknesses,
Also of the dark time
That brought them forth.

For we went, changing our country more often than our shoes,
In the class war, despairing
When there was only injustice and no resistance.
—Brecht, "To Posterity"

4

Paul Baran:

The Longer View

Paul Baran (1910–1964), was, above all, a Marxist intellectual committed to reason as the principal mode of understanding the historical process as a whole. He characterized the intellectual as "in essence a *social critic,* a person whose concern is to identify, to analyze, and in this way to help overcome the obstacles barring the way to the attainment of a better, more humane, and more rational social order. As such he becomes the conscience of society and the spokesman of such progressive forces as it contains in any given period of history."[1] Hence, to the usual condition of being an intellectual—the desire "to tell the truth"—Baran added a second: "courage, readiness to carry on rational inquiry to wherever it may lead, to undertake 'ruthless criticism of everything that exists, ruthless in the sense that the criticism will not shrink either from its own conclusions or from conflict with the powers that be' (Marx)."[2] As the only Marxian economist teaching in a major American university in the 1950s, Baran, even more than Mills, experienced the frustration and isolation of working in the numbing atmosphere of "the great American celebration." Earlier tests had prepared him for the cold-war years. Born in Russia in 1910, he studied in several important European intellectual centers, including the Plekhanov Institute in Moscow and the Frankfurt School for Social Research. There, too, he was plagued by the irrational historical forces he sought to understand: he left the Soviet Union in the late twenties because, after the accession of Stalin, serious intellectual work became impossible. And he found Germany in the early thirties an inhospitable environment for a Marxist, a Jew, and an ex-member of the Young Communist League. Following an interlude in Warsaw and London as a sales representative for his uncles' timber business, Baran came to America intent upon an academic career. But the war intervened, delaying his plans for nearly a decade. After completing a master's degree at Harvard in 1941, he accepted a fellowship at the Brookings Institution, then held positions in the Office of Price Administration, the United States Army (as a technical sergeant), the Strategic Bombing Survey, and the Federal Reserve Board. Toward the end of the forties, he went West to an academic post at Stanford, where he lived and worked until his death.[3]

As an economist and social critic, Baran was preoccupied with the definition and resolution of radical paradoxes. His postwar writings focus on what he considered "the three dominant themes of our age": the plight of underdeveloped countries in the shadow of the "free world"; "the vicissitudes of monopoly capitalism during its current period of decline and fall"; and "the outlook for the nascent socialist societies in Europe and Asia. . . ."[4] *The Political Economy of Growth* (1956) represents his most sustained effort to account for the absence of rapid economic development in large areas of Latin America, Asia, and Africa. *Monopoly Capital,* written with Paul Sweezy and published posthumously in 1966, tentatively charts the decline of American capitalism and prophesies its eventual fall. And *The Longer View* (1970), a collection of some twenty essays, reviews, and occasional pieces, presents Baran's most important explorations of the third principal theme: the prospects for socialist development in relatively advanced countries—the U.S.S.R. and Eastern Europe—as well as in such comparatively backward nations as Cuba and China.

Confronting Reality with Reason

The essays on Marxism and the commitment of intellectuals in *The Longer View* sketch out the philosophical perspectives that inform Baran's analyses of the "three dominant themes of our age." He contends that Marxism, contrary to the views of sectarians and dogmatists, was never intended to be primarily a "positive science" consisting of a set of empirically verifiable "statements about past and present facts, or a set of predictions about the shape or timing of future events." It was from the outset "an intellectual attitude . . . a philosophical position the fundamental principle of which is continuous, systematic, and comprehensive *confrontation of reality with reason.*"[5]

Baran argues that the "meaning of reason" and the "nature of reality" are intertwined "aspects of historical development." In the "long run . . . of the entire historical process," the "content and the injunctions of reason" as well as the structures of reality are relative.[6] This recognition, however, did not lead him into the impasse of skepticism; for though the content of reason and the structure of reality are ultimately relative, they can be approximately defined in any particular historical period: "The determining factors are the level of social development, society's achieved fund of scientific insight, the accumulated wealth of practical human experience."[7]

Baran appropriated the general aims of reason from the main tradition of Western thought: the satisfaction of man's basic needs for food, clothing, housing, medical care, and education; the need for useful work, satisfying human associations, and fulfilling leisure; the need for freedom and creativity. But merely to proclaim these values abstractly without stipulating the historical conditions under which they may be realized seemed to him an abdication of the Marxist intellectual's primary responsibility of approximating the content of reason in the short run, at the intersection of the present and its possible futures. Replying to a critique of his version of social theory in the late fifties, he asserted that "what is . . . central to the Marxian position is the capacity and willingness to look beyond the immediately observable facts and to see the tree of the future in the tiny shoots barely perceptible in the present. It is the combination of historical vision and the courage to be utopian—with the vision sternly disciplined by an analysis of *tendencies* discernible at the present time, and with the utopia rendered concrete by the identification of the *social forces* that may be expected to further its realization."[8]

Each social system, Baran insisted, must be examined critically and empirically, assessed in the light of changing injunctions of reason and the evolving structures of reality. Accepting Marx's general conception of uneven historical development as a point of departure, he maintained that in class societies, the exploiting class (or classes) has a vital interest in preserving existing constellations of power. When its interests coincide with the short-run injunctions of reason, a period of progress ensues. But when "the particular interests of the ruling class come into conflict with the interests of society as a whole," the confrontation of reality with reason "reveals the irrationality of the existing social order."[9] At such junctures, the intellectual serves as "a guidepost to the next steps in mankind's forward movement," helping exploited classes to articulate what they experience, and to discover a way out—in extreme situations through a social revolution under the auspices of an emerging dominant class.[10]

This abstract pattern of the growth and decline of social systems repeats itself with endless variations throughout history, at least until the abolition of capitalism. As an intellectual attitude, then,

Marxism retains its contemporary historical relevance, even in cold-war America, where no group combines the capacity and the will to overturn an irrational social system. "For Marxism is nothing if not a powerful magnifying glass under which the irrationality of the capitalist system protrudes in all of its monstrous forms."[11] Baran suggests that "Marxism will have outlived itself only when it has reached the end of its historical journey: when the confrontation of reality with reason has become redundant because reality will be governed by reason."[12] Generally avoiding grandiose utopian visions of communism in the foreseeable future, Baran used this symmetrical formulation as a theoretical construct, a limiting case that illuminated the irrationalities of the historical present. Like Mills, then, he worked mainly within a sociology of change.

The root metaphor of society as a dynamic whole with essential and inessential parts formed the center of Baran's view of historical movement in our time. As a Marxist, he maintained that monopoly capitalism is irrational as a whole, however rational its parts may have become, and that the various forms of socialism are rational as a whole, despite irrationalities in their parts. The plausibility of this highly abstract vision of the present epoch as a dialectic between declining capitalist and rising socialist nations depended upon what Baran termed the longer view. In this wider perspective, radical paradoxes assumed the form of historically temporary problems. Resisting what Mills termed "the intellectual default" of the Eisenhower era, Baran also avoided the radical debacle of the next decade, though he did not live through the most trying final years. Refusing to adopt any prefabricated position—orthodox, revisionist, Maoist, or anarchist—he generally remained aloof from the surrealistic explosion and fragmentation of Left social criticism in the sixties. Along the Marxist spectrum, he might be classified somewhere between orthodox and revisionist. But only provisionally, for even though his positive contribution to an understanding of the present as history reflects aspects of several established ideological perspectives, it proceeds mainly from his theoretical commitment to a continuous confrontation of reality with reason.

Baran's distinctive vision cannot, however, be understood merely as the impact of a disciplined mind on a powerful method. His biography and temperament also figure importantly in the formation of a judicious historical perspective. Molded by conflicting national and cultural styles, he was a fascinating assemblage of contraries: a passionate man committed to reason, a Marxist and an arrogant aristocrat, an admirer of women and by contemporary standards a male chauvinist. He was a radical and a man of convention; a brilliant intellectual with broad cultural interests and rather narrow personal tastes; a wanderer always without a real home, yet capable of warm, generous, and sustained personal friendships. His critical balance and sanity largely depended on the dynamic interplay of a pessimistic temperament and an optimistic perspective on history. A man cast partly in the ironic mode, Baran usually tempered his own enthusiasms and the romantic dimensions of Marxism with detachment and skepticism. While on a visit to Moscow in 1962, he wrote Paul Sweezy, his closest friend and collaborator, that "one is either made to oppose, to fight, to criticize, or to be a part of the Establishment. I am definitely no good for *any* Establishment. Schumpeter's disturbing, restless intellectual—a nuisance everywhere. Maybe this is the eternal function of the intellectual after all—in all times and in all places."[13] Wanting to belong yet unable to affiliate with any political group, desiring faith yet plagued by doubts, Baran found some security in the longer view, which provided a firm intellectual matrix for the many ambiguities of his temperament and biography.

Toward the end of his life, however, a convergence of historical and personal forces disturbed the critical balance that characterized him at his best. During the late fifties and early sixties, his formulations of radical paradoxes approached the breaking point. The anticipated transformation of Eastern European and Soviet socialisms into humane environments seemed increasingly problematic, while, with the apparent exception of Cuba and the other underdeveloped socialist countries, vast portions of the third world were trapped in an endless cycle of misery and backwardness. Finally, there was no American political movement capable of offsetting the trends of domestic capitalism and foreign imperialism: radical criticism fell into a cultural and political vacuum. Yielding to a mood of despair brought on by a European tour in 1957, Baran remarked in a letter to Sweezy that "The best thing would be to have money, to sit *sous les toits de Paris où les jeunes filles sont jolies,* to drink Courvoisier, and to devote oneself to the study of literature. For I cannot get rid of the feeling that the whole thing is going to pot not with a bang but with a whimper."[14]

Baran's sense of a historical ending was inseparable from intimations of his own impending death. Plagued by declining health, he suffered the first of three heart attacks late in 1960. Moreover, the immediate contexts of his life during the final decade augmented the deep pessimism, alienation—even morbidity—that dominate the tone and quality of his private reflections. Life in the far West, at the moving edge of a vulgar culture, contributed heavily to lengthening cycles of depression, as did his experiences at Stanford, where he felt increasingly estranged from his colleagues in the Economics Department.

A reluctance to criticize openly the Soviet Union partially accounts for this widening disparity between public optimism and private despair. In a memorial tribute, Isaac Deutscher remarked that "Baran had few, if any, illusions about Stalinism; but he thought that a Marxist in America had more urgent and difficult tasks to perform than to expose Stalinist myths. He saw to what use reactionaries and cold warriors were putting some such exposures, and what a demoralizing effect Stalinophobia had on many ex-Stalinists and ex-Trotskyists."[15] At the unexposed center of this dubious political defense of withholding a part of what one regards as the truth lay personal fears about the direction—indeed the fate—of socialism around the world. By consciously separating public utterances from private reflections, he held onto a hopeful critical assessment of socialism in the longer view.

In his best moments as a critic, Baran's pessimism seeped into his optimistic historical framework and tempered it. On balance, however, the separation of public and private discourse marred his achievement by choking off important sources of critical energy: disenchantment and doubt. His compartmentalized criticism of advanced and underdeveloped socialisms precluded a full definition and discussion of radical paradoxes in these parts of the world. Moreover, this mode of exorcising doubts brought out the weaknesses implicit in his special (though not highly original) version of Marxism. Abstracting from the bewildering particulars of experience, he projected large generalizations and then qualified them through detailed empirical investigations. Frequently, however, this essentialist mode of criticism overpowered him: schematic patterns of the decline of capitalism and the rise of socialism clouded the realities he sought to elucidate. Plagued by a personal sense of the growing obsolescence of his dominant perspectives on socialist development and capitalist decline, Baran gradually yielded to the excesses of his method, approaching a major intellectual crisis that he did not live to meet head-on. This pattern asserted itself in his formulations of radical paradoxes in every part of the world, and his own confrontation of reality finally verged on the irrational.

Socialism and Democracy

Though Baran never doubted that capitalism as a global system had utterly failed the test of reason in the twentieth century, or that most backward countries required at least an economic form of Stalinism in order to survive and establish conditions for less repressive varieties of socialism, his attitude toward the Soviet Union and other relatively advanced nations grew increasingly ambivalent toward the end of his life. Charles Bettelheim recalls Baran's mixed personal reactions to a Soviet tour in 1957, after the second wave of de-Stalinization: "Hopes stimulated by the democratization of public life, by the development of greater freedom of discussion. Fears impelled by the 'depoliticization' of a part of the Soviet population . . . and by the growing appetite, unchecked by a revolutionary spirit, for immediate material benefits on the part of an important sector of the cadres."[16] Yet Baran publicly expressed the hope that the new phase of development would result in a "free socialist democracy." And he maintained this position during his last years, insisting in "Thoughts on the Great Debate" (1962) that since the vast achievements of Stalinism had canceled its authoritarian premises, the Soviet Union and other Eastern European countries *must* greatly liberalize the economic and social conditions prevailing in their societies if further economic, cultural, and political advancement is to be assured. For here, as elsewhere, there is a powerful dialectic at work: the very system of extreme pressure on consumption, of unquestioned subordination to authority, and of rigidly dogmatic concentration on principal targets, which was imposed by Stalin and which enabled the Soviet Union to get over the 'hump' of initial industrialization—this very system has turned, in the current phase of history, into a prohibitive obstacle to further economic and social growth."[17]

By fulfilling the first phase of economic development under Stalin, Baran believed, the Soviet Union had greatly expanded the potential boundaries of social and individual freedom. Moreover, since terroristic practices that formerly kept the system in precarious balance had been significantly reduced, democracy could be more or less rapidly extended: "I am . . . convinced that . . . [the pressure of Soviet youth] which gains momentum with every success that it attains will sweep before it whatever may come into its way. It is the pressure of a great and irreversible awakened people that will transform Russia—perhaps more rapidly than frequently assumed—into a free, socialist democracy."[18] Until the late fifties, this two-stage theory of Soviet development from authoritarian to democratic socialism had the obvious advantage of accounting for the absence of democracy under conditions of backwardness. Thereafter, the second stage of the theory was put to the test of history in the advanced nations. And Baran's private doubts about the emerging shapes of these societies caused him to bend his theory of transition to its outer limits, to the edge of the utopian Marxism that Sweezy came to accept by the middle sixties.

At the base of his miscalculations lay illusions about the value of tight central planning at all stages of socialist development. Discussing trends at the close of the fifties, Baran assumed that plans to increase the "Soviet national product by 500 percent in twenty years" and to raise "real per capita income . . . by 350 percent" could be fulfilled.[19] Had these economic expectations been met, political liberalization and democratization *might* have come sooner and with less sacrifice. But the introduction of a number of qualifying political, social, cultural, and ideological assumptions would have helped him arrive at more realistic economic forecasts. He would then have had to confront the crucially important theoretical and practical issues of Soviet and Eastern European socialisms in the 1960s: whether a transition from authoritarian to democratic socialism is possible even in the longer view, and how this crucial transformation might come about. For without the safety valve of enormously rapid growth that would create wider areas of potential freedom in advanced socialist nations, the problem of the uses of existing social freedoms becomes even more troublesome. By miscalculating the rate of potential and actual democratization, Baran avoided an analysis of the more crucial question of the possible—and probable—directions of Soviet society in the sixties and beyond.[20]

Consider first the interrelated economic and political problems of democracy. Though respectable, the growth of the Soviet economy in the sixties fell far short of Baran's expectations. The actual economic growth thus reduced the raw amount of *projected* social and individual freedom and consequently restricted the possibilities for striking a more democratic balance between the two. Moreover, the achievement of even moderate growth depended on greater efficiency and a better balance of the output mix: the relative shortage of labor required greater efficiency than was achieved under centralized planning, and the growing complexity of the economy, including a greater variety of products and increasingly sophisticated consumers, required a better balance of output and a stress on goods of higher quality. Both criteria entailed significant decentralization of decision-making, increasing reliance on mechanisms of the market, and an expansion of the role of consumer preferences, because central planners could no longer dictate output quotas with minimal attention to the quality and mix of goods or the amount of labor required to produce them. Nor did they possess the technical resources or information to make a vast number of decisions that properly belonged at the enterprise level. Hence the debate over economic change turned on the *kind and degree* of decentralization that would be both economically practical and morally and politically desirable for a socialist country that has completed its argricultural and industrial base, and these factors are apt to remain the historical parameters of the controversy for several decades.[21]

Whatever position the various countries finally assume along the spectrum of planned and market socialism, it is clear that the relatively narrow range of economic imperatives carries with it certain broad individual, social, and political consequences. Actual and contemplated economic reforms are predicated on roughly the same *basic* policy of individualistic incentives that has prevailed in the Soviet Union since the inauguration of the first Five-Year Plan in 1928. While socializing the economy as a whole, the Soviet political elite nevertheless always organized production (and the producers) along classically hierarchical lines that made individual gain serve the immediate ends of socialist economic development. In the post-Stalin era, when survival came to depend on steady and balanced growth, the greater portion of surplus available for consumption eliminated the need to stress negative individual incentives, or rather turned such a system into an economic impediment as well as a political liability. Moreover, the economic imperatives of balance and efficiency required a stronger emphasis on positive incentives and rewards. For example, the Brezhnev-

Kosygin reforms inaugurated in 1965 provided more efficient means of measuring the performance, and hence the pay, of managers and workers. Since both abstract models—the Stalinist and the reformist—operate on similar assumptions about the basic organization of work and the motivations on which it is predicated, the general principle "from each according to his ability, to each according to his work" has remained the guiding practical and moral norm during every phase of development.

Though the form of this principle persists, the content has changed considerably because of the rise in the total amount to be distributed and the creation of more sophisticated modes of measuring work. With these improvements, the quality of individual life has, on the whole, greatly improved. Still, in one crucial respect the average structure of consciousness (insofar as it is shaped by the organization and relations of production and the possibilities for consumption) has not substantially altered: primarily motivated by the prospect of personal gain rather than by the spirit of socialist solidarity, most citizens retain a largely individualistic psychology and moral outlook. Of course material incentives continue to be used within an overall context of socialist planning. Income differentials widened by such incentives may be partially offset through the regulation of wages, prices, and taxes. And a portion of the added wealth generated by material incentives is distributed according to the criterion of need. For these reasons, advocates of material incentives argue that as the proportion of collective consumption (free goods and services) gradually increases, the importance of the market, of private consumption, and hence of "bourgeois" incentives will decline, opening the way to communism.[22]

Whatever one thinks of this dubious scenario for the peaceful transition from socialism to communism, it is probably safe to assume that despite increasing collective consumption and the survival of communist ideology, individualistic structures of consciousness will persist in advanced socialist countries as far into the future as it is useful to look. Yet Baran believed that "it can only be a socialist society itself—in which people are not governed by the profit motive and in which the individual is steeped not in the 'values' and mores of the marketplace but in the consciousness emerging from the new socialist relations of production—which will give rise to a new structure of individual preferences and to a new pattern of allocation of human and material resources."23 According to his implicit theory of transition, elements of the new communist man would emerge in societies modulating from authoritarian to democratic socialist phases.

This is the nub of his confusion (and ambivalence) about the possibilities for democracy and community under socialism. For the unrestrained pursuit of a socialist (i.e., communist) community in the post-Stalin era would still have entailed the massive coercion that might have been necessary to a degree under conditions of extreme underdevelopment but could hardly have been morally justified during a period of rising affluence. Moreover, such a synchronization of social and personal relations was, as I have argued, economically and politically out of the question in the 1960s. Decentralization entailed more rather than less consumer "sovereignty"; and economic reforms as well as economic achievements entailed a heavy emphasis on individualistic incentives. The necessity for work and the possibilities of leisure thus converge to "mold" and preserve essentially individualistic—bourgeois, if you like—structures of consciousness.

And more: Soviet economic development has also heightened the desire and the need for other elements of bourgeois democracy. If a highly centralized, politically rigid, and economically underdeveloped socialism severely restricted individual behavior—largely through coercion—the movement toward decentralization at higher levels of output creates a fresh range of tensions among individuals and groups, and between all the individual and institutional parts and the social whole. The impossible dream of an orchestrated, fully harmonious communist order that Baran finally cherished dissolves as the socialist sphere of disorder and unregulated behavior expands. Under present circumstances, these tensions may lead to resolutions that institutionalize more personal freedoms. The existence of popular desires and the material prerequisites for their fulfillment does not, however, ensure either easy or rapid transition to full democracy. For the rate of democratization has been retarded and its scope systematically restricted by the history and shape of Soviet society and politics, an inertial force that Baran consistently minimized. Throughout Soviet history, political control has been exercised by a small minority, sometimes against the immediate wishes of a large majority, sometimes not. Whatever elements of grass-roots democracy existed in the Stalin era were arbitrarily extended and withdrawn in accordance with the needs of the small ruling group. That these needs were affected by popular moods does not change the basic structure of power, which has always flowed from the top down; it rather indirectly demonstrates the main flow by accounting for weak and intermittent countercurrents.[24]

In my view, the primary impulses for democratic change will come mainly from intellectuals, journalists, scientists and engineers, professionals, students, and trade unionists, rather than from party bureaucrats. Nor does it appear likely that the struggle for democracy will be easy, rapid, or even assured of reasonable success. Those who wish to forge a genuine economic and political democracy still lack several crucial means: they do not have sufficient protection from the state to pursue their aims, they are without local bases of power, and they must proceed without very clear models. Barrington Moore's observation in the middle sixties is therefore apt to remain relevant to the advanced socialist countries for some time: ". . . the claims of existing socialist states to represent a higher form of freedom than Western democratic capitalism rest on promise, not on performance."[25] Still, it would be foolish to write off the chances for real democracy merely because the concrete steps and processes cannot be charted in advance. The current social options in the Soviet Union and the countries of Eastern Europe suggest that the contest for democracy is at the very least not utopian, a fact that in itself constitutes grounds for hope without illusion.

The historical possibility of establishing democratic norms, procedures, and institutions within advanced countries raises the important question of their compatibility with other socialist and communist goals. To posit elements of bourgeois democracy as historically realistic socialist aims implies an acceptance (cheerful or otherwise) of the proposition that the original ends of the Bolshevik Revolution have been indefinitely postponed and probably forever compromised. The Leninist vision of an equality of authority has been overwhelmed by the authoritarian economic and political means; the Marxist dream of abolishing the division of labor has been shattered by the necessities of rapid industrialization and modern technology; and the goal of equality of rewards has been overshadowed by the anti-egalitarian means of material (i.e., individualistic) incentives. Whatever the precise mixture of necessity, chance, and choice responsible for the defeat of these ends may have been, the fact remains that the medium-range future of advanced socialist countries largely depends on the past half century of Soviet history. As Moore suggests: "The Bolshevik experience . . . reveals the need for inequalities of power in an industrial society. At the same time, it reveals the needs for a functional division of labor and for inequality of rewards. All of these requirements add up to the necessity of organized social inequality."[26] If these modest conclusions are accepted (and they strike me as inescapable), then the best hope for decent societies that will enlarge the scope of human freedom lies in the development of representative democracy in the context of affluent socialist economies. Such norms and institutions provide the most comprehensive protection of individuals and groups against the unbridled exercise of power by a tiny minority in the presumed (or even actual) interests of the social whole, and they provide the most reliable guarantee that all citizens will have some voice in society's political and economic destiny.

During the 1960s, as we shall see in the chapters on Sweezy and Marcuse, many critics who shared Baran's basic outlook came to oppose the main internal drift and the foreign policy of the Soviet Union, partly because hopes for political decentralization in the reasonably near future appeared slim, but more importantly because the very *aim* of bourgeois democracy within the framework of planning represented an unconscionable violation of communist ideals—ideals that such critics as Baran and Sweezy previously believed would be gradually realized once the vast obstacles of underdevelopment had been overcome. Assessing the economic reforms in the early sixties, Harry Braverman (a regular contributor to Sweezy's *Monthly Review*) observes that the Soviet Union "badly needs more than a new technique in economics. It needs a new socialist spirit, which is after all the biggest *control* that socialism aims for and which it claims as its badge of true democracy, true humanity, and superiority in every other way over capitalist forms of control and incentive."[27]

By the end of the 1960s most critics, including Sweezy, had theoretically dissolved the tension between their ideals and current realities by defining the U.S.S.R. and the nations of Eastern Europe out of socialist existence and transferring their sympathies to China, Cuba, and militant revolutionary groups throughout the third world. They thus reinvested communist ideals with a tenuous historical relevance, and tacitly (or openly) classified European failures as an aspect of the more general disintegration of "Western" civilization.

Whether Baran, who was after all somewhat of a Russian chauvinist, would have similarly resolved this form of radical paradoxes is an open question, since he did not live long enough to clarify the theoretical and practical incompatibility between his hopes for democracy and his fears about the decline of socialist élan. It is impossible to guess whether he would have agreed to the historical costs of socialist democracy, once he had calculated them. For the price is nothing less than abandonment (or the indefinite shelving) of the socialist (communist) vision of community. Only a sterile formula similar to Braverman's could have averted Baran's fears about "depoliticization": the uninterrupted transition to communism depends upon a rebirth of "socialist spirit," which would function analogously to the previous combination of central planning, coercion, and political dictatorship. In place of the involuntary orchestration of the social whole out of backwardness and toward communism, a new socialist spirit would theoretically propel the movement to bring the dialectic of liberation within the purview of a viable sociology of change. In place of compulsion there would arise a voluntary collectivity of individual wills devoted to transforming gradually the Soviet Union into a communist community. The formula, however, has two fatal defects. First, it lies wholly outside the range of historical possibilities and is therefore utopian in theory. Second, considering the present social conditions and general structures of consciousness, in practice this proposed mode of meshing individual parts with the social whole would require new forms of coercion. Such a course would therefore indefinitely delay the growth of socialist democracy in favor of the pursuit of an illusory communist community.

Stanley Moore neatly summarizes what strikes me as the most hopeful direction: "A major economic tendency of liberalization movements in [European] communist countries is to increase the role of commodity exchange. A major political tendency is to increase the role of representative government. The socialist society resulting from such trends would differ from capitalist societies in being classless. Yet in other respects its economic organization, political processes, and cultural values would resemble those of a developed capitalist society more than those of a precapitalist or a communist *Gemeinschaft.*"[28] It is quite possible that, having recognized this, Baran would have rejected the advanced socialist countries as impossibly corrupt, beyond redemption. But I do not think he would have replaced the historical forms of radical paradoxes with a bogus formulation that would set the real though limited prospects for socialist democracy (*and* socialist alienation) against the utopian vision of a communist community beyond alienation and beyond bourgeois democracy. Baran might have attempted to define the ways in which an advanced socialist society could increase the substance of democracy and reduce the most obvious and unnecessary sources of alienation. Such a recasting of reason to reflect the actual and potential realities of advanced socialist nations might have appealed to Baran's rational side. But it would have tested his desires for the creation of a communist community within history. Baran could not have survived the sixties, then, without encountering a deep personal crisis of faith and reason that would have compelled him to revise drastically—or shelve—his inadequate theory of transition to socialism and communism.

Capitalism, Socialism, and Underdevelopment

The deficiencies in Baran's fragmentary theory of socialist evolution become evident once a developing country more or less completes the grueling task of primitive accumulation. In underdeveloped parts of the world, however, the assumptions about the emergence of democracy and community at advanced stages of social and economic growth remain untested—and in the foreseeable future, untestable. Despite enormous differences in history, demography, and culture, countries like China and Cuba must maneuver within very narrow political straits if only because rapid growth—the precondition to national survival—requires a considerable degree of authoritarian control over all the major institutions of society. Individual needs must be sharply restricted in the interests of the social whole—actually, in the battle for survival, and ideologically, in the name of distant goals. Throughout this protracted period, the limited structures of reality simplify the broad short-range injunctions of reason.

In his important studies of underdevelopment, Baran delineated the stark alternatives of misery and starvation under imperialism or survival and painful growth under "backward socialism" as trenchantly as any Marxist critic of his time. To facilitate these studies, he developed the concept of "economic surplus," initially (and provisionally) defined in an essay on "Economic Progress and Economic Surplus" (1953).[29] Based on Marx's category of surplus value, Baran's more general definition of surplus links "the economic foundation of society with what Marxists have in the past referred to as its political, cultural, and ideological superstructures." For analytic purposes, he projected several variants of surplus. The *actual* economic surplus" is a measure of the difference between a society's current output and its consumption. *"Potential* economic surplus" constitutes the "difference between the output that *could* be produced in a given natural and technological environment with the help of *actually* employed productive resources and what might be regarded as *essential* consumption."[30] The elements of the potential surplus may be roughly identified in a society's waste—the output squandered by upper-income groups, as well as the potential output lost through the existence of unemployed or socially useless workers and idle equipment. Together, these partially overlapping concepts comprise an abstract way of comparing what is with what could be.[31]

Underdeveloped nations whose actual surplus is inadequate to meet even the barest needs for food, clothing, and housing cannot make "the steep ascent" as long as they remain under the domination of local oligarchies allied with multinational corporations based in the United States, Western Europe, and Japan. Their only route of escape, Baran maintains in *The Political Economy of Growth,* lies in an alternative organization of resources, a social revolution that will permit redistribution of the actual economic surplus and its expansion toward the potential surplus. By eliminating excessive private expenditures and establishing everyone's consumption at minimum levels, a backward nation can invest a portion of its limited surplus in agriculture initially and in industry subsequently. Though Baran did not ignore the enormous personal sacrifices entailed by such a course, he nevertheless favored authoritarian forms of socialism on the grounds that they constituted the most reasonable (and the only possible) *historical* alternative for the majority of people in Africa, Asia, and Latin America. "Socialism in backward and underdeveloped countries," he remarked, "has a powerful tendency to become a backward and underdeveloped socialism."[32]

Baran clearly sketched the formidable international and internal obstacles confronting any backward country upon completion of the first phase of its social revolution. Since the victory of revolutionary forces is "merely a success 'in the first round,' " a nation quickly encounters serious postrevolutionary "roadblocks"—principally the threat of foreign invasion, which requires a substantial diversion of resources to defense.[33] The other main area of difficulty is the creation of an agricultural supply to meet the expanding demand. This bottleneck, Baran observed, "is primarily due to the fact that while in countries with considerable underemployment in the villages, the productivity *per man at work* could be raised *relatively* fast, the increase of productivity *per acre* has proved to be an extremely slow process."[34] Since agricultural output in an industrializing socialist country cannot be expected to keep pace with rising standards of living for a considerable time, the growth of the economy as a whole must proceed at a disappointingly slow pace.

But Baran's estimates of the prospects for socialism in underdeveloped parts of the world also suffered from the same theoretical lapses and temperamental biases that seriously mar the discussions of advanced countries. In fact, toward the end of his life Baran tried to exorcise fears and misgivings over the course of advanced socialist countries by concentrating his hopes on underdeveloped nations, especially Cuba. Like Mills, he *needed* to be hopeful about the Cuban revolution for personal reasons. Mounting anxieties over the direction of the Soviet Union in the late fifties doubtless called into question the justification of the Russian version of Stalinism as a prelude to advanced socialism and communism. Hence the partial demystification of the future of European Communism magnified hopes that new arrivals would be able to make the "steep ascent" without the needless sacrifices exacted from the Soviet people. But the wish conflicted with Baran's firm grasp of the realities confronting developing socialist nations as well as with his theoretical understanding of Stalinism.

After the official Soviet revelations about Stalinism in 1956, Baran did not accept crude explanations of that complex historical phenomenon. Along with Sweezy, he rejected the idea that the brutalities of "Stalinism are inevitable consequences of a serious all-out effort to develop an underdeveloped country" as an instance of simplistic historical determinism.[35] He also dismissed the apologetic notion that the "abuses" were "historical accidents caused by the fortuitous rise to power of evil men" as a species of the great-man—or evil-man—theory of history. Instead, he insisted that revolution in a backward country creates "conditions conducive to excessive political repression, to abuses of power, to unnecessary curtailment of individual freedoms."[36] Defending the economic policies associated with Stalin's name and acknowledging tendencies toward authoritarianism inherent in similar historical situations, he nevertheless hoped that other socialist countries would discover less repressive political modes of achieving rapid and humane economic growth.

It is against the lucid recognition of the basic forms of radical paradoxes in underdeveloped parts of the world that his overly optimistic reactions to Cuba must be understood. Recalling Baran's ambivalence about visiting Cuba, Sweezy remarks that "After the stormy events of the summer of 1960 . . . [Leo Huberman and I] were anxious to return and persuaded Paul to go with us. At first, he was skeptical of our enthusiasm, fearful, I suppose, of allowing his hopes to run too high and thus courting deception. But he too was carried off his feet in the island's heady revolutionary atmosphere."[37] And he remained enthusiastic about the experiment until his death. As Sweezy observes: "If, in spite of all disappointment and international danger and personal illness, he retained to the end an optimistic faith in the future, the reason was at least in part that brief glimpse of mankind's astonishing potentialities which we were privileged to have in revolutionary Cuba."[38]

Unfortunately, the illusory hopes for the Cuban revolution were compounded by Baran's typical theoretical failures—a too literal use of the part-whole metaphor of social analysis, and an overly abstract application of the concept of economic surplus to historical contexts. In an otherwise admirable brief analysis of the revolution, he predicted that Cuba would avoid the harshest economic aspects of Stalinism and the terror, violence, and repression that accompanied it in the Soviet Union. "The Cuban Revolution," Baran declared, "was born with a silver spoon in its mouth."[39] Having come to power with tremendous popular support and comparatively minor internal opposition, the Cuban revolutionaries, he believed, could bypass an extended period of collective sacrifice. In this "paradisaic garden," the agricultural problems would melt away as the potential economic surplus, which "assumes . . . gigantic proportions," was rapidly actualized. "Enabled . . . to organize an immediate improvement of the wretched living conditions of the masses, the Cuban Revolution is spared the excruciating but ineluctable compulsion that has beset all preceding socialist revolutions: the necessity to force a tightening of people's belts today in order to lay the foundations for a better tomorrow."[40]

With its ability to satisfy the basic needs of the people, the revolutionary government can also "carry out the most far-reaching transformation ever accomplished in human history—the transition from capitalism to socialism—with a minimum of repression and with a minimum of violence, in an atmosphere of freedom and enthusiastic participation of a resurrected nation."[41] Of course Baran realized that the enormously popular government based "on direct democracy in action; [and] on the people's unlimited confidence in and affection for Fidel Castro," would soon require a more formal democratic organization. But these and other problems, he concluded, were "manageable": "all of them can be dealt with rationally, given peace and given time. . . ."[42]

In less than a decade, these optimistic forecasts were invalidated by harsh realities that Baran should have predicted. According to Castro himself, Cuban economic failures have turned individual sacrifice into a semipermanent way of life. Baran's illusions rested in part on a characteristic simplification of his theory to fit the structure of his sentiments: vastly overestimating the rate of realizing the potential surplus, he imagined an economic safety valve that would dramatically ease the political atmosphere during the period of primitive socialist accumulation.

The illusions also derived from an unreasonable belief that Fidel and the Cuban leadership could resist indefinitely the attractions (and even the subtle corrruptions) of unlimited internal power. Confronted with unforeseen economic difficulties, the regime has been subject to the same tendencies that Baran recognized as typical of the early phases of socialist development: "excessive political repression," "abuses of power," and "unnecessary curtailment of individual freedom." Nor has Castro been willing or able to divest himself of awesome personal power and to institutionalize democratic norms and procedures.[43] Still, there are important differences among backward socialisms—differences that profoundly influence the quality of individual life during the arduous time of modernization. Surely not every country in the underdeveloped areas of the world will have to endure the economic *and* social horrors of Stalinism, if only because of important cultural differences that Baran largely ignores. (Whereas China seems to have an adequate substitute for the Puritan ethic as a motive force for development, other nations such as Cuba will need to undergo enormous cultural changes in order to create viable economies.) Yet the historical evidence of the postwar period plainly suggests the inescapability of Baran's general formulation of the slim options open to an industrializing socialist nation. Even Cuba, the presumed exception, seems to have turned into a normal case.

Baran's theoretical resolution to this dilemma—through the "preservation of popular controls over leaders," the extension "of the democratic institutions and civil liberties of the working people," and the confinement of "repression to active counter-revolutionaries"—remains less than satisfactory on two counts. Though preferable to Stalin's political practices, democratic centralism in an industrializing nation can at best provide a limited form of democracy, a slender theoretical counterweight to the economic and political power concentrated at the top. More crucially, this Leninist concept has never functioned as a genuine guide to social practice anywhere for extended periods of time. Though it may yet become a viable alternative in parts of the underdeveloped world, including Cuba, the preponderance of historical evidence suggests that the hope of success ought to be sharply distinguished from the high probability of failure. In the absence of a democratic revolutionary majority, the emergence of a bureaucratic dictatorship is virtually inevitable.

Baran projected other safety valves that might ease the transition from backward to mature socialism, arguing that the cumulative strength of the socialist areas of the world helps other countries in transition. Thus the material and technical aid extended Cuba by the Soviet Union "corroborates the crucially important proposition that every new arrival in the socialist camp finds the going easier than the country which preceded it, that the strength of socialism in the world is cumulative. . . . Just as the cost of modern industry and technology was paid for during the Industrial Revolution by the lives and health and happiness of generations of English and Indian and Irish workers and peasants, so the sweep of socialism in our time is the fruit of the heroism, endurance, and toil of the Russian workers and peasants in the era of the Five Year Plans."[44]

Though partially accurate, this sweeping declaration includes rash and unsubstantiated claims. Doubtless the Soviet Union's military power protected Cuba during the early years of the revolution. And in the sixties both the Chinese and the Russians extended some technical and military assistance to other countries, especially Cuba and Vietnam. On the other side, the costs of defecting from the "free world" rose sharply, as the long war in

Indo-China demonstrates. Nor has any advanced socialist country offered the massive amounts of aid required to reduce significantly the complex problems of economic development in any area of the underdeveloped world. The hard fact is that no *deus ex machina* can appreciably ease the obstacles to internal socialist development in most of the countries of Africa, Asia, and Latin America.

Deteriorating relations between advanced and underdeveloped socialist nations in the early sixties only compounded the difficulties of eliminating backwardness. Unlike most Marxist critics attached to parties, movements, or fixed ideologies, Baran insisted that the doctrinal dispute be analyzed critically and historically rather than debated fruitlessly on purely ideological or ethical grounds. He recognized that no single formula could be sensibly proposed for countries with dissimilar historical backgrounds, conditions, and options. Hence the initial and most important theoretical distinction concerned the quite different histories and uneven stages of economic and social development in the countries of the socialist part of the world. By 1960 the Soviet Union and several nations in Eastern Europe had reached the point where the economic policies of Stalinism (not to mention remnants of its social, political, and cultural components) impeded the progress of reason. Countries like China, however, still required a long period of individual and collective sacrifice to escape the morass of backwardness and underdevelopment: ". . . what constitutes a necessary and positive development in the Soviet Union's advance to a socialist democracy is wholly premature for China, which still has a long way to go until it reaches the Soviet Union's level of industrialization and per capita output."[45] Under these circumstances, the "liquidation of austerity, relaxation of pressure on consumption, and a measure of 'demobilization' of national effort are certainly not on the immediate agenda."[46]

Though Baran did not live to see China's "immediate agenda," it is probably safe to assume that he would have struck a balanced view of the Cultural Revolution. Nothing in his work suggests that he would have regarded that complex phenomenon as the gateway to communism, the social womb of a "new man," though he did predict that the "moral center" of world revolution would shift from Moscow to Peking in the sixties. Stark realities and narrow options contracted the range of ideologies and political structures available to the backward socialist countries. Until it managed to cross the threshold of primitive socialist accumulation, each nation required *some* ideology and political organization consistent with economic Stalinism as well as with its past, its culture, and its geopolitical situation. While suggesting the desperate need for stern economic policies in China, Baran also ventured to hope that they might be administered without the social, political, and cultural abuses associated with Stalin's despotic rule. To the degree that Maoism has fulfilled these injunctions, I believe he would have found the Cultural Revolution rational; thus far it has been a less painful historical alternative than protracted underdevelopment under capitalism or the nightmare of Stalinism.

By isolating the differing needs of the various countries, Baran refuted that arid strain of abstract (antihistorical) internationalism which some critics have invoked to defend China and wholly condemn the U.S.S.R. If advanced socialist countries were to ease the transition in the backward nations with massive amounts of aid, their own consumption and rate of growth would be severely restricted. And the programs of liberalization, on which the political stability and progress of advanced nations rest, would be aborted.

Baran offered a similarly reasoned survey of the differing foreign policies of advanced and underdeveloped nations. The domestic course of the Soviet Union required the easing of relations with the West, a policy of coexistence aimed at averting a nuclear disaster. Threatened with armed intervention from the West, and caught up in endless civil wars, Asian Communists generally took the opposite view that a "hard, uncompromising stand against imperialism would greatly contribute to the awakening and radicalization of the masses in the underdeveloped countries and thus to the strengthening of their socialist movements."[47] These opposing concerns, Baran suggested, raised the crucial question whether the *"short-run* interests of the Soviet people are not now coming into a *genuine* contradiction not only with those of the underprivileged socialist countries but also with those of other backward nations striving for independence and socialism."[48] In the vast literature on the Sino-Soviet conflict, it would be hard to find more than a few Marxist critiques that discuss so lucidly and judiciously the painful dilemmas concerning the direction of the fragmented socialist movement in the early sixties.

Baran's insight into the Sino-Soviet dispute complicated attempts to imagine a credible short-range resolution to his own formulation of radical paradoxes in the backward socialist nations. But he should not be blamed for this failure, since to my knowledge no other social critic has presented a workable historical and political alternative. Baran was, on balance, a better critic of underdeveloped countries than of advanced socialist nations, primarily, I suppose, because his general formulations of radical paradoxes were least ambiguous when applied to Asia, Africa, and Latin America —though most painful in human terms. Devoting a major part of his intellectual energy to problems of underdevelopment, he could not evade recognizing the central needs and narrow options of these countries. Moreover, the inadequacies of his theory of socialist development did not fatally distort his perspective on nations in the throes of primitive socialist accumulation. Apart from illusions concerning Cuba near the end of his life, then, Baran measured up to his conception of the intellectual by plainly delineating the obstacles to development while insisting on the possibilities for substantial change in the third world.

The American Impasse: 1950–1964

Unlike Mills, who worked his way toward a full characterization and resolution of radical paradoxes, Baran came to his studies of the American economic and social order with a set version of these dilemmas, which he elaborated but did not substantially change during the postwar era. As early as 1950 he offered a classic statement of radical paradoxes in a symposium on the ailing American Left sponsored by Leo Huberman and Paul Sweezy, the coeditors of *Monthly Review*. After commending them for launching the badly needed open discussion (generally taboo among the sects), he bluntly observed that "there is hardly any room for political cooperation on the *Left* at the present time because there are no politics of the *Left*."[49] This frank admission of political powerlessness presupposed a belief in the unique stability of American capitalism at midcentury, a stability ensured by a social tapestry with interwoven economic, political, and ideological strands.

Maintaining that the economic system "is on the whole as 'depression-prone' as it ever was,"[50] Baran also acknowledged that the combined power of government and the increasingly monopolistic sector of "big business" could avert a major catastrophe. Faced with the chronic problem of monopoly capitalism— the absorption of otherwise uninvestible portions of a rising surplus—the "ruling class" relies increasingly on military spending to create additional income and employment. But a growing military budget requires political justification. By 1950, Baran argued, the cold war furnished "the political formula for the concerted struggle for preservation of capitalism abroad and for its strengthening and, if necessary, fascization at home."[51] The anti-Communist crusade provided the political rationale for a large program of military spending; it bound the labor movement to the new framework of domestic prosperity, destroying its independence; and it protected the informal American empire in various parts of the world. "Everything," as Baran noted, "synthesizes beautifully in its general effects."[52]

Since most people remained loyal to the system despite relatively hard times, the major obstacles to the growth of the Left were ideological rather than merely economic: "the impotence of the American Left . . . cannot be understood without a full appreciation of the *ideological* stability of American capitalism."[53] Baran contended that without "major shocks," the economic, political, and ideological hegemony that thoroughly neutralized anticapitalist perspectives might survive indefinitely: ". . . in the humdrum of slow evolution the status quo reproduces itself continuously with only such changes as the manipulative machine wishes to induce."[54] By emphasizing—perhaps too strongly— ideological (or "subjective") considerations, he preserved a limited role for critical rationalists, contending that ". . . just now the issues are ideological, and ideological problems cannot be solved by organizational makeshifts."[55] Radicals who understood this were left with the slim alternative of developing a "blueprint of intellectual activity, of enlightened economic, ideological, political thinking and discussion that should be free of dogmatic fetters and petty political considerations."[56]

While amplifying his perspectives on American society during the fifties and early sixties, Baran nevertheless stuck closely to the stark 1950 formulation of radical paradoxes in "Better Smaller But Better." Toward the end, however, his public optimism about the "spontaneity of rational and socialist tendencies in society" yielded to a muted despair. Understandably so, for his studies of underdevelopment deepened his conviction that the growing American entanglement in parts of Asia, Africa, and Latin America constituted the main obstacle to socialism and survival for countless millions of people. At the same time, his preliminary studies of monopoly capitalism reinforced his belief in the necessity and the impossibility of socialism in America. He thus continued to define radical paradoxes *as paradoxes,* a stance that entailed ambiguous and ultimately unsatisfactory answers to the perennial political question of what to do.

Baran steadily refused to yield to the ultimate "logic" of his position, which, if followed from theory to politics, might have landed him in a sect. In a *Monthly Review* symposium on the 1952 Presidential election, for instance, he took the position that Stevenson was a "lesser evil" than Eisenhower. "Denying this is tantamount to regarding the ruling class and the millions who live, think, and act under its ideological spell as one undifferentiated, united, reactionary mass."[57] This decision, however, was basically tactical: ". . . there is a difference between fundamental and unalterable principles on the one hand and the expediencies of the daily political struggle on the other. The ability to recognize this difference marks off a political movement from a sect."[58] Yet Baran's argument against sectarianism hinged on a distinction without an immediate political difference. In the attempt to avoid the futile logic of a politically marginal group, he often lapsed into a sectarian position even as an independent intellectual.

Nor was he disposed to ameliorate the dilemma by advocating progressive reforms. In fact, his whole analysis of American society, begun in the fifties and amplified in *Monopoly Capital,* reinforced the notion that the system cannot be significantly reformed. While granting the *theoretical* possibility of achieving economic stability through a welfare (rather than a warfare) state, Baran consistently denied the practical or political likelihood of such a turn in the medium-range future. In later years he even argued against the desirability of reforms that rationalized parts of a social order without removing its irrational core.

By refusing to abandon his Marxist analysis of American capitalism or to give up his long-range aim of socialism, Baran placed the elements of radical paradoxes in total if not permanent opposition. The safety valve that Mills projected in the late fifties held little appeal. In an obvious though indirect reply to Mills, Baran maintained that unwarranted optimism concerning "the worldwide revolt" of the young intelligentsia violated the central Marxian concept of social classes as "the prime agents on the historical scene."[59] It implied that *"intellectuals* constitute a separate social stratum, an 'elite' above classes which plays an independent and indeed a decisive role in history." Baran then proposed that empty formulas concerning global revolts be put aside in favor of more concrete critical analyses: "The problem is . . . under what historical circumstances do intellectuals become drawn into such movements, under what conditions are they capable of affecting the course of events in any particular way, and what forces determine the specific part which they play."[60]

If the collapse of an autonomous labor movement sharply limited the political influence of a minority of intellectuals turning toward the Left in the early years of the sixties, it also prevented Baran from becoming sentimental about the students' chances of creating an alternative politics. After a radical meeting in San Francisco during the spring of 1963, he recorded his bleak impression of the "crackpots" who attended such affairs: "Until recently they were old-timers, health-food eaters, and Wobblies; now those have died out or are too old to move about but their place is taken by young bearded psychotics, one crazier and queerer than the other. *This* youth is no more likely to create a decent movement than the old [ones] to take up arms. Where is anything to come from in this desert?"[61]

In one of the last pieces published in his lifetime, Baran once again advocated critical rationalism as the only acceptable stance for American socialists. His reply to an essay by W. H. Ferry suggests that the then fashionable rhetoric of the peace movement—a declaration of a plague on both the Soviet and American houses—contributed to the ideological confusion he had described some fifteen years earlier in "Better Smaller But Better": "I submit that if this price has to be paid for the right to raise one's voice . . . *everything one says becomes automatically nullified,* indeed tends to discredit the cause of reason." Thus, by the early 1960s, the tone of personal optimism that marked the 1950 version of radical paradoxes had worn thin. The open letter to Ferry ends on a rhetorically positive note that fails to erase the dominant image of an isolated man: ". . . in the lonely battle in which one is engaged it is a minimal source of satisfaction to have reason on one's side. . . ."[62]

By the end of his life, Baran had in effect given up his slim hopes for a significant American socialist movement in the reasonably near future. The entire analysis of the internal workings of the economic and social order in *Monopoly Capital* reinforces the perspective of radical paradoxes, though the coda seems to offer a way out of the impasse. Borrowing the most sanguine Marxist illusions about foreign influences from the middle fifties, Baran and Sweezy hypothesize that when the Communist countries become glittering showcases, opposition to socialism in America will decline. Adding a dominant radical illusion of the middle sixties for good measure, they predict that as the "world revolution" gathers momentum in Asia, Africa, and Latin America, the domestic irrationalities of the system will intensify, altering objective conditions currently beyond the influence of the American Left.[63]

Although the closing paean to the world revolution represents one imaginative (if unoriginal) resolution to Baran's earlier characterizations of radical paradoxes, the general tenor of the remarks differs from the bleak mood of his final essays on the American condition. But since the coda to the last chapter includes references to events that postdate Baran's death, it probably expresses Sweezy's mood. In any event, the apocalyptic speculations preserve Baran's conception of the basic forms of radical paradoxes in America, and they therefore do not change the social functions of intellectuals. Ending on a strongly Baranian note, the book consigns American radicals to the role of critical rationalists. Between now and the revolutionary apocalypse, "what we in the United States need is historical perspective, courage to face the facts, and faith in mankind and its future. Having these, we can recognize our moral obligation to devote ourselves to fighting against an evil and destructive system which maims, oppresses, and dishonors those who live under it, and which threatens devastation and death to millions of others around the globe."[64] But the rhetoric only momentarily diverts attention from the sticky political problems of how this "fight" might be carried on.

The tissue of assumptions and arguments that buttress these somber conclusions about capitalism, socialism, and revolution receive their fullest development in the earlier chapters of *Monopoly Capital,* Baran's last sustained work. Since they are terrible conclusions not to be lightly adopted, the book requires careful scrutiny. The authors set out to show that the American social order is irrational in two quite distinct senses. They indict the system on moral grounds: against the criterion of the historical— or material—capacities for satisfying human needs that the nation possesses, the actual system has become bankrupt, antithetical to the whole humanist tradition. Because it is irrational at the economic core, no partial political, social, or cultural changes can temper (or even seriously qualify) the totally negative moral judgment. The social mechanisms of monopoly capitalism prevent most proposed reforms from becoming public policies, while those which further reforms only prolong the life of a decadent system. But Baran and Sweezy want to claim much more. Not only does the system richly *deserve* to collapse; it *will* do so at some unspecified point. Monopoly capitalism, in their view, is becoming existentially irrational, doomed by growing contradictions throughout society. They thus assume a variant of the Hegelian dictum that equates reality with rationality: whatever is irrational cannot be real for long.

My critique will be directed initially at the strong version of the arguments. For it is the extreme, uncompromising character of this Marxist case against contemporary capitalism and for revolutionary socialism that distinguishes the work from most other serious Left critiques of America in the early and middle sixties. Most people on the Left agree with much of Baran and Sweezy's indictment and critique. The emphasis on economic phenomena and the interdependence of all aspects of the social whole are not at issue. Nor are the conceptions of America as largely irrational on moral grounds, of advanced capitalism as an economic anachronism, or of the political system as weighted heavily—perhaps even hopelessly—in favor of propertied groups. The central question, rather, concerns the extreme version of the case against contemporary America: is an unlikely socialist revolution the sole alternative to a protracted doom?

A synthesis of Baran's three variants of the surplus—actual, potential, and planned—provides the Archimedean point of the book and dictates its organization and argumentative structure. "The economic surplus," in the briefest possible definition, "is the difference between what a society produces and the costs of producing it." The "size" of the surplus, an "index of productivity and wealth," indicates the quantity of "freedom a society has to accomplish whatever goals it may set for itself." And the composition—or forms—reveals the structure of freedom in society: "how much it invests in expanding its productive capacity, how much it consumes in various forms, how much it wastes and in what ways."[65] Hence the concept of surplus is not only a theoretical tool for analyzing the "purely economic functioning of the system" but also a means of approximating its actual and potential rationality.[66] For the typical ways of using surplus "constitute the indispensable mechanism linking the economic foundation with what Marxists call its political, cultural and ideological superstructure."[67] Focusing on the "generation and absorption of the surplus under conditions of monopoly capitalism," Baran and Sweezy begin with an analysis of the typical economic configurations of the system, and then, in separate chapters, discuss the interrelated political, social, cultural, and ideological shapes and tendencies of American society.[68] In the movement from the economic core to the farthest ideological reaches of the social order, the indictment gathers momentum, preparing the way for the final judgment of total irrationality in the last chapter.

A series of highly abstract models of the economy, the state-system, and the sociocultural sphere brings the fluid interplay between the parts and the social whole into focus. The purpose of these models, the authors suggest, is not to provide a "mirror image of reality," a realistic portrait of society, but rather to "single out and make available for intensive investigation those elements which are decisive."[69] As early as the first chapter, however, they betray the unbridgeable gulf between their aims and methods on the one side and the essayistic mode and exaggerated style on the other. For the method of abstraction requires scrupulous qualification, which the mode and style preclude. "The purpose of this book," they announce, "is to begin the process of systematically analyzing monopoly capitalism on the basis of the experience of the most developed monopoly capitalist society. This statement, however, needs to be clarified; for in science, as in art, a beginning can be of two kinds: a sketch of the overall conception, to be elaborated and filled in later, or the actual commencement of the final work. Our effort is in the nature of a sketch, a fact we have sought to underline by labelling it an 'essay.' "[70] Moreover, as the preface indicates, the essay-sketch intentionally runs to caricature (i.e., a series of exaggerated abstractions): "We shall probably be accused of exaggerating. It is a charge to which we readily plead guilty. In a very real sense the function of both science and art is to exaggerate, *provided that what is exaggerated is truth and not falsehood.*"[71]

As a preliminary sketch, however, *Monopoly Capital* could only support its dire and largely unqualified conclusions if, as the authors note, "what is exaggerated" is true. But that is precisely what the authors must demonstrate—and what they cannot show within the scope and design of their work. Nor does the acknowledgment of limitations make them any less limiting. *Monopoly Capital* is thus deeply flawed in its basic design. But let us examine the interlocking economic, political, and cultural models to determine what sort of case Baran and Sweezy manage within the limitations of their essay-sketch.

The Model of the Economy. To predict a realignment of reason and reality—or, in Baran's terms, a fresh encounter in comparatively rational social circumstances—the authors needed a model that would explain the decline and project the fall of the entire social order, and in particular of the economic system at its center. During the thirties and forties they were especially attracted to theories of stagnation. Understandably so, for these fitted the times. When visions of stagnation virtually disappeared from the literature of economics during the postwar period of relative affluence, Baran and Sweezy retained elements of the perspective, for it fitted their ideological requirements while allowing a marked degree of intellectual suppleness. Assuming an ultimate fall with the aid of the stagnationist emphasis, they were able, as were few other Marxist economists of comparable talent and education, to examine the long decline, using the tools of Marx and those of his latter-day antagonists as well.[72]

The stagnationist perspective informs their most fundamental conclusion about the American economic system:

Twist and turn as one will, there is no way to avoid the conclusion that monopoly capitalism is a self-contradictory system. It tends to generate ever more surplus, yet it fails to provide the consumption and investment outlets required for the absorption of a rising surplus and hence for the smooth working of the system. Since surplus which cannot be absorbed will not be produced, it follows that the *normal* state of the monopoly capitalist economy is stagnation. . . . Left to itself—that is to say, in the absence of counteracting forces which are no part of what may be called the "elementary logic" of the system—monopoly capitalism would sink deeper and deeper into a bog of chronic depression.[73]

To reach this theoretical insight into the "elementary logic" of the system, the authors construct an abstract model of the economy along with several key arguments in support of their basic contention concerning the "normal" tendencies toward stagnation. They suggest that over the past century American capitalism has passed from a competitive to a monopoly phase, a major transformation anticipated by Marx, developed by Lenin, but never fully recognized as a decisive shift by later economists in the tradition. "The dominant element, the prime mover" of twentieth-century American capitalism "is Big Business organized in giant corporations. These corporations are profit maximizers and capital accumulators. They are managed by company men whose fortunes are identified with the corporations' success or failure. They—and here the pronoun stands for both the corporations and the men—look ahead and calculate with care. It is their initiative that sets the economy in motion, their power that keeps it moving, their policies that get it into difficulties and crises."[74]

Because monopoly capitalism remains essentially unplanned, the large corporations relate to one another, to labor, to smaller business, and to consumers mainly through the market. "And since market relations are essentially price relations, the study of monopoly capitalism, like that of competitive capitalism, must begin with the workings of the price mechanism."[75] Baran and Sweezy contend that the operation of the entire system can best be understood in terms of monopoly pricing theory. Within certain limits, large corporations tend to set rather than to accept prices. To maximize profits, oligopolistic groups behave corespectively toward one another, banning price competition and normally following the leadership of the "largest and most powerful firm in the industry—such as U.S. Steel or General Motors. . . ." Though price setting assumes various forms, it has the general effect of driving prices upward.[76]

If the complex pressures of the system of oligopolies push prices upward, they also drive costs down. Baran and Sweezy rest this claim on two decisive aspects of nonprice competition: the obvious advantages in the struggle for shares of the market held by firms with "lower costs and higher profits" over "higher cost rivals"; and the cost-cutting proclivities of the producer-goods industries, whose customers are typically less interested in status and novelty than in equipment that will expand their profits by reducing the costs of production.[77]

Both tendencies—for prices to rise and for costs to decline— form integral aspects of the search for larger profits, which is, after all, still the fundamental economic engine and rationale of the system. By provisionally equating "aggregate profits with society's surplus," Baran and Sweezy turn their principal hypothesis about the generation of surplus into a *tendential* law of monopoly capitalism: "the surplus tends to rise both absolutely and relatively as the system develops."[78]

To round out their exposition of the stagnationist hypothesis, the authors must show that what can be generated cannot be absorbed, at least within the parameters of the economic system described by their model. This they do by arguing that the combined effect of capitalists' consumption and investment is insufficient to offset the swelling surplus.[79] The model is qualified through the introduction of three types of "exogenous" investment, which take "place independently of the demand factors generated by the normal workings of the system": investment to satisfy the needs of a growing population, investment to encourage technological innovation and new products, and foreign investment.[80] Arguing that none of these, separately or in concert, can provide the investment outlets to absorb a swelling surplus, the authors reach their principal conclusion concerning the internal characteristics and behavior of the corporate system: "the *normal* state of the monopoly capitalist economy is stagnation."[81]

The model thus far accounts only for those aspects of economic reality which the authors regard as "normal" proclivities of the system, its "elementary logic." Left to itself, the corporate economy would generate more surplus than it could absorb through capitalists' consumption and the combined impact of "endogenous" and "exogenous" investment. Obviously, however, the monopoly capitalist economy exists in a historical and social matrix, not in a vacuum. The authors argue that two sorts of historical factors have provided powerful external stimuli to investment: wars and their aftermaths, and "epoch-making innovations" such as the steam engine, the railroad, and the automobile, which reconstitute the entire pattern of economic geography. Both types have counteracted the "normal" workings of the economy, inducing periods of rapid growth in the course of American monopoly capitalism.[82] Moreover, from sheer necessity the social order has evolved regular patterns for absorbing excess surplus: the private sector itself now engages in a massive, continuous "sales effort" to increase effective demand, thereby raising income and employment and resisting the built-in death wish of the economy. But the state—principally the federal government—has assumed the major role of regulator and pump primer of the economy in this century; it therefore prevents the fundamental economic logic of the system from asserting itself.

Critics have objected to *Monopoly Capital* on the grounds that the Baran-Sweezy model does not fit the economic facts, that it is too stark to account for the actual functioning of the American economic order. In their eagerness to demonstrate the stagnation thesis, the authors may have simplified corporate behavior by exaggerating that part of the surplus appearing as investible profits and by minimizing the potentialities of what they classify as "exogenous" investment. Both distortions buttress the perspective of stagnation.[83]

A more basic battery of objections concerns the architecture of the economic model itself. Some critics have argued that it rests on a pointless designation of essential and fortuitous factors.[84] To account for the past and present, the authors must employ the "sum" of what they arbitrarily label essential and inessential, intrinsic and external elements. Such a procedure may serve the interests of theoretical purity, but it also diminishes the importance of their model as a means of gauging the future, for its value comes to depend on the off chance that the fundamental logic of the economic system will at some point decisively manifest itself. Otherwise we can expect an interplay of tendencies and counter-tendencies to keep the system afloat on the sea of rising surplus. Deprived of its main predictive force, the model also loses much of its political usefulness. Maurice Dobb notes that "a practical difficulty . . . with an exclusively 'stagnationist' emphasis is that it encourages the political attitude of 'waiting for another 1929' to happen, even apocalyptically—an attitude which has had some serious negative consequences for the leftwing movement in European countries over the past ten or fifteen years."[85]

Baran and Sweezy's description of stagnationist tendencies does, however, establish the context for their major argumentative and rhetorical assault. Considered in isolation, the economy will remain *potentially* irrational on existential grounds for as long as its depressive tendencies continue to operate. But the fatal flaws of capitalism have ceased to be primarily economic, for if sufficient outlets for the growing surplus can be devised in the larger society, it might persist indefinitely. To find the economic and social order morally *and* existentially irrational (albeit in the longer view), the authors must relocate the "irreconcilable contradictions" at several junctures throughout society.

The State System. The principal aim of the model of the state system is to demonstrate the impossibility—and the irrationality— of arresting the decay of the whole by patching up the parts. Having shown this, Baran and Sweezy hope to expose the futility of any politics of the Left not explicitly "revolutionary" and "socialist." They approach these aims with a depressingly simpli- fied conception of the state: "Under monopoly capitalism it is as true as it was in Marx's day that 'the executive power of the . . . State is simply a committee for managing the common affairs of the entire bourgeois class.' "[86] If the state constitutes a complex mechanism for regulating the affairs of the corporate rich and for preserving their interests, the political system of bourgeois democ- racy serves essentially the same ends. Democratic in form, pluto- cratic in content, it comprises yet another important dimension of class power and domination: "In constitutional theory, the people exercise sovereign power; in actual practice, a relatively small moneyed oligarchy rules supreme."[87]

To recapitulate the problem: the corporate sector of monopoly capitalist society generates increasing amounts of uninvestible surplus. Since such a system normally operates at less than capac- ity production, the alternatives to stagnation must come from sources outside the private sector. Only the government, through its taxing and spending policies, can prevent the system from drowning in its own unrealized potential surplus; for if "idle re- sources can be put to work, they can produce not only necessary means of subsistence for the producers but also additional amounts of surplus."[88] Because government spending benefits all classes by saving the economy from stagnation, steady increases now evoke little political opposition. The central question is no longer whether "there will be more and more government spending, but on what."[89] The authors insist that the conflict between economic imperatives and the evolved structures of the state and politics defies any rational resolution as long as "supreme" power resides in the "moneyed" oligarchy, because the common concerns of the oligarchy exclude the possibility of more than minimal expenditures on human welfare—the alleviation of poverty, the reconstruction of cities, the promotion of health and education. And they include, almost by default, growing amounts on warfare and other forms of waste. The oligarchy thus strikes a negative consensus that multiplies moral irrationality and drives the social order toward its ultimate collapse.

Baran and Sweezy offer a brief theoretical account of how the interests of the oligarchy conflict with social needs, illustrating their contentions empirically by reference to the American experience in the twentieth century. Assuming the growing need for federal spending, they attempt to establish a theoretical outer limit to *civilian* spending by identifying "the particular interests of the individuals and groups which comprise the oligarchy and the ways these interests are affected by the various types of spending."[90] As an initial approximation of spending patterns on any given item in the civilian budget, the authors assume a minimum amount that receives general approval and/or evokes no major opposition. But "As this amount is exceeded, approval for further increments gradually declines and opposition builds up until an equilibrium is reached and further expansion stops."[91] Moreover, the political customs of lobbying and logrolling reinforce the web of opposition to large expenditures through what Baran and Sweezy term "the interdependence effect"; for example, real-estate interests usually combine with groups representing the medical profession to oppose large increases in both public housing and public health. With this abstract mode of analysis, the authors suggest, "It would be possible to run through the gamut of civilian spending objects and show how in case after case the private interests of the oligarchy stand in stark opposition to the satisfaction of social needs."[92]

There are, according to Baran and Sweezy, two principal "class motives" for the opposition to adequate federal expenditures on human welfare: projects that interfere with private enterprise are generally taboo (except in times of crisis); and measures that erode the class structure—including the oligarchy's power, privileges, and prerogatives—are similarly deprived of much legislative support. For instance, ambitious public-housing and public-health proposals that do not respect the autonomy of the individual entrepreneur meet the combined opposition of vested interests primarily on economic grounds, while substantial federal aid to education, which might undermine the existing class structure, encounters political, social, and ideological resistance. Thus the conventional paradox of mounting resources (or surplus) along with mounting social needs defies rational political solution.

Baran and Sweezy find this theory of federal spending amply confirmed by their reading of the statistical record. For nearly half a century, federal outlays on war and preparations for war have represented the chief difference between stagnation and collapse on the one side and growth and survival on the other. In 1939, 17.2 percent of the labor force was unemployed and 1.4 percent was dependent on military spending. In 1961, the unemployment figure had dropped to 6.7 percent while the proportion of those supported by military outlays rose to 9.4 percent. The comparative totals—18.6 percent and 16.1 percent—point to a depressing conclusion: "the percentage of the labor force either unemployed or dependent on military spending was much the same in 1961 as in 1939. From which it follows that if the military budget were reduced to 1939 proportions, unemployment would also revert to 1939 proportions." The difference between the "deep stagnation of the 1930's and the relative prosperity of the 1950's is fully accounted for by the vast military outlays" during the latter period.[93]

The statistical record therefore buttresses the second part of Baran and Sweezy's theory of federal spending. Precluding economic and social survival through enlarged expenditures on human welfare, the negative consensus of the oligarchy seeks economic viability through a warfare state. By way of establishing the limited "rationality" of arms expenditures during the cold-war era, the authors devote a chapter to "Militarism and Imperialism," which situates the United States as the chief neoimperialist power in the context of the global battle between capitalist and socialist forces. They offer a wholly one-sided caricature of the cold war, suggesting that the need for a huge military derives from a synthesis of the dominant economic, political, and ideological motives, needs, and interests of the American oligarchy. To preserve and where possible to extend its informal economic empire, the United States oligarchy must devote resources to policing the "free world" and to combating socialism. In fact, military outlays in excess of the needs of empire have become an integral part of the system. The benefits are clear. The military establishment neither creates nor involves competition with private enterprise. And it offers obvious economic advantages such as risk-free government contracts and steady profits while consolidating the class position of the oligarchy: unlike massive expenditures on human welfare and education, "militarization fosters all the reactionary and irrational forces in society, and inhibits or kills everything progressive and humane."[94]

Everything fits together (rather too neatly) in this characterization of the political economy of monopoly capitalist society. In cold-war America, the genuine political "choices" are reduced to variations of two modes of irrationality: "the mass unemployment and hopelessness characteristic of the Great Depression" or "the relative job security and material well-being provided by the huge military budgets of the 1940's and 1950's."[95] But the historically temporary moral irrationality of the cold-war consensus is itself unstable, because military spending cannot be considered "a perfectly free variable." Rather it is subject to the same relentless process of technological rationalization as other branches of industry. And though profitable to large corporations, the impact of military spending on "investment and employment" threatens to diminish at some point not far off.[96] Moreover, the logic of the arms race with the Soviet Union (during the first stage of the cold war) has become self-defeating, for what began as a search, in part, for national security has ended in a condition of perpetual insecurity. That is the present uneasy standoff between the major nuclear powers. And the authors foresee no solutions to this impending economic and military threat: as in every other area, monopoly capitalist society generates new problems but no rational solutions.

The most promising external source of existential irrationality lies in the underdeveloped parts of the world, which have become the "real battlefields between capitalism and socialism."[97] There the nature of the conflict, as well as its direction and eventual outcome, is predetermined. Baran and Sweezy flatly predict that counterrevolutionary interventions "will continue and grow. They will undoubtedly lead to a long series of catastrophes, crises, and confrontations—of a kind with which we are already too familiar."[98] Projected onto a global screen, the moral irrationalities of the economic, state, and political systems will become existential. America will be destroyed in combat with revolutionary forces throughout the world, or else destroy most of civilization in a nuclear holocaust. In the meantime, the conflict between the needs of the oligarchy and those of society will exacerbate domestic social tensions and problems.

In order to project deepening crises issuing from the unresolvable conflicts between the common interests of the oligarchy and the mounting needs of society, Baran and Sweezy must follow out the logic of their prefabricated thesis. It is, briefly, this: the assumption of the oligarchy's inflexibility presupposes an impossibly narrow definition of its "interests" and an overestimation of its ideological limitations. The assumption of a rigid state system requires a broadening of the conception of the oligarchy to include nearly all reactionary segments of society, and a narrowing of the political process to exclude other individuals and groups. In *Monopoly Capital,* the terms "ruling class" and "oligarchy" never acquire precise theoretical or operational definition. Without warning the reader or explaining the shift, the authors modulate from one conception in the economic model to a second in the model of the state system. In the discussion of the economy, the oligarchy clearly stands for the small corporate elite—the owners, managers, and agents of the decisive economic institutions of monopoly capital who by virtue of their class position and commitment to big business exert an enormous influence on the state and the political process. In this context, the oligarchy is equated with the ruling class. But in the model of the state and politics, the oligarchy includes other classes and strata that retard needed change: the middle sector of business, small business, a significant number of professionals. In fact, it comes to include nearly everyone—from major actors to bit players—who might take part in the negative consensus. The "oligarchy" finally becomes an abstract notion standing for all the forces promoting what Baran and Sweezy consider "moral irrationality." Bound to the logic of their thesis and committed to a deliberately exaggerated style, Baran and Sweezy produce a distorted and misleading moving picture of power and politics in America—a cartoon whose minimal predictive value deprives it of much relevance to a politics of the Left.

To build their case for the inflexibility of the oligarchy, the authors contend that expenditures involving competition with the private sector or interference with class privileges "must be resisted." The additional phrase "at any cost" turns a very rough first approximation toward caricature. Defined in this way, the inelastic interests bar progressive proposals conceived by the oligarchy, shaped through the political and legislative process, and administered at one or another level of government. By definition, nearly every public policy proposal, from expanded health care to improved education, implies a modification of the existing balance of class power and privilege. Clearly, however, the "real" common interests of the corporate oligarchy are more inclusive: it can tolerate—indeed its members ought to promote—a far wider range of reforms, if only because continuous changes, some of them far-reaching, constitute the base price of class survival.

A more useful initial approximation of the chance for alleviating major and minor social problems and reducing injustices should begin with a tentative assumption about the *outer* limits of politically induced social change consistent with the oligarchy's common interests. In place of Baran and Sweezy's cramped definition, I would substitute the "criterion of political eligibility."[99] Here the relatively small though important band of the wide spectrum of proposed measures that may be realized through political activity must meet at least one basic condition—they cannot entail the dissolution of the American corporate structure. Although the criterion of political eligibility illuminates no more than the *potential* future space and adaptability of advanced capitalist society, it seems preferable as a point of departure to Baran and Sweezy's geometric projection of the worst of past and present performances.

Since these theoretical limits may encompass a partial or even a full nationalization of some industries, not to mention a broad panoply of measures to advance all forms of human welfare, they are elastic. Obviously the criterion of political eligibility needs to be qualified in a number of ways: the actual course of change depends upon a bushel of other factors such as the perceived interests of the oligarchy, governmental and political structures, and the politics of nonowning classes. I propose it here as a limiting case, a way of defining the unified interests of the oligarchy that does not place it inevitably and consistently at odds with social needs in general and with the needs of the lower classes in particular. This criterion shows no more than a probable general direction that may be acceptable to the oligarchy as a means of alleviating mounting social crises. It introduces the possibility, to vary "Engine Charlie" Wilson's dictum, that in some instances what is good for the country may be necessary for General Motors.

There is, of course, no reason to suppose that the oligarchy—or even a significant proportion of its members and representatives—will define its interests in this way and voluntarily push for legislative and executive action designed to realize these outer limits. But there is still less reason to suppose that the oligarchy will stubbornly cling to the inner core of its interests "at any cost." Unless, of course, we include what might well amount to class suicide in the calculus. And that is precisely the supposition the authors must press in order to type-cast the oligarchy in their tragic scenario. At every turn, Baran and Sweezy insist that the oligarchy will—as in the past—perceive its concerns narrowly and oppose every change that encroaches on the private sector or erodes class privileges. This part of the argument demands the assignment of the darkest possible motives, the meanest intentions, and the feeblest collective intelligence to the oligarchy.

The ultimate lineup of nearly unlimited power on the side of the irrational "oligarchy" and impotence on the side of the potentially rational opposition (elements of the working class, blacks, the young, and the dispossessed) amounts to a caricature of the American political system at its worst. It is at once a revealing and a misleading caricature—revealing because it suggests the lopsided division of economic and political power; misleading because it blots out all counteracting forces, labels every nonrevolutionary action on the political landscape directly or indirectly irrational, and transforms the most extreme options into *the* certain path to destruction. The authors thus fail to draw a balanced picture of the imbalances of power, or to present a sophisticated view of the possibilities for partially rational adaptation. Insisting that the oligarchy's pursuit of survival entails *only* destructive modes of adaptation, they ignore the prospects for constructive change through assimilating "token" reforms into the larger design of the irrational whole. In the end, the analysis of the state and politics moves beyond the framework of a plausible sociology of change toward the mythic regions of an ambiguous dialectic of liberation. It threatens to become an antipolitical myth, a vision of destruction that must precede revolution and the construction of socialism.

Had Baran and Sweezy evolved a more comprehensive—or rather a more complete—model of the state system, they would have confronted a spate of critical questions concerning class, ideology, power, and politics in America. And the consideration of these issues would have raised other questions about the actual and potential modes of flexibility within the interrelated economic, political, and social spheres of monopoly capitalism. At the very outset of the study, however, the authors deliberately omit the labor process: "We make no attempt to inquire systematically into the consequences which the particular kinds of technological change of the monopoly capitalist period have had for the nature of work, the composition (and differentiation) of the working class, the forms of working-class organization and struggle. . . ."[100]

Having consciously put these considerations to the side, Baran and Sweezy should also have refrained from indulging in massive, unqualified generalizations about the fate of American society. For their generalizations about political alternatives on the Left presuppose an analysis of "the relation of class incomes and interests to the generation of surplus. . . ."[101] An adequate class model, then, would include the relation of each important group to the creation and disposition of surplus. It would delineate the general and special interests of each class, rather than focusing exclusively on the single moment in which all irrational interests are in phase. Similarly, a useful model of the political process would enlarge our understanding of how tension, conflict, and consensus operating within and among various classes and strata are translated into political terms and public policies. Finally, to acquire predictive value, it should allow for and anticipate indeterminate change over time. For when fatal contradictions cannot be plausibly ascribed to the social order, the chances for its survival—in more decent economic, political, and social forms—become the most vital area of concern for people on the Left. Without convincing assumptions and analyses of class, power, interests, ideologies, and politics, it is risky to attempt an assessment of the general thrust of American capitalism.

Baran and Sweezy clearly do not earn the right to dismiss cavalierly the entire range of nonrevolutionary socialist and even liberal analyses, strategies, and tactics, the more so because the burden of persuasion, so to speak, properly falls on advocates of a convulsive social revolution. There is, as the authors note, no "magic formula for converting the oligarchy" to a program of Left-liberal reform;[102] there may even be no viable *political* formula. Over the medium haul, however, any program of the American Left must begin with a search for the political means of meeting the chief economic imperative through a reversal of priorities in the public sector. That is only a beginning, perhaps even an unpromising one. But it represents a political alternative to Baran and Sweezy's own magic formula for wishing the system away by predicting a disaster that probably will not come about, at least in the relevant future. Since their economic and political models, taken together, do not project a convincing fatal contradiction, the authors fail to establish the context for a revolutionary program. Willing to settle for nothing less, however, they end up without any domestic politics at all. And the search for the denouement of monopoly capitalism must be transferred to the cultural and ideological spheres.

The Sociocultural Sphere. The part-whole metaphor of society constitutes the paradigm of Baran and Sweezy's wide-ranging discussion of the ubiquitous crisis of capitalist culture. They view all facets of contemporary American life through the paradoxical lens of partial rationality advancing in a context of total irrationality. Every crevice of society, every typical ideological pattern and emotional set, expresses the same overriding contradiction "between the rapidly advancing rationalization of the actual processes of production and the undiminished *elementality* of the system as a whole."[103] Though everyone experiences its debilitating effects in one way or another, most cannot even comprehend the elementality of a society that "is governed as though by great natural forces, like wind and tide, to which men may adjust but over which they have no control."[104]

Identifying "irrationality" and "elementality" with the social whole, Baran and Sweezy lead the reader through the capitalist chamber of horrors, showing at every turn that the unresolvable conflict between the "elementary needs of human nature" and "the compulsions of the system" is becoming "ever more insupportable." Millions lack the material prerequisites for a decent existence: an adequate diet, housing, and medical care. And nearly everyone, according to the authors, confronts needless misery and loneliness because of alienating work and debilitating leisure, not to mention the breakdown of community, the increasing barriers to satisfying personal relationships, and the slow "destruction" of family life. The "logical outcome" of these tensions generated by the political economy and expressed in the cultural, ideological, and personal spheres "would be the spread of increasingly severe psychic disorders leading to the impairment and eventual breakdown of the system's ability to function even on its own terms."[105]

The treatment of alienation typifies the consequences of employing utopian assumptions to assess historical realities. Baran and Sweezy begin with the notion that the capitalist division of labor has prepared the way for general abundance, the material prerequisite for communism in classical Marxism. They further suppose that the productive achievements of advanced capitalism have obviated the need for the "all-engrossing system of specializing and sorting men. . . ."[106] Instead of freeing people, however, the irrational capitalist order must preserve alienating patterns of work: "Men are still being specialized and sorted, imprisoned in the narrow cells prepared for them by the division of labor, their faculties stunted and their minds diminished."[107] Moreover, the authors presume that alienated labor constitutes the paradigm for other spheres of personal life: "Forces similar to those which destroy the worker's identification with his work lead to the erosion of his self-identification as a consumer."[108] Work and consumption thus turn into an enervating round from which there is no escape and little relief: "while fulfilling the basic needs of survival, [work and leisure] increasingly lose their inner content and meaning."[109]

There is an important core of truth in this characterization of work and leisure. Much labor, "judged by genuine human needs," is indeed "useless, wasteful, or positively destructive."[110] Millions of dull, routine jobs offer only meager personal satisfactions. But the point should not be bent out of shape. Intellectuals, especially those on the Left, tend to simplify the complex, subtle, and ambiguous psychological fabric that most men weave around their jobs. Consequently they underestimate the genuine needs that even unpleasant jobs may fill, as well as the small though important pleasures of human association and accomplishment they afford.

Baran and Sweezy must press their case beyond its useful limits in order to reveal the *complete* bankruptcy of capitalist society and culture, its total opposition to the fulfillment of human needs. In this final section of the book, the authors cannot afford to separate myths from historical and political possibilities. Instead they intend to use assumptions from the dialectic of liberation to load the case hopelessly against contemporary capitalism. In this process, however, valid points and useful insights typically disappear in the folds of a larger utopian myth. Hence their method of judging American society as utterly irrational exacts the heavy price of substituting imagination for reason in the ceaseless human confrontation of reality. In its ultimate vision of America, *Monopoly Capital* becomes a symbolic gesture of revulsion, a sweeping negation of the present. The authors replace political possibilities with an undifferentiated moral judgment that confines the critic to the margins of society and recasts him as a prophet of doom.

Thus the early advantages of intellectual latitude that the authors shared as politically independent intellectuals returns to haunt them in the final chapters of *Monopoly Capital*. As one Communist critic remarked: "In eliminating the working class as the revolutionary force in American society, Baran and Sweezy eliminate what Marx and Engels considered the motive force of social change in a class society—the internal class struggle engendered by its exploitative character."[111] Of course the authors report only the current nonrevolutionary condition of the working class. At the same time, however, they discount all "working class" politics within the system on the ground that no group in America possesses the capacity and the will to stage a successful socialist revolution. Having made this reductive assumption, they avoid Marxist political sects altogether, though for incomplete reasons and in the pursuit of the even more remote end of the world revolution. Hence, by continuing to place the revolutionary vision of Marx at the center of their efforts, they gravitate toward scenarios of destruction and re-creation that lack a "motive force" in history. Finally, then, politics modulates into antipolitics, and frequently shrewd analyses serve the larger ends of a futile vision, one with no applicability in America and with only tenuous relevance elsewhere.

By pressing all their evidence into an apocalyptic mold, Baran and Sweezy cancel out the predictive value of their work. Having abstracted basic tendencies from monopoly-capitalist and socialist societies, they imagine a simplistic interplay of their own symbols that leads inescapably toward the destruction of capitalism and the creation of socialism. Their failure, as Robert Heilbroner aptly describes it, "lies . . . in a fatal Marxian predilection for 'closed systems' of thought that can then proceed with a delicious inexorability to their assigned destinations. In such systems, it is very hard to incorporate models of thought or action that partake of uncertainty, indeterminateness, or changeability."[112] Consequently, Heilbroner continues, "beliefs and attitudes that are perfectly correct as first approximations of social behavior—such as the predisposition of the American government and business class to defend its system of privileges—are frozen in ways that leave no room for compromise, retreat, adaptation, or learning. No wonder, then, that the historic drama has so often defied Marxist predictions."[113] In this crucial respect, *Monopoly Capital* falls neatly into a long tradition of Marxist prophecy. Though based in part on an "overly abstract conception of power and class," as Heilbroner suggests, these failures, I think, are at bottom based on the authors' submission to the dialectic of liberation as a critical perspective *and* as a goal in history.

After reducing the historical roads in our time to two, Baran and Sweezy do not evolve a plausible image of socialism as the *specific* historical form that abstract rationality must—and ought to—take in the next decades (even centuries). Their narrowing of means is matched by a feeble vision of the socialist end. Throughout, images of socialism are muted, and their dismal manifestations elsewhere not carefully distinguished from ideals. For example: "In a rationally ordered socialist society, no matter how richly endowed it might be with natural resources and technology and human skills, 'too much' could only be a welcome signal to shift attention to an area of 'too little.' Only under monopoly capitalism does 'too much' appear as a pervasive problem affecting everyone at all times."[114] At every juncture the comparisons are one-sided, and often simply wrong. Apart from invoking Marx's utopian concept of man, Baran and Sweezy do not articulate a viable theory of persons, a view of human nature—its past, present, and possible futures. Without some theory of persons, however, a socialist vision quickly crumbles for lack of basic assumptions about the impact of human intellect and sensibility on social forms. In part, this omission reflects the authors' growing uncertainty about the forms of socialism in the U.S.S.R. and Eastern Europe; it also implies the inadequacy of their minimum definition of socialism as the abolition of exploitation, and the prelude to the end of alienation under communism.

The narrow paths of history illuminated by the later chapters of *Monopoly Capital* thus represent a retreat toward rigidity. They obliterate less deterministic projections in Baran's earlier works that allow for a broader range of possibilities resulting from confrontations of reality with reason. Concluding his case against American policy toward Cuba, he remarked in 1961: "must we now assume that the United States government . . . will follow the example of the Portuguese rather than the example of the British? I cannot accept this as inevitable. . . . There is no way of writing an insurance policy for the capitalist system for an indefinite period of time, either in this country or anywhere else in the world. There may be, however, a way of assuring the world's survival provided the 'furies of private property' can be—if only partly—tamed, if the ruling class of this country can be prevented from committing suicide out of fear of death."[115] The difference between this grimly realistic statement and the apocalyptic matrix and tone of *Monopoly Capital* may be a thin one, a matter of degree; but it marks the hazy border between a vision of guarded hope and a submission to despair. It also separates a rational consideration of options in an imperfect world from a simplified conception of contemporary history as tragic drama, with the dominant class of the leading capitalist nations assigned stereotyped motives and a predetermined part in a suicidal script.

Conclusion

Any attempt to estimate Baran's overall contribution to Left-wing thought suggests, I think, a paradoxical or at least an ambiguous conclusion, since his inseparable strengths and deficiencies were ultimately expressions of a man in deepening conflict—with his changing surroundings, to be sure, but more crucially with his own impulses and ideology. His perspectives on the present as history from the end of World War II until his death remained stable in fundamental respects. This critical sanity generally enabled him to resist dubious contemporary intellectual fashions. At the same time, Baran's vision of the world was buckling under the weight of events in the fifties and early sixties. Toward the end of his life, the sense of the tragic disturbed his critical balance, without impelling him to launch a full-scale revision of his main perspectives on the "three dominant themes of our age."

Failing to distinguish theoretically between the abolition of exploitation under socialism and the eradication and alienation under communism, he was increasingly unable to connect current realities with historical trends in the Communist countries of Europe. Sensing this, he banished private doubts from public utterances. Had he lived, however, Baran would have been compelled to confront radical paradoxes in the advanced and the underdeveloped socialist countries head-on. He might have moved —with Sweezy—toward a new synthesis of personal desires and historical options by regarding the advanced countries as betrayers of the socialist vision and placing all hope in the Chinese, Cuban, and other revolutionaries. Or he might have surrendered the communist vision and redefined the goal of socialism as the abolition of exploitation and the creation of a genuine political democracy. He would have then characterized radical paradoxes *as paradoxes* with different implications in the advanced socialist nations, in the underdeveloped world, and in the United States, Japan, and Western Europe.

Such a fragmented view, however, is uncongenial to a radical who temperamentally and theoretically sought to connect a unified vision of communism to the historical present by adopting the longer view. Nor is it congenial to someone with an urgent sense of his own ending. Plagued by a lingering illness in the early sixties, Baran held onto his central perspectives and hopes, yielding occasionally to his profound pessimism about the United States—indeed, the world—as in the vision of psychic decline at the end of *Monopoly Capital.* His last personal letter described plans for a sabbatical in Europe, which he looked forward to as an escape from Stanford and an opportunity to bring his intellectual life to a close. Baran hoped to complete a book of essays and "work further on a half-done ms. of 'An Essay on Marx,' " which, he remarked, "I would like to bestow on an astonished and grateful humanity sometime in 1966. Thereafter I plan not to touch pen or pencil anymore, to dispose of my . . . [typewriter], and to conclude my days reading novels, listening to records, and engaging in *dolce far niente.*[116] He never had the chance to attain this desire for an aesthetically appealing ending, a resolution of the tensions that in large part accounted for his important insights as well as for his intellectual blind spots. Neither history nor his own experience granted him that.

The materialist doctrine that men are products of circumstances and upbringing, and that, therefore, changed men are products of other circumstances and changed upbringing, forgets that it is men that change circumstances and that the educator himself needs educating. . . .

The coincidence of the changing of circumstances and of human activity can be conceived and rationally understood only as *revolutionizing practice.*

—Marx, *Theses on Feuerbach*

"Allons en Icarie!"

—Étienne Cabet

5

Paul Sweezy:

The Pursuit of Communism

Baran and Sweezy (1910–   ) are usually thought of as an inseparable pair, since for a quarter of a century—1939 to 1964—their personal and intellectual lives were so closely intertwined. Assessing Baran's contribution to *Monthly Review,* the journal that has formed the core of his own intellectual work since 1949, Sweezy observed that "while he did not always agree with us . . . it is hardly an exaggeration to say that the editorial ideas and opinions expressed in *MR* over the years have been as much his as ours."[1] Yet there are important differences between the two men—differences in background and temperament, education, and class, and most important, in their conceptions of the present as

128

history. Sweezy comes from the American upper class, having been educated at Exeter, the London School of Economics, and Harvard, where he taught until 1949. During the sixties, his search for a sign of communism in history demanded definitions and proposed resolutions to radical paradoxes that differ appreciably from those he earlier shared with Baran. In fact, Sweezy's later intellectual development can best be understood as one representative direction out of the theoretical and political impasse which Baran approached toward the end of his life.

As cofounder and principal editor of *Monthly Review,* Sweezy has created an open-ended historical document of considerable importance. Devoted "to analyzing, from a socialist point of view, the most significant trends in domestic and foreign affairs," the more than twenty volumes of *MR* also provide a monthly barometer of Sweezy's own pursuit of communism in history.[2] His most dramatic shift—from a mildly critical supporter of socialism in the Soviet Union and the Eastern European nations in the fifties to an enthusiastic interpreter and follower of the Chinese in the sixties— has thus far received scant critical attention. Unaccountably so, since he is at once the most distinguished American Marxist economist of his generation, and one of the most influential social critics of the far Left of the 1960s.[3] When not ignored (or merely quoted), Sweezy has been ignorantly attacked from a variety of sources, if only because his disenchantment with authoritarian aspects of Soviet socialism did not take him down a usual path of retreat. As Irving Howe facetiously observed: "The logic is clear: begin with theoretical inquiry and concern over the perpetuation of dictatorship in Russia and end with 'full trust and confidence' in China, where the dictatorship is more severe."[4]

Though it explains nothing, Howe's evaluation of Sweezy's changing allegiances does obliquely indicate his deepening disillusionment with every branch of Western civilization in the late 1950s. His revulsion with American society and culture and a growing skepticism about the chances for significant social change account for one principal source of his disenchantment. The other stems from a gradual and reluctant realization that the Soviet Union was not moving toward socialist democracy and communism. In 1958 he wearily observed that "world leadership, for better or worse, is on the point of passing out of the hands of Western white civilization and into those of a new Eastern and predominantly colored civilization. One can regret it, but I don't think I do. I only hope that the new civilization that is coming succeeds better than ours has in realizing what I still hold to be the great potentialities of the human race."5

His increasing drift toward pessimism was offset by a rebirth of hope in the early sixties—a belief at first tentative and later beyond question (if not beyond doubt) that the Cubans, Chinese, and other revolutionaries in underdeveloped areas of the world were reclaiming the betrayed promises of socialism and communism, and beginning to enact them in history. Though important, this dialectic of hope and despair only traces out the patterns of Sweezy's faith, which finally required him to substitute China for Russia as the primary historical manifestation of socialism and the harbinger of communism as well. Since he is also a man of reason, the more interesting side of the story revolves around his theoretical development, his movement from one paradigm of socialism/communism, largely derived from classical Marxism and Soviet experience, to a second, largely distilled from Maoist and Cuban perspectives. The first paradigm, which he used with considerable confidence until the Hungarian uprising in 1956, fell apart during an interlude of doubt, disillusionment, and revaluation—roughly from 1957 until 1960. After visiting Cuba in the spring of 1960, Sweezy began to develop a second paradigm, gradually elaborating it into a coherent perspective on the transition from capitalism to communism via perpetual revolution.

Thus the intricate interplay between Sweezy's personal dialectic of hope and despair on the one side, and his changing analyses of the nature and prospects of socialism, communism, and capitalism on the other, does exhibit a theoretical and emotional logic that neither Howe nor other critics have managed to reconstruct. I shall argue that the dramatic shift in theory and the corresponding relocation of his vision resulted primarily from tensions between images of socialism and communism in the 1950s and their disappointingly slow progress in various societies.

The First Paradigm: 1949–1956

During the early postwar years, Sweezy adopted Marx's general distinction between socialism and communism, dividing the long process into two theoretically and historically distinct phases. In the inaugural issue of *Monthly Review,* the editors define socialism as "a system of society with two fundamental characteristics: first, public ownership of the decisive sectors of the economy; and second, comprehensive planning of production for the benefit of the producers themselves."[6] For Sweezy, then, "the essence of socialism is production for use in accordance with a comprehensive plan."[7] The principle "from each according to his ability, to each according to his work" summarizes the initial stage of the transition from capitalism to communism. This "first phase" must display the noneconomic marks of its origins: "the workers as the new ruling class will need their own state (the dictatorship of the proletariat) to protect them against their enemies; man's mental and spiritual horizon will still be colored by bourgeois ideas and values. . . ."[8]

In time, however, the achievements of socialism will permit a peaceful transition to communism, a higher phase of man's historical development. At this distant juncture, the "limitations imposed by the capitalist past will . . . [have been] transcended. . . ."[9] Specifically, economic progress under socialism should guarantee the inauguration of communism by "gradually . . . [raising] the [material] well-being and education of everyone."[10] Hence "all classes and class distinctions would be done away with. When that happened," Marx predicted, "the state as a repressive apparatus for dealing with class and other forms of social conflict would 'wither away.' " Delivered from the constraints of scarcity, men would construct an egalitarian society in which " 'the free development of each is the condition for the free development of all.' " Moreover, when the socialist mode of production evolves into the communist mode of distribution, differential wages and commodities will become obsolete forms: each man will produce according to his ability, and consume what he needs. Sweezy envisions societies rooted in "scarcity and alienation" giving way to societies of "abundance and brotherhood."[11]

This paradigm of socialism and communism fitted most of the requirements of independent Marxist intellectuals at midcentury. The two-stage theory of transition preserved the ideals of communism—abundance, equality, democracy, and the conquest of alienation—from the historical present: the achievement of communism, in Sweezy's schema, "remains what it was a century ago, a goal for the future."[12] At the same time, these assumptions invested independent Marxists with contemporary historical if not political relevance, because existing Communist countries satisfied the bare criteria of socialism. By deliberately leaving open the question of political forms, Sweezy implied that socialist societies may be authoritarian or democratic, depending on their stage of economic, technical, and cultural development. Moreover, socialism in backward countries must pass through an authoritarian phase before becoming democratic. But the same forces of rapid economic growth and massive "socialist education" that propel authoritarian socialist societies toward the eventual destination of communism also push them toward the intermediate point of democratic socialism. Despite all sorts of unanticipated zigzags, democratic socialism and communism were considered distinct points on a one-way path into the next great epoch of human history.

Sweezy's analysis of advanced socialist nations during this period turned on two related themes. First, he constructed a fragmentary historical explanation of the ethical paradoxes that are still plaguing the U.S.S.R., using Marx's method to correct nineteenth-century predictions about the course of socialism in history. Second, he conducted periodic critiques of the pace of Soviet progress, measuring swiftly changing socialist realities against the paradigm. The first explanation accounted for the nature and direction of Soviet socialism; the second accounted for the tempo.

On several occasions in the late forties and early fifties, Sweezy reviewed Marx's general scenario for the transition from capitalism to socialism, concluding in 1949 that "the *Manifesto* has stood up amazingly well during its first hundred years. The theory of history, the analysis of capitalism, the prognosis of socialism, have all been brilliantly confirmed."[13] Responding to the overriding question "Was Marx Right?," Sweezy reiterates the answer seven years later: "In the broadest sense, I do not see how it can be denied that Marx was brilliantly vindicated." A powerful socialist movement developed in his own lifetime; the Russian Revolution of 1917 brought socialism directly into history, and more crucially, it survived and spread to other countries: "Today, something like a third of the human race has definitely abandoned private enterprise and, under Communist leadership, is building up a network of planned economies."[14]

But history did not follow Marx's image of transition: the cruel goddess "has decreed that the world transition from capitalism to socialism, instead of being relatively quick and smooth, as it might have been if the most productive and civilized nations had led the way, is to be a long drawn-out period of intense suffering and bitter conflict."[15] Sweezy accepted this spin of the historical wheel, along with its implications for the backward countries—especially the hardships involved in the steep ascent from economic underdevelopment to abundance, and the consequent delay in the formation of democratic institutions. "The new order" in the U.S.S.R. "could not build directly on the achievements of the old. It had no developed industrial base, no educated and trained labor force, no political democracy. It had to start from scratch and work under conditions of utmost difficulty."[16] Such circumstances sealed the short-term fate of freedom and democracy: "Intellectual freedom and personal security guaranteed by law . . . have been virtually unknown to the peoples who are now blazing the trail to socialism. . . ."[17]

Sweezy nevertheless continued to assert that democracy was not part of the minimum definition of socialism, but rather the determined product of its essential characteristics—public ownership and central planning—operating over time. In the light of this version of the opening stages of socialism in history, he defended Stalinism (and Stalin) as the only available course in the late twenties. Immediately after Stalin's death early in 1953, the editors declared that "there can be little doubt that history will account Stalin one of the greatest men of all time."[18] Their flattering obituary highlights Stalin's "achievements" while generally excusing his harsh "methods."[19] Sweezy concluded that "only Stalin of all the Soviet leaders had the vast organizing ability, the unerring judgment, the steady nerve, and the iron will that were required." Lenin was the Russian Moses, "the true leader and inspirer of victory in the October Revolution and the ensuing Civil War"; Stalin was its Joshua, "the architect of socialism in its first homeland and the generalissimo of victory over fascist barbarism."[20]

After Stalin's death, the system of terror, violence, and illegality seemed less justifiable. The harsh facts of the political dictatorship, especially its past but also its contemporary modes, were increasingly inescapable and inexcusable. Still, in his comments on the fall of Malenkov in 1955 Sweezy exaggerated the positive implications of the power and policy struggle, noting that the succession of leaders took place, for the first time, "in an orderly and civilized way," without "violence and bloodshed." A tradition of nonviolent succession, he predicted, would represent "a very long step on the road to establishing a true reign of law in the socialist world. . . ."[21] At that point, progress in liberty meant no more than the suspension of terror, the cessation of domestic political violence, and the establishment of elementary legal guarantees.

After the XXth Party Congress in 1956, the matter of democracy could no longer be so easily finessed. The socialist paradigm and corresponding theory of Soviet development needed to be brought more closely in line with Soviet realities, past and present. The problem was clear: to vindicate the paradigm, Sweezy had to put Stalinism into a contemporary perspective and offer theoretical assurance of the gradual democratization of Soviet society. It became imperative, then, to explain both the achievements and the horrors of the Stalin era as inseparable parts of an historical process leading to democratic socialism and communism. This required elaboration rather than abandonment of the paradigm. Along with Baran and Isaac Deutscher, Sweezy approached the problem dialectically, arguing that the Stalinist state "embodied a gigantic contradiction: in its aims and achievement it can fairly be described as superhuman; in its methods and attitude toward the rights and dignity of the individual it was subhuman."[22] Stalinism was thus "a self-contradictory phenomenon. It accomplished good ends by bad means."[23] Moreover, it appeared to be a self-liquidating phenomenon, because the ends it achieved—economic growth, education, and survival—canceled out the means. But this theoretical projection still did not constitute grounds for excessive optimism about the character and rate of democratization. In his assessment of the XXth Congress, Sweezy issued an "implicit warning against exaggerated hopes or expectations," noting that "the Soviet dictatorship is cleaning house, not abolishing itself."[24] Hence it was reasonable to expect an end to capricious terror and arbitrary police rule, frame-ups, and willful falsifications of history, but not to the secret police, political trials, or official views of history. And "above all, there is no ground for expecting an abandonment of the one-party state or any abdication of its monopoly of leadership by the Communist Party."[25]

However limited, these minor reforms seemed both a vast improvement over the recent past and the token of a more democratic future, for in Sweezy's opinion they would "set in motion or accelerate certain trends in Soviet society which *in the long run* will make further and more basic changes necessary and inevitable."[26] Though shaken, his belief that developments in economics and education were driving the Soviet Union toward a more civilized socialism and communism survived the Khrushchev speech. The revelations of the Congress, however, moved him to formulate a fragmentary theory of socialist democracy that accommodated current changes and hoped for trends. Sweezy began by offering a simplistic and obviously inadequate definition of democracy as "popular sovereignty," the opinion of the majority. Since public opinion had become the most crucial form of popular sovereignty in modern societies, the key to power lay in "control over the public mind." Without this, leaders could not govern effectively. Hence the ruling classes of capitalism and the self-perpetuating elites of socialism systematically attempt to create and control public opinion by monopolizing as many channels of information as necessary. In a "genuine democracy," however, *"public opinion is in a real sense self-forming."*[27]

Since this theory rests precariously on the questionable dichotomy between controlled and autonomous public opinion, no existing society, needless to say, embodied it. Without ceasing to be itself, capitalism could never achieve genuine democracy, because the real interests of the ruling minority and those of the vast majority exist in permanent opposition. The Soviet Union did not practice "genuine democracy" either, though for very different reasons. Under conditions of backwardness, the Stalinist dictatorship had to mold an amorphous public opinion and press it "into the service of socialist construction." Moreover, the leadership used "capitalist thought-control systems, including physical coercion, deliberate falsification, hiding or glossing over of contradictions. . . ." But only as means to the quite different end of building "a new system with limitless possibilities for expansion and progress." Thus, by a dialectical somersault, Sweezy concluded that techniques of thought control helped to produce "an increasingly rational and enlightened public opinion," which was modulating into an even more powerful force.[28]

In the fifties, and especially after Stalin, Soviet leaders began to confront the force that they had called forth and previously bent to their own purposes. They could either adapt to public opinion or intensify the old techniques of formation and control on the off chance that they might arrest "the further growth and enlightenment of public opinion."[29] Sweezy contended that to avoid enlarging tensions the leadership relaxed former methods without changing the form of its political rule, a strategy with prospects of immediate success and eventual failure. The abandonment of obsolete methods "necessarily . . . [implies] that the element of autonomy in the formation of public opinion will be increased." Rather than assuming that the political elite would seek—and discover—more subtle ways of molding attitudes, then, he predicted that public opinion would gradually emancipate itself from the spell of a "self-chosen political elite. Then, but not until then, we shall see in the USSR a genuine socialist democracy, one in which a *rational and enlightened* public opinion is supreme and the political leadership is merely its chosen instrument."[30]

Sweezy paid only slight attention to underdeveloped countries during this first period, for in his essentially linear, deterministic theory of socialist evolution, the Soviet Union's course during its first forty years prefigured the main path that other backward countries would be compelled to follow: it was the image of their future. And the United States, as the primary locus of world reaction following World War II, constituted the chief threat to existing socialist nations—whatever their stage of growth—as well as to other nations that in the absence of American pressure would adopt socialism very quickly. In underdeveloped parts of the world, then, the paradox of powerlessness dominated Sweezy's view of the historical present. There, the crucial questions revolved around modes of transition, their political management, and the stand of the United States.

The Chinese Revolution, of course, marked the most significant shift in the global balance of capitalist and socialist forces during this period. Sweezy immediately grasped its main significance, noting in the spring of 1949 that the "impending victory" of the

Chinese Communists "is a world-shaking event comparable in importance to the Russian Revolution of 1917. Then, one-sixth of the land surface of the globe; now, one-fifth of the human race."[31] The vague outlines of China's immediate future were imagined on the analogy of the postrevolutionary course of the Soviet Union: an initial period of "War Communism," designed to restore order following a protracted civil strife, then an intermediate phase along the lines of Lenin's New Economic Policy to alleviate vast problems in agriculture and secure the "commanding heights" of the narrow industrial base. And finally, Sweezy predicted that in a decade, after reaching its own 1928, China could introduce a Five-Year Plan to mark "the transition from a 'mixed' economy to full-fledged socialism."[32]

The application of Soviet experience to China was not merely mechanical, since Sweezy allowed for a certain slack in the relations between the paradigm and its enactment in different cultures at different times. Historical analogies, he cautioned, should be used tentatively. For example, China's international situation in 1949 differed from Russia's in 1917; and "the very fact that the Soviet Union . . . [had] already been through the transition to socialism is of enormous importance." Still, at a higher level of abstraction, Sweezy expressed confidence in the analogy: "when full allowance has been made for all these factors, it remains true that the problems which China faces today are basically the problems that Russia faced at the beginning of the 1920's."[33] And he argued that China must find similar means of resolving them.

Thus the largest outlines of the course of world history seemed charted in advance. In the epic struggle between the two systems of socialism and imperialism (each embodied in countries at different stages of development or decline), the adoption of socialism by backward nations would gradually tip the balance in favor of the new world order. Sweezy never doubted the "necessity" of socialism; underdeveloped countries simply could not solve their massive problems as long as they retained some combination of feudal and capitalist arrangements and remained economically subservient to one or another imperialist power.[34] But he did not devote much energy to the details of the shift in social systems during these years. Generally committed to the basic Marxian premise that nations *usually* recapitulate all the stages of social evolution, though at varying rates, he hypothesized that in Latin America essentially bourgeois revolutions with the aim of sweeping away "indigenous feudalisms and foreign imperialisms" might precede and facilitate the emergence of socialism.[35] Though revolutions in underdeveloped nations, whether peaceful or violent, generally pass through a nationalist phase, they sooner or later must become socialist.

For the underdeveloped world, then, socialism was the end, and some form of national revolution the means. In the early fifties, the global stage was set for "the Great Contest," the battle between advanced socialist and capitalist nations for the allegiance of hundreds of millions in the underdeveloped world. Sweezy adopted this general Communist perspective, though his writings suggest a growing uneasiness about it. Summarizing the Soviet policy of "peaceful coexistence and competition between the systems" in his assessment of the XXth Party Congress, he observed that with more than a third of mankind living under socialism—"and more than half in a 'zone of peace'—legal and non-violent forms of transition to socialism become possible in some countries and under some conditions."[36] Acknowledging the consistency of this position with Marxist theory, Sweezy nevertheless found Khrushchev's explanations of the specific conditions for peaceful transition "not entirely satisfactory." The viability of such scenarios depended mainly on United States policy.

If the Soviet Union and China provided the main source of Sweezy's historical optimism during the early fifties, the domestic and international course of the United States brought out his anxieties. The paradox of powerlessness haunted him, as it did other plain Marxists. And not merely because the resolution of radical paradoxes required a considerable stretch of history: the precondition of time applied to socialist countries and underdeveloped nations as well. For these regions, however, Sweezy advanced a theory whose first stages could be "verified" by direct inspection of the countries in question. But he did not have a parallel theory for the decline and fall of American capitalism: though doomed in the long run, it exhibited disturbing signs of economic and political stability while the tiny Left disintegrated.

In its outward thrust, America had become the principal obstacle to the evolution of socialism everywhere. But in Sweezy's view, foreign policy was essentially a projection of the interplay of domestic forces and interests, notably the changing options of the American ruling class. Radical paradoxes, especially the dilemma of powerlessness, were therefore both a domestic matter (for America, too, needed socialism) and one with profound international ramifications. As long as the ruling class remained unhampered by a strong Left, it could be expected to formulate and execute foreign policies that subverted the progress of socialism elsewhere, and in an atomic age threatened the very survival of mankind.

Sweezy's domestic version of radical paradoxes in the early fifties was similar though not identical to Baran's. Since these paradoxes were deeply imbedded in the historical situation, Baran argued, they remained for the present beyond political control, even beyond political influence. He therefore focused on the limits of the dilemmas, whereas Sweezy (who covered some aspect of American affairs on the average of six or seven times each year) vacillated between identifying the paradoxes *as paradoxes* and charting a way out, or at least a way off dead center. Despite critical attempts to break out of the impasse, however, it was only through the lens of the longer view that Sweezy could plausibly adapt postwar American realities to the first paradigm of socialism/communism. Exhibiting an "unforeseen margin of expansibility" in the late nineteenth and early twentieth centuries, advanced capitalist nations avoided the decline, fall, and resurrection through socialism predicted by Marx. Instead, "imperialism prolonged the life of capitalism in the West and turned what was a revolutionary working-class movement (e.g., Germany) or what might have become one (e.g., England) into reformist and collaborationist channels."[37]

America also had the space to expand, and by midcentury with other imperialist powers in decline, it emerged as the chief center of world "reaction."[38] Sweezy acknowledged the current situation candidly, placing the apparently exceptional American case in the perspective of the longer view: "to say that capitalism has enjoyed an unexpectedly long life in the most advanced countries is very different from saying that it will live forever. Similarly, to say that the Western European and American working classes have so far failed to fulfill the role of 'gravediggers' of capitalism is not equivalent to asserting that they will never do so."[39]

The crucial questions, of course, were how socialism would come to America and whether its long delay would cast the ruling class as gravediggers of civilization before the working class could abolish capitalism. Sweezy's discussions of domestic affairs stressed patterns of economic change that for a Marxist economist were central to the fate of American capitalism. From 1949 through 1956 Sweezy moved away from traditional Marxist assumptions of boom and bust toward the perspective of "creeping stagnation," which informs the economic analysis in *Monopoly Capital*. In the early fifties, the periodic analyses of economic realities and trends in *MR* generally turned on tensions between the system's presumed propensity toward depression and collapse and its contrary impulses toward survival and growth. Though expressed abstractly as an interplay of economic theory and statistically visible economic trends, this tension also bore the weight of Sweezy's emotions. His hopes were bound up with the theory of decline, whereas his fears were sustained by the system's apparent durability. In these analyses, then, he highlighted theoretical contradictions and prophesied eventual decline without engaging in the depressionmongering that marred the work of more orthodox Marxist economists.[40]

The related political analyses followed a similar pattern: a general emphasis on the paradoxes, with periodic oscillations of mood and stress ranging from apocalyptic visions of disaster to mildly hopeful anticipations of an opening on the Left. Sweezy's dominant view was that the American political system and the constellation of class forces precluded every solution to the problem of excess surplus except one: "all roads lead eventually to the war-preparations economy as capitalism's answer to its own fundamental contradiction."[41] Though theoretically possible, genuine reform leading to a welfare state represented an illusion since it worked against ruling-class interests. Moreover, without a strong liberal-Left, such changes did not stand a chance of being imposed on the powerful ruling minority.

This was the main view of the drift toward economic and political crisis. Especially in the early fifties, Sweezy imagined a greatly accelerated tempo of decline, declaring in 1952 that the United States was "going fascist" at a "frightening pace."[42] In two subsequent and much-neglected analyses of domestic anticommunism and McCarthyism, however, he concluded that the moment of crisis had passed; the movement toward fascism had turned out to be a surface phenomenon without a viable class base. Hence, after 1954, he considered "the outlook for McCarthyism . . . distinctly poor, *provided that there is no serious deterioration in the international situation.*"[43] In retrospect these fears of an impending American fascism may seem exaggerated to us, as they did to many at the time. But in the early fifties the very real assaults on civil liberties appeared as tangible signs confirming Sweezy's evolutionary theoretical bias.[44] In a world turning socialist according to his determinist paradigm, the last bastion of capitalism might well be expected to approach *its* final stage by making the transition from bourgeois democracy to fascism. To articulate his deepest fears (which were inseparable from his fondest hopes), Sweezy periodically projected a domestic catastrophe. Though of dubious critical value, these exercises provided symbolic release from the very real impasse of radical paradoxes.

On the other side, he occasionally imagined a new politics of the Left that would open another (theoretically well-worn) road to "reform and gradual replacement" of capitalism by socialism, through the agency of a Labor Party.[45] This theoretical alternative to drift, and ultimately to fascism and war, took the form of a "New New Deal" that "would proceed in domestic affairs along the lines clearly indicated by the old New Deal": improved "health care . . . educational facilities, more social security, decent housing . . . in short . . . a rising standard of life."[46] Sweezy thus endorsed immediate liberal programs on the basis that they were a *possible* response to the economic imperatives of the system—a response that also conformed "to the interests of the overwhelming majority of the American people."[47] If pursued, however, this turn toward reform would not be socialist, nor would it represent a substitute for socialism. Moreover, it could easily backfire: *"the only way to keep a New New Deal from suffering the fate of the old New Deal is to turn it into a socialist movement in good time."*[48] Otherwise the system would soon exhibit its normal tendencies toward polarization of wealth, periodic crisis, and underconsumption.

The recommendation that socialists (a small fraction of a broadly conceived liberal-Left) pursue a politics of reform without abandoning their principal aims suggests Sweezy's determination to avoid a sectarian policy of " 'socialism or nothing.' "[49] But the facts could not be evaded. There was little life in the trade-union movement and less in the fragmented far Left. A tiny ruling class wielded economic and political power. Though the neocolonial foundations of the informal American empire seemed to be "crumbling into dust" by the middle fifties, its enormous domestic strength was plainly evident. Even the projected "New New Deal" presupposed crisis, division, and temporary immobilization in the ruling class. Despite its urgency, then, a rapid turn to the Left, with reformist politics eventually becoming socialist, remained what it had been throughout the decade: an illusion to which Sweezy occasionally turned but invariably turned away from.

American foreign policy was easily his major concern between 1949 and 1956 because it powerfully influenced the course and character of socialism everywhere. It also set limits on any "New New Deal": a large and growing annual military expenditure, for example, precluded imperative reforms in housing, health care, and education. Sweezy's general theory of American policy in these years turns on the incompatibility between its central aims and contemporary global trends. Without American intervention after World War II, other nations would have adopted socialism more quickly—in some instances peacefully, in others after protracted civil war. History would have clearly embodied the first paradigm. But the United States did make its presence felt around the world, from Western Europe and Asia to Africa, the Middle East, and Latin America. In the most abstract sense, America's policies were designed to divert irresistible historical forces from their inevitable course. That these designs had no chance of success over the long haul did not detract from their immediate importance. For, according to Sweezy, the American ruling class had three choices in the fifties, each with global consequences. It could acquiesce in the slow historical drift toward socialism under a "sane foreign policy"; it could launch a general, conventional war ending in certain defeat; or it could destroy civilization in the process of consuming itself through a nuclear blitzkrieg.[50]

The main rationale for Sweezy's slim hopes for peace lay in his estimate of the process of decision-making in American foreign policy. The paradox of powerlessness in the United States deprived the Left—indeed any mass organization—of a shaping hand. Foreign policy was wholly designed by competing factions of the ruling class that Sweezy roughly identified as the "Party of War" and the "Party of Caution." The war party included the right wing of the Republican Party ("especially the [Nationalist] China Lobby and its stable of Senators and Representatives"), the higher echelons of the Air Force and Navy, and capitalists dependent on arms spending, whereas the "Party of Caution" included "the largest part of the Republican Party, based on Big Business and the aristocracy of inherited wealth," the Army, and many liberal Democrats who understood the terrible risks of a general war.[51] Though it had no direct part in the formation of foreign policy, the Left might reasonably hope to affect the struggle between the reckless and the merely aggressive factions of the ruling class through peace campaigns aimed at influencing public opinion. Working for peace was thus consistent with the aims of the first paradigm.

Sweezy nevertheless felt the weight of the ethical paradoxes: by pressing for reforms, socialists inevitably supported liberals who were actively encouraging the prevailing anti-Communist—and by implication antisocialist—foreign policy, however cautiously. In the main, then, the stark version of radical paradoxes constituted his fundamental perspective on America: socialism remained an aim in search of a politics. During the early fifties, "objective conditions" prevented the formation of an effective socialist program. And unless the surviving Left groups could break out of their imprisoning sectarianism, they would, in Sweezy's estimate, "remain isolated and ineffectual even if the objective situation becomes considerably more favorable."[52] Like Mills and Baran, then, he cast himself in the role of a critical rationalist, repeatedly declaring that American Leftists must "tell the truth" about the prospects for socialism everywhere, and about the menace of capitalism to the survival and progress of mankind.

The Breakup of the Paradigm: 1956–1960

The moment when Sweezy's latent crisis of faith turned into a dominant concern cannot be fixed with precision, since intellectual crises of this sort usually gather emotional force over several years. Then an incident, often a minor one, plunges a man into a time of doubt, disillusionment, and theoretical confusion. For Sweezy, Hungary appears to have been the triggering event. After the Soviet invasion of Budapest in November 1956, the *MR* editors did "not see how the feelings of any socialist toward the Soviet Union . . . [could] remain unchanged. Any claim the Soviet

Union had to moral leadership of the world socialist movement is now extinguished."[53] Until the death of Stalin, as I have shown, Sweezy confidently elaborated the first paradigm while applying it to past and present Soviet experience. Thereafter, misgivings about the pace of Soviet progress toward democratic socialism and communism claimed increasing amounts of his critical attention. In these years of the middle fifties he publicly allayed doubts by modifying the socialist paradigm to include "socialist legality" in the essential criteria and by reassessing the historical tempo of Soviet development.

After Hungary, however, doubts about the direction of socialism in advanced countries compelled Sweezy to question the entire paradigm. Since at no point in his intellectual career was he a mere believer, articles of faith always demanded a convincing structure of reason. Unlike many Communist intellectuals, Sweezy was finally more interested in defending socialism than in defending the Soviet Union.[54] Thus, during this time of disenchantment and confusion, he reassessed his theory, measuring earlier predictions against contemporary historical realities rather than tailoring realities to his theory. This critical exercise cast doubt on the minimal definition of socialism that had been at the very center of his previous analyses. Humbled by the course of events in the middle fifties, Sweezy evolved some of his most reasoned, measured analyses of the historical fate of socialism in this interlude between two periods of strong faith. He patched up parts of the paradigm while discarding others that had been plainly discredited. At the same time, however, the center of gravity of his entire outlook shifted: confronting the ethical dimensions of radical paradoxes in advanced socialist countries, he gradually proceeded from a historical to a utopian framework—from questioning the absence of democracy in the socialist nations to questioning the persistence of alienation.

Two important essays published late in 1957 pose the problems of dictatorship and democracy clearly for the first time.[55] Though the harshest features of the Soviet regime had been tempered, it was nevertheless "true that even the mildest of dictatorships is not a democracy."[56] Sweezy questioned his previous conviction "that when the conditions which produced the dictatorship—economic backwardness and international insecurity—had been overcome, the Soviet regime would, in some unspecified manner, democratize itself." The overriding question "now is: will it, and how?" Internal conditions that gave the dictatorship its character of inevitability had been overcome; and internationally, the Soviet Union was "at least as secure as any country in the world." Hence the "theory is being put to the test of practice. And so far—let us face it frankly—there is precious little evidence to confirm it."[57]

Maintaining that Soviet society is composed of "a collection of interest groups, which have both competing and common interests," Sweezy contended that "the problem of such a society is to devise some substitute for class rule, to keep the groups working together for their common interests and to prevent them from ganging up on each other in the pursuit of their separate interests." Stalin "solved this problem by means of the secret police," through which terror held the parts of the system in balance.[58] Democracy, of course, provided the most desirable substitute. Having rejected its inevitability, however, Sweezy fell back on the less plausible hypothesis that the party might voluntarily democratize its rule. The other possible substitute for the Stalinist apparatus was a military dictatorship, which in 1957 he considered the more likely course. In any case, the implicit deterministic foundations of the first paradigm had visibly cracked: instead of a smooth, automatic transition from authoritarian to democratic socialism, Sweezy came to expect an era of indeterminism and crisis. For if the economic transformation of the Soviet Union continued and the party resisted democratization, then the dictatorship would certainly "be subjected to increasingly heavy strains at the top as the competing interests push and pull their way toward the levers of power."[59] By doubting the key element of determinism, Sweezy took a crucial intellectual turn: thereafter he could never again regard the transition to democratic socialism and communism as an irreversible historical process largely beyond the control of political elites.

As doubts about the historical relevance of the first paradigm multiplied, Sweezy began a tentative reformulation of his criteria of socialism that included democracy (liberty) but emphasized the other "historic aims" of the socialist movement: equality and fraternity. In their assessment of the Soviet Revolution after forty years, Sweezy and Huberman argued that unless a nation achieves democracy, equality and brotherhood, it cannot be designated a "good society."[60] A tour of the U.S.S.R., Poland, and Yugoslavia in late 1957 confirmed Sweezy's disenchantment with the mixed character of European socialisms and added to his theoretical confusion. Lecturing on his reactions to the advanced socialist countries, he felt moved to preface sharp criticisms with a public reaffirmation of faith: "Some of the things that I am going to say . . . will sound highly critical to you and you may be inclined to interpret them to mean that I am wavering in my belief in and support for socialism. Please do not make that mistake." On the positive side, he returned with the conviction that the Soviets had fully overcome economic backwardness and that under centralized planning (with perhaps some administrative decentralization), "progress will be fast from here on." He confidently concluded that "in terms of economic achievement and promise, the Soviet system is perhaps history's greatest success story." Moreover, his observations strengthened the view that since there are "no vested interests in war preparations" apart from the Soviet military (!), "only socialism can assure" peace, the precondition of human survival in a nuclear age.[61]

But Sweezy quickly sketched in the darker tones, progressing from the first paradigm within his sociology of change to what would become the utopian basis for the second in the sixties. He suggested that "the historic aim of the socialist movement has been to create a new society of human brotherhood and solidarity, a society in which man would no longer be dominated by his own products and from which not only all forms of exploitation but also all forms of alienation—from self as well as from fellow human beings—would be abolished." Now he was less troubled by the failure to create such a society than by his inability to uncover any "evidence of trends pointing in the right direction." Though exploitation "has been largely eliminated . . . new forms of alienation seem to have taken or to be taking the place of the old." Young people appeared cynical about politics and public life, typically preferring to pursue personal success. Nor were there other signs of the beginnings of a good society: "If one looks for what I would call *socialist* ideals, a *socialist* ethic, *socialist* motivations in the Soviet Union today, forty years after the world's first socialist revolution, one finds disappointingly little." Sweezy frankly confessed that he did "not understand all the reasons for" this state of affairs. In retrospect, however, it is clear that during the interlude of doubt he began to suspect that democracy, though desirable, might not be enough: "Despite all disappointments . . . I have not given up hope that I shall live to see a good society in the making. I do not know that a democratized Soviet Union will fit the description, but as of now at any rate it seems to me to be the world's best chance."[62]

In another report on European themes, Sweezy suggested that none of the advanced countries had solved the problem of "generating a whole new moral and ethical climate in which the traditional aims and ideals of socialism can be brought to fruition." And "in the long run . . . it will be in this area, and not in the sphere of technology or economics, that socialism will be judged a success or a failure."[63] It may at first seem curious that the criteria of egalitarianism and dealienation were added to the earlier definition of socialism just when the less ambitious aim of democracy had finally become a *historical* possibility. Though the theoretical implications were still hazy, Sweezy's shift toward a dialectic of liberation preserved the ideals of socialism and communism from the historical present by rescheduling the "real" test of socialism once again. Since gloomy realities demanded more elaborate hopes, the political unlikelihood of rapid democratization probably provided another reason for formulating the beginnings of a utopian theory that would replace the first paradigm in the sixties. Still, the new test required more than a different paradigm; it demanded a new historical setting. For the Soviet Union and other European countries were plainly not moving toward full socialist democracy and a communist community beyond alienation.

Sweezy's expanded conception of socialism provides a negative index of his pessimism in the late fifties. The tentative definition of a "good society" came to serve primarily as a mirror of Soviet shortcomings rather than as a vague image of its future. As the deterministic underpinnings of the first paradigm fell away, he found it increasingly hard to imagine a dynamic pattern of current shapes and trends in Soviet society gradually converging on the ideals. Hence the present could no longer be confidently justified as the necessary prelude to a brighter future. Nor could it be wholly absolved on the grounds of the Russian past, since Sweezy never adequately accounted for the persistence of older cultural patterns. He therefore maintained that as the Soviet Union moved well beyond economic backwardness toward abundance, the gap between what was and what could be at any given moment steadily widened.

Moreover, the search for a new historical location for the expanded ideal of socialism must not have seemed promising at first, if only because underdeveloped nations confronted the difficult task of liquidating backwardness that had forced the Soviets off the main road to communism in the late twenties. But as he became progressively more disenchanted with the advanced nations, Sweezy turned his attention toward China.[64] Analyzing the Great Leap Forward in 1958, he argued that the communes might solve the major agricultural problem of underdeveloped socialism while also advancing the nation toward a good society of economic abundance, equality, and community. The communes constituted "a system which is the avowed enemy of individualism; seeks the end of the small family as the basic unit of society; wants to wipe out the key distinctions of society as we know it in the West (between workers and peasants, between town and country, between mental and manual work, between peasants and intellectuals, between collective ownership and ownership by the people); and aims at the eventual disappearance of wages and even of money itself."[65] The Chinese had apparently hit upon a better solution to the problem of socializing agriculture than the brutal Soviet collectivization drive of the late twenties. At this point in his transition to a new paradigm, however, Sweezy still regarded the Soviet course as the necessary alternative to a "much slower rate of industrialization and quite possibly total defeat in World War II."[66] But he no longer assumed that every backward nation would be forced into a similar solution to the admittedly staggering problem of development.

He expressed but one reservation about the Great Leap Forward. Though the Chinese had taken a long step toward a society of abundance, equality, and brotherhood, they had yet to register much progress in liberty. But the grandeur of the ideal of a good society (an amalgam of the criteria of socialism and communism in the first paradigm) justified the negative side effects of the experiment: "Puritanism, fanaticism, arrogance, enforced intellectual conformity—these are qualities which recur in periods of revolutionary advance."[67]

In the late fifties, the American scene only added to Sweezy's pessimism. Instead of deliquescing into fascism or moving toward another New Deal, American society passed through a stagnant period of "immobilism." The old Left had completely disintegrated, and there were few tangible signs of a new movement, though at the end of the decade Sweezy tentatively predicted that the steel strike "may be the first sign that we are even now emerging into the light of a new day of labor militancy and social struggles."[68] "Creeping stagnation" at home and continued failure in the quest to dominate the world—this was the bleak outlook for

America in the late fifties. *"Up to now, the decline of the United States as a world power has had only minor repercussions on the domestic economy and has therefore left undisturbed the pattern of class interests that determines foreign policy. As long as this remains true there is no reason to expect a change in foreign policy or an interruption in the process of decline."*[69] The disappointing attenuation of American capitalism provided an objective correlative for Sweezy's pessimism. History was moving too slowly and its destination no longer amounted to a certainty. By the end of the fifties, socialism had failed the first test of history, and capitalism refused to die. In moments of pessimism, then, the search for signs of communism in history must have seemed futile. But Cuba provided a context for yet another beginning.

Toward a New Vision of Communism: 1960–1970

Sweezy's trip to Cuba in 1960 ended his interlude of doubt. Swept "off his feet" in the "island's heady revolutionary" ambience, he summarized his pilgrimage in essentially religious terms:[70] "To be with these people, to see with your own eyes how they are rehabilitating and transforming a whole nation, to share their dreams of the great tasks and achievements that lie ahead—these are purifying and liberating experiences. You come away with your faith in the human race restored."[71] These were just the experiences Sweezy needed: purification for having shared a corrupted faith in the fifties, and liberation from the ethical paradoxes that cast doubt on the entire socialist experiment.

The restoration of faith required a second paradigm that would include a revised vision of socialism and communism, a theory of armed revolution as the only means of destroying capitalism, and a fresh perspective on postrevolutionary development. Unlike the original paradigm, which Sweezy *applied* to historical events and trends in the fifties, the second had to be *forged* gradually in the shadow of earlier defeats and under the difficult circumstances of a decade of massive, swift, and unprecedented changes within and among nations representing capitalism (imperialism) and social-ism. In the new paradigm, two sets of criteria merge into a single standard. Retaining the minimum definition of socialism as public ownership under comprehensive planning, Sweezy added the other essential conditions that he had reclaimed from the Marxist past in the late fifties: democracy, equality, and fraternity.

In the sixties he came to regard the present epoch as essentially a single (though multifaceted) struggle between a dying imperial-ism and "the world revolution." But the certain defeat of im-perialism by armed revolutionaries with socialist aspirations no longer guaranteed a smooth evolution from authoritarian to demo-cratic socialism, and then to communism: the traffic patterns of history now seemed more intricate. For having once gained state power, revolutionaries encountered formidable perils beyond the traditional dangers of counterrevolution, foreign intervention, and the moral and psychological "remnants" of the bourgeois past. They had to contend with the larger threat of a peaceful reversion to capitalism. In place of linear metaphors and rigid analogies, Sweezy's new faith required an exercise of historical imagina-tion.[72] Though no general theory could cover all contingencies, he cautiously began to formulate comparative perspectives on so-cieties in transition from capitalism to socialism, using Soviet failures as well as Cuban and Chinese experience.

The argument for the necessity of revolution rests on several assumptions about the connections between capitalism and under-development. Whereas in the fifties Sweezy reluctantly endorsed the Great Contest hypothesis, which presupposed a "third world" between capitalism and socialism, in the sixties he adopted an altogether different view: "Capitalism in its homelands advanced from the very beginning by subjugating, plundering, exploiting, and re-shaping the environment in which it existed. The result was to transfer wealth from the periphery to the metropolis, and corre-spondingly to destroy the old society and re-organize it on a dependent satellite basis."[73] By broadening the definition of the "capitalist world" to encompass a network of nations, Sweezy discovered a modern use for Marx's general notion of the system's fatal contradictions: the exploited and impoverished masses at the peripheries are the new revolutionary "gravediggers" of capitalism, not the working classes of the advanced centers. Revolution is therefore possible in theory and, as Cuba proved, possible in history as well.[74]

It is also *necessary* everywhere. Viewing development and underdevelopment as opposite sides of the same coin, Sweezy argued that as long as the backward nations remain in the capitalist world—economically dominated by a coalition of foreign imperialists and domestic capitalists—they cannot break the vicious cycle of underdevelopment. This position also presumed continuous American intervention to rescue governments in Asia, Africa, and Latin America, a supposition largely borne out by events of the sixties. He concluded that in Vietnam and elsewhere, this process prefigured disaster, declaring in 1965 that "the course of the Decline and Fall of the American Empire has now been charted for all to see."[75] The United States would have to intervene periodically to rescue tottering regimes until it reached material and moral exhaustion. In the meantime, however, visions of reform or gradual transition in various nations were cruel illusions. The masses at the edges of the capitalist world must confront a stark imperative: "starve or fight."

Sweezy came to this view of the necessity of armed revolution slowly, following Chinese leads though not always playing Chinese tunes. Analyzing the Sino-Soviet split in late 1961, the editors of *MR* assumed that the central issue dividing the two socialist powers was strategic: *"what course of action [ought] . . . the socialist countries . . . follow in order to minimize the threat of World War III."* Following an admirable summary of the competing positions, they bluntly declared that "the Russians are right and the Chinese wrong" because the Maoists had lapsed into "a kind of dogmatic leftism that has appeared again and again in the history of the international socialist movement." In their aggressive ideological stance, the Chinese underestimated the force of nationalism, lumping together all opposition "in an undifferentiated reactionary mass."[76] Ironically, the editors sided with the Chinese two years later, arguing that the struggle against imperialism must take precedence over the pursuit of peace at current Soviet prices: "Real peace will never be achieved, much less guaranteed, as long as imperialism exists."[77] By 1966 Sweezy and Huberman declared that "it is no longer enough to proclaim the necessity of armed struggle: that battle has been won. It is now necessary to learn *how* to fight a *successful* armed struggle."[78]

Until late 1963, disagreements over the most effective mode of opposing imperialism seemed the most urgent matter in the Sino-Soviet dispute. Thereafter, the second set of questions concerning postrevolutionary social change received more sustained attention. Sweezy's preliminary search for adequate perspectives on transitional societies proceeded in two directions at once: he both explored the negative lessons of Soviet experience and assessed socialist countries at the beginning of the long transition. The reevaluation of the Soviet experiment—its past, present, and probable future—logically preceded the examination of socialism's fragmentary beginnings in China and Cuba, for Sweezy had to determine what had gone wrong in the advanced countries and whether the "mistakes" were "necessary." Without a convincing statement that the Soviet course was either avoidable or necessary only in the specific cultural context of Russia, there would be no good reason to hope that other backward countries might evade a similar fate later on.

Sweezy abandoned the deterministic elements of the first paradigm gradually. Commenting on the progress of de-Stalinization in 1962, he concluded that "Stalinism is *not* the inevitable superstructure of socialist revolution: on the contrary, it is a transitory historical phenomenon which owes its existence to very special historical conditions." Although moral and spiritual leadership of the international socialist movement may temporarily pass from

Moscow to Peking, it should return as the "Soviet Union catches up with and surpasses the developed capitalist countries. . . ."[79] But this hope, based on economic assumptions in the first paradigm, soon faded as the more advanced countries, beginning with Yugoslavia, turned increasingly to the market and to material incentives for solutions to the mounting economic difficulties of centralized bureaucratic planning.

Though Yugoslavia and later Czechoslovakia were the most advanced cases of this shift in emphasis, they prefigured the course of all the nations in the Soviet bloc. "The trend toward capitalism is built into the present system: Control of enterprises in the enterprises themselves, coordination through the market, and reliance on material incentives—these three factors, taken together, make inevitable a strong tendency toward an economic order which, whatever one may choose to call it, functions more and more like capitalism." A network of enterprises producing commodities for the market with a view to sharing the profits creates the essential economic and social relations of capitalism: "Appropriate juridical forms will develop in due course. . . ." Hence "whoever acts to strengthen the market instead of struggling against the market is, regardless of intentions, promoting capitalism and not socialism."[80]

The logic of the process is, briefly, this: "First comes the consolidation of power by a bureaucratic ruling stratum (not yet a ruling *class*), accompanied and followed by the depoliticizing of the masses." Once revolutionary enthusiasm and mass political participation falter, centralized planning becomes increasingly rigid and authoritarian, precipitating economic problems and failures. Faced with mounting economic troubles, leaders "turn to capitalist techniques, vesting increasing power within the economic enterprises in management and relying for their guidance and control less and less on centralized planning and more and more on the impersonal pressures of the market." In time, real power "gravitates into the hands of the managerial elite," which "tends to develop into a new type of bourgeoisie."[81] It favors extending material incentives and the market, a strategy designed to alleviate economic difficulties while strengthening its own political position. Older functionaries in the tradition of bureaucratic centralism resist for a time. Lacking either economic remedies or mass support, however, they wage a losing battle against the new elite of technocrats and managers. Gradually, then, the privileged stratum consolidates its power and eventually may turn into a full-fledged ruling class.

Though defenders of advanced socialist countries argued that reliance on the market and material incentives was a stage in the transition from socialism to communism, Sweezy rightly maintained that this dominant thrust subverted all the criteria in the second paradigm. Greater reliance on the market and profitability subverts the goal of egalitarianism by widening rather than narrowing divisions of wealth. At the same time, the cause of "genuine democracy" suffers as the elite assumes hierarchical power and the masses remain politically disenfranchised. Finally, a "depoliticized society *must* rely on private [material] incentives," which ensures a general flight into private life, perpetuates alienation, and delays the creation of a *Gemeinschaft* community.[82] In a word, economic progress comes at the heavy price of forging social relations that reproduce the old bourgeois man. Since these structural trends could withstand any amount of socialist ideology, the course of Soviet development undermined what Sweezy loosely referred to as "socialist education," one of the two driving forces of the transition to communism in the first paradigm.

In 1967 there was still hope that these tendencies toward the restoration of capitalism might be reversed. By the end of the decade, however, Sweezy was "more and more inclined to accept Charles Bettelheim's contention that Soviet society today is a form of state capitalism ruled by a new state bourgeoisie. If this is true, it means that the world's first attempt to build a socialist society was abortive." Having reluctantly abandoned the Soviet experiment, he confronted the "crucial question" of whether new attempts to build socialism in China and Cuba "are doomed to follow the Soviet Union on the road back to class-dominated societies, or whether they have succeeded in creating genuinely new social structures which have a reasonable prospect of moving forward toward the historic goals of socialism (and ultimately) communism."[83] The answer, as I have indicated, depended heavily on the weight of "necessity" in Soviet history.

Relinquishing the deterministic base of the first paradigm, Sweezy began the analysis by positing that "Marxism is . . . both determinist and voluntarist." That is, "at any given time the range of possibilities is determined by what has gone before (determinism), but within this range genuine choices are possible (voluntarism)." Moreover, there is a dialectic between determinism and voluntarism in history: once a new social order becomes established "and its 'law of motion' is in full operation, power naturally gravitates into the hands of those who understand the system's requirements. . . . In these circumstances, there is little that individuals or groups can do to change the course of history. . . ." In periods of revolutionary upheaval, however, the range of social choice expands, "and groups (especially, in our time, disciplined political parties) and great leaders come into their own as actors on the stage of history."[84]

Applying this dialectic provisionally to Soviet history, Sweezy characterized the first decade from 1917 until the forced industrialization and collectivization of agriculture in the late twenties as a "voluntarist" period "during which the Bolshevik Party and its leaders, meaning primarily Lenin and Stalin, played a decisive role in shaping the course of events." Of course there were, as always, limits, but Sweezy suggested that they were sufficiently wide to encompass Stalin's policies at one extreme and those of Bukharin at the other. In recent years, the Soviet Union entered a "determinist" phase in which the "Party and its leaders are hardly more than cogs in a great machine. . . ." But the nature of the machine dominating the "determinist" period was shaped during the "voluntarist" phase by party leaders and especially by Stalin. This intermediate stage—roughly between 1928 and the end of

World War II—was "certainly the crucial formative period of present-day Soviet society. . . ." In contrast to earlier versions of Soviet development, Sweezy concluded that "we *know* that different courses were possible in the decisive years after Lenin's death because we know that great struggles and debates racked the Bolshevik Party in that period." There is no reason to accept the inevitability of Stalin's victory or the necessity of his policies: "The options were real, and the Soviet Union is what it is today because some were embraced and others rejected."[85]

According to Sweezy, depoliticization of the masses constitutes the fatal decision that reverses the socialist direction of a society in transition. Everything follows from this: when revolutionary enthusiasm winds down, a system of private incentives (accompanied by stringent modes of coercion in periods of scarcity) becomes the driving force of development. In turn, the economy *"must* be shaped to turn out the goods and services which give the appropriate concrete meaning to money incomes and demands." The only way to break "this seemingly closed circle would be a *re-politicization* of . . . society which would permit a move away from private incentives and hence also a different structure of production and a different composition and distribution of additions to the social product."[86] In a word, advanced countries need what they cannot have—"an all-out campaign to rouse the masses, to elevate the general level of political consciousness, to revitalize socialist ideals, to give increasing responsibility to the producers themselves at all levels of decision-making."[87]

But a cultural revolution does constitute a genuine political option in nations at a relatively early "voluntarist" stage of transition similar to the first phase of Soviet development. Sweezy interpreted the Cultural Revolution as essentially an attempt to avoid depoliticization among the Chinese people. Personifying the main internal enemy as "those in authority" following "the capitalist road," the Chinese were in fact launching an all-out campaign against a postrevolutionary *social* trend—the growth "of an increasingly privileged and powerful . . . stratum in command of society's politico-economic apparatus." Sweezy posited the inevitability of this trend "in any country in a period of rapid economic development from a condition of technological backwardness and low labor productivity." In China, with a per capita income of only about fifty dollars a year, scientists, managers, technicians, and bureaucrats require far more than an equal share merely to perform their jobs. In such circumstances, the economy and the privileged stratum grow in tandem; privilege hardens into "vested interests" and new social structures perpetuate the old values of "selfishness, individualism, separation from the life of the masses."[88]

What can be done about these forces and tendencies? Clearly, Sweezy acknowledged, no individual or group can "completely . . . [prevent] the emergence of a privileged stratum which has the potential for evolving into a new ruling class"; that is included in the price of economic development. But the power and privileges of this stratum can be limited, and its tendency to become a ruling class checked, by an alliance of pure revolutionaries and the underprivileged. Though all the dispossessed are potential allies in the battle against excessive privilege, an effective counterforce must be organized by a powerful minority with a conscious interest in the outcome of the struggle. Sweezy maintained that in China this group includes "those . . . who made the revolution . . . and remain uncorrupted by the temptations of actual or potential privilege."[89] The Cultural Revolution, then, was mainly a desperate effort by Mao and other revolutionaries to mobilize the energy of the underprivileged (especially the uncorrupted youth) and direct it against the most aggressive elements of the privileged stratum of managers, scientists, and bureaucrats.

At a comparable stage of Soviet development, Stalin welded together a system of terror to check the power of the potential ruling class. But he neither created a mass base to counterbalance the privileged stratum nor adequately prepared for the future by training a "new generation of genuine revolutionaries to lead and carry on the struggle against the restoration of class rule." Hence when the system of terror was relaxed, the privileged stratum in the Soviet

Union asserted itself rapidly and with only nominal opposition. Beginning with a stronger mass base, the Chinese used periodic "education and rectification campaigns" in place of Stalinist terror. The Cultural Revolution was thus the most spectacular in a series of campaigns to ensure the development of socialism in history: "The Party leadership evidently believes that if the privileged stratum can be contained and controlled and the young can be won for the Revolution and its goals, then the country can be kept from taking the capitalist road for at least one more generation while economic development brings closer the day when general abundance will make possible the real elimination of inequality and privilege."[90] Sweezy believed that by substituting "education and persuasion" for Stalinist terror, the Chinese had discovered a humane means of holding a planned society together in the early stages of development while also ensuring its advance toward full communism at higher levels of production.

Ideological conformity, in effect, replaces terror as the primary unifying substance of a backward society in transition. Discussing the Chinese stress on decentralized decision-making as an alternative to rigid bureaucratic planning and the market, Sweezy noted that "for a decentralized socialist system . . . to work smoothly, it is essential that those who make the important decisions should think alike on fundamental problems of economy, society, and morality."[91] But he did not explore the conflict between ideological conformity and democracy. Though a uniformity of outlook constitutes the price of economic development and the promise of a communist community moving beyond alienation, it also frustrates development of a genuine democracy characterized by a "self-forming public opinion."

At the end of the sixties, Sweezy converted his specific analyses of Soviet failures and Chinese experiments into a tentative general perspective on societies in transition to socialism. He argued that twentieth-century socialist experiments discredited previous Marxist theories of analogous transitions between social systems. In the movement from feudalism to capitalism, which took up an entire epoch, "bourgeois man" had a chance to mature alongside the old feudal man: "The establishment and expansion of capitalist economic and social relations were practical human activities which molded human beings with appropriate attitudes, motivations, 'instincts'—cupidity, means-and-ends rationality, individualism, and so on."[92]

The transition to socialism must take another course, for "socialism itself cannot take root and grow within the confines of capitalist society. . . ." According to Marx, capitalism produces its own gravediggers. But that is only half of a theory of transition, since it does not specify the kind of "revolutionizing practice" required to bring "socialist man" into historical existence. Sweezy thus rejected the earlier equation between the "proletarian" and the "new man," maintaining that Marx nowhere outlines the means of converting "a mere fragment of a man into a fully developed individual" whose values, attitudes, and instincts express the criteria of the second paradigm. Unable to discover a full answer in Marx, Sweezy turned to Lenin, arguing that his insistence on the need to teach revolutionary consciousness to proletarians through a vanguard party implies that "it is not capitalism as such but the revolutionary struggle to overthrow capitalism which creates men with the will and ability to go further and begin the construction of socialism." Hence, "Revolutionizing practice, in Lenin's view, was nothing more nor less than the practice of revolution." The revised line of genuine revolutionaries now runs from Marx and Engels to Lenin and Mao: "All history, Marx said, is the continuous transformation of human nature. What is Mao telling us but that even after the overthrow of class domination the positive task of transforming human nature never ceases?"[93] (Stalin, the Soviet Joshua in Sweezy's first paradigm, becomes its Judas in his second.)

Within two eventful decades, then, Sweezy nearly inverted the ratios of necessity and choice. In the first paradigm, economic forces drove postrevolutionary societies along the road to communism, transforming consciousness on the way. In the second, men must simultaneously change their nature and their circumstances through revolutionizing practice or else revert to "capitalism." Earlier, one revolution seemed sufficient to guarantee a society's transition to communism. By the seventies, however, Sweezy had to posit an unlimited number of revolutions or else abandon the new vision of communism. Even so, the odds on success, previously rated nearly certain, lengthened considerably. Instead of evolving out of the past, both socialism and communism would have to be insinuated onto the stage of history. And China, now the most ideologically advanced post revolutionary society and the largest as well, held the answer to the momentous question of socialism's historical future.

The American Impasse

During the sixties, the United States more than ever emerged as the chief villain in the drama of contemporary history. Consequently, international considerations increasingly dominated Sweezy's characterization of radical paradoxes in America and narrowed the possibilities of resolution. Doomed to play out a counterrevolutionary role at the peripheries of its empire, capitalism was headed for certain dissolution. Especially toward the end of the decade, Sweezy frequently yielded to self-indulgent, apocalyptic visions of this impending disaster: "One can only conclude that the downfall of the American Empire and the end of United States capitalism may be much closer at hand than we have been accustomed to think. It will be at best a frightful process, but one cannot deny at any rate that these monstrous social formations deserve the fate which now threatens them, and that their destruction would at least make it possible for mankind to reconstruct in peace. Perhaps on a very long view of history it is better that it should be so."[94] Having abandoned all hope for a sane foreign policy under capitalism, Sweezy took an ever harder line on domestic forms of radical paradoxes, as we have seen in the discussion of *Monopoly Capital*. The Manichaean perspective on imperialism and the world revolution obliterated conflicts between democratic values and various modalities of Left-wing politics. The ethical dimensions of the paradoxes merged into the single issue of power for two related reasons. First, the system had become altogether too monstrous in its outward thrust to merit any support, however indirect. Second, in the new paradigm the concept of revolutionizing practice canceled distinctions between personal and political morality in the context of a hopelessly corrupt society. Radical, or more precisely, revolutionary powerlessness constituted the sole paradox (with many facets) confronting serious American Leftists.

By arguing for the necessity of socialist revolution in America, Sweezy must remain at the edge of sectarianism, however much he resists joining a sect. Though unlikely in his view, a domestic new New Deal would pacify potentially revolutionary segments of society and strengthen America's counterrevolutionary activities throughout the world. Rejecting every form of gradual transition, Sweezy adopted Baran's part-whole metaphor as a way of dismissing all political activities except his own version of revolutionizing practice: "those who are really for peace, and not simply against wars the United States may lose, should steer scrupulously clear of ruling-class electoral politics." In fact, "until we can change the system, our primary aim must be to weaken it, to reduce as much as possible its capacity to fight wars of aggression against other peoples."[95]

If Sweezy continued to regard socialist education as the primary concrete form of revolutionizing practice available to white revolutionaries (more than thirty years old), he assigned more ambitious and perilous roles to blacks and to the young. Here at last were signs of the long-awaited revolution. As early as 1963 he observed that "only through pressing their demands for 'integration now' and finding out how pitifully little they can achieve will Negroes become convinced of the necessity for revolution. . . . In this sense, Negroes have enrolled in a cram course for the indefinite future."[96] Five years later he was convinced that blacks had achieved the beginnings of a "mass movement with a revolutionary will . . . [and] potential. . . ." In these circumstances a program of selected reforms—control of the ghettos and jobs—should advance rather than retard revolutionary aims. The danger of losing the revolutionary driving force was there, of course. But it was slight, for in a period of perpetual crisis, minor concessions can be won only "in direct proportion to the organizational strength, militancy, and combativity of the black community." Moreover, the great majority of American "blacks are in a very real sense part of the Third World which can survive and develop only by carrying through to the end the revolutionary people's war against United States imperialism. . . ." A few reforms, therefore, were "not likely to divert the fundamentally revolutionary thrust of the black movement."[97]

Sweezy also turned briefly to the new Left as it became ever more militant. Toward the end of the decade, he assessed the old Left and the new against his criterion of revolutionizing practice: "Whatever the ideological pronouncements of some of its segments, the Old Left was in fact a thoroughly reformist movement which aimed to achieve its goals within the framework of the existing capitalist society." The young Left of the sixties took a different turn, beginning with reactions "at a gut level" and gradually discovering theoretical perspectives to match their "anger and frustration." By 1969, "advanced elements" of the new Left leadership had developed into "an outspokenly revolutionary movement." In "place of the reformist Old Left which dreamt of uniting whites and blacks under a single leadership and achieving its aims through pressure politics, we now have a New Left which understands and accepts (1) the necessity of revolution and (2) that at least for the foreseeable future whites and blacks must organize separately while struggling together."[98]

Of course, Sweezy attempted to put these hopes into critical perspective: "the New Left, like its predecessor, is still small. It has hardly touched the masses of blue- and white-collar workers; and where it has, the reaction has tended to be negative rather than positive. And without the masses, what Paul Baran said in 1950 is still true, 'there are no politics of the Left.' "[99] It would be hard to imagine more serious handicaps for a revolutionary movement. Despite his own withering qualifications, however, Sweezy invested some faith in the new turn. Ironically, his assessment of the "advanced revolutionary consciousness" of the white student leadership rested largely on dispatches from the 1969 meeting of Students for a Democratic Society in Austin, Texas—an organization issuing bold revolutionary pronouncements as it split into hopelessly impotent factions.

Thus within the second paradigm Sweezy redefined socialism and communism, rescuing the ideals from the Soviet failure and identifying them with revolution in the third world and postrevolutionary experiments in China and Cuba. These were his principal intentions. But the new paradigm did not fit the American scene any more closely than the first.

Conclusion

It would be a mistake to regard Sweezy as a mere reflector of ideological fashions, beginning with pro-Soviet biases in the fifties and ending as a partisan of the Chinese. His intellectual odyssey between 1945 and 1970 traces a more intricate design. Though obviously influenced by the concatenation of international events and by important controversies within the world socialist movement, the logic of his development seems decisively shaped by subjective concerns. His socialist faith and impatient radical temperament form the thread of continuity in a tapestry of intellectual change. More than anything else, then, Sweezy's generally resourceful, often brilliant criticism expresses the dynamics of his personal quest for a sign of communism in history. Each major shift—the rejection of the first paradigm, the reconsideration of ideals during the interlude of doubt, and the formulation of the second paradigm—represents a reaction to what he regarded as stark choices between socialist ideals and historical relevance on the one side, and abandonment of the quest on the other. By reaffirming his faith at each juncture, he was trapped in a narrowing circle of theoretical and political options. Though perhaps ultimately determined by temperament, these were nevertheless conscious choices of an independent political intellectual.

An evaluation of Sweezy's contribution to radical thought in the postwar years, then, depends upon how well the movement from hope to disillusionment and back allowed him to illuminate contemporary history. Did his commitment to communism sharpen or blur critical insight into its present shapes and probable future? Though the question resists a definitive answer, I believe that on balance the requirements of faith increasingly distorted the lenses of reason. Under the weight of postwar events, Sweezy's radical impatience with the progress of socialism impelled him to move latent utopian ideals to the center of his vision. Finally he had to resort to the general concept of "revolutionizing practice" as the principal moral test of individuals and the principal political test of a nation's advance toward communism. This reliance on ever more abstract versions of the conflict between imperialism and the world revolution constricted his vision of contemporary realities and trends. Sweezy virtually wrote off Western civilization—capitalist and socialist nations alike—because neither group could embody the specific form of revolutionizing practice that he and others prescribed. Nothing less than a cultural revolution could restore socialism to the U.S.S.R. and the nations of Eastern Europe, and nothing less than an armed revolution could end capitalism in the West. Such inflexible formulations of radical paradoxes defined Sweezy out of political existence, consigning him to the role of critical rationalist. Even more importantly, they seriously handicapped his criticism of "the most significant trends in domestic and foreign affairs."

Sweezy's changing attitudes toward advanced socialist nations illustrate the fundamental weaknesses that progressively marred his criticism. Even the pragmatic two-stage theory of transition, imagined in the first paradigm, implies his radical impatience, for the minimum characterization of socialism as public ownership under central planning allowed him to include backward nations in the definition while exempting the more ambitious ideals of socialism from the test of history. The projected modulation from authoritarian to democratic socialism, however, rested on the flimsy argument that economic development and its by-product, "socialist education," would not merely *permit* but *guarantee* progress toward communism. Sweezy's miscalculation stemmed in part from an overestimation of bureaucratic central planning, whose promise turned out to exceed its performance as the Soviet economy reached new stages of complexity in the late fifties. And he correspondingly minimized the inertial tendencies of political and cultural institutions. Had he accounted for the vast cultural differences between prerevolutionary Russia, China, and Cuba, Sweezy would have recognized the impossibility of searching for a single general theory of socialism, communism, and the politics of transition.

But the chief error involved implicit assumptions about the impact of education on human nature. While elaborating the first paradigm, Sweezy never really examined the relationships between what he termed "socialist education" and the emergence of a new man. He rather assumed that desirable changes were occurring. Both halves of this assumption are at least questionable. Though obviously important, such achievements as the elimination of illiteracy and the swift rise in "trained manpower" have little to do with the formation of "socialist man."[100]

Also, to have described even the firm beginnings of a profound alteration of human consciousness on the basis of a mere half century of public ownership and planning in any culture was surely naïve. Sweezy came to recognize this in the late fifties. Instead of examining the desirability of a massive change from an essentially individualist to an essentially collectivist personality, however, he focused initially on its absence and later on its political impossibility in advanced socialist countries. This critical exercise, begun after the Soviet invasion of Hungary, did partially illuminate the main ethical paradoxes, the disparities between actual conditions and the ideals of liberty (democracy), equality, and fraternity (dealienation in an egalitarian community). But only briefly and not very clearly, for Sweezy did not steadily confront the intricate questions of the apparent incompatibility between communist ideals and the relatively narrow historical options in advanced countries—or anywhere else, for that matter. He simply refused to accept the central political and cultural implications of economic imperatives that required decentralization, market mechanisms, and material incentives—namely, an indefinite perpetuation of substantial inequalities of wealth and power that precluded the emergence of collective man in an egalitarian community beyond alienation. To have accepted these basic implications would have entailed abandonment, or indefinite postponement, of communism as a historical ideal and goal. Sweezy quite predictably chose not to follow this course as long as he could plausibly relocate his vision in a new historical setting.

But the vision was salvaged at a considerable price. In the sixties, he used the second paradigm to define advanced countries out of the socialist movement rather than to examine prospects for democracy, the one historically possible element of his vision that did not presuppose socialist man. As a critic of advanced socialist societies, then, he held two impossible theories of transition. The first assumed an automatic evolution from authoritarian to democratic socialism. When it crumbled after Hungary, he appeared to be casting about for a perspective that would account for the failure and chart the historical problems and potentialities of transitional societies. But in the end the imperatives of his temperament and the demands of his faith moved him to create another impossible paradigm that formed the rationale for condemning advanced socialist countries. That was one aspect of his estrangement from Western civilization. The other, on which I have commented at length, was the correspondingly rigid formulation of radical paradoxes in the West, especially in the United

States. In both instances, Sweezy exchanged political and historical criticism for myths of total rejection.

Sweezy's predilection for stark characterizations of radical paradoxes made him in some ways a more acute critic of underdeveloped countries, where actual conditions and options were also stark. Though his arguments for the necessity of armed revolution suffer from a characteristic tendency to exaggerate, to foreclose all options except one, they are in my view not far off the mark. To have a reasonable chance for economic development, people in backward nations must surely break out of the "free world" and retire their small ruling classes. And since rapid growth constitutes the alternative to a brief and miserable existence, some form of social revolution becomes the leading priority throughout the underdeveloped world. In many cases, the liquidation of capitalism will be violent, the result of a long, exhausting guerrilla war. But surely not everywhere, as Sweezy argues.

Socialism in underdeveloped countries is thus a flawed phenomenon. "It is," as Robert Heilbroner observes, "likely to emerge both as the salvation of its otherwise doomed people, and also as the source of a moral and intellectual infection from which it may take generations to recover."[101] But Sweezy's whole intellectual thrust in the fifties and sixties precluded such a balanced characterization of the paradoxical noneconomic implications of socialism in backward nations. To retain his faith in the historical enactment of socialist (and communist) ideals, he needed to regard moral incentives as more than a preferable substitute for Stalinist terror at comparatively early stages of socialist development; they had to be interpreted as tokens of a communist future. The argument, cast initially in the evaluations of the Cultural Revolution, is elaborated in Sweezy and Huberman's second book on Cuba. Before the revolution, they argue, Cuban peasants worked out of fear of starvation. In the course of a decade, however, the economic achievements of the revolution had the effect of breaking up old patterns of incentives. To maintain an adequate rate of growth, the leadership could rely heavily on material incentives, but this line of least resistance would entail enormous coercion, since Cuba lacks the resources to support an all-out program of positive financial incentives. Thus individuals would have to work more under the threat of the stick than out of a desire for carrots. More important, a stress on material incentives would defer the transition to collectivist consciousness and hence subvert the revolution by reinforcing the individualist traits of the prerevolutionary man.

Sweezy advocated implementation of moral incentives, a sustained effort to raise "social and political consciousness to the point where people will work hard because . . . they find a positive value in work and/or . . . they feel a sense of responsibility to the collectivity." If the Cubans overcome the difficult stage of primitive socialist accumulation through a policy of moral incentives and the new man begins to dominate the social landscape, the material well-being of the citizens can rise slowly, simultaneously. And the transition to communism will have reached a new and firmer plateau. But in the meantime, Cuba must undergo a "semi-militarization of . . . work" to accomplish economic tasks and preserve an austere version of the communist principle, "from each according to his ability, to each according to his needs."[102] As a matter of course, then, each person will be encouraged to contribute maximum effort and "voluntarily" restrict his consumption. Whoever fails to carry out both parts of the ideal willingly must be coerced.

The genuine historical questions here center on the immediate and longer-range consequences of stressing moral incentives and coercion over material incentives and coercion. But they cannot even be candidly approached without the paradoxical perspective of authoritarian socialism as the necessary though flawed mode of salvation for underdeveloped countries. Sweezy understands the necessity but minimizes the flaws. His formulation of the second paradigm prevents the lucid examination of various ideologies of socialist development because, in his insistence on relocating the communist vision in history, he invests moral incentives with exaggerated and unearned moral import. Though admitting the possibility of failure, Sweezy does not calculate the immediate and intermediate prices of moral incentives. For example, he suggests that in a country like Cuba this structure of incentives is consistent with communist ideals of fraternity and equality. Now it is perfectly true that this system should reduce inequities of wealth during initial phases of development. But for Sweezy it also presupposes the desirability and possibility of creating and preserving selfless individuals at higher levels of industrialization, technology, and productivity.

Though the desirability of Sweezy's version of communist man is finally a matter of personal preference, the possibilities for his emergence in the relevant future seem less controversial. At the very least, the burden of proof falls to the proponents. The historical experience of advanced socialist nations plainly suggests the enormous difficulties of such a change and its virtual impossibility within a few decades. Even the beginnings of the transformation in underdeveloped nations apparently elude utopian communists. Commenting on Sweezy and Huberman's discussion of corruption among small businessmen in Havana during the late sixties, Heilbroner observes that "if the rise of a worker to the precarious status of a small shopkeeper is enough to endanger the sentiments and institutions on which socialism is based, then socialism must constantly live in fear of betrayal from the secret corruptibility of the people."[103]

Sweezy's crucial miscalculation of the prospects for "genuine" socialism in underdeveloped countries, then, stems from his justification of Chinese and Cuban ideologies of socialist development on criteria drawn from a dialectic of liberation rather than from a viable sociology of change. Perceiving current realities through the utopian lens of communist ideals, he imagines that moral incentives can substantially reduce inequalities of wealth and establish the rudiments of an egalitarian community and the beginnings of the end of alienation as well. If this position preserves the ideals, investing them with a dubious historical relevance, it also obscures the political dimensions of radical paradoxes in the sociology of change—principally the thorny questions of power and democracy. His characterization of moral incentives requires on the one side a uniformity of opinion concerning basic issues, and on the other "extensive democracy" in smaller decisions. Under any social circumstances, such an equation raises serious if not fatal problems. In conditions of scarcity, the tension must yield to an unsatisfactory resolution, since uniformity is necessary to keep the system afloat whereas limited democracy is merely desirable and therefore expendable. Sweezy recognizes that should deprivation and austerity continue in Cuba, "there is a grave danger that the ties between people and government will continue to erode and that the diabolic logic of the process will lead the government deeper and deeper into the ways of repression."[104]

His remedy for this probable turn—"an attempt to change the character of the relationship" from "paternalism" to a "sharing of power and responsibility"—is more a hope than an expectation.[105] And it depends, I think, on a serious ideological confusion with far-reaching consequences. For if moral incentives under austere conditions encourage a crude form of egalitarianism and community, they may also discourage the development and expression of independent critical thought. The whole enterprise rests on a foundation of stifling conformity, in part "voluntary" but largely coerced. This in turn not only insures the emergence of clumsy bureaucracies, despite campaigns to increase flexibility in decision-making; it also guarantees the monopolization of power by a minority, usually personified by a maximum leader, who decide on the nature of the ideals and set the specific tests of compliance. And when the official ideology entails nothing less than communist ideals, leaders will predictably become suspicious of the majority who are so easily "corrupted."

Moreover, emergency measures have a way of surviving. As Sweezy acknowledges, "bureaucratic rule, once entrenched, is extremely resistant to change."[106] Despite all this, he resists the obvious conclusion that underdeveloped countries cannot escape a long period of authoritarian socialism. It is the price of their salvation, which must be paid in installments—alike during the time of austerity and at higher stages of development, when representative democracy and personal freedom become slim political options rather than historical certainties. The severity of socialist dictatorships—and their effectiveness—will, of course, vary according to geographic, social, and cultural factors. Within these limits people in underdeveloped socialist countries may be able to devise systems of incentives that minimize the pain associated with their progress. But critics, especially if they are situated in advanced capitalist countries, do not help matters by confusing ideology with analysis, and desire with genuine possibilities.

Sweezy thus pushes traditional Marxist modes of analysis and the orthodox dream of a communist man and society beyond the outer limits of historical possibility. The second paradigm connects the present with an impossible future by means of an unlikely theory of transition. Slighting the real problems and limited prospects of socialism everywhere, he has created narrowing perspectives that virtually guarantee a succession of disappointments as one postrevolutionary society after another confronts the manifold problems of survival and growth. Betting on the off chance that a mythic communist future may yet redeem the past, Sweezy ends by distorting his perception of an unsettling present.

When we lose the comfortable formulas that have hitherto been our guides amid the complexities of existence . . . we feel like drowning in the ocean of facts until we find a new foothold or learn to swim.

—Werner Sombart, *The Quintessence of Capitalism*

There is no ground on which theory and practice, thought and action meet.

—Herbert Marcuse, *One-Dimensional Man*

6

Herbert Marcuse:

From History to Myth

None of his critics, to my knowledge, has ever imagined that Herbert Marcuse would perish in a sea of facts: from the beginning, he responded to the defeats of socialism by learning to fly. Whereas Mills set foot tentatively on revisionist ground toward the end of his critical explorations, and Sweezy swam from one Marxist foothold to another following his disenchantment with Soviet socialism, Marcuse has always conducted his social philosophy from the air, searching for a political landing strip that he could never find. Mills remained steadily antiutopian, though he wanted to be hopeful about the historical progress of socialism in the late fifties and early sixties. Baran publicly clung to his original conception of socialist evolution. Sweezy yielded to Maoist mythology only late in life, having preserved his faith in orthodox Communism long after most politically independent Marxists abandoned theirs. But Marcuse begins and ends with a double

175

optic—with premonitions of an apocalypse and revolutionary visions of a new man in a new society beyond alienation. He therefore anticipates and completes the theoretical trajectory of the plain Marxists who gravitated from social theory toward myth during the cold-war years.

The pattern of Marcuse's life sets him apart from the native American plain Marxists. Born in Berlin in 1898, he studied philosophy at the universities of Berlin and Freiburg, completing a doctoral dissertation on Hegel's ontology in 1922.[1] At the invitation of Max Horkheimer he joined the Frankfurt Institute for Social Research, only to be forced out of the country when the fate of Left-wing Jewish intellectuals under the regime of Hitler became clear. After a year in Geneva, Marcuse, like Baran, emigrated to the United States, joining the Institute of Social Research at Columbia, where he worked on and off from 1934 until 1940. During these years he published a number of essays and finished *Reason and Revolution* (1941), his first major study in English.[2] In World War II he began a career in government, working initially with the Office of Strategic Services and later on at the State Department as acting head of the Eastern European section. After a decade of public service Marcuse returned to the academy to complete his mature work: *Eros and Civilization* (1955); *Soviet Marxism* (1958); *One-Dimensional Man* (1964); and *An Essay on Liberation* (1969).[3] He taught philosophy at Brandeis from 1954 until his initial retirement in 1965 and then went West to teach at the quiet ocean-front branch of the University of California at San Diego, only to be transformed into a figure of international controversy, an unlikely guru of the new Left.

This biographical sketch underplays the pervasive ironies that characterize Marcuse's life and shape his major works: the social prophet of a global society forced into exile; the semiretired academic lifted from obscurity largely against his will; the isolated revolutionary thinker adopted late in life by a new generation of utopians quite unlike his own. Nor does it give proper weight to the paradox of a "buoyant" pessimist whose personal success, first as an academic philosopher and later as a public figure, was carved out of the historical matter of tragedy and political defeat.[4] Marcuse has endured an unbroken succession of defeats spanning five decades: the collapse of the European revolutionary Left after World War I, the Stalinization of Russia, the grim episode of fascism and nazism, and the resurgence of American capitalism following the Second World War. Since the early twenties, then, his critical stance as a utopian realist—or, if you will, a utopian pessimist—has compelled him to formulate distinctive and stark versions of radical paradoxes. Throughout, he has been a revolutionary thinker without political portfolio, a Jeremian witness to a series of revolutions delayed and revolutions betrayed. Following a brief period of activism with the German Sparticist movement in his youth, Marcuse's disenchantment with politics deepened, though he did not lose faith in the revolutionary thrust of the working class until the middle thirties. In a retrospective assessment of his early writings, he comments that "the end of a historical period and the horror of the one to come were announced in the simultaneity of the civil war in Spain and the trials in Moscow."[5] The failure of socialism, in his view, removed the last obstacles to the proliferation of modern totalitarianism—fascist, democratic, and Stalinist.

The strong current of pessimism, frustration, and anger running through his major works is therefore hardly surprising. It is rather the survival of historical optimism that suggests the problem of Marcuse. Whereas other critics responded to crises of socialism by abandoning Marxism altogether, casting their lot with one of the major currents of the world Communist movement, or diluting their visions of communism to fit some species of revisionist politics, Marcuse attempted to compensate for every political loss and dark turn of the historical wheel by extending and deepening his vision of utopia. This is the basic structure and dynamic of his work. He constructs (and periodically remodels) an elaborate symbolic world in which steadily diverging visions of the future and versions of the present are forced into ironic focus by the double optic of "critical theory." And though these magnified projections of man's hope counterbalanced an increasingly dystopian present, evoking a thin illusion of historical credibility, they gradually led to a rejection of the old man in favor of a series of incredible mythic figures allegedly capable of creating and inhabiting the new civilization.

As I shall argue, Marcuse blends quasi-historical analysis, utopian speculation, and myth into a distinctive mode of social criticism that is essentially symbolist fiction—an impossible view of the world with a surface of verisimilitude. But he never fully evades the implications of radical paradoxes, for the specter of political impotence and the revolutionary's apparent impulse toward self-defeat remain the dominant concerns of his entire critical enterprise. The freewheeling examinations of the history of Western philosophy, culture, and society; the abstract studies of Hegel, Marx, and Freud; the highly allusive and syntactically bewildering excursions into Kant, Plato, and Aristotle are all variations on a single theme. Despite its dense variety, Marcuse's work is essentially a heterodox political defense of an orthodox version of utopian Marxism, a steady assertion and elaboration of the dialectic of liberation against any plausible sociology of change, of vision against history, and of the future against the social past and present.

Marcuse's Critical Theory—the Prewar Phase

Marcuse's wish to conduct a political defense of his Hegelianized version of Marxism at abstract levels of philosophical discourse welds the prewar and postwar phases of his work into a single enterprise whose unity derives from two constant attitudes: an inflexible utopian-revolutionary impulse and a steadily realistic assessment of the ultra-Left antipolitics that usually follows from such visions. The changing subjects and surfaces of his critiques are elements of the attempt to sustain this basic version of the paradox of powerlessness amid deteriorating social contexts throughout the capitalist and socialist worlds—an effort which brings on the mood of despair that increasingly pervades the postwar work, overshadowing even the faint resurgence of hope in the late sixties.

Marcuse establishes the main lines of his later utopian visions through an examination of Marx in *Reason and Revolution*.[6] His sympathetic—and selective—reading relaxes the tensions between Marx's dialectic of liberation and his sociology of change, reducing the substantive distance between the early philosophical anthropology and the mature examinations of political economy.[7] Marcuse claims that Marx's overriding philosophical interests always centered on the disparity between man's essence and his miserable historical existence, especially under capitalism. The early Marx locates the central causes of deprivation and unhappiness in various modalities of alienation. " 'Misery,' " he observes, " 'springs from the *nature* of the prevailing mode of labor . . .' " which narrowly circumscribes man's entire historical existence and provides a rough negative index of the separation from his essence—from his potentialities for reason, freedom, and happiness. More than a mere economic activity, labor in any society is the " 'existential activity' of man," the characteristic way he reproduces, expresses, changes, and fulfills or distorts himself. Under capitalist forms of commodity production, the worker enlarges the power of capital while reducing his own capacity "for appropriating his products." Since he confronts his creations as alien entities, the basic form of alienation is exploitation, an economic fact that implies the psychic mutilation of man under capitalism. The worker also becomes estranged from his own activity—from himself—because his labor time literally belongs to others. He can therefore be free only when not on the job, " 'at home when he does not work and not at home when he does.' "[8]

The capitalist division of labor enforces two additional modes of alienation: it isolates individuals from others in a lonely, competitive existence and it gradually destroys any sense of community, of solidarity with the species.[9] Cut off from their potential selves, individuals cannot escape an organization of labor that expresses the economic rationality of the dominant classes while blocking the full development and satisfaction of human needs and faculties. Enlarging society's material wealth, the working class contributes to its own economic, intellectual, and spiritual impoverishment. Trapped in a reified world where distorted human relations take on the appearance of objective relationships among things, man loses not only himself but even the *consciousness* of his essence.

The modalities of alienation—from the products of labor, from self, others, and the human community—thus constitute interconnected aspects of a total psychic and social disease that requires the total cure of communism. As Marcuse puts it: "The negativity of capitalist society lies in its alienation of labor; the negation of this negativity will come with the abolition of alienated labor."[10] To liberate his potentialities, man must destroy those outer historical forms which express and perpetuate the inner disease of alienation. This version of the dialectic of liberation encompasses Marcuse's notion of an ideal harmony between the one and the many, between man as an individual and social being. "The true history of mankind," he asserts, "will be . . . the history of free individuals, so that the interest of the whole will be woven into the individual existence of each."[11] In such an " 'association of free individuals' "—a community beyond scarcity and alienation—men can repeal previous patterns of domination and exploitation.

For Marcuse—and Marcuse's Marx—the vision of community simultaneously forms the underlying goal of human activity and establishes dominant criteria for understanding and condemning the present. Assuming from the outset that "the labor process determines the totality of human existence and thus gives to society its basic pattern," Marx turned to political economy to fashion an "exact analysis of this process." His categories, according to Marcuse, "are negative and at the same time positive; they present a negative state of affairs in the light of its positive solution, revealing the true situation in existing society as the prelude to its passing into a new form." The labor theory of value, elaborated in *Capital,* simultaneously specifies the indictment of capitalism and implies the communist vision of human potentiality.[12]

This utopian perspective entailed general imperatives of action, for the philosophical conflicts first revealed by Hegel as historical dilemmas demand political resolution: with Marx, philosophy "devolved upon social theory" and politics.[13] But not any politics of the Left, because the utopian goal adopted from Marx requires nothing less than revolutionary means. As the ultimate negation of humanity, the proletariat of industrial society formed the only class capable of abolishing itself and all other classes through a final revolution to end the inner and outer antagonisms of the old civilization. Here Marcuse comes upon the first version of the central paradox of powerlessness—the disparity between Marx's revolutionary-utopian projections and the course of the first four decades of twentieth-century history. Why has the working class failed to take up its historical challenge and opportunity? Marcuse protects the analysis and utopian vision from the failures and betrayals of this century by insisting that Marx's scenario projects a *possible* rather than a *necessary* future. Maintaining that the mature analyses of capitalism illuminate its necessary laws of growth and decline, he argues that the realization of communism in history remains an open question, a matter of man's conscious revolutionary activity. To be sure, revolution presupposes a configuration of objective conditions—"a certain attained level of material and intellectual culture, a self-conscious and organized working class on an international scale, acute class struggle." But these factors become aspects of a promising revolutionary *situation* only "if seized upon and directed by a conscious activity that has in mind the socialist goal."[14]

Since the only end worth pursuing dictated revolutionary means, Marcuse spurned the theories and politics of social democracy: "Revisionist writing and thought, which expressed the growing faith of large socialist groups in a peaceful evolution from capitalism to socialism, attempted to change socialism from a theoretical and practical antithesis to the capitalist system into a parliamentary movement within this system."[15] He opposed all forms of "economism" on the ground that a mere improvement in living standards, while not objectionable in itself, had nothing to do with the main goal of communism. Nor did he regard the preservation and extension of capitalist democracy as indispensable values: though preferable to brutal forms of authoritarian rule, these caricatures of true freedom were valuable only to the extent that they permitted the growth of a genuinely revolutionary opposition. But the ideology of bourgeois democracy also extended the bondage of the working class, delaying, perhaps tragically, the recognition and fulfillment of man's hope.[16]

For similar reasons, Marcuse remained aloof from the orthodox Communist movement in the thirties, contending that "the socialization of the means of production is as such merely an economic fact. . . . Its claim to be the beginning of a new social order depends on what man does with the socialized means of production." Skipping over Sweezy's first paradigm, Marcuse rejected the evolutionary view of postrevolutionary development through a long period of authoritarian socialism, a gradual transition to a democratic phase at higher levels of productivity, and eventually a modulation to communism. If socialized forms of production "are not utilized for the development and gratification of the free individual, they will amount simply to a new form for subjugating individuals to a hypostatized universality" (i.e., a false community).[17] Perhaps because he was a philosopher rather than an economist, Marcuse never submitted to the fetishism of planning, recognizing always the possibility of planned misery.

Identifying false consciousness as the central reason for the revolutions not made in the West and the revolution betrayed in the East, he insists from the beginning that the riddle of Marx's third thesis on Feuerbach be solved by "revolutionizing practice." Since consciousness—of the alienated present, the communist aim, and the revolutionary means—is the indispensable condition of any qualitative change in the human condition, the problem of educating the educators defined Marcuse's critical project. For in the absence of revolutionary social conditions (especially of a significant working-class movement) the chief possibility of political action becomes the liberation and transformation of consciousness—one's own and others'—through sustained rational effort. Though the practice of revolutionary theory seemed virtually hopeless by the middle thirties, it struck Marcuse as the only way of preserving man's slim chance of emerging from the cave of his long history. In contrast, all other varieties of politics were so many forms of shadow boxing.

Through his associations with Max Horkheimer and other members of the Institute for Social Research, Marcuse carved out his own version of "critical theory," the basic organon which connects possible futures with past and present social realities. Its principles are essentially general guidelines of inquiry abstracted from classical Marxism which Marcuse uses to manipulate (and in the early postwar years, to disguise) orthodox concepts and categories.[18] Critical theory is essentially a double optic with two main analytic dimensions—a version of the present and a vision of the future. Together, these two lenses bring a third, implicit political dimension into obscure and changing focus. Insofar as he concerns himself with political economy, the early Marcuse merely appropriates Marx's tendential laws, estimating the extent to which capitalist society fulfills them at any moment of its long, unavoidable decline. His assessments of the social trajectory of the first four decades of twentieth-century capitalism are therefore bleak—in fact necessarily dystopian, for he assumes a general though not always mechanical correspondence between cultural and social spheres.[19] Then, in his principal role of cultural astronomer, Marcuse turns to various "reactionary" philosophical configurations—"universalism," "naturalism (organicism)," and "existentialism"—arguing that each perspective anticipated and aided the transition from competitive to monopoly capitalism. This procedure sets the pattern and tone for the postwar examinations of contemporary styles in philosophy.[20] The studies of positivism, empiricism, and scientism all revolve about the one fundamental, essentially political issue of whether the position in question is good for the revolution. If not, Marcuse invariably concludes, it probably aids the forces of reaction.

Just as the dystopian lens of critical theory isolates—and magnifies—the negative contours of contemporary reality, the utopian optic enables the critic to see the negation of the negative, or the positive outlines of a better future. Once again, Marcuse draws heavily on his Hegelianized reading of Marx, arguing that Marx's critique of political economy illuminates the concrete potentialities for realizing man's hopes that are imprisoned in capitalism's perverse ordering of economic, social, and psychic environments. In contrast to my use of the term,[21] then, Marcuse defines "utopian" as the historically widening horizon of man's hope. As the fantastic dreams of one epoch become materially (i.e., economically and technically) feasible, they turn into historical possibilities. And their political chances, however bleak, only set the intellectual's task.[22] Though Marcuse, like Marx, refuses to draw blueprints for a society that only "liberated mankind" can create, he must nevertheless outline the "determinate negation" of the present order by distinguishing those specific values which apparently cannot (and yet ought to) be realized under capitalism from the larger category of logical and material possibilities. He does this by scanning the past, assuming that past futures can be retrospectively discerned in the cultural galaxies. He recognizes, of course, that the whole of Western philosophy and culture, by virtue of its separation from power, has reinforced the successive historical and social forms of man's misery. But this tradition also contains a progressive second dimension of theoretical opposition, extending from the classical period (the later dialogues of Plato, and Aristotle) through Kant, Hegel, and Marx, culminating in Marcuse's own Frankfurt school of critical theory.[23]

Through the power of reason, "the fundamental category of

philosophical thought," figures in the Western tradition have identified the basic antagonisms between subject and object, fact and value, actuality and potentiality, existence and essence. Before Hegel and Marx, however, these dualisms were defined ontologically, as conditions of being reconcilable only in pure thought, rather than as conditions of history, subject to revolutionary political transformation. The goal of contemporary man, which earlier philosophers both concealed and foreshadowed, is to discover and reconcile these antagonisms, to bring historical reality under the rule of reason. In this sense, reason presupposes freedom. Marcuse completes his utopian triad by adding happiness, whose images survive mainly in art, the other principal branch of Western culture.[24] Only by abolishing alienation (including exploitation and material deprivation) can man finally fulfill his essence as a rational, free, and happy social being. At this juncture, the exploration of the philosophical and cultural galaxies links up with the utopian vision adapted from Marx; for the materialization of reason, freedom, and happiness requires nothing less than the annihiliation of all forms of *Gesellschaft* society and the creation of a *Gemeinschaft* community.

Marcuse thus begins his intellectual odyssey with the belief that critical theory constitutes a prelude to revolutionary politics by shaping, at every turn, a correct awareness of what is, what ought to be, and what can be brought about by man's collective activity. Toward the end of the thirties, however, the utopian lens became increasingly cloudy as capitalism moved into its totalitarian phases and even the rational elements of the second dimension of the Western experience were being rapidly absorbed into forms of total social control that threatened formerly free areas of consciousness. "The abyss between rational and present reality," Marcuse concluded, "cannot be bridged by conceptual thought"; intimations of the future previously buried in philosophy would henceforth have to be remembered through art. This decisive shift in emphasis from reason to imagination deeply influenced the character and direction of Marcuse's subsequent thought. "Without phantasy," he declared in 1937, "all philosophical knowledge remains in the grip of the present or the past and severed from the future, which is the only link between philosophy and the real history of mankind."[25] As the social world darkened the dystopian lens of critical theory, Marcuse began to see ever more fantastic shapes through the utopian optic. This balancing perspective enabled him to predict disaster—to expect the worst—while expanding his vision of human possibility. But since the critical prelude never led to a main movement, it became a surrogate, a symbolic mode of simultaneously confronting and evading radical paradoxes during the long prerevolutionary wait.

The Drift into Despair: 1940-1964

Between 1941 and the appearance of *Eros and Civilization* in 1955, Marcuse published very little—a longish piece on Sartre's *Being and Nothingness* (1948) and a handful of minor essays and reviews.[26] But this was nevertheless a decisive period in his intellectual life, a major turning point within a larger circle of continuity. The postwar work divides conveniently into two phases: a descent into despair culminating in *One-Dimensional Man* (1964), his chief contribution to the literature of dystopia, and a revival of hope during his curious association with the new Left in the late sixties. Within each phase, however, Marcuse employs the double optic of critical theory that he fashioned in the thirties, balancing the apocalyptic drift of civilization with fresh visions of utopia.

Commenting on his early work, he observes that "Auschwitz deeply separates it from the present. What was correct in it has since become, perhaps not false, but a thing of the past."[27] Auschwitz dramatically symbolized the horror of Western civilization, demonstrating the barbarous capacity of the fascist strain of late capitalism and prefiguring its growing potential for destruction on a global scale.[28] And if the democratic variants of Western capitalism took on increasingly subtle and grotesque shapes after

1945, the even grimmer contours of socialism in the East offered no immediate consolation and only a slim long-range hope, as Marcuse contends in *Soviet Marxism* (1958).

From several Marxist vantage points, the strength of each principal dystopian trend—the rise and decline of fascism, the recovery of Western capitalism, and the perversion of the Bolshevik Revolution—depended upon the impotence of the "workers' movement."[29] Both its virtual collapse in the West and its reversal in the East could be understood as, among other things, a failure of socialist education to introduce and sustain revolutionary consciousness and will among the masses. Those who stayed in or around the Western Communist parties—and even politically independent Marxists like Baran and Sweezy—continued to find some variant of this hypothesis plausible well into the cold war. But Marcuse could not follow this strategy after World War II, because his utopian vision of socialism lacked even preliminary historical confirmation. More than a century of socialist education had failed to transform any proletariant into a class-for-itself, discrediting the assumed theoretical links between rational education, the qualitative reconstruction of consciousness, and revolution. Though events and trends in both worlds largely confirmed earlier apocalyptic premonitions, deepening his pessimism, there was never any question of abandoning the Hegelianized version of Marxism that formerly invested radical pedagogy with long-range political significance: critical theory validated itself even in the drift toward dystopia. As a practical matter, of course, the issue was never really live, since Marcuse's opaque critical theory always resisted accurate translation into any readily comprehensible political language.[30] The loss of the theoretical illusion of potential political relevance, however, raised the more immediate and fundamental problem of accounting for the massive resistance to rational modes of socialist education, a question Marcuse took up initially in the late thirties when he began an extensive study of Freud.[31] The inquiry was complicated by the need to find answers that would also reestablish the historical credibility of his prewar utopian speculations.[32] Confronted with an increasingly repressive actual situation, Marcuse raised the utopian stakes and plunged into the realm of myth.

It may at first appear odd that Marcuse's initial response to postwar dilemmas took the form of an ambitious projection of man's hope, anchored in a selective reading of the pessimistic metapsychology of the later Freud. But *Eros and Civilization,* I shall argue, clearly follows the logic and dynamic of his entire intellectual venture. Without slighting the complex, occasionally brilliant fabric of the central arguments, I think it fair to suggest that the work is fundamentally animated by the desire to clarify both dimensions of radical paradoxes—to explain the paradox of political powerlessness in the West and the ethical paradox of receding socialist ends (the corruptions of power) in the East.[33]

According to Freud, the origins, development, and preservation of civilization rest on the tragic premise of continuous repression of the instincts.[34] From the obscure beginnings of his journey into history, man is cut off from a life of pleasure (or happiness) by his environment: "The animal drives become human instincts under the influence of the external reality. Their original 'location' in the organism and their basic direction remain the same, but their objectives and their manifestations are subject to change." In the transition from the animal to the human state, capricious natural forces and persistent scarcity form and reform the relatively plastic instincts, bending the changing imperatives of the pleasure principle to fit the harsh demands of reality: immediate satisfaction, pleasure, joy (play), receptiveness, and the absence of repression give way to delayed satisfaction, the restraint of pleasure, toil (work), productiveness, and security.[35]

In return for the renunciation of happiness, man achieves a measure of reason by transforming the collection of animal drives into an organized ego. "Under the reality principle, the human being develops the function of *reason:* it learns to 'test' the reality, to distinguish between good and bad, true and false, useful and harmful." Man then becomes a "conscious, thinking *subject*" whose criteria of rationality enable him to alter the environment in the interests of survival. But the environment he shapes, shapes him: throughout history, nature and society have remained beyond *collective, rational control.* In the hard bargain of civilizing himself, then, man attains only partial rationality while losing genuine freedom: "neither his desires nor his alteration of reality are . . . his own: they are now 'organized' by his society. And this 'organization' represses and transubstantiates his original instinctual needs. If absence from repression is the archetype of freedom, then civilization is the struggle against this freedom."[36]

Marcuse employs the myth of the primal horde to illuminate the tragic pattern of domination and repression that has plagued all forms of civilization: "The rule of the primal father is followed, after the first rebellion, by the rule of the sons, and the brother clan develops into institutionalized social and political domination. The reality principle materializes in a system of institutions." Freud's myth thus exposes the fatal link between history and biography, between the phylogenetic development of the human species and the early ontogenetic development of individuals. As Marcuse puts it, "repression from without has been supported by repression from within: the unfree individual introjects his masters and their commands into his own mental apparatus."[37] Hence the individual subject—the ego and the superego, reason and morality—is in bondage to the outer forms of history and to its own inner world. Chained to the reality principle by seemingly inescapable psychic ties, man retains but one historically and politically impotent sphere of freedom—phantasy, ranging from dreams and daydreams to the highest artistic achievements of his culture.

With the main elements of this Freudian myth, Marcuse fashioned an explanation of the inadequacy of rational socialist education and the reversal of all revolutions—an explanation that includes but goes beyond traditional Marxian categories of power, the state of productive forces, and class consciousness. In the succession of revolts against real and institutionalized fathers, there is a point at which the sons, moved by their guilt, identify with "the power against which they revolt." A measure of "self-defeat" therefore "seems to be involved. . . . In this sense, every revolution has also been a betrayed revolution."[38] Brief openings onto genuine liberation close, and the repressive dialectic of civilization reasserts itself through social and/or psychological counter-revolution. The root of the failure of revolutions, then, is the postlapsarian Adam, man himself. As long as he continues to identify with false fathers, no mere reordering of the institutional network in the outer world can break the internal reproduction of domination and servitude. Marcuse's reading of Freud thus implies that the educator cannot be reeducated, because false consciousness only manifests the deeper malaise located in the tangled roots of civilization and the instincts. He must therefore be *cured*, liberated from his old self, if the repressive pattern of civilization is ever to be shattered.

From this perspective, the paradox of radical powerlessness emerges as a hopeless contradiction beyond political remedy. Though Freud's analysis accounts for some variations within history,[39] it encloses all social formations in a larger, more abstract web of frustration and defeat. To rescue the analysis from its pessimistic implications, Marcuse "extrapolates" the hidden historical or "sociological" character of Freud's pivotal assumptions, arguing that man's repressed existence results not only from the general fact of scarcity but also from its specific organization and maldistribution at various stages of historical growth: "the *distribution* of scarcity as well as the effort of overcoming it, the mode of work, have been *imposed* upon individuals—first by mere violence, subsequently by a more rational utilization of power."[40] In the most abstract view, man's commitment to the reality principle—and hence to a life of alienated labor—emerges as a constant feature of civilization; the long history of external and internal repression is in this sense circular.

But Marcuse suggests that history also exhibits a potentially progressive, linear dimension. Through science, technology, and capitalism, man has moved to the threshold of the complete conquest of scarcity, a condition that turns old utopian dreams into genuine historical possibilities. Material progress occurs, but always within contexts of domination. Here Marcuse combines a deeply conservative metaphor of historical recurrence with a liberal metaphor of linear progress, in order to reintroduce the main elements of his own utopian revolutionary Marxian position (without ever referring explicitly to Marx).[41] To distinguish theoretically between progress and reaction, he first substitutes the "performance principle" for Freud's reality principle.[42] Designating the changing social shapes of the reality principle, Marcuse's concept enables the critic to search out the specific modes of domination required at any historical moment to continue the struggle for survival *and* to perpetuate the prevailing class system. At this level of abstraction, the growth of civilization can be understood as a dynamic of class conflict, precisely in Marx's sense. If social order and the general conquest of scarcity entail a basic, minimum quantity of organized repression at any particular time, the maintenance of class societies has demanded "additional controls," or what Marcuse terms "surplus repression." This obvious psychic analogue to Marx's economic category of surplus value serves as a theoretical index of the general irrationality of man's existence in civilization, and as an initial approximation of the needless repression in any particular period.[43]

The apparent departure from the utopian Marx in *Eros and Civilization* thus moves back upon itself. Enabling Marcuse to locate the internal causes of revolutionary failure in the shifting patterns of surplus repression, this selective reading of Freud rescues the utopian quest from the refutation of twentieth-century history, including the horrors of Stalinism. The historically relative concept of the performance principle also illuminates the widening material horizons of man's hope. In fact, the paradox of increasing domination and repression in the framework of growing abundance gives modern societies their especially grotesque appearance in the dystopian lens of critical theory, a theme that Marcuse elucidates in *One-Dimensional Man*. Although *Eros and Civiliza-*

tion focuses mainly on utopian possibilities, the credibility of the exercise depends upon the dystopian contours of the present, upon vast material progress encapsulated in perverted social and psychic forms. This curious version of "the worse, the better" hypothesis provides the material foundations for what many critics consider Marcuse's most optimistic vision of human potentiality.[44]

The utopian vision in *Eros and Civilization* conforms to the general criteria taken over from Marx in the thirties.[45] Though happiness now occupies the central position, Marcuse retains reason and freedom, the other elements of the original triad. And he continues to insist that the realization of these values requires a global community beyond alienation. But the character of the defense changes: having used Marx to liberate Freud's metapsychology from its conservative and allegedly antihistorical straitjacket, Marcuse proceeds to extrapolate the outlines of a nonrepressive civilization from Freud's theory of instincts. His complex strategy revolves around an attempt to connect the forgotten, precivilized past with a "forbidden" future through an examination of the aesthetic dimension of man's existence.

The theoretical defense of the new order rests on parallel myths of a golden past and a utopian future. Because of its continuing fidelity to the id, "imagination preserves the 'memory' of the subhistorical past when the life of the individual was the life of the genus, the image of the immediate unity between the universal and the particular under the rule of the pleasure principle."[46] Though impotent in a civilization ruled by the performance principle, the artistic achievements of the imagination constitute their own sphere of truth that indicts the present and demands a better future. Imaginative truths "are first realized when phantasy itself takes form, when it creates a universe of perception and comprehension—a subjective and at the same time objective universe." Marcuse selects Orpheus and Narcissus as the archetypal antagonists of life under the reality principle, for they front the world passively rather than aggressively, receptively rather than productively, sensuously rather than rationally. In them "the opposition between man and nature, subject and object is overcome. Being is experienced as gratification, which unites man and nature so that the fulfillment of man is at the same time the fulfillment, without violence, of nature." Orpheus overcomes death and cruelty—"his language is *song,* and his work is *play"*—whereas Narcissus follows a life of beauty, a contemplative existence. Revealing the possibility of fulfillment through a release of libidinal forces[47] rather than through domination and exploitation, both mythic figures imply that the characteristics of a new reality principle are buried in the history of aesthetics.

Following his earlier practice of collecting insights from various philosophers, Marcuse constructs his aesthetic mosaic of a new man and civilization out of fragments from Kant and Schiller. "Art," he declares, "challenges the prevailing principle of reason: in representing the order of sensuousness, it invokes a tabooed logic—the logic of gratification as against that of repression. Behind the sublimated aesthetic form, the unsublimated content shows forth: the commitment of art to the pleasure principle." The new aesthetic form of reason, of order, then, conforms to the logic of sensuousness: a new society must make reason sensuous and sensuousness rational. Only then will the freedom of each be in harmony with the freedom of all. "In a truly free civilization, all laws are self-given by the individuals . . . 'the will of the whole' fulfills itself only 'through the nature of the individual.' Order is freedom only if it is founded on and sustained by the free gratification of the individuals."[48]

In past and present civilizations, especially in industrial societies, however, reason and sensuousness are tragically separated, placed in a perpetually antagonistic relationship. And "since it was civilization itself which 'dealt modern man this wound,' only a new mode of civilization can heal it." According to Schiller, from whom Marcuse borrows liberally, the basic antagonisms between reason and sensuousness, nature and freedom, the particular and the universal, are governed by two opposing impulses: the essentially passive "sensuous impulse" and the domineering rational "form-impulse." The "play-impulse," which aims at beauty and freedom, can reconcile these opposites, but only momentarily, in art. Taking Schiller's analysis out of the aesthetic realm, Marcuse posits it as the basis of a new mode of free, rational, and happy existence. Alienated labor would be transformed into play, and repressive productivity into "dis-play" under conditions of abundance.[49] Sensuousness could then be self-sublimated rather than generally repressed and occasionally set loose. The desublimation of reason (the form-impulse) would complete the reconciliation of opposites. And man could fully confront the problems of time and death, which place obvious barriers on sustained gratification.

Before dealing with these penultimate questions, Marcuse must defend his pastoral vision of utopia and its mythic inhabitants against the serious charge that the liberation of the instincts from the performance principle would release vast quantities of destructive or antisocial energy. Rather than establishing a new, higher form of civilization, such liberation might lead to the destruction of culture. He conducts the defense by examining sexuality, the "most 'disorderly' of all instincts,"[50] taking the argument down a predictable path. By requiring "genital supremacy" and the corresponding de-eroticization of other areas of the body, the current ordering of labor prevents the spread of libidinal energy within and among men and their surroundings. Nonrepressive conditions, however, might release and transform libidinal energy, minimizing its merely sexual manifestations "by integrating them into a far larger order, including the order of work."[51] Moreover, Eros may come to exhibit a " 'natural' self-restraint" that would make delay, detour, and arrest, voluntarily imposed, the main routes to genuine and lasting gratification.[52] The nonrepressive self-sublimation of sexuality, then, indicates "the culture-building power of Eros," the prospect for the emergence of a new reality principle with its own rationality and morality: "Eros redefines reason in his own terms. Reasonable is what sustains the order of gratification." Marcuse acknowledges that the chances of self-sublimation—of the transformation of sexuality into Eros—depend upon a global social transformation. As an unrepressed force, libidinal energy "can promote the formation of culture only under conditions which relate associated individuals to each other in the cultivation of the environment for their developing needs and faculties." The utopian notion of a community beyond alienation is thus reestablished on the thin hypothesis that the instincts may become the basis for a harmonious, orderly fulfillment of each individual's needs and capacities—within a unified social whole.[53]

The manipulation of the dystopian and utopian lenses in *Eros and Civilization* brings the political dimension into partial focus. As I have shown, the theoretical credibility of Marcuse's entire argument depends upon the material or historical possibility of abolishing scarcity, a point he emphasizes without ever establishing empirically.[54] Its historical relevance, however, presupposes a viable political solution. But on this issue Marcuse is nearly silent, and wisely so. Discussing Schiller, for example, he notes that the end of repressive civilization would probably be accompanied by a short transitional dictatorship of the passions, a storm preceding the new order of tranquillity.[55] A later passage on the political implications of this transition to a nonrepressive civilization suggests that conflicts between the one and the many may be reconciled *either* by the emergence of a " 'general will' " *or* by an educational dictatorship, a trap he falls into more than once in his mature work.[56] Approaching the ethical dimensions of radical paradoxes almost casually, Marcuse then claims that educational dictatorships have become "obsolete" since knowledge of the Good no longer need be confined to a small elite: "The facts are all too open, and the individual consciousness would safely arrive at them if it were not methodically arrested and diverted." In the same paragraph, he apparently reverses himself: "That . . . [individuals] cannot make this distinction [between rational and irrational authority] now does not mean that they cannot learn to make it *once they are given the opportunity to do so.*"[57] Presumably, then, the (obsolete) educational dictatorship will be shorter and more merciful than a dictatorship of the proletariat—if it is not brutalized and indefinitely extended by a tyranny of the passions.

These allusions to the political issues of revolution and the transition to a new society are as unsatisfactory as they are brief. Their main function within the larger work is to invest the myth of a new man in a utopian society with the illusion of credibility, to blunt the inevitable suspicion that the whole effort amounts to a fanciful exercise rather than a historically possible (though politically preposterous) vision of the future. An extended discussion of modes of transition, however, would have detracted from the fictional surface by underlining the deeply antipolitical implications of Marcuse's utopian vision. Despite its highly abstract character, then, *Eros and Civilization* is clearly a work of the fifties, a projection of man's hope cast in the social circumstances of a depressingly stable, relatively affluent capitalist society that largely resisted significant political reforms and fully repelled—or absorbed—utopian reveries. And it is a work of Marcuse's own fifties that indirectly indicts his defeated generation by imagining a curiously middle-aged mythic man—Orphic rather than Promethean, passive and receptive rather than productive and aggressive. It thus begins as an implicit attempt to resolve radical paradoxes and ends by evading them through a disastrous confusion of aesthetic and historical categories. The vision of a new man and a new society may be taken as a celebration of human potentiality, but it is a potentiality to be unfolded on the other side of a cataclysmic leap out of the present, out of history. In the absence of any conceivable path toward that future, we are left with the mirror image of the old man, for whom Marcuse has little use— political or other.

If *Eros and Civilization* defines man's hope in the early cold-war years, *One-Dimensional Man* depicts a hopeless world, balancing reality against vision once more in the double optic of critical theory. It also marks a dramatic break in mood from the strained, almost escapist optimism of *Eros and Civilization* to a bitter pessimism brought on, perhaps, by too many years of disenchantment and defeat. Deemphasizing the historical prospects for a new man and civilization, Marcuse employs the familiar criteria of the dialectic of liberation more ironically than ever, and the result is a savage indictment of existing men and institutions. Focusing relentlessly on the apparent dead ends of revolutionary theory and politics, this essay in speculative sociology addresses the principal elements of radical paradoxes directly rather than obliquely, through a Freudian glass.

One-Dimensional Man opens with a series of massive ironies that foreshadow its entire dramatic structure: "Does not the threat of an atomic catastrophe which could wipe out the human race also serve to protect the very forces which perpetuate this danger?" Again: "We submit to the peaceful production of the means of destruction, to the perfection of waste, to being educated for a defense which deforms the defenders and that which they defend."[58] At the highest level of abstraction, "advanced industrial society" (Marcuse's euphemism for postwar American capitalism) thrives on these ironies which link the growing material well-being of individuals to a social structure generating waste and destruction on a scale unequaled in history.[59] As life becomes more comfortable and man extends his control over nature, the whole takes on the appearance of reason. But this deceptive façade conceals the opposite reality: America's "productivity is destructive of the free development of human needs and faculties, its peace maintained by the constant threat of war, its growth dependent on the repression of the real possibilities for pacifying the struggle for existence—individual, national, and international."[60]

This grim overview of the present dictates the basic strategy of argument: to enforce the case for irrationality, Marcuse had to initially bring all the worst features of the American landscape into critical view, an effort that parallels the form of his speculations on the condition and fate of capitalism in the thirties. Then he assumed that Marx's tendential laws of capitalist crisis and decline would manifest themselves in history unless repealed by the conscious, revolutionary action of the proletariat, a rapidly diminishing chance within the larger realm of necessity. Since critical theory would validate the "laws" of political economy in either case, it anticipated the impending political failure of the working class, while providing the critic with the modest security of vague foreknowledge. In *One-Dimensional Man* Marcuse returns to Marx for a theoretical explanation of the survival and astonishing material growth of postwar capitalism. This time, however, he refocuses the dystopian lens by emphasizing an alternate projection of political economy found in the *Grundrisse,* an important manuscript written in 1857–58 but not widely known among Western scholars until the early 1950s.[61]

In this remarkable probe, Marx seeks to define the *ultimate* contradiction of capitalism, the theoretical point beyond which the system would cease to be itself. Abstracting the revolutionary proletariat from the analysis, he contends that the major contradiction between the social character of production and the private appropriation of wealth reaches its logical limits when the advancing productive forces come to depend primarily on science and technology rather than on direct labor time: " 'As soon as human labor, in its immediate form, has ceased to be the great source of wealth, labor time will cease . . . to be the measure of wealth, and the exchange value must of necessity cease to be the measure of use value.' " At this imaginary point, the capitalist mode of production would crumble in practice as well as in theory. For "complete automation," according to Marcuse, entails the conquest of scarcity *and* the elimination of alienated labor—two major obstacles to the emergence of a "new civilization."[62]

Though he uses this theoretical formulation to indicate centrifugal tendencies within the current technological organization and thrust of advanced industrial societies, it has the opposite effect of strengthening the pessimistic prediction that "qualitative" (or revolutionary) change will be contained within a framework of private property: the distant theoretical boundaries of the system accentuate its resilience as well as its potentially broad historical parameters.[63] On a higher though less illuminating level of abstraction, then, this formulation functions analogously to Sweezy's conception of "creeping stagnation." Both bring the classical Marxian prediction of the ultimate fall of capitalism into line with the realities of an interminably long decline. Both preserve the Marxian evaluation of capitalism as a *morally* irrational, dehumanizing social order. But Marcuse is even less successful than Baran and Sweezy in pinpointing the structural sources of *existential* irrationality in advanced capitalism.[64]

It is, of course, the lost proletariat that suspends this "historical freak" between capitalism and genuine socialism.[65] Along with other plain Marxists, Marcuse rejects the contemporary working class (old and new) as a revolutionary or even progressive agency of change.[66] What once seemed a class-in-itself with the prospect of becoming a class-for-itself through political education and action is now being rapidly absorbed into the leviathan of late capitalist society: "In the medium of technology, culture, politics, and the economy merge into an omnipresent system which swallows up or repulses all alternatives."[67] This actual integration of formerly antagonistic classes is at once a consequence of the growth of the technological apparatus and a chief condition of its survival. Following a leading strategy employed in *Eros and Civilization,* Marcuse puts the issue of social change effectively beyond rational human control: the genus Man makes his own history, but living men have little to do with shaping their collective and individual destinies—a deeply conservative view that often drives radicals to revolutionary fantasies or to despair.

Marcuse moved toward the second alternative in the early sixties, convinced that the thrust of advanced industrial society preserves the deforming features of capitalism—gross economic inequities, alienation, domination, and repression—within a framework of growing affluence.[68] The system is thus a "totalitarian" whole whose development effectively suffocates "those needs which demand liberation—liberation also from that which is tolerable and rewarding and comfortable. . . ."[69] Obliterating distinctions between public and private spheres of life, the organization of the whole reproduces individuals and classes with "false needs" which perpetuate the system. Whereas *Eros and Civilization* purports to show the psychic mechanisms by which revolutions have been betrayed throughout history, *One-Dimensional Man* depicts a current social and psychic economy immune to qualitative change: the old man who always betrayed revolutions can no longer even contemplate them.

With these loose assumptions about an irrational whole that must and yet cannot be decisively changed, Marcuse turns to his main task of exploring the ideological regions of society. The freewheeling characterizations of one-dimensional thought—that is, all nonrevolutionary, "undialectical" mental activity—begin with comic-strip sketches of popular ideology. "The people," Marcuse flatly remarks, "recognize themselves in their commodities; they find their soul in their automobile, hi-fi set, split-level home, kitchen equipment."[70] And the potshots land over the whole range of philosophy, mathematics, and the natural and social sciences. I shall not pause over these lengthy, abstruse discussions of the postwar intellectual default, since they have received wide and devastating criticism elsewhere.[71] Apart from the virtual disappearance of the second (or progressive) dimension of philosophy, which enables the only notable departure from previous explorations of the ideological regions of late capitalism, the rest is quite familiar vintage Marcuse; each analysis buttresses the thesis of one-dimensionality by showing how material trends are reflected and reinforced in conservative (or nonrevolutionary) forms of philosophy and art.

A dark corollary haunts this relentless, thesis-ridden critique of modern ideology: Marcuse's self-conscious dystopian construction threatens to shatter the double-optic of critical theory because the more he insists on the thesis of one-dimensionality, the less criticism and gestures of political opposition seem to matter. In advanced industrial society, the "introjection" of social controls affects "individual protest . . . at its roots." When even the precarious role of critical rationalist is seriously threatened, the "intellectual and emotional refusal 'to go along' appears neurotic and impotent."[72] Increasingly, then, this dystopian version of the present oscillates theoretically between the two contradictory hypotheses of containment and catastrophe. Projecting an indefinite enlargement of the welfare state as the more probable course, Marcuse envisions a social script that roughly corresponds to Aldous Huxley's *Brave New World*. But this domestic prophecy unfolds within a larger, Orwellian world whose superpowers maintain a precarious peace through continual preparation for an apocalyptic showdown.[73] Retaining the perspective of critical theory while abandoning all hope in the working classes of advanced industrial societies, Marcuse is compelled to hypothesize the indefinite blockage of history or its catastrophic ending.

Since *One-Dimensional Man,* like *Monopoly Capital,* rests on the paradox of partial rationality within an overall context of total irrationality, Marcuse must also argue that even apparently progressive achievements—rising living standards, a range of civil rights and liberties, and the retention of remnants of pluralist democracy—fit into the larger dystopian design. This he does in each instance by assessing actual conditions against utopian criteria drawn from the dialectic of liberation: every silver lining conceals a dark cloud. At several junctures, for example, Marcuse professes ambivalence toward postwar affluence: "It is a good way of life—much better than before. . . ." Yet "as a good way of life, it militates against qualitative change," against a revolution that would unleash the utopian potentialities within current forces of production. Similarly, the liberalization of sexuality is vaguely acknowledged and then dismissed as yet another instance of apparent or partial rationality. Marcuse invites the reader to "compare love-making in a meadow and in an automobile, on a lovers' walk outside the town walls and on a Manhattan street" (at the clear risk of being run down by a chestnut peddler). These ludicrous juxtapositions presumably illustrate the general hypothesis that "technological reality *limits the scope of sublimation.*"[74]

Properly understood, the observable desublimation is actually repressive, for the increase in sexuality conceals a decrease in total erotic energy and a corresponding rise in aggressive energy. With this crude hydraulic metaphor, Marcuse obliterates a complex reality by absorbing it into his dominant thesis.[75]

Finally, he argues—or rather declares—that the surviving elements of bourgeois freedom and democracy also reinforce the repressive whole. Rather than doing away with pluralism, advanced industrial society preserves it in petrified forms, for the "countervailing powers do not include those which counter the whole." Nevertheless, "for the administered individual, pluralistic administration is far better than total administration. One institution might protect him against the other; one organization might mitigate the impact of the other; possibilities of escape and redress can be calculated. The rule of law, no matter how restricted, is still infinitely safer than rule above or without law." Yet these comparative advantages become insignificant when set against the notion that democracy subverts formation of revolutionary consciousness and politics. In advanced industrial societies, "free election of masters does not abolish the masters or the slaves. Free choice among a wide variety of goods and services does not signify freedom if these goods and services sustain social controls over a life of toil and fear—that is, if they sustain alienation."[76]

Here Marcuse explicitly confuses historical with utopian categories of criticism, condemning complex realities in the light of his dialectic of liberation. He deemphasizes the concepts of individual freedom and democracy, which remain historical possibilities, by asserting that they do not entail the abolition of alienation, a utopian impossibility. This confusion makes it impossible to characterize adequately the fragile historical status of democracy in America, or to assess its slim prospects within any nonutopian social framework, capitalist or socialist. Consequently, ethical tensions between personal values and the possibilities for political action never come into clear perspective because the double optic of critical theory finally blurs all distinctions between democratic ideology and practice.

Yet left-liberal and democratic socialist critics[77] who labor the *feasibility* of large-scale reform fail to subvert the leading thesis of *One-Dimensional Man*. Marcuse does not posit a society closed to change, but rather one closed to revolutionary transformation, the only kind of change he ever considered worth pursuing. Nor was the thesis open to damaging political criticism from far Leftists who shared vaguely similar utopian and revolutionary ends while objecting to the quietistic implications of the analysis.[78] Some, of course, criticized Marcuse's glib faith in containment of fundamental social change through technology and his related underestimation of the potential impact of third-world revolutionary movements on the stability of advanced capitalist nations. But on the essential point of the political chances for revolutionary transcendence in the West, no one presented a convincing rebuttal.[79] Though none of the significant radical movements of the sixties are anticipated in the elaboration of the central contention, none of them necessarily altered the basic argumentative thrust either, as Marcuse points out in the coda. Existing beyond "the democratic process," a "substratum of the outcasts and the outsiders"—ethnic and racial minorities, "the unemployed and the unemployable"—share at least one characteristic with the old proletariat: they are uncorrupted by the system. Because their "opposition is revolutionary even if their consciousness is not," the "fact that they start refusing to play the game may be the fact which marks the beginning of the end of a period." Yet "nothing indicates that it will be a good end" because the established societies can probably contain qualitative change through a combination of technology and terror. Like all other old men, the outsiders and outcasts are only uncorrupted, not uncorruptible. The argument finally enforces and sustains the mood of despair summarized in the closing quotation from Walter Benjamin: " 'It is only for the sake of those without hope that hope is given to us.' "[80]

Marcuse's utopian vision and his political refusal to settle for less thus invests the gloomy thesis of one-dimensionality with a formal political and moral consistency. A *possible* version of the present, it represents a highly abstract formulation of radical paradoxes built around the stark proposition that the ideological and structural absorption of the working class precludes a significant revolutionary theory and politics.[81] Since the paradox of powerlessness appears totally unalterable in the calculable future, any discussion of the ethical dilemmas of contemporary politics becomes sterile. The argument, as I have shown, dispenses with the traditional radical dilemmas of synchronizing immediate political activity—legal or illegal, open or underground, peaceful or violent—with long-term revolutionary goals.[82] Even "traditional ways and means of *protest*" may become "dangerous because they preserve the illusion of popular sovereignty." There is, finally, *"no* ground on which theory and practice, thought and action meet."[83]

For radicals committed to social change, the moral force of this antipolitical choice depends solely on the long-term plausibility of the utopian alternative; otherwise despair turns into utter hopelessness. Yet the case for utopia in *One-Dimensional Man* is even less convincing than the similar argument of *Eros and Civilization*. Explicitly disavowing the contemporary relevance of politics as a way toward a new civilization, Marcuse fails to represent his utopia as a convincing historical possibility. The historical relevance of the vision of a world civilization beyond scarcity and alienation presupposes at least the availability of resources for the abolition of poverty and scarcity in every corner of the globe, a possibility that Marcuse glibly assumes: "quantifiable is the available range of freedom from want. Or, calculable is the degree to which, under the same conditions, care could be provided for the ill, the infirm, and the aged. . . ."[84] To be considered seriously, however, this premise should form the conclusion to a complex argument involving an empirically verifiable definition of abundance and a corresponding statistical projection of the natural, scientific, and technological resources needed to eliminate scarcity everywhere. Rather than summarizing the conflicting testimony or offering calculations of his own, Marcuse simply invests his fantastic premise with the illusion of credibility by asserting that the new civilization could be launched without *unlimited* abundance for all. This revised material condition merely entails the ending of hunger, misery, disease, and ignorance throughout the world![85]

The dubious assumption of even minimal "abundance," then, forms the centerpiece of a wildly implausible argument. For according to Marcuse, the deployment of these "calculable" resources depends upon nearly complete automation, which would presumably enable the elimination of the worst manifestations of alienated labor. But he provides no reason to suppose that relative abundance through automation would reduce the multiple tensions and frustrations associated with mental labor at any point in the imaginable future. Maintaining his ambivalence about the degree of abundance that a reorganized technological base might achieve, Marcuse ends up in a vicious cycle. As George Kateb puts it: "there can be no liberation without abundance, but there can be no abundance without alienation. The means for abundance hurt the ends for which abundance is itself the means."[86] To shatter this cycle, Marcuse must add several familiar qualifying premises that turn a social contradiction into pure fantasy: the vast reduction of labor time, a nearly complete shift from physical to mental labor, full workers' control (an old demand from the thirties), and a new man with new instinctual structures—all within a technological base preserved and reconstructed so as to transform life into an art! When we recall the necessary though impossible political revolution throughout the capitalist and socialist sectors of the world, the fanciful idea of a vast increase in automated production accompanied by the abolition of alienated labor may seem a comparatively minor flaw.

By depriving *One-Dimensional Man* of historical relevance, however, this flaw invests the temporarily antipolitical stance with permanence, thereby seriously weakening the apparent moral forces of Marcuse's decision to opt out of what he considered a possible—even probable—politics of reform. Viewed "dialectically," then, the thesis of one-dimensionality turns in upon itself, pointing back toward history and suggesting the need for a reconsideration of the politically and morally ambiguous space between the present and the possible forms of capitalist (and socialist) societies. Marcuse attempts to close off his implication as much through his rhetoric as through the consistently abstract level of argument. Reifying rather than respecting radical paradoxes, he nearly always fails to hear the rhythms, idioms, and nuances of contemporary speech. The rare attempts to specify the quality of attitudes and ideological subtleties are generally disastrous, as this typical comment on religious moods of the early sixties suggests: "there is a great deal of 'Worship together this week,' 'Why not try God,' Zen, existentialism, and beat ways of life, etc."[87] Far from representing a mere failure of rhetoric, this eerie atmosphere of aloofness from the diversity of hopes and disappointments common to various age, class, ethnic, and racial groups obscures the moral implications of refusing political involvement; it finally reinforces the rejection of the "old man"—which is to say, of a people and their concerns.

Nor could Marcuse follow Sweezy's strategy of relocating his vision in the Soviet Union, China, or countries of the third world. His analysis of the chances for nonrepressive societies in the socialist sectors generally reinforces a growing pessimism during the late fifties and early sixties. Measured against the utopian vision, Soviet experience fits the abstract pattern of repressive societies. Moreover, even the post-Stalinist organization of society ran a poor second to the American variety of totalitarianism.[88] In *Soviet Marxism* and *One-Dimensional Man,* however, there is a deep ambivalence about the course and prospects of Soviet development.[89] Following his custom of freely adapting materials from philosophers in the Western tradition, Marcuse assembles a paradoxical argument out of fragments from twentieth-century Marxist criticism. His contorted position includes remnants of old Marxist sentiments along with weary acknowledgments of a succession of disappointments covering five decades. For Marcuse, the central question concerns the reasons for the Soviet departure from the classical scenario of a two-stage transition from capitalism to communism. Granting partial validity to the "argument from historical backwardness," he nevertheless insists that "socialism must become reality with the first act of the revolution because it must already be in the consciousness and action of those who carried the revolution." Otherwise men cannot act freely and collectively against the material "necessity which limits their freedom and their humanity."[90] Higher productivity is therefore a necessary but not a sufficient condition for the transition to communism.

According to Marcuse, the "situation of hostile coexistence" rather than economic backwardness constitutes the overriding external reason for the betrayal of the Soviet Revolution since the middle twenties. But these international imperatives, which "may explain the terroristic features of Stalinist industrialization," also "set in motion the forces which tend to perpetuate technical progress as the instrument of domination." The past haunts the socialist present and sharply limits its future prospects. Existing in the shadow of nuclear catastrophe, the Soviet Union will probably achieve a comfortable domestic dystopia through containment: Marcuse casually predicts rising living standards, reduction of the working day, and "continued liberalization of controls." Once again, the confusion and imprecision of utopian and historical categories make it impossible to tell whether he projects "liberalization" within a dictatorship (socialist legality, for example) or the emergence of a truly representative socialist democracy. Since both modes of "liberalization" are compatible with a system that prevents the construction of utopia, Marcuse lets the matter dangle, ambiguously.[91]

Forced into a dialectical dance, both superpowers may be pursuing essentially similar forms of dystopia in order to prevent the "catastrophe of liberation" or the catastrophe of nuclear annihilation. Yet the "socialist base" of the Soviet system constitutes a "decisive difference" that may eventually invalidate this loose version of the convergence thesis.[92] Whereas classes in American society are organic to the capitalist process of production, Soviet classes, according to Marcuse, remain *theoretically* separable from the material base. In this view, the " 'immediate producers' " lost control of the Soviet economic apparatus in the Stalin era by virtue of a series of *political* decisions.[93] Moreover, the pattern may be politically reversible, for according to Marcuse, "the ruling strata are themselves separable from the productive process—that is, they are replaceable without exploding the basic institutions of society." Using the outmoded metaphor of base and superstructure, Marcuse hypothesizes the possibility of a political revolution that would liberate Soviet society while preserving the "foundation of a fully nationalized and planned economy."[94]

Piecing together these scraps of arguments more fully developed by other plain Marxists such as Baran, Sweezy, and Deutscher, Marcuse ends his inadequate analysis on an ambivalent note. On the one side, the "entrenched bureaucracies" can be expected to resist a political revolution by a skillful synthesis of terror and technology: "The more the rulers are capable of delivering the goods of consumption, the more firmly will the underlying population be tied to the various ruling bureaucracies." On the other, the theoretical separability of economic growth from political control may ultimately present the ruling group with the Hobson's choice of either yielding their privileged positions "once the level of a possible qualitative change has been reached" or retarding the "material and intellectual growth at a point where domination still is rational and profitable." But if international economic competition forecloses the apparent option of slowing material progress, the imperatives of the "great contest" may "prove stronger than the resistance of the vested bureaucracies."[95] A nostalgic wish thus precludes a clear argument: rather than assessing the historical and political chances for a democratic socialism, Marcuse ends by projecting the abolition of alienation as a formal possibility without historical substance.

There was literally no route of escape. For unlike other far Left critics in the early sixties, Marcuse did not transfer the broken hopes of a utopian socialism to developing nations. As helpless pawns in the dominant struggle between the two major superpowers, "the backward areas are likely to succumb either to one of the various forms of neo-colonialism, or to a more or less terroristic system of primary accumulation." In this bipolar scheme, advanced capitalist societies largely determined the course of Soviet development after World War I, and by midcentury both giants precluded the emergence of a nonrepressive pattern of industrialization elsewhere. Marcuse does project a formal alternative— a "new confluence of" industrial development and "liberation"— for third-world nations, but without conviction.[96] By 1964, then, the trends toward a polycentric global dystopia seemed irreversible.

It may be argued that Marcuse met his moral obligation as a radical theorist during this period merely by continuing to ply his trade, fronting an intractable world without illusion. Perhaps. But the argument of *One-Dimensional Man,* which spins out illusions of its own, seems to exist for the sake of the pervasive mood of despair. It is, of course, a possible mood, one that periodically overcomes every rational person. Yet when despair turns into the sole outlook, it blurs perception of the slim chance for survival and the creation of just societies within history. In *One-Dimensional Man* critical theory becomes primarily a mode of therapy, a symbolic defiance of men and institutions beyond the control of utopian radicals. It appears as a myth of consolation that pretends to be more or other than what it essentially is, a cathartic form of popular art. Adhering steadily to his utopian vision as well as to his grimly realistic assessment of its political chances in the early sixties, Marcuse remained at once a romantic utopian and a hard-boiled realist.

Ferment of Hope: 1965–1970

History, Marx wrote in his assessment of Napoleon, always repeats itself—the first time as tragedy, the second time as farce. Marcuse's critical odyssey might easily have ended in 1964 with his tragic view of human waste. Sustaining the dual commitment to an essentially Marxian vision of utopia and to a dystopian version of the present (also rooted in a loose adaptation of Marx's political economy), *One-Dimensional Man* brings the logic of Marcuse's thought to a consistent conclusion: from the thirties on, his critical exercises centered on successive attempts to define and resolve radical paradoxes by locating *agents* and *agencies* of revolutionary change.[97] Though this steady adherence to the double optic of critical theory constituted the dynamic force of his work, it always drove him into a political cul-de-sac. Until the middle thirties, reason seemed the last repository of truth that critical theorists might use to rouse a dormant proletariat. But the advance of fascism in Europe (along with the betrayal of the Soviet Revolution) irreparably broke the hypothetical chain between critical reason, socialist education, and the emergence of a revolutionary class. Since the old man could no longer be *reached* through this process, he could revolutionize neither himself nor society.

Searching for new modes of liberation in *Eros and Civilization,* Marcuse defined the aesthetic dimension as the surviving locus of truth that tenuously connected man's psychic past and present with images of a possible future beyond scarcity and alienation. The fatal lockstep of psychic and social history accounted for the reversal of all revolutions, completing the case against the old man and his civilization. By a curious logic, Marcuse confused the "truths" of art—its preservation of the repressed claims of the pleasure principle—with a scenario of the future constructed on an aesthetic model. This modulation from historical criticism to myth called for a new man to populate the utopian fantasy. But when he turned his attention once more to contemporary trends in *One-Dimensional Man,* there was no sign of a new Orphic man, who in any case would have been an unsuitable agent of qualitative change. And the historical agency of classical Marxism had already reappeared as the "conservative base" of advanced industrial society. Ironically, then, the baroque texture of Marcuse's critical essays obscures the classically simple version of radical paradoxes that informs all of his work. If the refusal to abandon either the essential constituents of the utopian vision or the dystopian assumptions about actual trends invests the entire critical edifice with a forbidding grandeur, it also prefigures the tragic impasse of *One-Dimensional Man.*

Rather than closing on a tragic note, however, Marcuse offers another repetition—or variation—of his central position in the late sixties, provisionally ending his critical odyssey as farce, indeed, as an international farce involving the new Left and the media of the United States, England, and Western Europe. These new external factors significantly influenced the latest rendition of critical theory. As the young Left shifted from a politics of reform to complete disenchantment with contemporary shapes of American society, including the existing machinery of change, many discovered consoling, even flattering explanations in Marcuse's earlier writings. His basic image of modern totalitarianism not only justified the suspension of democratic theory and practice in the pursuit of a new man and society; it also accounted for the inadequacies of the old man, personified by the fathers.[98] *Eros and Civilization* became an important document in the cultural revolution, providing images of a wholly new man which dialectically fit the mood of a disillusioned minority who experienced postwar affluence along with a kind of spiritual and emotional poverty.

His popularity in Western Europe, especially in France and Germany, rested on firmer historical and theoretical ground.[99] Beginning as a young revolutionary intellectual in the early twenties, Marcuse survived without abandoning his commitment to the utopian Marx (however carefully he disguised it in his early postwar essays). Unlike orthodox Communists, social democrats, and weary independent Left intellecutals, he could be apprehended as an old comrade of the young, and ally in their revolt against bourgeois establishments of Western Europe, including the established Left. At the peak of the French uprising in May 1968, students walked the streets of Paris chanting "Marx the god,

Marcuse his prophet, and Mao his sword." Bookstores quickly sold their supplies of Marcuse's works (and his wall posters as well). For a historical instant, the new romantic revolutionaries found a living embodiment of their utopian strain of Marxism, a link with the past that foreshadowed the future they intended to create.

The dramatic alliance between the old philosopher and the rebellious young soon commanded the attention of the European and American media. Marcuse made especially good copy because his association with new Left figures suggested such easy and satisfying interpretations.[100] Journalists and critics accounted for the unlikely alliance in pop Freudian terms, characterizing Marcuse as a surrogate father who encouraged and sanctioned political and sexual rebellion.[101] A seducer of innocent youth, he became a convenient scapegoat, a personified cause of social tensions that troubled middle Americans as well as academics no longer in touch with their students. This motif reached its seriocomic extreme in southern California when American Legionnaires and other local groups of "concerned citizens" conducted a vicious campaign to remove Marcuse from his teaching post at San Diego.[102] After receiving an anonymous threat on his life, he retreated to the hills, guarded by a group of loyal students.

By 1970, when Marcuse had been exhausted as a media figure, many of his followers had already brushed him aside as a "political fink," a "metaphysician" who hedged his ideas when the political chips were down.[103] But the swirl of publicity—ignorant, malicious, and ill-timed as much of it was—contributed to his brief celebrity among the young, as well as to the diffusion of his leading hypotheses. A proud man, Marcuse retained his dignity and humor while being made into a marketable personality. "I can become part of the Establishment," he remarked in an interview with Harvey Wheeler, "and it serves me right."[104] Moreover, on several occasions he publicly refused the part of spiritual guide: "I never claimed to be the ideological leader of the left and I don't think the left needs an ideological leader. And there is one thing the left does not need, and that's another father image, another daddy."[105] The textual evidence generally supports these disclaimers. In 1960 Marcuse explicitly distinguished the kind of cerebral political opposition that critical theory entails from forerunners of the cultural revolution—"all pseudo- and crackpot opposition, beatnik and hipsterism."[106] And apart from the coda to *One-Dimensional Man,* none of the movements of the early sixties figure in his work prior to 1965.

The new constituency, then, doubtless came as a surprise. Once cast as a chief philosopher of the new Left, however, Marcuse fell somewhat reluctantly into the role, trying to bring his unsolicited audience into focus by perceiving them as the legitimate political heirs of the utopian Marx. *An Essay on Liberation* (1969), the culminating work of this period, records the sad results of the enterprise. One critic commented that Marcuse had finally "caught up with his following."[107] That is only half of the story, for the followers had also caught up with Marcuse, allowing him to be explicit once again about what he had essentially been all along—a romantic, revolutionary intellectual. In this adumbrated recapitulation of earlier exercises in critical theory, a huge gulf still separates the new man of *Eros and Civilization* from one-dimensional man, since there is, as always, no class agency of qualitative change in the West. Rather than ending in despair, however, Marcuse offers the qualified hope that advanced sectors of the young Left may constitute a new agent of change, a transitional figure between the old man and the Orphic creature of *Eros and Civilization.* Though the introduction of this transitional man does not resolve radical paradoxes, it reestablishes the historical possibility of a resolution in the long run. This is the only genuinely novel element in his work after 1964.

Marcuse's transitional man combines fragments of the utopian figure of *Eros and Civilization* with certain characteristics of the classical Marxian proletariat.[108] He anticipates Orphic man by opting out of the aggressive cycle of production and consumption enforcing repressed modes of consciousness and behavior in advanced industrial societies. But in addition to enjoying play and display, transitional man is part Promethean, an active agent literally forced into political and sexual opposition to established totalitarianisms. As Marcuse awkwardly puts it, this pop-art figure mixes "the barricade and the dance floor, love play and heroism"—political and cultural revolution.[109] A qualitatively new historical agent, transitional man is superficially analogous to the old Marxian class agency insofar as the lack of social alternatives largely determines his initial refusal. Marx's proletariat might have attained revolutionary consciousness had its structural imprisonment at the bottom of capitalist society been adequate insurance against corruptions of the old man. Because it was also psychically tied to repressive patterns, however, the old working class could be bought off and integrated into new modes of domination in the West and in the East as well.[110] Marcuse further reduces the scope of individual choice in *An Essay on Liberation* by attributing psychic uncorruptibility to transitional man, who as a consequence of his political and sexual rebellion evolves a new structure of needs that advanced industrial societies cannot satisfy. Thus theoretically exorcised is the old specter of material, moral, and spiritual "economism" that haunted revolutionaries, including Marcuse, throughout the Marxian tradition.

Beyond the reach of external forces and institutions, transitional man is, more importantly, beyond his own reach once the complex process of psychic transformation is under way. Marcuse suggests that the educator educates himself—in spite of himself: "The radical change which is to transform the existing society into a free society must reach into a dimension of the human existence hardly considered in Marxian theory—the 'biological' dimension in which the vital, imperative needs and satisfactions of man assert themselves. Inasmuch as these needs and satisfactions reproduce a life in servitude, liberation presupposes changes in this biological dimension, that is to say, different instinctual needs, different reactions of the body as well as the mind." Expelled from the historical continuum of social and psychic repression that Marcuse defines in *Eros and Civilization,* transitional man marches to the beat of his new "metabolism."[111] In this mythic microcosm of the revolutionary process, changes in the biological base of individuals produce alterations in the psychic superstructure—chiefly a liberated consciousness and imagination that Marcuse calls "the new sensibility."[112]

Though initiated by a conscious refusal (which is itself based on narrow public options), the inner metamorphosis quickly becomes irreversible. "Political radicalism . . . implies moral radicalism: the emergence of a minority which might *precondition* man for freedom. This radicalism activates the elementary, organic foundations of morality in the human being."[113] Once in possession of a new metabolism and sensibility, transitional man strives to act out dreams which have been preserved in the aesthetic sphere throughout the historical epochs dominated by reason and the reality (or performance) principle. As a political/cultural revolutionary, he can aim at nothing less than the conversion of life into an art. In his Promethean role, transitional man may be obliged to destroy an old civilization. But no matter: his new sensibility also moves him to construct a community of social men.

The modulation from history to myth, which entails displacement of radical paradoxes from the larger historical stage to the psyche of individual actors, enables Marcuse to introduce a "free" agent into the otherwise determined, antirevolutionary versions of contemporary social systems. By drawing transitional man out of a dialectical hat, he breaks the pessimistic quandary of *One-Dimensional Man.* And since this figure is irreversibly revolutionary from the outset, transitional social forms that preoccupied other radical intellectuals lose their importance as determinants of qualitative change. In fact, unless they are designed and implemented by liberated men, new social forms will *necessarily* fail. Once in political control of society, however, transitional man will be set on a determined course toward communism, the outer form of his inner self-realization as Orphic man. Larger historical forces—the agents and agencies of the old man—may crush him along the way, but he cannot betray himself.

This theoretical projection of transitional man, however, raises the related problems of identifying members of the new genus, estimating their political chances in the historical long run, and defining provisional strategy and tactics. Here Marcuse does some casting of his own, locating the leading species of transitional man among radical students and intellectuals, defectors from upper and middle classes of advanced capitalist societies. Since the "diffused rebellion among the youth and the intelligentsia" triggers the process of psychic transformation, the "student movement" becomes *"the* ferment of hope in the overpowering and stifling capitalist metropoles," supplementing the corruptible outsiders and outcasts of *One-Dimensional Man*.[114]

By viewing political and cultural revolutionaries of the late sixties through the abstract lenses of critical theory, Marcuse generally managed to sustain the fiction that they would evolve into full-fledged embodiments of transitional man. The new revolutionaries did, after all, loosely fit the paradigm: they were in complete opposition to society and culture (capitalist and socialist alike); they easily mixed "the barricade and the dance floor." And more than a few accommodated themselves to the grandiose role of new men—the last, best hope of a dying civilization.[115] But the tenuous connections between real figures and the stereotype cast a shadow over the whole enterprise. Like the elect of certain Christian sects, transitional man could not be positively identified by his appearance, or even by his political deeds. Fools and impostors who merely took on "weird and clownish forms" mingled indiscriminately with genuine revolutionaries.[116] But the new men were nevertheless *there,* somewhere in the crowd. And their presence confirmed (or at any rate did not refute) the theory.

Authentic representatives of the new species "resolved" radical paradoxes informally only to confront them once more in history. Marcuse emphasizes the paradoxical situation of the opposition, "the striking contrast between the radical and total character of the rebellion on the one hand, and the absence of a class basis for this radicalism on the other." Rejecting their middle- and upper-class origins, transitional men dwell on the margins of one-dimensional society as revolutionaries in search of a class. And for Marcuse, who remains orthodox on essential questions, there can be no revolution without the decisive participation of the working class—old and new.[117] Thus the paradox of powerlessness holds its central position on the Marcusean critical landscape. But the existence of genuine revolutionaries changes the tone from the bleak pessimism of *One-Dimensional Man* to a tenuous optimism.

Since the mythic agent carries the embryo of the new society within himself, internalizing values that a revolution under his auspices would manifest in a new social order, he exists beyond the ethical ambiguities that plague the old man: "revolution would be liberating only if it were carried out by the non-repressive forces stirring in the existing society."[118] Utopia remains the central historical goal, revolution the chief political means, and transitional man the agent in search of the agency. For the new men, moral injunctions are therefore indistinguishable from general political imperatives: above all, transitional man needs to survive and multiply. And he must also function as a catalyst "of rebellion within the majorities." The two tasks merge because transitional man is born—or reborn—in the caldron of total opposition to his society and culture. His moral regeneration depends on radical action, just as his ultimate political effectiveness entails rebirth. For the foreseeable future, however, actual powerlessness dictates a familiar stand toward the problem of action: "Historically, it is again the period of enlightenment prior to material change—a period of education. . . ." Marcuse adds a new twist, advocating "education which turns into praxis: demonstration, confrontation, rebellion."[119]

By way of delimiting the meaning of such education, he impatiently excludes all traditional political modes, including participation in pressure groups, committees, and parties: "This entire sphere and atmosphere, with all its power, is invalidated. . . ." Moreover, contemporary varieties of revisionism and social democracy cannot even *tempt* transitional man: "the protest and refusal are parts of their metabolism." Happily so, for according to Marcuse, efforts at significantly altering the composition of Congress might take a century. Hence "to work for the improvement of the existing democracy easily appears as indefinitely delaying attainment of the goal of creating a free society."[120] This antipolitical analysis leaves transitional man a narrow sphere of public action. Confined to demonstration, confrontation, and rebellion, his politics becomes chiefly a form of radical education, or therapy, that initiates and accelerates the internal metamorphosis.[121] Without qualifying assumptions, such a view entails ominous consequences. As individuals, transitional men exist beyond "contaminated" moral and political norms of behavior. They generate their own ethical standards, which cannot be publicly verified. Nor are their actions even monitored by the pragmatic imperative of conventional politics, a weak enough restraint on otherwise uninhibited moral imaginations. Ironically, then, transitional man, who aims at becoming a *social* creature, cuts himself loose from a society where, according to Marcuse, "the general will is always wrong": he remains potentially responsible only to other *Übermenschen.* Moreover, the metabolic resistance to nearly all forms of politics, combined with the need to act, creates a tendency, as Marcuse admits, for radical protest to "become antinomian, anarchistic, and even nonpolitical"—not to mention, irresponsible, violent, and apocalyptic.[122]

The absurd argument that Eros shapes and curbs the moral imagination of liberated men does not even thoroughly convince Marcuse. He follows the mythic arc of his own speculations and then, lapsing into momentary political sanity, tries to draw back, as the ambivalent discussion of democracy suggests. In one-dimensional society, "working according to the rules and methods of democratic legality appears as surrender to the prevailing power structure." And yet, he immediately adds, "it would be fatal to abandon the defense of civil rights and liberties within the established framework." But the "democratic struggle" waged by transitional man will "come into increasing conflict with the existing democratic institutions." Marcuse "solves" this puzzle with a dialectical somersault: "if democracy means self-government of free people, with justice for all . . . the realization of democracy would presuppose abolition of the existing pseudo-democracy." In "corporate capitalism," then, "the fight for democracy . . . tends to assume antidemocratic forms."[123]

The texture of irony thickens: disappointments, frustrations, and defeats that culminated in the hopeless conclusion to *One-Dimensional Man* also shaped the main features of transitional man, principally his metabolic inability to lapse into antiutopian, nonrevolutionary consciousness and behavior. Yet these very characteristics that guarantee uncorruptibility are indissolubly linked to his unaccountability, his status as a figure beyond law, political conventions, and moral responsibility. In the attempt to regain a tenuous historical relevance by connecting the young Left to his utopian projection, Marcuse implicitly justifies any oppositional activity that *seems* to proceed from transitional man. But the tortured discussion of democracy shows that the same political frustrations that led Marcuse to forge the myth compelled him to propose moral and political boundaries for transitional man. The dystopian versions of critical theory contain a succession of cautionary lessons distilled from the radical betrayals and defeats of the century: ominous threats from the political Right in late capitalist societies, the failures of the Soviet Revolution, the impotence of sectarian and authoritarian Marxist groups in the West, all testified to the limitations and dangers of ultra-Left ideology and politics.[124] *In* An Essay on Liberation, *however, there are no theoretical connections between the utopian argument for the existence and potentialities of transitional man and the restrictions which Marcuse periodically feels compelled to propose.* Hence the dialectical acrobatics—the confused, clumsy qualifications—are capricious, contrary to the main theoretical design.

Though transitional man is the only conceptually new element in *An Essay on Liberation* and the later pieces, he does not remain a completely isolated figure at the edges of advanced Western nations. Marcuse situates the new agent in the larger international matrix of the "Great Refusal."[125] This highly abstract construction includes all the forces that "seem to be animated by . . . [the] same subversive impulse: liberation." Those who have broken out of the "continuum of repression" are provisionally designated as participants in the Great Refusal: "In Vietnam, in Cuba, in China, a revolution is being defended and driven forward which struggles to eschew the bureaucratic administration of socialism." "Guerrilla forces" throughout Latin America and Southeast Asia apparently share similar goals. When added to the transitional men of Western nations and the "ghetto population" of the United States, these third-world revolutionary groupings complete the impressive numerical inventory of the worldwide legions of opposition.[126]

Though hazy, Marcuse's conception of the potential interplay of forces in the entire capitalist sector of the world generally follows the pattern more fully worked out by Baran and Sweezy. Since corporate capitalism can be expected to pursue its counterrevolutionary policies militarily, guerrilla warfare becomes *the* dominant mode of revolutionary change in the third world. But it cannot succeed without the simultaneous weakening of enormously powerful forces in the heartlands of capitalism: "The chain of exploitation must break at its strongest link." Appropriating the leading conclusions of Baran and Sweezy's *Monopoly Capital* without so much as a footnote, Marcuse foresees a psychic crisis in the metropolis when the system, weakened by growing economic contradictions, can no longer "deliver the goods." Taken "in conjunction with the objective economic and political strains to which the system will be exposed on a global scale," these "subjective factors" may eventually assume "material force." Until then there can be no "mass basis for the new forms of organization required for directing the struggle."[127]

But Marcuse refused to adopt uncritically the usual *political* orchestrations that accompanied similar ultra-Left themes in the late sixties. He generally distinguished between theoretical designations of the common interests of everyone in opposition to the continuum of repression and the actual factors which now divide them. Two examples illustrate this basic pattern. Endorsing a weak version of the internal colony model that connects the interests of black Americans to those of third-world peoples, he nevertheless observes that "at this stage," the actual "links are practically non-existent."[128] The chances of political solidarity within the metropolis are similarly ambiguous: those excluded from the middle classes and the conservative working class—the young intelligentsia and the ghetto population—represent "the very real common interest of the oppressed."[129] But these common interests are not—or not yet—politically real.

In contrast to Sweezy, then, Marcuse's hopes did not depend *wholly* on the success of an ultra-Left politics that matched the vaguely similar utopian visions of both men. While the myth of transitional man requires *some* characterization of contemporary historical and political forces, it does not hinge on a *particular* analysis.[130] The double optic of critical theory, which can accommodate a range of assessments, provides a convenient safety valve. "None" of the forces Marcuse designates *"is* the alternative": they merely "outline, *in very different dimensions,* the limits of the established societies, of their power of containment. When these limits are reached, the Establishment may initiate a new order of totalitarian suppression." The actual groups arrayed against corporate capitalism, according to Marcuse, are "the symbols but also the embodiments of hope." This formulation conveys the studied ambivalence of his assessment of prospects for liberation on a worldwide scale. In abstract terms, *all* the forces included in the Great Refusal constitute symbols of hope. But the extent to which these forces actually embody hope varies because they operate in such "different dimensions," or sociohistorical contexts. The present *agencies* of revolutionary change—principally the external proletariat—are still psychically corruptible, as are the ghetto populations of the metropolis, which may form the mass basis of revolt but not of revolution. Since they are struggling simultaneously for liberation from massive economic exploitation and from alienation, these groups may submit to a "new order of totalitarian suppression" or even create one of their own. Only transitional man, the mythic figure whose authentic representatives inhabit mainly the Western societies, remains immune to the vagaries of unreconstructed men: it is finally the student revolutionaries "who have taken the idea of revolution out of the continuuum of repression and placed it into its authentic dimension—that of liberation."[131]

In the end, Marcuse seems to regard the mythic dimension as more vivid, more real, than his largely borrowed historical analysis.[132] And yet without the fragmentary body of assertions and predictions concerning medium-range trends, the myth would be naked, simply incredible. Moreover, as I have indicated, both the myth and the historical analysis depend heavily—indeed, almost exclusively—on ingenious though ultimately rather mechanical adaptations of old Marxian formulas. Marcuse, of course, claims to have soared past classical revolutionary thinkers by imagining the new man—Marx's "all-round individual"—as builder rather than mere inhabitant of the new society.[133] Since Marx conceived the realm of genuine freedom as existing beyond the area of work, progress in freedom consisted in the vast reduction of labor, not its elimination.[134] But Marcuse "envisages the ingression of freedom into the realm of necessity, and the union between causality by necessity and casuality by freedom." The first, he claims, "would mean passing from Marx to Fourier; the second from realism to surrealism." By developing a new mode of reason based on imagination, transitional man would transform "the process of production" into "a process of creation."[135]

In an obvious sense, then, Marcuse is right: his new concept of freedom does depart from classical Marxism. But it also proceeds from an imagination deeply imbued with classical modes of Marxian thought. He responds to the dissolution of the Marxian synthesis—the dialectical conception of a transformation of consciousness and society through the agency of the proletariat—by splitting the problem into two parts, one mythic, the other historical. The creation of a mythic figure requires displacement of the revolutionary process into the self, whereas the characterization of social trends follows the variant of Marxian political economy found in the *Grundrisse*. The "progress" from Marx to Fourier, then, consists in mingling, if not wholly confusing, mythic and historical elements. Transitional man, the only reliable hope of an imperiled civilization, remains a mythic figure whose existence presupposes an "ingression" of the future into the present. Though perhaps acceptable in surrealist art, this temporal construction only confuses issues of social theory. At the same time, Marcuse employs orthodox assumptions to account for the objective historical forces and the contemporary *agencies* of revolutionary change. Accepting the inescapable historical fact that the revolution did not begin in advanced Western nations and radiate out into other areas, he relocates the principal *agencies* of change in the underdeveloped world. Ironically, however, he cannot escape his ethnocentric bias on the most important matter: the qualitatively new *agent*—the only sure one—still emerges in the West.[136]

In both its domestic and international dimensions, then, *An Essay on Liberation* upsets the precarious balance of contrary impulses—between the sentimental utopian and the disenchanted realist, the idealist and the political pragmatist, the believer and the rational skeptic—which Marcuse spent his adult life articulating and trying to resolve in the double optic of critical theory. The myth of transitional man attains coherence at the heavy price of excluding reservations, hesitations, and qualifications from the main theoretical design. And yet Marcuse's rational, skeptical voice, which recalls the tragic dimensions of twentieth-century history, cannot be wholly silenced. Intruding occasionally, it makes sense. But by virtue of being isolated from the theoretical structure of *An Essay on Liberation* it makes only fragmentary and arbitrary sense. Accounting for a certain energy and coarse complexity in his essays after *One-Dimensional Man,* this emotional and theoretical ambivalence between the utopian and the sensible Marcuse distinguishes his work from the general run of unambiguously ultraradical nonsense that helped to pollute the ideological atmosphere of the late sixties.

But it lends a dimension of pathos to his later work as well. Setting out to accommodate a new audience in his declining years, Marcuse ends by destroying the precarious internal balance of his symbolic world, the only realm where the illusions of critical theory could be preserved against the realities of history. It would be pointless to cite every instance in the late essays where the intrusive rational voice leads him into embarrassing and indefensible dilemmas. The pattern of mythic thrust, interrupted by rational though theoretically capricious qualification, dominates these essays and interviews.[137] It accounts for Marcuse's disposition to take several sides of major questions concerning the nature, fate, and politics of the new Left.

If the persistence of the rational voice illuminates the failures of theory, it also has cost Marcuse a large portion of the audience that he attempted, diffidently at first, to incorporate into the last version of critical theory. Transitional men preferred their Marcuse undiluted by annoying qualifications and seemingly arbitrary restrictions. When they wanted to express their new sensibilities by pushing campus rebellions to the point of destroying academic institutions in the late sixties, Marcuse drew back, revealing himself as a political "fink." "I have," he declared after the 1968 revolt at Columbia, "never suggested or advocated or supported destroying the established universities and building new anti-institutions instead." American universities, "at least quite a few of them . . . are still enclaves of relatively critical thought and relatively free thought. So we do not have to think of replacing them by new institutions." But he adds that "this is one of the very rare cases in which I think you can achieve what you want to achieve within the existing institutions."[138] Once legitimized in theory, however, transitional man no longer needed either Marcuse or his arbitrary caveats. The most militant members of his audience had surpassed him, leaving the last version of critical theory in a shambles, a fate engineered partly by the ironies of history and partly by Marcuse himself. By 1970, the sorcerer had become an apprentice—and a dispensable one at that.

Conclusion

The shabby treatment of Marcuse by ex-followers, representatives of the press, and critics all along the ideological spectrum compounds the already difficult problem of assessing the value and continuing importance of his work. It is safe to assume that his public moment has forever passed: as a fusion of symbolic leader, critical theorist, and prophet, Marcuse, in contrast to Marx and Mao, obviously lacked staying power. Whatever influence his thought may exert in the seventies and after will therefore be less dramatic. Many of his leading themes have found their way into pop radical vocabulary, where they will probably survive in disguised and diluted forms as long as utopian impulses persist among people on the Left. A few younger critics who take Marcuse as a point of entry into the murky regions of dialectical theory will continue to elaborate his ideas and, judging from the first fruits of these ventures, incorporate them into ever more convoluted exercises in critical theory.[139] It would seem, then, that Marcuse's work, which depends so heavily on bits and pieces mined from philosophers, artists, and social theorists in the Western tradition, will survive in fragments. This is, of course, an inescapable condition of the growth and development of social theory. But in the case of Marcuse such fragmentation obscures major achievements and distorts central flaws. As *elements* of radical thought, most of his hypotheses remain useless: we have seen that they are neither precisely worked out nor empirically verifiable. Key terms never receive careful, extended definition. And although occasionally arresting, the "provocative" insights generally lack originality. Elusive, stylistically clumsy, ambiguous, and excessively abstract, his work consists of a tissue of pronouncements and naked assertions that transcend the usual canons of argument and evidence.[140]

In one sense, then, this whole body of work is intellectually and politically sterile, a long dialectic without issue. Yet it is an interesting and in some ways admirable failure, a white elephant well worth looking at and remembering. Taken as a whole, the critical odyssey displays a remarkable interior unity and singleness of purpose. Despite the variety of critical surfaces he constructs, Marcuse rigorously defines and redefines a simple version of radical paradoxes. As each work, beginning in the thirties, unfolds within the double optic of critical theory, the whole takes on the character of a long fugue. The shapes of the visions of utopia and the versions of dystopia change with changing historical and political circumstances. But the development moves around the still point of Marcuse's steady adherence to the main outline of Marx's utopia—rational, free, and happy men inhabiting a global community beyond scarcity and alienation.[141] As each critical synthesis began to dissolve under the weight of events and trends, Marcuse tried to keep the idea of utopia historically alive by constructing fresh images of a possible future that balance his grim views of the present.

But as the distance between conceptions of utopia and dystopia widened in the late thirties and the forties, he had to restore critical balance by modulating from social theory to social mythology. Marcuse invented Orphic man to populate his remote utopia and then, as if to underscore the ahistorical status of his creation, countered with one-dimensional man, a savage caricature of the man that failed. Finally, he makes one last effort to break out of despair in the sixties, forging a link between the present and a utopian future by casting new Leftists as transitional men, half Orphic and half Promethean. But none of these mythic agents could compensate for the lost historical agency, the working class of nineteenth-century Marxism. Marcuse, of course, knew this— and yet resisted its implications for his utopian hopes with his full critical power. But the insistence on dialectical coherence ensured a disastrous result, or so it seems in retrospect: what began as an effort to imagine a truly human future soon exhibited deeply misanthropic theoretical biases.[142] This is perhaps the most poignant irony of the entire critical voyage: in the course of seeking large solutions to match the ubiquitous evil and cruelty of man's condition, Marcuse subverted the values he intended to define and uphold.[143] It would, however, be smug to leave the matter there, a deceptive half judgment. The critical trap that he both prepares and tries to evade may appear baroque and alien, quite unlike our own. But as a possible version of the ethical components of radical paradoxes, it differs from other formulations only in degree.[144]

In his exaggerated way, he illustrates and perhaps brings to a historically temporary climax the worst utopian tendencies of the independent intellectuals whom we have been examining—Mills, Baran, and Sweezy. Marcuse provides a negative illumination of the theoretical and practical consequences of blurring distinctions between utopian fantasy and historical criticism. Refusing to abandon the communist vision as the supreme goal of history, he fails to offer convincing assessments of prospects for various modes of socialism around the world. Like others who yield to the dialectic of liberation, Marcuse cannot estimate the slim historical and political chances of doing away with capitalist forms of exploitation and establishing democratic norms and institutions in socialist societies. The luminous goal of ending alienation obliterates these tortuous paths. But this quasi-religious aim is more than a harmless mirage, as Marcuse's work plainly implies; it also obscures the complex relationships between exploitation and alienation in specific historical settings. Surely capitalist exploitation, which intensifies the division of labor and binds men in the West to an ideology of lonely consumerism, generates and sustains certain dimensions of alienation that socialist orderings of society might attenuate. But Marcuse's perspective precludes a careful examination of these issues. And it deflects attention from other possible sources of alienation that probably lie beyond human control.[145] Finally, as a prelude to politics, the theoretical investigations lead to a radical despair that may manifest itself in quietism or in a nihilistic antipolitics.

Such exclusively theoretical considerations, however, cloud the aesthetic dimensions of Marcuse's work, which assured his appeal during the sixties. Jeremy Shapiro, a younger critic indebted to Marcuse, observes that "the original impetus of the current radical movement . . . was the experience of one-dimensional society and the attempt to formulate this experience and turn it into a source of radical social change motivated its theory and practice."[146] The negative myth of one-dimensional man and the positive myths of Orphic and transitional man surely fit varied structures of sentiments shared by considerable numbers of new Leftists in the sixties. But I rather doubt that these mythic images will continue to figure prominently as vehicles for articulating and legitimizing utopian impulses. The impulses themselves will doubtless endure and help to re-create the tragic rhythm of American radicalism—a continuous imbalance between the desires of radical minorities and historically possible political and social change. Some tension between desires and possibilities may be useful; but the impassable gulf that Marcuse's work suggests, along with the moods it justifies, is surely not. Thus, if Marcuse's thought persists in largely useless fragments, his mythic images may also be torn from their total contexts and absorbed into the pop counterculture. In that event, the isolated mythic figures should be the more easily exposed for what they are: alienating and distorted conceptions of old men and naïve stereotypes of a nonexistent new man. But this conjecture may be too facile—a rational illusion that underestimates the continuing need for radical fictions.

Moreover, such a fate would slight the major aesthetic achievement and the most important cautionary lesson of Marcuse. I have argued that he carefully encloses his utopian visions and mythic creations within a structure of social theory. In his major works, this synthesis creates the illusion of verisimilitude, of historical if not political credibility. Marcuse finally produces a kind of fiction that he represents as social theory.[147] The implicit fictional form ironically parallels the disastrous confusion of social theory and aesthetics that his postwar essays often exhibit. In the end, the strategy of imagining the future on aesthetic models demeans the positive and negative functions of art—and of human life as well. The utopian image of perfectibility allows him to move imperceptibly from social theory to myth, to condemn the old men unfairly in the name of imaginary substitutes. The experience of the sixties demonstrates, once again, the high political and human costs incurred by those who *act* as if they were authentic representatives of a new man, irresponsible precursors of an impossible communist utopia. We may have got beyond Marcuse, but not beyond his central mistake of confusing political and aesthetic categories. It is a fitting irony that the didactic master of negation embodies this negative lesson more fully than other postwar radical critics—a lesson at once so obvious and so elusive.

Part II

THE REVOLUTION DELAYED

Men often take their imagination for their heart, and they believe they are converted as soon as they think of being converted.

—Blaise Pascal, *Pensées*

7

The New Left

As the stultifying fifties drew to a close, a new generation of radicals promised fresh directions in American politics. Idealistic, bright, and energetic, these young people revived the confidence of weary men on the Left. Of course the new radicals had obvious limitations: they possessed no clear program, no viable organization, not even a formidable constituency. And they were innocent of the disastrous potentialities of moral vision insufficiently tempered by political realism. But these were the inseparable strengths and weaknesses of youth. Vision would be modified by experience, it was supposed. What counted was their idealism and their enormous energy—indeed, their very existence after an arid season on the Left. As Mills declared in 1960: "Let the old men ask sourly, 'Out of Apathy—into what?' The Age of Complacency is ending. Let the old women complain wisely about 'the end of ideology.' We are beginning to move again."[1]

After a decade of movement, however, the question that Mills brushed aside had to be asked once again. For the hopes of a generation of radicals soured; their visions took on disturbing shapes; their politics turned into fantasies of an impossible revolution. Born in the optimistic climate of the New Frontier, the move-

233

ment reenacted "the tragic rhythm of American radicalism" within the brief span of a decade. The two most publicized styles of radicalism at the end of the sixties—Students for a Democratic Society and the Yippies—revealed the intense frustration and impotence of those who thoroughly reject the present social order. If the political revolutionaries acquired the usual symptoms of exhaustion—sectarianism, dogmatism, and elitism—the cultural revolutionaries displayed the opposite marks of radical incoherence. Both groups exchanged the complexities of history for simplistic myths.

The impasse that this new radicalism had reached toward the end of the sixties is compellingly illustrated by Tom Hayden's visit to St. Patrick's Cathedral after the death of Robert Kennedy. Diana Trilling writes that "the cathedral was dark, empty except for the guard around the coffin. Holding in his hand the field cap which reputedly was given him by Castro, Hayden sat alone in the shadows, weeping, until someone who saw him invited him to stand a watch at the coffin, which he did, probably glad of the invitation. . . ."[2] The mannerist portrait of Hayden standing in front of the bier, holding the Cuban fatigue cap and weeping for Kennedy, graphically summarizes the state of the new Left in 1968—caught between the memory of reform and the desire for revolution. By then, however, the balance had already shifted toward a militant revolutionary romanticism. The origins in liberalism were dismissed as part of a dead past, a necessary step along the way to mature revolutionary consciousness. Though defenders of the movement acknowledged internal divisions as well as mounting external repression, they nevertheless expected that somehow, through an undefinable interplay of revolutionary theory and action, it would turn into a mass organization capable of staging a Marxist revolution in corporate America.

For a brief period, this myth transcended theoretical as well as empirical considerations, dissipating the enormous weight of negative evidence, as Barrington Moore suggests in his careful assessment of the possibilities for a minority revolution in America. He concludes that "any temporary collapse within the next twenty or thirty years would probably have utterly tragic consequences. Even if it succeeds in taking power, a revolution that tries to remold society against the mores and folkways of the mass of the population must turn to terror and propaganda on a gigantic scale in order to stay in control. . . . It would almost certainly be a failure."[3] By the early seventies, revolutionary rhetoric could no longer shield even the faithful from the hard realities of failure. In their confessional history of the new Left, Greg Calvert and Carol Neiman observe that the movement has not "achieved one single radical reform which transferred power from the corporate elite to the people. The military posture of the Black Panther Party has produced many martyrs but not armed self-defense of the black community; the experiences of the 1960s, with all their pain and struggle, have not left one mass-based organization which has the power to resist either repression or co-optation."[4]

Plain Marxists and the New Left

What went wrong? How did sizable elements of the new Left, which began as an optimistic, democratic, anti-ideological youth movement, so rapidly acquire the characteristics of nihilistic, marginal revolutionary sects? Christopher Lasch suggests a substantial part of the answer: "Both the strengths and the weaknesses of the New Left derive from the fact that it is largely a student movement based on 'alienation.' From the beginning, the New Left defined political issues as personal issues. How does one achieve personal integrity—'authenticity'—in a mechanized, bureaucratized, dehumanized society?" Because the new Left has acted "out of an ideal of personal heroism rather than from an analysis of the sources of tension in American society and the possibilities for change," it "vacillates between existential despair and absurdly inflated estimates of its own potential."[5]

Lasch's interpretation is essentially accurate, though I shall argue that he underestimates the political *intentions* of the founders of SDS. By focusing on several leading characteristics of new Leftists—their feelings of alienation, their youth, and their lack of political sophistication—Lasch sees the end of the movement implicit in its origins. Probably he is right. The theoretical trajectories of the plain Marxists, which we have examined in detail, provide the basis for a fuller interpretation of the rise and decline of the new Left of the sixties. Each plain Marxist confronted the problems of defining visions of an alternate society and stipulating political means for their realization. Those who lived through the sixties responded to radical frustration and defeat in various parts of the world by projecting utopian visions of communism. Beginning with the intention of finding ways to overcome exploitation and establish democracy, they ended by demanding the abolition of alienation through the creation of community.

This progression from historical to utopian perspectives entailed the construction of mythic men whose interests, needs, and desires would be in complete harmony with the principles of a *Gemeinschaft* community. For Sweezy, who adopts a Maoist perspective, the new man is essentially Protestant, even Puritan: he willingly denies many of his own potentialities in order to ensure the progress of an orchestrated social whole. For Marcuse, the new man is not bound by the real constraints of scarcity in underdeveloped societies or by the artificial barriers of overdeveloped ones. Liberated from the distorting influences of previous civilizations, he discovers freedom and happiness in a confluence of genuine individual needs with the nearly limitless possibilities of a communist community. Though Sweezy and Marcuse essentially deduce their new man from utopian variants of classical Marxism, their visions fall into a more abstract paradigm in which the cure for alienation requires a postcapitalist, postsocialist community. But as I have maintained throughout this study, the quest for community on such a grand scale sooner or later requires abandonment of the values of socialism and democracy.

The experience of the new Left of the sixties clearly illustrates this central contention. During the early stages, the search for ways to end alienation assumed the form of a democratic politics of radical reform. In fact, the leading concept of "participatory democracy" expressed the activists' hope of establishing democratic modes of decision-making within the context of nonalienated communities. But this multivalent concept yoked together mutually exclusive aims. What the plain Marxists discovered through tortuous exercises in theory, the new Left learned largely through trial and error in arenas of action. The quasi-religious kernel burst out of its political husk relatively quickly, and by the middle sixties the desire to eradicate alienation eclipsed the idea of democracy. From an initial perspective largely based on the work of Mills, the organized sectors of the Left moved to revolutionary variants of Sweezy's second paradigm and to versions of Marcuse's utopian and dystopian fantasies. They moved, in a word, from a rudimentary sociology of change to a self-defeating dialectic of liberation.

The new Left thus confirmed, once again, Max Weber's dictum that whoever wants to save his soul should avoid politics. For the predictable result of acting out the wish to end alienation was political disaster, and in many instances spiritual impoverishment. This debacle was partly a function of the social obstacles to a successful Left-liberal politics of reform in the sixties. But political failures only accelerated the emergence of the fundamentally antidemocratic implications of the activists' desire to overcome alienation. In retrospect, then, the tension between the capacities, needs, and desires of the new Left and the relative inflexibility of American society seems destined to have resulted in sectarianism, extremism, and an emerging cult of violence on the one side and in a massive withdrawal into metapolitical forms of fundamentalism on the other.

The Political Revolutionaries

Although largely repudiated by later leaders of SDS factions, "The Port Huron Statement" is in many respects a remarkable document, a powerful record of the dominant moods of an articulate minority of the young in the early sixties. The wide disparities between the rhetoric and the realities of American life stirred them into radical action. Everywhere they looked, students confronted specific manifestations of radical paradoxes: the American creed of racial equality and the grim facts of bigotry; the celebration of domestic progress and the aimlessness of much work and most leisure; the myth of affluence and the realities of poverty; the rhetorical commitment to assisting underdeveloped nations and the ever more lopsided global polarization of wealth; and most ominously, the proclamations of peaceful intentions amid furious preparations for a catastrophic nuclear war.

At the outset, then, the young Left displayed a partial awareness of the chief dilemmas of contemporary American radicalism: the paradox of powerlessness and the moral ambiguities of politics. Their youth allowed them fresh, vivid perceptions of the intolerable dilemmas that parents and teachers had distanced through a variety of perspectives, best summarized in Daniel Bell's concept of "the end of ideology."[6] Since the chance of total revolutionary change in advanced nations of the West had vanished, Bell contended, progress would henceforth come about less dramatically, in slow, relatively even stages. By emphasizing the enormous complexity of modern societies and the unavailability of revolutionary levers of change, the "end of ideology" theorists—Bell, Seymour Martin Lipset, and others—also tended to minimize the moral dimensions of domestic and international injustices, and the urgency of acting against them. In the end, these intellectuals "resolved" the dilemmas by obliterating the paradox of radical powerlessness; they came to accept the basic features of the American system, if only because there seemed to be no politically viable alternative.

A political conflict between the generations became imminent as the new radicals focused on what their elders no longer wanted to look at directly. The young had no good reason to accept the resignation of the intellectuals, for their own radical odyssey had just begun. And older, ex-Left intellectuals were still adjusting to the crushing losses of an earlier radicalism. For a variety of reasons, then, neither group could accept the basic position of the other. The fresh, unmediated perceptions of American dilemmas reinforced the mood of urgency among the young radicals at Port Huron: "Our work is guided by the sense that we may be the last generation in the experiment with living."[7] Still, they understood that most of their fellow citizens did not care—or had learned not to care—about the drift toward apocalypse. "We are," they frankly admitted, "a minority. . . . In this is perhaps the outstanding paradox: we ourselves are imbued with urgency, yet the message of our society is that there is no viable alternative. . . ." The received wisdom of resignation struck the young as a counsel of despair that they sought to exorcise with hope, with a "yearning to believe there *is* an alternative to the present."

To reestablish radical vision after its virtual disappearance in the 1950s, activists formulated an optimistic though tentative statement of their values. They asserted that man is "infinitely precious and possessed of unfulfilled capacities for reason, freedom, and love." But in America the myth of unlimited consumption had dehumanized everyone—the affluent who had too much and the poor who had too little. The expression of man's dormant capacities required a new social setting, "a democracy of individual participation, governed by two central aims: that the individual share in those social decisions determining the quality and direction of his life; that society be organized to encourage independence in men and provide the media for their common participation."

Recognizing the initial need for enlarging their campus constituencies, founders of the movement cast about for political equivalents of the existential moods of students. In the early phases, it was assumed that success could not be measured by political victories or even by "the intellectual 'competence' or 'maturity' of the students involved. . . ." The leaders harbored no illusions about prevalent student attitudes or the dismal state of higher education. After portraying the defensive ennui and the flight into private life by the vast majority, "The Port Huron Statement" provisionally traced individual frustrations to structural causes, noting that "apathy is not simply an attitude" but rather "a product of social institutions and of the structure and organization of higher education itself." Hence the primary opportunity of the new movement lay "in the fact [that] the students are breaking the crust of apathy and overcoming the inner alienation that remain the defining characteristics of American college life."

Within this general framework, specific targets were brought into focus: the outmoded character of the *in loco parentis* theory, the excessive specialization and compartmentalization of knowledge, the alienating effects of value-free social science, and a cumbersome "academic bureaucracy" that contributes "to the sense of outer complexity and inner powerlessness." University authorities now openly acknowledge the validity of nearly every criticism of higher education in "The Port Huron Statement." And the beginnings of reform are evident in the abandonment of *in loco parentis* by major institutions, in the development of interdisciplinary curricula, and in the search for new modes of teaching and learning. But in 1962 few academics understood (or would acknowledge) the breadth and depth of student discontent. It is probably not too cynical to assume that the guardians of higher education would have accelerated their drive toward specialized undergraduate programs of study as long as students remained outwardly docile (and funds for rapid expansion remained available). The most impassioned critics of the new radicalism frequently display notoriously bad memories; whatever SDS was to become, it played a serious part in nudging the complacent into an awareness of the profound conflicts that were to dominate colleges and universities throughout the sixties.

Though sketchy, the radicals' analysis of the larger political scene had the solid virtues of identifying the primary problems that would haunt the nation throughout the decade, and of outlining the intricate social, psychological, and political dimensions of a fresh departure from the pace and direction of American life. Drawing heavily on the work of Mills, they clearly identified the dominant trend toward increasing private power under the public façade of democracy. American politics was sinking into an "organized . . . stalemate: calcification dominates flexibility as the principle of parliamentary organization, frustration is the expectancy of legislators intending liberal reform, and Congress becomes less and less central to national decision-making, especially in the area of foreign policy."

To rescue the essential values of American liberalism from the complacency of intellectuals and from the crude deformations of philistines, the founders charted a vague politics of radical reform that included protest and confrontation as well as electoral activity. In general, the early SDS advocated a Left-liberal coalition of students, civil-rights and peace groups, labor, the poor, and the conscience constituency of affluent professionals. Since the wide range of available tactics was to serve the larger ends of their vision, they ruled out violence, which "requires generally the transformation of the target, be it a human being or a community of people, into a depersonalized object of hate."

Though flawed by strains of pretentious romanticism, "The Port Huron Statement" generally struck a balance between the articulation of ideals and the recognition of social realities. The founders intended to combine the best elements of the liberal tradition—its sense of the fragility of democracy and of the complexity of modern social problems—with a critique of its failures. They fused an awareness of the problematic with their passionate determination to solve radical paradoxes by embarking upon a sweeping politics of reform. But it was far easier to draw up a statement of political intentions than to execute it. The founders of SDS did not anticipate the devastating effects that the impending clash with the larger society would have on their efforts to develop a radical analysis, vision, and politics. Unable to calculate the narrow range of American politics, they could not know how quickly their activity would dramatize the inherent weaknesses and limitations of a radical youth movement in an advanced capitalist society. This interplay between their own expectations and the resistance of society propelled the drive toward sectarianism.

In *Rebellion and Repression* (1969), Tom Hayden, the principal author of "The Port Huron Statement," casts the history of the new Left in the context of its most representative theme—disillusionment and the loss of innocence. At the outset of the decade, he recalls, the hopes of the young were raised by the election of Kennedy and the establishment of the Peace Corps which "represented an alternative symbolically, a way out of the Cold War: and at the same time, an alternative to the ratrace careers that most young people faced unhappily." But the Peace Corps turned out to be little more than a façade which for a time blinded people to the "more brutal and exploitative patterns of American foreign policy. . . ."[8] Of course the principal encounters that turned the new Left away from conventional liberalism were domestic, chiefly the civil-rights movement. (A good deal of the history of the young radicals must be understood as a series of reactions to shifting currents in the black movement.)[9] Students went South "with a confidence that the conscience of the United States" was on their "side," only to discover that racism permeated the institutional structures and consciousness of the entire nation. The South, they learned at first hand, was organically connected to the rest of the country by complex tissues of economic, social, and political power. Hayden observes that the "federal government and Democratic Party could not and would not offend Southern officials." For political reasons, the Justice Department refused to protect "people conducting sit-ins or voter registration."[10]

The series of rebellions in northern cities after 1964 dramatized and extended the lessons of the South. Local structures of power everywhere resisted change. The poor—black and white—were locked into ghettos, oppressed by city governments, and for the most part unrepresented. "There is," Hayden observes, "no community machinery for control of the police, the landlord, the merchant, the social worker, or other parasitic elements which patrol and exploit the ghetto."[11] Instead of responding humanely to the desperate needs that the rebellions underlined, however, a majority of whites became defensive, arrogant, and insensitive, while local, state, and national governments resorted to force, unconvincing rhetoric, and very little genuine aid.

Beginning in 1965, this same rhythm of defeated expectations unfolded on a global scale as the war in Vietnam echoed the "violence and racism . . . we were already seeing at home."[12] After supporting Lyndon Johnson as the peace candidate of 1964, a good many young Leftists (along with millions of others) felt betrayed as the war dragged on. Moreover, the variety of subsequent protest tactics—marches, sit-ins, teach-ins—had little tangible impact on the nature and direction of American foreign policy.

Throughout the decade, then, the experiences of activists seemed to fit the same basic pattern: rather than achieving integration, the civil-rights movement revealed a deep, structural racism throughout America. Rather than promoting substantial economic, social, and political gains, the promising work among the urban poor foundered against the solid resistance of a vast maze of local economic and political interests. And instead of reversing a neo-imperialist foreign policy, the antiwar efforts highlighted its apparent irreversibility. Despite relatively rapid growth, the experience of failure and the accompanying sense of impotence soon corroded the fragile balance of theory, politics, and vision which the founders had intended to maintain. Hayden's selective history of the new Left suggests the activists' need for full explanations of minor achievements within the larger framework of defeat. The search proceeded on two interrelated fronts—one theoretical, the other mythical.

The early frustrations of SDS—in the areas of civil rights, peace, and community organizing—led many to ask more fundamental questions: who makes domestic and foreign policy? What are the decision-makers' sources of power? Who benefits from these policies? If activists could not provide thoroughly convincing answers, they nevertheless stuck to the central questions. And the seasoned critics didn't help much. Establishment liberals such as Nathan Glazer proved more skillful at diagnosing the weaknesses of the new Left than in defining the anatomy and dynamics of American society. In his generally sound critique of the state of the movement in 1968, Glazer suddenly goes blank when attempting to refute the new Left's contention that Vietnam is an especially ugly aspect of neo-imperialism: "In the end, I cannot help believing, the Vietnam war must be understood as the result of a series of monumental errors. The key point to me is this: *America would not have had to be very different from what it now is for some President to have gotten us out of Vietnam rather than deeper and deeper into it.*"[13] This is rather like arguing that the rapist who accidentally killed the girl only intended to molest her. It may be so; with a second chance, the man might avoid another murder. But the argument begs the main question of why (or even whether) he is a habitual rapist.

How, then, were these fundamental questions to be approached if older intellectuals of the establishment provided no comprehensive frameworks of analysis? It would not do merely to suggest that grand syntheses were outmoded, to declare that basic questions about the American economic and social order could not be analyzed and refined. So in the absence of alternatives, the young turned uneasily to the radical past, and as the decade wore on, to such plain Marxists as Mills, Baran, Sweezy, and Marcuse. In spite of the many revisions and distortions accumulated over a century, Marxism remained the only comprehensive intellectual point of departure available to the young Left, or at least to the minority who pursued theory. Hoping to resist the ideological straitjackets and sectarianism of the old Left (of the men who, along with their God, had failed), the new radicals returned to Marxism, arguing all the while that they would recast it in a contemporary mold.

Throughout this study, I have assumed that without an essentially Marxian perspective it is hard to understand the largest contours of twentieth-century history—the global polarization of wealth through various forms of capitalism and neo-imperialism, the major wars, and the decisive revolutions. Marxism, as Sartre has observed, is the fundamental philosophy of our time. But it may also be the philosophy that, in the America of the sixties and seventies, cannot be widely understood in its nonutopian forms. At the very least, Marxist theory did not have a full chance to develop in the politically active segments of the movement. Of course, the frustrating experiences of radicals after the Port Huron gathering did move some to a serious analysis of American society, and by the middle of the decade the perspective of radical paradoxes was lucidly articulated by leading spokesmen of the movement.[14] Carl Oglesby's eloquent address at the November 1965 March on Washington summarized the growing understanding of the separation of liberal values from the American corporate system:

Let's stare our situation coldly in the face. All of us are born to the colossus of history, our American corporate system—in many ways, an awesome organism. There is one fact that describes it: with about 5 percent of the world's people, we consume about half the world's goods. We take a richness that is in good part not our own, and we put it in our pockets, our garages, our split-levels, our bellies, and our futures.

On the *face* of it, it is a crime that so few should have so much at the expense of so many. Where is the moral imagination so abused as to call this just? Perhaps many of us feel a bit uneasy in our sleep. We are not, after all, a cruel people. And perhaps we don't really need this super-dominance that deforms others. But what can we do? The investments are made. The financial ties are established. The plants abroad are built. Our system *exists*. One is swept up into it. How intolerable—to be born moral, but addicted to a stolen and maybe surplus luxury. Our goodness threatens to become counterfeit before our eyes—unless we change.[15]

The tremendous potential of Marxist theory was barely tapped if only because, as Oglesby's speech implies, it led straight to the cul-de-sac of radical paradoxes. And most young Leftists found radical paradoxes an intolerable perspective that failed to meet personal needs through a public ideology and politics. In part because of their youth, in part because of their anti-intellectual cultural legacy and their affluent middle-class origins, young Leftists needed moral clarity, not moral ambiguity. They needed an ideology that justified decisive action, not a theory that raised unanswered and perhaps unanswerable political questions. Above all, they needed an apocalyptic and utopian vision of a future beyond alienation, not an anxious view of endless crises under various forms of capitalism and socialism.

By the late 1960s, nonutopian variants of Marxist theory were eclipsed by the complementary myths of disillusionment and revolution, both of them responses to the fundamental experiences of alienation. Hayden's interpretation of new Left history suggests the power of the myth of disillusionment whose personal and political cycle includes the loss of innocence through the discovery of evil, the resolution to eradicate it, the encounter with popular and institutional resistance to dramatic social change, and finally disenchantment and frustration. This myth had obvious appeal to young Leftists for reasons beyond its partial truth. It placed frustrating political losses (and minor successes as well) in a tolerable perspective; more importantly, it reinforced their morally absolute views of the world. The myth of disillusionment explained the alienation of the young, justifying their search for "authenticity" through an unyielding opposition to this culture. When the most immediate institutions—the family, the school, and local authorities—proved immovable, the myth revealed its built-in safety valve of infinitely expanding contexts. To justify specific defeats and to sustain their momentum after marginal victories, it was now possible for young radicals to identify ever more formidable and more inclusive enemies: capitalism, imperialism, socialism, and more recently civilization itself.

Once set in motion, however, the pattern of expanding contexts blurs vision and destroys values. When reasonable criteria of political success and failure collapse, specific actions lose their meaning; there is nothing to measure them against. Paradoxically, thought diminishes in value because it does not lead to satisfying public action. Inaction and increasingly desperate forms of behavior turn out to be the frustrating poles of expression; for as the parameters of imagination continuously expand and the "enemy" takes on mythical proportions, the possibilities for significant, purposive action narrow: sooner or later, violence—the least ambiguous form of direct action—becomes the chief criterion of personal and political "authenticity." From this perspective, any concession on the part of the undifferentiated opposition must be rejected as a form of tokenism. Cooptation emerges as the principal external political threat, and selling out becomes the chief moral temptation. Thus, in the late 1960s, the logic of extremism—in ideology, style, and ultimately in action—came to be the driving force of the movement's most highly organized sectors.

By itself, however, the negative myth of disillusionment tends to suppress the quest for authenticity through direct political action. Those who do not choose to drop out, sell out, or to engage in random acts of violence, must seek a positive resolution to this myth. The most militant elements of the new Left sought relief from the strains of radical paradoxes by opting for revolution.

Faith in the revolutionary myth seriously crippled the theory, politics, and vision of the movement. When one considers the changes in Marxist perspectives during the postwar era, which includes the collapse of the old Left and the rise of the new, the parallels are as striking as the differences. Old Leftists based their overall strategy on the general Marxian notion that capitalism was creating the objective conditions for its own demise. Capitalist development had formed an exploited class-in-itself, which the radical elite would help convert into a revolutionary class-for-itself. If Marx provided the general scenario(s) for the dialectics of qualitative change, the Soviet Revolution demonstrated the historical possibility of staging the opening scenes of the drama of human liberation (even for Trotskyists who believed that the revolution was subsequently betrayed). Although this basic framework allowed ample scope for fierce sectarian squabbles, the general theoretical task of the old Left seemed clear: to continuously take the pulse of a dying system, bringing an essentially valid theory up to date. The political aim was equally unambiguous: to organize a disciplined vanguard party, and to raise the level of consciousness of the masses through continuous education, propaganda, and political action, at times within the Democratic Party, at times not.

More than fifty years of failure by the old Left, however, destroyed the belief in the industrial working class as the principal revolutionary force in advanced capitalist nations, especially in the United States. But when the new Left rejected a politics of reform in the middle sixties, it turned back to utopian Marxian patterns of revolutionary change, seeking external models once again—this time Chinese and Cuban rather than Soviet—in order to revitalize the belief that some oppressed class would take hold of its revolutionary mission. After the new Left began to adopt the general faith (and soon after, the dominant organizational forms) of its predecessor, every revolutionary group in the United States settled on at least one proletarian heart to execute the desires of its own head: the oppressed of the third world, the poor, the blacks, the new working class, the counterculture, the students themselves, and finally, to complete the circle, the old working class. Each surrogate proletariat has been theoretically groomed for a role in a new version of an old drama that none is able or even willing to play.[16]

Compared with the intellectual efforts of plain Marxists, this theoretical activity is of generally poor quality. It all follows from and sustains the revolutionary myth that there *must* be a surrogate proletariat somewhere in America or at the peripheries of its informal empire. By absorbing theory, mythical modes of perception reduce reason and history to caricatures. And once the moral and political perspectives of radical paradoxes disappear into revolutionary myth, it is a relatively simple matter to justify any action or strategy proposed by the several small vanguards, as the argument in Marcuse's *Essay on Liberation* clearly implies. In place of trying to define the structural limits of the American social order— and hence the free space for creative politics within and against that changing system—extremist sectors of the new Left retained their revolutionary fervor by emphasizing the subjective elements of will, courage, and desire. If the old Left exaggerated the determined elements in history, the new revolutionaries relied almost exclusively on a romantic voluntarism. (To metaphrase the New Testament: "Revolution in me, the hope of glory.") Within this mythicized, existentialized Marxism, personal needs and desires take on a public, pseudo-historical significance. The alienated, passive victim can suddenly imagine himself an important actor in a mythic drama. He becomes a member of a community of outcasts who intend to create a new civilization without alienation. As Tom Hayden put it, apparently without embarrassment: "Whether repression works depends basically on our spirit. If we are cautious or paranoid, if we focus only on our defense and forget the issues that made us originally rebel, our feelings will spread and weaken the morale of the people. If we keep a fighting spirit, and define the issues over and over, the people will support us as their warriors."[17]

If the desperate need to act out the myths of disillusionment and revolution reduced Marxist theory to a shambles, the organizational and political consequences flowing from this theoretical muddle were even more disastrous. Once set loose, the extremist dynamic allowed the most militant minorities to assume control of nearly every organization and wreck it. The extreme form of the substitution of faith for reason, of myth for history, and of mindless action for theorizing is exemplified by the Weathermen, an SDS splinter group that put forth the most rigid revolutionary solution to radical paradoxes. Accepting the paradox of powerlessness and obliterating the moral ambiguities of radical activity, the Weathermen concluded that white revolutionaries in America can act only as a support group to the blacks (the chief internal colony) and to revolutionaries in underdeveloped parts of the world. To define socialism in "national terms within so extreme and historical an oppressor nation" was, according to the Weathermen, an instance of "imperialist national chauvinism." They contended that "any attempt to put forth a strategy which despite internationalist rhetoric, assumes a purely internal development to the class struggle in this country is incorrect. The Vietnamese (and the Uruguayans and the Rhodesians) and the blacks and the third world peoples in this country will continue to set the terms for class struggle in America."[18]

The implications drawn from this analysis are frightening. For the Weathermen virtually dissolved economic, political, social, moral, and cultural ties with nearly everyone in America: all groups, except the lumpenproletariat and the "colonized" blacks whom they support from a distance, are guilty—of national chauvinism, imperialism, and "white skin privilege." So guilty, in fact, that the overwhelming majority cannot participate in their own salvation; white America, the Weathermen concluded, must resign itself to being ruled by a coalition of blacks and third-world revolutionaries. Solving the perplexing question of the revolutionary agency of change by denying its existence in the United States, the Weathermen renounced all seriously political pretensions. Freed from social, political, and moral obligations, they could operate freely—and irresponsibly—at the edges of American society, acting out personal fantasies of guilt and rage against an undifferentiated and dehumanized enemy. The following account of Bernadine Dohrn's keynote address at the Weathermen "War Council" in December 1969 illustrates the logic of extremism pushed to absurdity by unrelieved frustration and despair:

Dohrn characterized violent, militant response in the streets as "armed struggle" against imperialism. . . . "We're about being a fighting force alongside the blacks, but a lot of us are still honkies [unable to overcome "white skin privilege"] and we're still scared of fighting. We have to get into armed struggle."

Part of armed struggle, as Dohrn and others laid it down, is terrorism. Political assassination—openly joked about by some Weathermen—and literally any kind of violence that is considered anti-social were put forward as legitimate forms of armed struggle. . . .[19]

Other sectors of the revolutionary Left such as the Progressive Labor Party, the Young Socialist Alliance, and local remnants of SDS did not yield to the uninhibited rantings and pointless violence of Weathermen. Lacking the theoretical sophistication to understand the implications of utopian faith, however, militant elements of the new Left were and are destined to engage in a string of political disasters, isolating themselves further and further from potentially radical constituencies. Even on the campuses, the main center of white radical activity in the 1960s, the revolutionary rhetoric and wildly disruptive actions of tiny minorities increasingly alienate students and faculty. Whatever limited successes radicals had in prompting educational reforms did not keep pace with the expanding myth of revolution in the 1960s.

Unable to chart the historical present accurately, incapable of developing a politics of transition, the new Left of the sixties also failed to imagine the outlines of a decent future. The social vision of young revolutionaries was essentially a simplistic negation of the worst features of the present. It proceeded from the fundamentalist premise of the absolute depravity of a world where, under capitalism, each man bears the marks of the Original Sin of alienation, which turns him away from himself and against others. Dehumanized people continually reproduce a dehumanized world of bureaucracy, technology, and centralized control over ever wider areas of public and private life. Blind to their own unfreedom, the vast majority of the people do not even consciously desire liberation. Overadministered and ceaselessly manipulated individuals do not want what they need, and they generally do not need what they want. Since the disease of alienation resides both in contemporary social structures and in individuals, the movement's theorists had to posit a new society and a new man. They therefore confronted the perennial Marxian dilemma of whether to revolutionize the social context and man simultaneously or by stages.

Whatever priorities the several far Left groups established, all agreed on the necessity and the possibility of doing both—a perspective that entails a clean break with the past.

The vague images of a new man and society vacillated between the revolutionaries' desire for total liberation and their need to submit to tightly structured collectives, between Marcuse's Orphic figure and Sweezy's Puritan. Liberation turned into a growing charter of "freedom from": it signified release from stultifying work and enervating leisure; from social convention; from corrupt, media-dominated politics; from sexual inhibitions; and from the culture of the past. In the widest sense, then, it represented a quasi-religious yearning to be free from "the things of earth," which is to say free from the complexities and ironies of history.

The loss of historical perspective implied by these images seriously subverted the political potentialities of the movement. Despite individual exceptions, those who controlled the organizations of the new Left tended toward ever more bizarre notions of liberation, until at last the distinction between capitalism and civilization blurred. Every institution, value, and social convention fell short of the simplistic criterion of egalitarianism. All notions of order, rank, hierarchy, and distinction came under sustained attack—along with the gross economic, social, political and cultural inequities built into monopoly capitalist society. From this vantage point, trivial and important issues ran together. The teacher who pretended to know more than his students was no less an elitist than the politician who believed that his constituents could not understand basic issues. The humanist who engaged in the modest fraud of publishing pointless anthologies became a "literary imperialist," scarcely less culpable than the executive who pursued corporate interests in the tin mines of Bolivia.[20] The parent who exercised any authority over the teenager was no less an authoritarian than the cop who wielded his nightstick indiscriminately. And so on, *ad nauseam.*

The belief in the imminence of a wholly new postrevolutionary man and society justified uncompromising moral attitudes toward contemporary realities: "future morality" obliterated the ethical ambiguities of the present. Revolutionary purity functioned both as a sign of individual moral worth and as a criterion of political action: all the impurities of the system had to be purged. The university, for instance, may be an instrument of military policy *and* a center of humane learning. Still, because of its mixed elements, it might as well be done away with. That campuses remain a primary context for educating and radicalizing the young could not register on polarized minds, as Mark Rudd demonstrates in recalling an encounter during which he "was asked, in the middle of a crowded faculty meeting, the following crucial question by Professor Alan Silver. . . . 'Mr. Rudd, is there nothing in the university worth saving?' Had I been as sure then as I was *several weeks later, after much study, experience, and discussion,* the answer *No* would have come readily."[21]

Such rigid stands turn politics into metapolitics by distorting the social landscape and reducing its inhabitants to caricatures. In the middle sixties, when SDS centered its activities in urban slums, the slow progress in organizing the poor soon became frustrating, especially when set against the goal of total change. The brief foray into the ghetto both confirmed and reshaped the radicals' view of the nature of human nature, a view heavily influenced by *One-Dimensional Man.* In theory, the poor could be counted on because they had nothing to gain from retaining the system. Their incorruptibility was therefore a social necessity. But in fact, radicals soon discovered what they should have known all along—that a vast majority of the poor want no more than a part in this society. The inflated view of human nature in the mythical form of a new man clashed with the intricate reality of human motives in this historical matrix. When real people didn't measure up, the militant sector of the new Left in effect abandoned the people in order to retain its illusions. After the revolution, of course, the curse of alienation would be lifted from all men. In the meantime, the poor, like every other deluded segment of society, would have to be manipulated insofar as they figured at all in the rapidly changing designs of the revolutionary Left.

The assumption that modes of consciousness and social systems could be erased like chalk on a blackboard also led to a vast miscalculation of the potential rate and direction of historical change in socialist as well as in capitalist societies. Despite continuous social change—from mild reforms to convulsive revolutions—the past weighs upon the present and narrows the options of the future, as even the most superficial glance at the socialist history of the twentieth century demonstrates. Neither the Soviet nor the Chinese Revolution, perhaps the decisive events of this era, has in fact approached the new Left's visions of liberated man. In response to these predictable shortcomings, the purists of the sixties redefined socialism so as to exclude the Soviet Union, saving the vision at the price of wholly condemning the ambiguous reality. Moreover, when they discover the human sacrifice it will take to bring China out of centuries of backwardness and imperial exploitation, the purists will condemn it, too, as a revolution betrayed. Or perhaps they will merely lose interest in it.

The precise merits and faults of the Soviet and Chinese Revolutions are not at issue here; it is rather the possibility of recognizing and discussing them in historical and political terms that seems to have eluded so many new Leftists.[22] Ironically, those who appropriated the mantle of Marx were unable to assess reasonably the varieties of socialism as imperfect historical phenomena, mainly because their quasi-religious frameworks precluded such analysis. And not surprisingly. Since religious images of the Heavenly City remain locked in the imagination, every attempt to realize them in history must sooner or later be condemned as inadequate or worse. The visions of liberation illustrate Marx's insight into religion as a negative index of actual misery expressed in the form of fantasy: "Religion," he observed, "is the sigh of the oppressed creature, the heart of a heartless world, just as it is the spirit of a spiritless situation." It is, however, only the beginning of criticism, according to Marx, not its final form, as many revolutionaries of the new Left would have it. Although the imaginative shapes of the concept of liberation may be cathartic for those living in advanced capitalist countries, they lie beyond the historical boundaries of possible change in the remaining decades of this century and probably well into the next. In a divided world, threatened by overkill, mushrooming population, famine, vastly inequitable division of wealth, and increasingly sophisticated forms of destructive technology and bureaucracy, visions of spontaneity and total liberation cannot be the basis of a remotely effective politics, even if one considers them to be the supreme ends of human existence. The gardens that survive in the machine will have to be carefully planned.

The Marcusean impulses toward liberation from civilization did not operate unchecked in the semiorganized political far Left. They mingled with authoritarian images and practices that characterized the social relations and mores of hard-core members of the various revolutionary factions. The authoritarian underside of the vision of liberation implies the new Left's inability to resolve the continuous historical dilemmas of the relations between the one and the many, the problem of democracy. To an essentially fundamentalist consciousness, the ambiguous theoretical and practical problem of maintaining a delicate balance between an individual's rights and his social responsibilities, between freedom and authority, between the desired and the desirable, is not treated as a dilemma at all. Someday, after the revolution, the paradox will melt away as individual motives and desires mesh with whatever social imperatives remain. In the meantime, the revolutionary goal requires an equally simplistic resolution: the committed individual must renounce his individuality; he must reshape himself into what Mao calls "a shining cog in the revolutionary machine." One defender of the Weathermen writes of "the necessity of building revolutionary collectives that demand total, wholehearted commitment of the individual to struggle against everything that interferes with the revolutionary struggle, and to struggle to transform oneself into a revolutionary and a communist: collectives through which we can forge ourselves into effective 'tools of necessity'. . . ."23

The borrowed social models of the new Left thus illustrate the authoritarian tendencies barely disguised by the concept of liberation. While denouncing the relatively developed socialist societies as impossibly corrupt, many admire the undeveloped countries for what seem to me the wrong reasons. The tight organization of human and material resources, a social necessity in Cuba and China, became a psychological requirement of political organizations of the new Leftists in America, satisfying their subterranean urge for order, security—even the denial of individuality—and for a sense of solidarity that our society largely precludes. At the same time, the apparently freewheeling, antibureaucratic ethos of China and Cuba appealed to the desire for liberation from the stultifying, tedious quality of their own lives in a postindustrial society.

Perhaps it is premature to announce yet another abortion of Marxism in America. But events and trends of the 1960s indicate that it has thus far been revived as myth rather than as theory. If the young Leftists looked briefly to Marxism for answers, they soon exchanged the theoretical challenge for liturgical drama, dressing up like revolutionary heroes and acting out their desires through ritualistic battles. The troubling perspective of radical paradoxes was officially dispelled by an orgy of nonsense: at one of the last SDS conventions when one faction chanted "Mao, Mao, Mao Tse-tung!" while another replied with "Ho, Ho, Ho Chi Minh," the dialogue had reached its outer limits. Assuming the surrogate form of drama, the play continued for a time, but the political revolution in America had been delayed once more. The brief ritual of blood was about to begin.

How could it have been otherwise? The seemingly opposed notions of liberation actually met on common ground. Both were politically impossible in the American context. And both were profoundly antidemocratic. After Port Huron, new Leftists groped toward the idea of a *Gemeinschaft* community because it was the only theoretically consistent solution to the riddle of alienation. But the concept of liberation, conceived as a charter of total freedoms from existing forms of civilization, presupposed a Marcusean context of a communist community in which all genuine needs of individuals would be met. Yet the political revolutionaries obviously could not enact this version of liberation in contemporary society: they could not become the new men they vaguely imagined. Nor could they, in the early stages, create an egalitarian, democratic political organization without leaders. Moreover, many radicals used this utopian concept of freedom, deduced from an impossible social vision, to judge and condemn the present. In the process, the idea of socialism as a goal lost whatever power it had, or might have gained. And the idea of democracy, both as a political means of inducing change and as an intrinsically important component of a fully developed socialist society, was deprived of much of its force.

This ideological pattern alone would have guaranteed political marginality and intensified feelings of alienation. But the final impetus toward sectarianism and organizational collapse was provided by the complementary notion of liberation considered as submission to the rigid dictates of an obviously repressive collective, a false community. The authoritarian version of liberation was repressive in practice, since it entailed the reduction of individual needs and potentialities to the narrow demands of the whole. Though such a diminished image of man was at least historically possible on a small scale, the dominant cultural pattern of individualism quickly blunted its main thrust. No amount of collectivist rhetoric could dispel the pervasive emotional attachment of large numbers of young radicals to the cluster of notions summarized in the concept of individualism.

Thus utopian radicals of the sixties ensured their own political powerlessness by refusing to accept the disparity between emotional individualism and collectivist rhetoric of community as a pervasive fact of American life. This fundamental paradox, I believe, illuminates the main internal cause of the organizational demise of the political "revolutionaries." Despite its many ambiguous meanings and mythical connotations, the central impulse of individualism survived, thwarting the efforts of utopian Marxists to establish disciplined political organizations. Individualism functions as a self-selecting mechanism by which people attracted to utopian ideologies leave—or never join—organizations based on authoritarian notions of "liberation." Or else it becomes a centrifugal force within vanguard parties, promoting splintering and, in many instances, total disintegration. This, at least, was the experience of the sixties.

The Cultural Revolutionaries

Plagued by similar frustrations, political and cultural revolutionaries shared a spirit of unremitting opposition to American society. This is not surprising, considering their common backgrounds: predominantly young, white, middle-class, and disillusioned, they demanded full release from the dull, affluent settings of their childhoods, no less than from the prefabricated adult roles in what they regarded as the same meaningless rituals of production and consumption.[24] Of course no clear line separates political from cultural revolutionaries; their moods, tactics, and personal styles were responses to the same society and culture. Though few people held a pure form of either position in the sixties, the extremes illuminate much of the interior social and psychic territory. On the continuum of liberation, cultural revolutionaries stand to the left of their political counterparts who cling (however tenuously) to language and logic, theory and political action as means of shaping men and history. The Yippies, representing the most flamboyant semipolitical force in the cultural revolution, found these lingering commitments a source of new frustrations, new orthodoxies, new prisons of the mind.

Unencumbered by the idea of reason and history, Yippies did not need to establish political priorities, to mediate between utopian desires and genuine historical options. Jerry Rubin, a leading spokesman, experienced the futility of sectarian politics at first hand: "For years I went to left-wing meetings trying to figure out what the hell was going on. Finally I started taking acid, and I realized what was going on: nothing. I vowed never to go to another left-wing meeting again. Fuck left-wing meetings!" By submitting wholly to the spirit of liberation through total opposition to American culture and society, they evaded the radical paradoxes of independent Left intellectuals and the radical problems of the new revolutionaries. "The Yippies are Marxists," Rubin declared facetiously: "We follow in the revolutionary tradition of Groucho, Chico, Harpo and Karl."[25]

The accent was on direct, unmeditated, frenetic action against every actual and imagined form of repression. *Do It!*, Rubin's bestseller, provided the cultural revolutionary's reply to the perennial question, "What Is to Be Done?" The vague parody of Lenin was sufficiently precise for Rubin's purpose: "Previous revolutions aimed at seizure of the state's highest authority, followed by the takeover of the means of production. The Youth International Revolution will begin with mass breakdown of authority, mass rebellion, total anarchy in every institution in the Western world. Tribes of longhairs, blacks, armed women, workers, peasants and students will take over." The subtitle—*Scenarios for Revolution*—is equally revealing. For the cultural revolutionaries sought to bypass radical paradoxes by obliterating distinctions between life (in particular, the categories of reason, history, and politics) and art, turning everything in sight into a gigantic set for a musical comedy in a violent key: "language," Rubin contends, "does not radicalize people—what changes people is the emotional involvement of action. What breaks through apathy and complacency are confrontations and actions, the creation of new situations which previous mental pictures do not explain, polarizations which define people into rapidly new situations."[26]

Personal and social salvation—and the two cannot be distinguished in this gestalt—begin when one externalizes his frustrations, dreams, hopes, and anxieties. Conformity and isolation turn into creative conflict and community. Once large numbers enlisted as revolutionary actors, it was claimed, old structures would crumble and power would pass into the hands of the people. And after the orgy of destruction? Rubin's scenario of liberation reads like pop drama, not historical prophecy. His projected revolution takes the form of a comic dance: "Millions of young people will surge into the streets of every city, dancing, singing, smoking pot, fucking in the streets, tripping, burning draft cards, stopping traffic." Concluding with a stage adaptation of Marx's vision of the communist future, Rubin prophesies that "People will farm in the morning, make music in the afternoon and fuck wherever and whenever they want to."[27]

Though anticapitalist, antiracist, and anti-imperialist, Yippies shunned the sectarian organization and scholastic games of the politically revolutionary elements of the movement. Largely immune to critical theory and politics even when both were infused with a "revolutionary content," they would tolerate no transitional periods before the state withered away. Abbie Hoffman, the most prolific spokesman for this amorphous tendency, suggests the similarities and differences between the two dominant radical tendencies in his five-day "book," *Woodstock Nation:*

When I appear in the Chicago courtroom, I want to be tried not because I support the National Liberation Front—which I do—but because I have long hair. Not because I support the Black Liberation Movement, but because I smoke dope. Not because I am against a capitalist system, but because I think property eats shit. Not because I believe in student power, but that the schools should be destroyed. Not because I'm against corporate liberalism, but because I think people should do whatever the fuck they want, and not because I am trying to organize the working class, but because I think kids should kill their parents. Finally, I want to be tried for having a good time and not for being serious. I'm not angry over Vietnam and racism and imperialism. Naturally I'm against all that shit but I'm *really* pissed cause my friends are in prison for dope and cops stop me on the street because I have long hair. I'm guilty of a conspiracy, all right. Guilty of creating liberated land in which we can do whatever the fuck we decide. Guilty of helping to bring WOODSTOCK NATION to the whole earth. Guilty of trying to overthrow the motherfuckin senile government of the U.S.A. . . . Just thought I'd let you know what I mean when I say, "I'm just doin my thing."[28]

This remarkable passage reveals the paradoxical character of the Yippie phenomenon. Self-consciously antipolitical, Yippies, unlike the political revolutionaries, were in touch with the moods of a sizable majority of America's young, mainly the children of affluence but also young refugees from all classes—the street people. But only briefly, for the Yippies represented no more than a flash on the cultural horizon, a figment of deeper impulses that will constantly appear in new forms.

Whereas theorists of the political Left were obsessively scholastic (however mad their points of departure), the Yippies regarded reason as a trap. As Hoffman put it: "It's only when you get to the End of Reason can you begin to enter WOODSTOCK NATION." Antitheoretical and antirational, the Yippies searched for new modes of expressing their revulsion against the PIG NATION. Since reason and language had been appropriated by the enemy, Yippies sought the only uncorrupted modes of expression—sensations and feelings. In their attempts to constitute new worlds, they thus begin with severe, partially self-imposed limitations. Through spokesmen such as Hoffman, the Yippies registered their opposition in concrete, intensely personal terms. Insofar as they depended upon language at all, they avoided alienating abstractions, sticking to a language of the nerves.

Since the aim was to make an instant cultural revolution rather than to define a long-range political one, Hoffman rejected theory and politics, relying instead on a self-consciously fashioned social myth to account for his revulsion against contemporary America. Like the political revolutionaries, he divided the world simplistically into two camps—the PIG NATION and the WOODSTOCK NATION, one perishing, the other rising out of its ruins. For Hoffman, the gathering at Woodstock in the summer of 1969 was not merely a rock festival but the birth of a nation, the formation of another country where the diseases of civilization would disappear. Let the tribe gather together, let everyone do "what the fuck he wants," and then the details of government can be worked out. There is in this comic-strip perspective no need for elaborate theory, no need for social vision, and no need for a politics of transition. The cultural revolution is NOW, and the only "politics" of this transformation is self-defense against the "fascist pigs," he declares, sweeping the details of strategy aside with the grandiose phrase "by any means necessary."[29] According to Hoffman, the flower children of the middle sixties were beginning to rise above their early innocence and passiveness. Like the political militants who graduated from liberalism to uncompromising revolutionary postures, Yippies had to drop their pacific fantasies in order to resist actively the harsh repression of the larger society.

The Yippies' primitivism obviously had little to offer in the way of ethical or political insight into contemporary dilemmas. The idea of doing one's own thing is not the culmination of ethics but its obvious precondition and cause. And the political and social consequences of everyone's pursuing his whims were predictably disastrous. Hoffman, who wrote his book while lying comfortably on the floor of his publisher's office, romanticizes the pathetic scene at Woodstock that provided the content for his fantasies. But the new "nation" survived only three days before paralysis set in. As the New York *Times* observed, "What kind of culture is it that can produce so colossal a mess: one youth dead and at least three others in hospitals from overdoses of drugs; another dead from a mishap while sleeping in an open field. The highways for twenty miles around made completely impassable, not only for the maddened youth but for local residents and ordinary travelers." Had the *Times* reporter been able to go beyond the perspective of a foreign correspondent and drop his mask of moral arrogance, he might have been able to recognize the responsible culture as his own.

For Hoffman, an insider, the tragic aspects of Woodstock disappeared into his fantasy of a new nation taking shape. He was as blind as most petty chieftains to the agony of the lower castes, of those who form the writhing backdrop to his own flamboyant fantasies. Except for a few media figures such as Joan Baez and Jerry Rubin, Hoffman revealingly portrayed Woodstock as a faceless nation. He saw only the incredible energy of the young, not the massive waste of human potential that such gatherings of aimless people exemplify. As one participant in Woodstock West observed: "I kept thinking we are so stupid, so unable to cope with anything practical. Push forward, smoke dope. But maintain? Never. We don't know how. We've been coddled, treadmilled, straight-teethed and vitamin-pilled, but we don't know what to do on our own. Reports of a revolution are vastly premature. We don't like the power structure. But we have to live together. We will be governed by others until we learn how to govern ourselves."[30]

But such moralistic criticism of the Yippies largely misses the mark, and not only by obscuring the devastating satire they level against the triviality of life in middle America. More importantly, it obscures the social and psychological roots of their dominant moods and styles. In his credo, Hoffman wants to locate himself *against* the family, the school, and the local authorities—against those who would prevent him from wearing long hair and smoking dope; against those who would restrict his sexual urges and force him to be serious. Destroy the schools and kill the parents (symbolically, one hopes), and you will be born into the sensate kingdom of the young. In reaction to those institutional and personal forces, Hoffman declared his independence by asserting his right to "do his thing." He needs to do what he *feels* like doing in order to *be* himself, which means, at the very least, to become the antithesis of whatever formerly controlled and repressed him.

At bottom, then, the Yippie quest is for authenticity, for a believable sense of self. Since the prevailing culture has appropriated and distorted rationality through its language and values, no less than through its disorienting pace of technological change, the search centers on feelings as the only remaining mode of authenticity. In *Woodstock Nation,* Hoffman presents himself as a representative character in revolt (though he makes it quite clear that he is cleverer and more intense than others). A picaro in search of himself, he neglects the creation of a coherent personality to emphasize consciousness as an ever expanding medium which generates and expends as much energy as possible. The more energy which passes through the multicircuitry of the self, the better. As Hoffman remarks, "WOODSTOCK NATION is built on ELECTRICITY. It is our energy, music, politics, school, religion, play, battleground and our sensuality."[31] One can be even more precise: when language and conventional patterns of behavior break down, the tokens of authenticity are largely reduced to sex and violence. Throughout his long rap, Hoffman tediously emphasizes his desire to seduce every women he can imagine. And he regards most of his encounters with important figures in pugilistic terms, even summing up his meeting with Joan Baez as "a draw." As the most extreme expression of raw energy, sex and violence form the poles around which Hoffman moves, rather like a Little League Norman Mailer, endlessly taking his pulse for signs of life. To be is to be in continuous motion, pouring energy out into the environment.

This stress on the quantitative expenditure of energy leads Hoffman to project a multiplicity of more specific self-images. But the quest for authenticity becomes curiously inauthentic when, in the frantic effort to become other than the culture he rejects, Hoffman accepts any and all characterizations of himself: "I suppose all this energy results from being an anarchist, Jewish, bottle-fed, stubborn, beautiful, white, spoiled brat, dedicated male, young, old, optimistic, Sagittarius, schmuck, revolutionist, communist, god, self-destructive, egotistical, horny, show-off, paranoid-schizophrenic, naive, fucked-up, big-mouth, not serious, brilliant, honest Yippie leader and non-leader and a whole lot more from Concord, Mass., and the Bronx, New York."[32] Hoffman may indeed possess every one of these characteristics (a list facetiously compiled from his critics), but his failure to structure and organize them is perhaps the most revealing trait of all: he emerges as a hollow man with a thousand faces. Obsessed with demonstrating his vitality, he piles up images of himself and accounts of his activities. Any effort at discrimination seems a concession to the entropic spirit of Thanatos, since such acts entail curbing some of these traits and developing others, which would make him less "real." Moreover, it is easier to plead guilty to all charges, especially if the mere admission of guilt is taken as the principal sign of innocence.

What renders the total performance unconvincing, however, is Hoffman's steady refusal to take himself seriously. All the confident pronouncements become tentative by virtue of his self-conscious comic pose. By disclaiming accountability for his fantasies, his thoughts, and his actions, he ultimately denies any responsibility for himself. The external and internal sense of reality he frantically tries to construct turns out to be no more than an illusion. Protesting that he's "only in it for kicks and stuff," he nevertheless emerges as the sad butt of his own elaborate gag. None of the roles he tries on so cavalierly fit—nor do all of them at once. They are so many unconvincing media images that fail to provide satisfying forms for the amorphous flow of energy. And so the endless cycle of expending himself continuously exposes his own emptiness.

It is as if J. D. Salinger's Holden Caulfield had reappeared in Hoffman. Both the character and the culture were fifteen years older—less idealistic, more callous. The disease of youth now extends through the twenties. Instead of being institutionalized, the hung-up kid can travel to Woodstock. In a word, the silent rebellion of the fifties modulated into the expressive rebellion of the sixties. Whereas Holden's fantasy life was tempered by external constraints and internal restraints, Hoffman embodies his fantasies in direct action, measuring his successes by the number of times he gets busted and laid. But the displacement of reality by media fantasies of the lover-warrior gone wild destroys the functions of each. By the end of *The Catcher in the Rye* Holden is at least paralyzed, consciously trapped between the two worlds of *his* imagination and *their* reality. At the end of the sixties, Hoffman was also imprisoned in his own moving world of fantasy, seemingly unable to combat his disease.

Like many of the alienated young, Hoffman could not even manage the world of his feelings and imagination. His repertoire of fantasies was even more prefabricated than Holden's—often exaggerated but always recognizable. Hoffman's inauthenticity is an authentic embodiment of some of the primary features of cold-war American culture. Listen to a portion of his summary of a year's activity:

a book and a half, three quick movies, one to design and edit, the other two to improvise-act in, and lots more to get absorbed into. . . . I also did a unique Yippie calendar, ten or so street theatre events, wasted time battling SDS, gave about seventy speech-performances, had hepatitis and almost died, flew about eighty thousand miles. . . . In between I managed to write about thirty articles, mostly under other names, for the underground press, and a few children's stories. I founded the Movement Speakers' Bureau—a very good idea—and helped to hustle bread and spread the word on the conspiracy trial. I took about twenty acid trips, fucked about 856 times and did a few things that only the FBI knows about and lots of other stuff they don't. I managed to get busted only ten times and face a possible thirty-seven years or so in prison. . . .[33]

With a few modifications, this fantastic combination of business and pleasure would be the envy of most young men on the rise in the straight world. Hoffman is always on the move (in "pig" planes), consummating deals (with "pig" publishers), yet managing to get laid 856 times! The fantasies of sex and aggression, the emphasis on action as opposed to deliberation, the quantification of pleasure—all testify to Hoffman's *machismo*. Rather than creating unique imaginative fantasies, then, he merely acts out surrealistic variations of the standard wish projections of the masscult hero. If the straight executive escapes through television and alcohol, Hoffman manages to numb himself through movies and drugs. Both appear to be on endless trips with no destination in mind. Process replaces purpose; means obscure ends. But what Mailer calls a "sense of the real" eludes both the executive and his "liberated" double.

Hoffman almost perfectly embodies the ideal type of the alienated young man in a consumer society. His celebration of quantity—in the form of reckless expenditure of energy—suggests the ultimate reification of individuals. The frantic consumption of things in the larger society takes the form of a frenetic consumption of self among many of the young. How could it be otherwise in this society? Energy is youth's principal capital. What could be a more perfect example of the deficit spending of energy than the spectacle of Woodstock? Like large sectors of the middle class, Yippies could not find personally viable and rewarding styles of life. And despite all the rhetoric of community, the premises of their search were as fundamentally antisocial and antipolitical as those of any isolated citizen. Instead of just considering all politicians crooked, however, the Yippies regarded the whole system as irredeemably corrupt. And they assumed that the only way to respond to a rigged game is to ridicule it or to break it up. But since it couldn't be wrecked, and since ridicule is easily absorbed into the game, the strategy failed in its outward thrust against the culture. Moreover, both the Yippie and his pale masscult double exemplified the inner isolation that results from elevating the infantile notion of perpetually doing your thing to the first principle of moral and political philosophy.

In the end, after the brief appeal of the Yippies had been exhausted by the media, Rubin and Hoffman cut their hair. And when the Democratic Party held its 1972 convention in Miami, they were there, inside the hall. Facing the television cameras once again, they looked rather like their former selves—innocent, ambitious high-school seniors of the middle fifties.[34] Meanwhile, remnants of the Yippies, camping out in a nearby park, complained that Jerry and Abbie had sold out. Actually they were only looking for new ways to buy in, to retain their tenuous roles as prophets of a new culture.

Like many leaders of the new Left, Rubin and Hoffman could not succeed in their quest for authenticity if only because they were individualists who rejected conventional ways of making it without ever really abandoning the aim of personal success. Their revolt against alienation demanded the establishment of community. Yet through savage caricatures of other revolutionaries who sought political roads to utopia, Yippies rejected the very idea of organization. As the underground writer Paul Krassner put it, "The Crazies have a rule that in order to become a member one must first destroy his membership card."[35] Lacking both the desire and the capacity for organization, Yippie leaders could not hope to retain the attention of would-be followers, who quickly dispersed, seeking new modes of metapolitical expression. Figures such as Rubin, who began as editor of his high-school paper, rose to prominence on the crest of a rebellion against prevailing cultural modes. They spoke the language of community to their loose constituencies—and perhaps even believed it. But they achieved an unearned success, a national visibility, because managers of the media were able to interest the American public in their quasi-political brand of vaudeville. Like other packaged entertainment figures without disciplined talent, however, new Left leaders could not hold an audience for long. Doubtless the media, as some claim, corrupted many ambitious young Leftists. But most turned out to be willing victims who sought publicity as avidly as publicists sought them. Having been weaned on such cultural fare as *Howdy Doody Time* and the *Mickey Mouse Club* in the fifties, Hoffman, Rubin, and others easily fell into their comic roles in the sixties. The cultural distance only seemed greater than it was. The leaders of leaderless groups committed to total change could not resist the most fundamental American imperative of making it.

Conclusion

As a major expression of the wider cultural revolt, Yippies articulated the antipolitical implications of the new Left's search for utopia. Each grouping exposed the utopian and apocalyptic character of the other. And though there is an endless variety to the themes, moods, and styles of metapolitical criticism, the underlying perspectives and social implications remain fairly constant. Insofar as contemporary visionaries reject social criticism and politics for modes of spiritual salvation from alienation, they join with multitudes of more conventional secular and religious figures in the American tradition. The basic paradigm of personal salvation experienced in small communities has a long heritage: the critic-preacher or prophet articulates hopes, fears, and frustrations, and then prescribes a means of personal relief, often with the stipulation that if everyone were to accept his prescription, the world would be quickly delivered from evil. This formula links the tracts of vegetarians, the sermons of Billy Graham, and the latest techniques of transcendental meditation imported from remote Indian villages.

Thus it was not surprising that by the early seventies, when Yippies and the political revolutionaries had passed from the center of the public stage, the Jesus movement was flourishing, along with a plethora of exotic religious fantasies that furthered the formation of small communities, or the establishment by fiat of "communities" of solipsists unable to distinguish their own from other worlds. As long as the disparity between the cultural aim of ending alienation through the enactment of community and the political aims of achieving full democracy and social justice persists, temporary, unstable groups of hippies, Yippies, and Jesus freaks will form colonies in the interstices of advanced industrial society. The rank and file will reject its pressures and the ethic of private material gain only to magnify the private virtues of passivity and self-involvement. As antipolitical minorities, however, these groups will be as harmless to the establishment as sanctified members of tiny fundamentalist sects: both renounce certain values of society only to legitimize and perpetuate them by acquiescing in the status quo.

By the end of the sixties, SDS and the Yippies emerged as the most extreme symbols of white protest and revolt in American society; they were at the same time among the most impotent radical groups, with their encounter with power ending in powerlessness. In their distinctive ways, political and cultural revolutionaries reinforce antipolitical attitudes in the wider society. Though not without some political importance, they exercise virtually no control over the uses of their public activity. Their analyses, visions, and politics preclude a coherent synthesis of motive and act, intention and execution. Hence, in addition to being self-defeating, the revolutionaries have become potentially dangerous insofar as they threaten less apocalyptic radical constituencies, intensifying political repression across the Left, and contributing to the erosion of civil rights and liberties. Even though the dominant forms of opposition of the sixties such as mass demonstrations, sit-ins, and limited modes of violent rebellion have lost their power, at least for the historical moment, the terrifying symbols of these activities will continue to be used by right-wing politicians, journalists, and publicists of the new conservatism, in much the same way that the bogey of the internal Communist menace survived in popular mythology long after the first stages of the cold war.

The most disheartening failure of the new Left, however, was one of omission. Revolutionaries not only repelled the majority of Americans: they also disillusioned a majority on the Left who refused to go over the psychological brink into holistic fantasies of total change. There is a terrible irony here: the new radicals who contributed in important ways to the emergence of anticapitalist modes of consciousness in the sixties were unable to organize the energies they helped to unleash. Driven to mythical modes of understanding that symbolically united their incompatible desires to establish social justice and end alienation, they could neither anticipate nor control the antipolitical consequences of their activity. Isolating themselves even as they were isolated by others, the new revolutionaries could revolutionize neither themselves nor society.

As a youth movement, the new Left quickly reached its predictable political limits, though not before having helped to shake the country out of the complacency of the Eisenhower years. Many of its graduates, and countless others whose outlooks have been influenced by the movement, will move into society, mainly as members of the service professions—law, medicine, teaching, social work, urban planning. Even though they temper the utopian visions of their youth, they will also retain their distrust of received ideology. Some will pursue experimental attitudes toward the questions of how to live within the dominant society. Others will drop out to pursue even more fluid alternative patterns of work and leisure. Thus, the primary importance of the new Left—in the widest sense of the term—may not be felt until the late seventies and the eighties. Though unpredictable, the impact of new ways of thinking and feeling on present social and political configurations may be significant. New departures in relations between the sexes, in family structures, child rearing, education, the meaning of work, and the possibilities of creative leisure all entail political consequences, and in the seventies some may assume political forms. Though it is too early to tell how these experiments will affect the structure of American society, it would be foolish to reject them as mere retreats from the enormous political challenge of moving toward a just society.

The most obvious—and most modest—lesson of the radicalism of the sixties, then, is a negative one that was implicit in the theory of plain Marxists and explicit in the practice of the new revolutionaries: visions of a *Gemeinschaft* community in twentieth-century America are "romantic and utopian in theory, oppressive and reactionary in practice." Mounting social problems may in fact lead to an apocalyptic seizure. But that real possibility ought not to license an uninhibited play of subjective visions of disaster. It is one thing to possess the capacity for imagining an apocalypse and quite another to succumb to the apocalyptic imagination. Those who looked forward to the greening of America, whether through the evolution of a new consciousness or after a destructive revolution, hopelessly blurred this distinction. Instead of evading radical paradoxes, the new revolutionaries submitted to ahistorical versions of them. They quickly discovered their powerlessness against the prevailing social order. And in their search for contemporary variants of communism, they sacrificed the power of the socialist vision.

The harvest is past, the summer is ended, and we are not saved.
—Jeremiah 8:20

8

Conclusion:

The Future of Socialism

"Marxism," Bernard Rosenberg declares, "is unthinkable apart from its premise of proletarian victory and its all-liberating effects. It is a philosophy suspended upon an event, a monologue in the drama of history which only the action of its mass hero can save from being a soliloquy."[1] The plain Marxists recognized that in America and the West, the old working class displayed no signs of becoming the transforming historical agency capable of vindicating the basic classical theory. But since they resisted the conclusion that Marxism had become "unthinkable," every critical attempt to link optimistic nineteenth-century visions with dismal twentieth-century realities initially required the organizing framework of paradox. Unable to identify a surrogate proletariat and unwilling to abandon their belief in a new society, plain Marxists continuously wrestled with the dominant radical paradox of political powerlessness.

As we have seen, they exhibited varied responses to encounters with powerlessness and the cumulative frustrations of defeat. The similarities of their collective response to the crisis of socialism, however, outweigh the differences. Having virtually discarded the idea that the American working class, old and new, would bring

273

about a revolution in social systems—either by a convulsive, dramatic act, or through a long, gradual politics of radical reform—plain Marxists looked elsewhere. Baran and Sweezy and, to a lesser extent, Mills and Marcuse attempted geographical relocations of their visions, first in the Soviet Union and the nations of Eastern Europe, later in China and Cuba. These several efforts to discover emergent connections between vision and history generally ended in disillusionment or in the construction of false hopes. And they exacted an enormous critical price: to preserve the illusion of the historical relevance of their radicalism, plain Marxists, especially Sweezy and Marcuse, substituted the utopian mirage of communism for the classical Marxian formulation of socialism.

The thrust of plain-Marxist theory in the sixties culminated in rejection of the old man in favor of mythic "new men," and in rejection of the very concept of society—capitalist and socialist—in favor of the idea of a communist community without alienation. It was the depth and intensity of the critics' despair that evoked such grandiose hopes. Plain Marxists vacillated between an awareness of paradox and a postulation of counterbalancing myths thinly disguised as critical theory. Their movement toward acceptance of the ideal of a *Gemeinschaft* community as the ultimate solution to exploitation and alienation amounted to a classic quasi-religious form of world rejection. Yet this sweeping, negative response to their perception of actual conditions and trends also implies the continuing power of Marx's articulation of a dominant Western vision of utopia. The desire for a community in which the needs of each are consonant with the needs of all, in which reason, freedom, and happiness converge in the real life and imagination of all people, is deeply woven into the design of Western art, philosophy, and religion. It is, in its multiple forms, a majestic, powerful vision of man released from the bonds of self and the limitations of history, a view of social harmony that transcends tensions between the one and the many, the self and others, characteristic of various modes of society.

Critically mismanaged, however, the vision can be antipolitical and ultimately antisocial. By mingling religious, aesthetic, and philosophical categories with those of history and politics, plain Marxists finally exceeded the fruitful limits of political imagination. They obliterated the dominant tension of utopian and historical elements in classical Marxism by discarding the vision of socialism and slighting the potentialities of democracy. This distortion of vision also impaired their analyses and evaluations of present social systems. Measuring the realities of advanced capitalist nations—and those of some Communist countries as well—against the ahistorical norms of *Gemeinschaft* communities, plain Marxists weakened their capacity to make crucial distinctions between modes and degrees of oppression and liberation in existing societies. Various formulations of the dialectic of liberation, used both as historical goals and as means of judging and condemning the present, ensured inaccurate predictions of the probable rate and direction of social change.

When acted out, these utopian tendencies culminated in a public debacle, as the experience of the political and cultural revolutionaries clearly demonstrates. The utopian corruption of political imagination thus impairs vision, distorts analysis, and predictably ends in political disaster where the successful achievement of power may constitute the worst species of failure. Many people had to experience the sixties to learn these old cautionary lessons concerning the radical quest for a just social order. But those on the Left who escaped this most recent manifestation of the utopian heresy encountered their own versions of radical paradoxes centering on the question of the contemporary relevance of socialism. Without a compelling socialist vision, any radical critique of the plain Marxists and the new Left must end in another, less flamboyant mood of despair. That variants of the communist vision are cruel political illusions seems to me as certain as any proposition in the treacherously vague region of social theory. While demonstrating this, the utopian dimension of Western radicalism in the sixties also obscured the more problematic question of what remains vital and politically plausible in classical and contemporary versions of socialism.

Socialism

The current crisis of socialism, as Robert Heilbroner has observed, is primarily a *crise de foi,* not a crisis of existence.[2] Almost half of the world's people now live in transitional societies whose dominant groups are constructing or moving toward some form of socialism. In most underdeveloped regions, socialism has emerged as the best hope of a decent future. Even allowing for the vastly increased tempo of historical change in the twentieth century, this global transformation is remarkable. But the translations of images into historical manifestations of socialism leave much to be desired. Wide discrepancies between classical ideals and contemporary enactments of socialism have cast serious doubt on the adequacy and relevance of its guiding principles and norms.

As a group, plain Marxists responded to the inner crisis of faith by gradually discarding classical definitions of socialism and adopting communist norms, exchanging the historical quest for a just society for larger myths of hope and consolation. However futile, the retreat to utopian vantage points, which plain Marxists took relatively late in comparison to other Western intellectuals, testifies to the shrinkage of viable critical and historical terrain. Doubtless the multiple failures of socialist experiments provide good grounds for skepticism, doubt, even disbelief. The conventional minimum definition of socialism, as public ownership and planned production for use rather than for profit, has thus far been an insufficient guide to the construction of new societies. This organizing principle of economic society has not permitted men anywhere to achieve fully what Stanley Moore terms the "negative" goal of revolution in the twentieth century—the abolition of exploitation and the elimination of social classes.[3]

In its early forms, as the Soviet experience suggests, central planning in the economic sphere entailed the construction of a vast, impersonal bureaucracy that became economically inefficient and technologically inadequate by the sixties. Controlled as they were by small political elites, bureaucratic organizations also frustrated democratic aspirations. After fifty years, the first socialist country had not moved very far in the direction of the classical goals of liberty, equality, and fraternity; in the process of creating a new organization of production and distribution, the Soviets failed to develop political and social institutions that facilitated enactment of the moral aims of socialism, not to mention the more ambitious goals of communism.[4] This experience, taken in conjunction with similar failures in Eastern Europe, enormous obstacles to modernization in underdeveloped countries, and the virtual collapse of radical visions in the West, raised deeper questions that people on the Left had been exploring in one form or another for more than a century.

Does the conventional minimum definition of socialism always compel the creation of new forms of excessive privilege in historical practice? Does it bring about the destruction of democratic hopes, the intensification of alienation, and the diminution of individual potentialities for a creative, satisfying life? If so, the basic socialist definition of the economic reordering of society is inherently incompatible with the realization of its social and moral aims. This abstract formulation of the ethical dimension of radical paradoxes, which goes beyond the issue of power and powerlessness, struck many as the final irony, the tragic end of an illusory search for just forms of social organization and human existence. It provided grounds for a variety of retreats from the socialist challenge—grounds for justifying the political status quo in the United States and the West, for rejecting all forms of political imagination in favor of a personal search for survival and meaning, and for embracing expressly religious visions of private and public salvation and doom.

Along with sectors of the new Left, the plain Marxists increasingly sought to attenuate the ethical paradoxes by widening the ethical parameters of radical vision. In the process of adapting the

Marxian vision of communism to contemporary conditions, they were able to raise the fundamental theoretical questions about the nature and historical failures of socialism that others had already posed and answered in various ways. I have argued that the plain Marxists pursued a false solution that finally obscured the problems and prospects of existing socialisms by reintroducing the impossible norms of a community beyond alienation into the radical vision of alternative societies. And furthermore, that sooner or later this response must provoke more profound crises of radical faith since the communist premises are even further removed from technical, economic, and social trends than ethical visions of socialism.

Questions about the future of socialism resist comprehensive answers precisely because it is an emergent historical phenomenon that has only begun to assume unpredicted and unpredictable shapes in every part of the world. New images and new manifestations will be fashioned in the contexts of differing cultures, national histories, geographical locations, and levels of technical and economic development. Obviously, no one can deduce the designs of the socialist future from even the best definition, and no one ought to try. Yet I find the temptation to conclude with a few speculations on the future of the socialist vision irresistible. More than a form of self-indulgence, such efforts constitute a practical necessity, for without some guiding notion, doubt turns into disbelief, pessimism becomes mere cynicism, and the need to act yields to resignation. A crisis of faith calls for a statement of faith, however qualified, problematic, and skeptical it must be.

Throughout this study, I have maintained that the minimum definition of socialism as public ownership under some form of planning is not inherently incompatible with reasonable versions of the larger political and moral aims of socialism. In fact, it is the precondition, the indispensable substratum, of a mature socialism. Let me, by way of summary, outline the reasons for maintaining this belief and suggest adjustments in vision and theory that the bitter experiences of this century require.

Public ownership and some mode of general planning still represent the best alternative to capitalist organization of complex, modern societies. It is true that advanced capitalist nations have already adopted elements of planning—and must adopt even more in the near future if they are to survive. But the division of wealth and power in these nations remains grossly inequitable; the planning primarily benefits the very wealthy and the moderately wealthy; and the dynamic thrust of the economy requires vast waste as well as a continuous, intensive campaign to expand private consumption of all sorts.

Nor does the postwar American experience add much weight to hopes for rapid change. The interests of private citizens seeking to protect and expand their wealth and income largely work against the progressive expansion of the welfare state. In such circumstances, relatively few individuals can be expected to develop a deep concern for the general welfare, for the interests of society as a whole.[5] And there are few institutional mechanisms of democracy that currently function to bring conflicting public and private interests into a politically progressive relationship.

Thus the mood of conservative resignation that followed the collapse of liberal hopes in the Kennedy years is solidly grounded in a recognition of important structural realities of American society. The familiar catalogue of social problems—poverty, deterioration of the environment, perpetuation of grossly unequal opportunities for various minorities—has been accepted in many quarters as a permanent condition. Neither the rational idea of government regulation nor the more antiquated and romantic notion of the spontaneous overflow of capitalist wealth as the antidote for poverty has worked very well.

Though some combination of these two strategies may ensure survival and perhaps even some progressive change, the idea of public ownership and planning remains a theoretically superior principle of economic organization. By eliminating specifically capitalist modes of wealth and privilege, a socialist reorganization of the economy would reduce the great distances between the very rich and the poor. It would also eliminate the capitalist mystique that these extremes are, if not altogether morally desirable, at least the result of generally fair competition.

There is clearly no guarantee that socialism, thus defined, would assure the full realization of equality and liberty. Quite the contrary. The dominant principle of socialism—"from each according to his ability, to each according to his work"—entails the emergence of a stratified society. It may be that since no one group will own the means of production, all classes will cease to exist in the classical Marxian sense of the term. But if everyone belongs to the "working class," then that category loses much of its functional meaning. The really interesting question is whether public ownership and planning can become the theoretical basis for developing institutions that will reduce inequality and expand liberty. The dynamic tensions between liberty and equality, between individual rights and society's responsibilities, require constant reworking because the varied institutional thrusts of both capitalist and socialist societies tend to diminish liberty while increasing inequality, and to narrow the scope of individual rights while widening the parameters of collective power. These, at any rate, are dominant tendencies that the mechanisms of democracy by themselves cannot offset. Whether the additional power of a free and educated citizenry in a socialist economic setting would achieve a satisfactory balance between equality and liberty is problematic, a slim historical possibility as opposed to the impossibility of enacting the communist vision. To put the issue conditionally, we can say that one index of a truly democratic socialism would be found in the existence of a dynamic tension between equality and liberty in which the ratios would change over time within tolerable limits.

I assume here a modified version of the character and relationship between equality and liberty that is at least implicit in the classical vision of socialism. By requiring structural and ideological connections between individual effort and reward, socialism presupposes the continuation of some form of the work ethic as well as a system of material incentives and differential rewards.

The existence of inequality of rewards precludes the establishment of perfect equality of opportunity. For even if great concentrations of wealth and power were dissolved, differential wages and specialized occupations would guarantee the formation of strata and the perpetuation of different moral, educational, and social environments. Yet one decisive advantage of socialism over capitalism lies in the possibility of substantially reducing the extremes of inequality through economic reorganization. Socialist governments can prohibit the formation of large concentrations of private capital, they can impose severe inheritance taxes, and they can reduce staggering disparities in income by regulating maximum and minimum parameters on wages and by establishing a sharply graduated income tax. Each of these measures contributes to the reduction of inequality.

The vague outlines of a society characterized by public ownership and planning thus include strata with fluid boundaries and a higher degree of equality of opportunity and rewards than existed in previous bourgeois societies. With the capacity for planning, such a society should be able to allocate increasingly large amounts of money for social services to cover the minimal needs of all.[6] And it would theoretically be in a position to make rational choices between private and public consumption on the one side and investment for future needs on the other. As I have suggested in the chapters on Baran and Sweezy, the idea of rigid central planning proved not only economically cumbersome—even potentially disastrous—at a certain point in socialist development; it also required from the outset the virtual abolition of democracy and the curtailment of individual initiative and autonomy in the spheres of production and consumption, work and leisure. The illusion of social orchestration through central planning turned into the reality of regimentation and a new concentration of excessive power at the top. Planners enacted the dictates of the most powerful elite of the party.

Thus, to prevent self-perpetuating elites from monopolizing power through political control rather than outright ownership of the economy, a fully developed socialism must be democratic. Genuinely rational and humane planning cannot be total planning that subverts any plausible version of the socialist ideal of liberty. In the economic realm, liberty entails at least the introduction of features of market planning. At the highest levels, planners may formulate basic goals; but beyond this, there must be flexibility at every lower level of production and consumption if socialist citizens are to exercise a tolerable degree of choice—not only of products but of career and general style of life as well. Because it can help to ensure a large measure of personal freedom, the substitution of market planning for tight central planning represents a crucial turning point in the development of socialist democracy.

But not necessarily a decisive one. Even if a flexible system of planning introduces some institutional checks on arbitrary excesses of power, lacking in the old Stalinist model, such a system implies that important economic choices with far-reaching political implications will continue to be made by small groups at the summit of political and economic hierarchies. In a stratified socialist society, then, there will obviously be a tendency for too much power to collect at higher levels, unless a counterbalancing system of participatory and representative democracy can be devised. If liberty entails a measure of inequality expressed in differential rewards and fluid strata, social inequality requires a political and legal system that guarantees a high degree of democracy.

I am inclined, doubtless partly because of ingrained cultural biases, to regard participatory democracy as a desirable goal and representative institutions as a necessary means in nonauthoritarian modern societies. Though vague, the idea of participatory democracy implies the widest possible involvement of people in shaping the public decisions that affect their lives. Since socialist citizens need access to a broad range of information and opinion in order to arrive at reasonable choices, there must be freedom of the press and freedom of assembly. Without this base of freedom, a representative system, which lacks the virtues of direct democracy, cannot effectively offset the concentrations of power and influence inevitable in any stratified society. Similarly, without a representative system, including mechanisms of periodic review and recall, no amount of enlightenment and participation can be effectively translated into public policy in complex societies.

The model of a democratic socialist society I have outlined thus includes a vast maze of conflicting group interests that can be satisfactorily resolved only through democratic mechanisms. Moreover, in a pluralistic society with a high degree of conflict and many centers of power, individuals need to be protected by and from potentially repressive larger units through a fair legal system and an extensive set of personal and political rights. A socialist citizen must have the public right to participate in political decisions affecting him and the personal right to a private life free from the fear of political intimidation. It would be pointless, even contradictory, to attempt a precise characterization of the specific parts of liberty and equality in the socialist equation. If for no other reason than that important questions concerning the tolerable limits of dissent and action within a socialist society must be the subject of continuing debate, the specific ratios between personal and social rights cannot be established in advance for all situations.

The vision of societies characterized by public ownership and planning, social strata that resemble classes, and political democracy may strike contemporary radicals as meager and atavistic, not worth pursuing. Compared to images of a *Gemeinschaft* community without alienation, this vision of socialism is surely a conservative one. In fact, a democratic socialism, as classical Marxists acknowledged, would resemble capitalism more than communism. It would provide for a large measure of individualism and perpetuate a system of material incentives, thereby preserving the work ethic in some modified form. Such a modest vision of democratic socialism is consistent with Barrington Moore's notion of a "decent society." This conception, Moore writes, "means no more than the elimination of that portion of human misery caused by the workings of social institutions. The historically recurring forms of suffering due to such causes can be grouped very roughly under the headings of war, poverty, injustice, and persecution for the holding of unorthodox opinions."[7] In a decent society, every individual ought to be guaranteed the prerequisites to freedom: an adequate diet, clothing, commodious housing; full medical care; education to the limits of his desires and abilities; and the opportunity to perform useful work and to pursue creative leisure. Beyond this, every individual ought to be encouraged (though not required) to have a part in decisions that determine the character of his several environments—his neighborhood, his place of work, his community and the wider society as well. Furthermore, each man should be free to develop and express his own views fully, without fear of punitive measures by a collective entity.

It is equally important to recognize the limitations of democratic socialism. Such a mode of social organization cannot ensure resolution of all major public problems. The vast destruction and deformation of human energies resulting from racism and the oppression of women cut across social systems. So do the myriad difficulties of achieving a balanced ecology at advanced levels of technology. No mere reordering of social institutions can automatically exorcise these public dilemmas. In the past, socialists surely claimed too much, arguing that the abolition of capitalist institutions would negate all human vices and obviate the motives for antisocial behavior: socialism was considered a patent social medicine for curing poverty, racism, crime, the evils of mass culture, and the oppression of women. Such perspectives have enabled detractors to claim that the presence of, say, racism in both modes of society provides sufficient grounds for rejecting the centrality of the controversy over the relative merits of capitalism and socialism. It does nothing of the sort. Such counterarguments only expose the naïveté of earlier claims about the curative values of socialism. A more credible position must include some estimate of *which* forms of human misery socialism might either eliminate or considerably reduce. Despite the sobering defeats of this century, I think it can still be plausibly maintained that the abolition of capitalist economic institutions and the establishment of genuine democracy would substantially improve the social environment in which the struggle against long-standing modes of oppression might occur. The creation of democratic socialist institutions would change the dominant forms of social oppression, eliminate dire poverty, and considerably reduce the pervasive economic dimensions of racism and sexism. Similarly, mechanisms of planning would permit a more rational approach to the preservation of the environment and to the allocation of scarce resources.

The inability of democratic socialism to remove the social causes of human misery guarantees the persistence of what Mills termed "private troubles," for the major public issues of racism, sexism, and the quality of the environment all intersect the personal sphere. Moreover, the notion of a democratic socialist society includes no provisions for eradicating a broad panoply of private troubles not directly attributable to social causes. The trauma of birth and the fear of death will continue to circumscribe every life even in a socialist society. In between, the painful search for personal coherence and meaning, the evanescence of success and the tragedy of individual failure, and the fragile, transient character of personal relationships will persist, ensuring a wide range of possibilities for individual happiness and misery. Of course, a new social context should alter the nature and intensity of the forms of human unhappiness. For instance, death may be less intolerable when it comes at the end of a fulfilled life. Similarly, the pain of personal failure would surely be dulled (but not obliterated) if there were adequate support systems for providing new opportunities for different kinds of achievement at various junctures of a person's life.

Thus, while socialism would very probably reduce the sources and manifestations of misery, it cannot be expected to guarantee the happiness of individuals. Happiness cannot be directly legislated into any social system. As I have argued, plain Marxists and other utopians in the radical tradition did not acknowledge this important constraint on politics and social organization. Their projections of happiness as a constituent quality of a community beyond society are mythical illusions that obscure the more limited real political choices within and between social systems. The ultimate ethical paradox of radical thought is that the pursuit of equality and fraternity in the form of a community without alienation must lead, in practice, to the suppression of liberty. This consequence strikes me as sufficient reason for abandoning politics and social organization as primary vehicles of the utopian quest for happiness.

A refutation of utopian variants of Marxism does not, however, dispose of the troublesome problems subsumed under the general heading of "fraternity." Granted, the image of happiness in a community beyond alienation is an impossible dream. We must nevertheless ask whether the achievement of greater equality and liberty in the matrix of a planned economy would necessitate giving up the search for the social, cooperative aspects of classical and contemporary notions of socialism. There are no clear answers, because this question raises a number of imponderable issues. Surely, none of the structural forms consistent with the basic premises of democratic socialism guarantees the emergence of wholly new modes of consciousness, new patterns of belief and feeling that stress collective values and the experience of solidarity. In fact, the image of a stratified democratic socialist society entails the continuance of multiple tensions between the one and the many. Even if the limited Marxian notion of alienation were accepted as a point of departure, the felt experience of alienation would persist because of the continuing need for specialized labor. Nor do the possible structures of democratic socialist society create more than minimal moral imperatives of cooperation. In both capitalist and socialist modes of organization, the social character of production creates vast networks of human interdependence. But the fact that an individual is inescapably woven into the web of society does not ensure the emergence of a social conscience and consciousness.

Yet I do not consider this incomplete dimension of democratic socialism fatal to the vision. The problem of creating a core of shared assumptions, of building moral and cultural contexts in which individuals may transcend their isolation, is endemic to any industrial or postindustrial society. It is true that the institutional and ideological frameworks of a democratic socialist society would not lend themselves to the establishment of strong, organic links between the individual and the social whole. Myriad forms of alienation would persist. The majority of interpersonal transactions would be carried out more or less impersonally. Large areas of asocial interior freedom and indeterminate patterns of public behavior are part of this notion of democratic socialism. These features represent the price of abandoning the utopian strain of Marxism: the establishment of a dynamic tension between liberty and equality in a planned economy entails a suspension of the quest for an organic community encompassing every individual.

Democratic socialism does, however, promise a new range of institutional possibilities for cultivating essentially social virtues. The persistence of utopian myths of community testifies to the continuing desire of individuals to overcome loneliness, boredom, and isolation. Nothing in the vision of democratic socialism precludes a new range of efforts at cooperation. Indeed, the quest for community should continue—between individuals, in small groups, and in experimental living arrangements. As long as these efforts are voluntary and are conducted on relatively small human scales, they remain consistent with the principles of the sort of democratic socialism I am advocating.

But communities cannot be legislated into existence. Nor can they be permanently institutionalized once they appear, since they have lives of their own: they come into existence, live, and die out mysteriously. Both in historical and personal terms, the experience of community is momentary. No one can fully explain, let alone arrange, the symbolic community of author and reader, the beauty of a moment of personal integration and peace, the intimacy of two lovers, the formation of the subtle bonds of friendship, or the complex emotional and intellectual sinews of a group pursuing common objectives. Such phenomena lie beyond the direct control of social planners. Indeed, the principles of a democratic socialist society imply definite limits to political activity and social organization: there can be no large-scale, involuntary sacrifice of liberty in the quest for happiness. If the limits of political imagination and action are not respected, the rights of individuals will be capriciously violated. This is the clear implication of the utopian heresy in radical thought that we have been examining—an implication which the conception of democratic socialism must avoid, even at the cost of accepting levels and zones of personal and social anarchy. A society organized around genuinely socialist principles must accommodate people who may never become socialists. To be sure, the quest for fraternity must occur within social space. And the institutional and ideological structures of a society do facilitate or retard the enactment of small communities. Yet in the abstract design of the main contours of an open-ended democratic socialism, the shape, tone, and texture of the parts are better left blank. These must be filled in, well or badly, by real people.

Doubtless this image of socialism goes against the grain of traditional radical assumptions concerning the nature of man. Major figures in the Marxian tradition, beginning with Marx himself, have spun out heroic images of a marvelous breed of new men. "Man," according to the rhapsodic projection of Trotsky, "will become immeasurably stronger, wiser and subtler. . . . The average human type will rise to the heights of an Aristotle, a Goethe, a Marx. And above this ridge, new peaks will arise."[8] Such notions of the nearly limitless perfectibility of man depended upon the possibility of a social evolution from society to community that, as I have insisted throughout this study, lies beyond the scope of current historical possibilities. At the same time, the vision of a historically possible democratic socialism, which strikes me as the most optimistic and humane projection of social organization, implies outer limits to engineering—limits that clearly preclude the social formation of substantially new men. Previous radical arguments concerning the plasticity of human character rested on the assumption that the perfection of man ultimately required the transcendence of social and historical barriers, even though the beginnings of the transition to a new consciousness could be made under capitalism (by a few) and under socialism (by a larger number). Without engaging the subtleties of the issue here, I merely wish to suggest that the narrow band of possibilities in the relevant future determines the limits of that portion of human nature which can be manifested in history. The framework of democratic socialism would permit the fullest development of man's creative potentialities without negating his unique, individual character. Even though no social system can eliminate the capacity for subtle and overt forms of destruction—of self and others—democratic socialism should diminish the forms and degrees of violence in society.

Far from representing a flaw in the socialist vision, the absence of a new breed of mythic figures is a positive feature. Neither the builders nor the inhabitants of a more humane society need to possess a radically different *nature*. The old men possess all the talents and qualities necessary to attempt a more rational social organization. However long the odds against political success may be, the venture nevertheless lies within the framework of human possibility. These essentially conservative insights into the limits of political imagination and action—which explode the myth of the unlimited perfectibility of man—add clarity to the socialist vision, giving it a contemporary plausibility and vitality.

After the decline of faith in the power of liberal approaches to capitalist reform in the fifties and after the utopian excesses of radicals in the sixties, this search for usable elements in the tradition of conservative thought should come as no surprise. After all, Marxism is in many ways an essentially conservative outlook. Or, to put the matter more precisely, the utopian cure to the human condition that Marx posited on occasion could proceed only from a deep recognition of the continuities of history and consciousness. Recognizing above all that the past always haunts the present, Marx had to posit a quantum leap beyond history into a new realm of freedom if his mythic men were ever to materialize. Knowing that such a leap is impossible in the light of twentieth-century experience, socialists are forced to examine once again the conservative underpinnings of Marxism and to work within the limitations that history imposes on human nature. Robert Heilbroner suggests that "however purified of apologetics, there remains a tincture of regret in conservatism."[9] Perhaps so, but I see no compelling reason to fear employing major insights from this tradition if they help to separate radical hopes from radical fantasies. Besides, the recent mood of radical conservatism grows organically out of an examination of radical theory and politics of the past half century. It is a possible, even a sensible, response to radical paradoxes. For the tropism of utopian critics and new Leftists toward myths of man and community ends in the sort of failure that implicitly suggests the wisdom of acknowledging the conservative dimension of Marxian socialism as a promising point of departure.

Radical Paradoxes Once More

I have suggested that the minimum definition of socialism as public ownership with comprehensive planning is not inherently incompatible with the larger aims of individual freedom and democracy within a context of greater equality of opportunity and rewards. Yet this formulation leaves open the crucial and probably unanswerable question of whether the aims of democratic socialism are in permanent historical conflict with the material conditions for its enactment. The affirmative arguments are at best dubious. On a global scale, the most abstract version of the radical paradox of powerlessness seems intact: nowhere have men been able to reorganize institutions and reform themselves in the image of democratic socialism. Must we then conclude that this alternative—like the vision of communism—is just another myth, a figment of the political imagination?

Cast in such a grandiose, global form, the problem is clearly unmanageable. If it cannot be conquered, however, the question may at least be divided into less formidable parts. To begin with, I would not claim universal relevance for democratic socialism. Throughout most parts of the third world, debates over the issues of democratic socialism amount to a luxury. In India and China, in Cuba and Haiti, in Tanzania and the Congo, the immediate issues concern survival and growth, not the creation of socialist democracy. If these nations are to escape the cruel legacy of underdevelopment and misdevelopment, they require some form of socialism involving a massive mobilization of institutions and human energies to satisfy the basic needs for food, clothing, shelter, and medical care. These efforts assume a variety of institutional shapes —from the Tanzanian ujamaa to the Chinese communes to variants of military socialism found in such diverse places as Peru and Syria.

Considered abstractly, all these collectivist strategies for survival and development involve the creation of authoritarian structures of power that in their initial stages subvert the political criteria of democratic socialism. But I do not consider it useful merely to condemn these efforts as authoritarian modes of collectivism. Surely authoritarian socialisms remain vastly preferable to misery, anarchy, and mass starvation; to their credit, plain Marxists grasped this stark alternative that nearly two billion people now encounter. Furthermore, as I have suggested in the chapters on Baran and Sweezy, there are important discriminations to be made among authoritarian modes of socialism, choices between the harsh forms of Stalinism and the milder modes of Maoism. In cases where survival entails the mobilization of mass energy, the social possibilities for individual expression must be sharply reduced to ensure the full public participation of each able member of society. The principal moral criteria of such political arrangements must center on the kinds and degrees of coercion employed to solve elemental economic and social problems. The orchestration of human energies in such circumstances should be primarily social and ideological rather than physical. And in matrices of underdevelopment, all forms of coercion should be kept at minimum levels—at a point no higher than necessary to accomplish the basic social objectives that assure individual survival. Though dictatorships exclude the establishment of full democracy, they need not entail the abrogation of legal protections for individuals.

No one can say whether the imperatives of survival, which result in authoritarian configurations of power, will permanently impede the emergence of democratic socialisms throughout the third world. At this point, though, the chances for democracy seem remote, if only because of the enormous obstacles to securing the essentials of a decent life. Moreover, in the process of modernization, antidemocratic institutions can be expected to take on a momentum of their own, a capacity to survive even when no longer economically imperative. Different modes of social organization and consciousness will emerge from different socialisms in underdeveloped countries. Perhaps more cooperative sorts of people will be molded by enforced collective patterns of work and living. Even so, the basic issues of social organization will persist, and at some juncture the enlarged possibilities for individual freedom resulting from development must be dealt with. Here as elsewhere, the exigencies of the past and present may preclude a democratic future. Without authoritarian socialism as a beginning point, however, most nations of the third world will not have the opportunity to fashion even limited modes of democracy and personal freedom that masses of people can use. Though it may yet become a relevant long-range goal, then, democratic socialism is surely not on the immediate agenda in most regions of the third world.

In the relatively advanced socialist nations, the chances of achieving democratic socialism seem less remote. But there, too, the past dominates the present in countless ways, strengthening the belief that the legacy of Stalinism may never be fully overcome. Clearly, the two-stage evolutionary model of transition from authoritarian to democratic socialism espoused and later discarded by Sweezy has proved simplistic. Economic development and education have not combined to produce a democratic socialism in the U.S.S.R. and the nations of Eastern Europe. It is true that important gains in the area of liberty have been registered, however unevenly, since the death of Stalin. Yet no country has designed a successful strategy for democracy. In Czechoslovakia, the first major attempt to establish socialist democracy was summarily crushed. And the entire Yugoslav experiment of workers' control unfolds within the framework of an essentially one-party state. It also remains a fragile probing, subject to the divisive cultural currents of such groups as the Serbs, Croats, Slovenes, and Montenegrins.

Despite all this, however, structural trends toward market socialism and intensified pressures for the extension of democracy and civil liberties should continue. Rather than specifying various sociologies of change or constructing predictive models of democratization, I want to stress the more modest claim that democratic socialism is the most appropriate political myth in these transitional societies. Unlike the idea of communism, which either conceals harsh current realities or, even worse, justifies needless oppression, the model of democratic socialism has become a useful ideal in countries where the battle for survival has been waged successfully following a reorganization of the economy. In the Soviet Union and the nations of Eastern Europe, democratic socialism represents the social and political side of a disciplined dialectic of liberation, for its principles are consistent with their material and structural potentialities.

To put the matter conditionally, then, if the relatively advanced Communist nations are to approach Barrington Moore's criteria of a decent society, they must achieve social forms and states of consciousness consistent with the principles of democratic socialism. That there is a chance of enacting this model in history reduces the paradox of powerlessness—or partial power—to a genuinely political problem, however massive. Even though it may ultimately prove inadequate, belief in democratic socialism need not lead immediately to a politically self-defeating resignation, despair, and nihilism characteristic of the *Gemeinschaft* notion of community used as the visionary core of a radical politics. Moreover, the vision of democratic socialism somewhat attenuates the ethical dimensions of radical paradoxes because the principles of individual liberty and democracy remain worthwhile values within contexts of semi-affluent, semi-authoritarian socialisms. Freed from the illusions of a perfect society and an infinitely perfectible man, people can attempt to exercise these values immediately, since liberty always requires both defense and extension. And they can simultaneously be employed as goals of a just society that may or may not be fully attainable, even in the long run.

These speculative comments should not be taken as a facile formula for *resolving* radical paradoxes in advanced socialist nations. Far from it. Democratic socialists exist precariously, as minorities; lacking anything like dominant power, they must confront a series of hard and often hazardous political and personal choices. The elements of radical paradoxes persist, as they must in any modern social environment. But the myth of democratic socialism provides reasonable grounds for hope, with a moral base for pursuing those aspects of human liberation which fall within the parameters of the political imagination.

I would also press, in tentative ways, a similar claim for the value of the model of democratic socialism in Western nations, particularly in the United States. Despite its obvious shortcomings as a political orientation, this vision seems to be as compelling as ever; at the very least, it is compelling in the absence of serious alternatives. Yet it is doubtful whether some version of democratic socialism can form the controlling ideological core of a viable Left politics in America during the seventies and eighties.

For one thing, many radicals do not accept the limitations on the political imagination that make the principles of democratic socialism the most desirable basis of social organization in relatively developed nations. It would be reassuring but wrong to contend that the radical debacle of the sixties after its extended bout with utopian fever ended in a clear recognition that democratic socialism represents the only political alternative and social ideal worth seeking. The new radicalism of the sixties was but one expression of diverse currents of belief—or the quest for belief—in the political usefulness of essentially religious and aesthetic fictions. This search for identity and community, for a sense of self in a harmonious social matrix, went beyond the symbolic parameters of democratic socialism. Moreover, the theoretical drift from political theory to utopian myth, exhibited by the plain Marxists, was in large measure a similar response to frustrations attending previous political defeats of socialism. (Both Baran and Marcuse had witnessed, at first hand, the failure of European social democracy in the thirties.) Thus those who went through the postwar American experience without much historical awareness—principally the young—rejected democratic socialism because it was not a moving ideal, an organizing myth that mitigated their alienation. And those who knew the history of the Left in Europe and America classified democratic socialism as a bankrupt ideal, if only because it was associated with a politics of betrayal and defeat—or at best with political activity with highly ambiguous results. In a word, democratic socialists had never achieved sufficient power to enact their vision.

We thus encounter radical paradoxes once more. The experiences of the sixties, however, have altered the specific forms of these paradoxes. Though the cautionary lessons illustrated by the plain Marxists and the militant sectors of the new Left do not imply an alternative politics of transition, it would be foolish to minimize their importance. If nothing else, the defeat of utopian visions of a community beyond society enables people to confront the problems and prospects of socialist politics directly, without the handicaps of debilitating illusions of a wholly new kind of man and social organization. The choice of social myths always affects the outcome of political activity. In the case of the utopians, the communist myth compelled failure. Similarly, pursuit of the model of democratic socialism may ultimately end in political defeat. But the result is not preordained. That makes the crucial difference.

Although the chances of piecing together a viable political coalition at the national level seem bleak at present, the need for a vision of democratic socialism as the only sane alternative to monopoly capitalism is clearer than ever. The sort of democratic socialism I have outlined is consistent with a number of major cultural premises held by the majority of Americans. It includes the work ethic, though under conditions of full or nearly full employment. It permits limited forms of competition without allowing small groups to amass great fortunes. As a loosely stratified society, democratic socialism preserves a measure of social mobility. It could also extend the forms and substance of democracy. And with the considerable reduction in military spending that such a system should entail, as well as the availability of larger sums for collective spending due to the breakup of large concentrations of wealth, it would be possible to begin massive assaults on major social ills through a revitalized public sector.

Yet there is no use in pretending that the major obstacles to achieving democratic socialism in the United States have been cleared away, even though many have shed earlier radical illusions. True, there are now elements of a potential Left-liberal coalition to be found among blacks, chicanos, women, the poor, the young, parts of the working class, and the relatively small conscience constituency of professionals. But at the national level, these groups display neither political unity nor adequate organizational modes to extend substantially the welfare state in the coming years, not to mention the capacity to move very far in the direction of democratic socialism. The coalition that Senator McGovern managed to put together in 1972, using the vehicle of the Democratic Party, was twenty-five years too late in terms of the social needs of this nation. Yet in practical terms it was probably ten years too early. The massive opposition among European ethnics and other voters from middle America underscored the current disparity of perceived interests among the various groups that might someday comprise a democratic socialist coalition.

Consider, for example, the issue of work. The current organization of the American economy does not provide anything like full employment. And yet the work ethic survives in modified forms among large sectors of the population. Working people resent paying taxes to support those who cannot find employment. More often than not, the unemployed feel a deep sense of personal inadequacy and failure largely enforced by their economic status. The issue is magnified by the fact that a sizable minority of young people now reject the idea of work as a mode of achieving self-respect, at least for a brief period in their lives. Within the framework of generally accepted assumptions about capitalism as the best possible mode of economic organization—or the least odious —there is ample space for endless political controversy among the economically disenfranchised, the working poor, and the more affluent sectors of the old and new working class. Forced into an endless game of political mirrors by his liberal ideology, McGovern shifted positions on welfare and tax reform with depressing regularity, precisely because he assumed that substantive progress could be made within the matrix of advanced capitalism—without affecting the current corporate system or the specific mechanisms for dividing the spoils within it.

Such a program, then, has obvious—perhaps fatal—political drawbacks. Just now there is considerable opposition to the enlargement of public spending which will probably become more entrenched over the next several years. Divisions along racial, ethnic, and class lines remain intense. Many carry on the search for solutions to the problems of alienation through nonpolitical ideologies and strategies of action—strategies that may conflict with the principles of democratic socialism. The massive cynicism about politics and politicians has the effect of strengthening the status quo. Disaffected people vacillate between moods of rebellion and resignation.

In fact, then, the paradox of powerlessness remains in effect.

Even the vision of democratic socialism, a historically possible alternative to advanced capitalism, seems to be a distant political possibility. And the view that a series of minor victories will culminate in the achievement of socialism has thus far not been lavishly substantiated. Thus the danger of abandoning those utopian formulations of radical paradoxes which lead to sectarianism lies in being swept toward a gradual acceptance and justification of existing structures of power. This danger increases when political power is pursued realistically—within and at the fringes of the existing system—in the name of what appears to be a reasonable vision of a more just society.

Despite these perils, and despite the narrow chances of building a democratic socialist society in the end, I believe that the vision remains the best moral basis from which to pursue public and political activity. Even if the ultimate consequence is failure to achieve a more humane social organization, the principles of democratic socialism allow individuals to work toward the reduction of public problems that overarch both social orders. As a system, capitalism retards progress against imperialism, racism, poverty, and the oppression of women. But it does not preclude a decent struggle against the tragic waste of human resources, a struggle with limited gains here and there.

This is, admittedly, a conclusion reached largely by default. Like the plain Marxists, I do not know how to participate in building a viable political Left. One thing is clear: there is no point in affiliating with any political, cultural, or religious sect dedicated to total revolution. For even if revolution is the only *theoretical* answer to the irrationalities of the American economic and social order, it is not, I am convinced, a practical option in the medium-range. "Total" questions yield partial, incomplete answers at best, as this study of the plain Marxists and the new Left clearly demonstrates. When measured against its human talent and material resources, capitalism has clearly failed. It maintains itself economically by militarism and its distinctive brand of imperialism, as well as by a cult of consumership whose absurd and destructive aspects should by now be apparent to all. Its dominant political and cultural styles are characterized more by slick salesmanship than by critical intelligence and concern for human welfare. It treats it own racial and impoverished minorities callously, responding primarily to threats and pressure if it responds at all.

It has surely failed the test of reason. More important, however, it has survived. No doubt oligopolistic capitalism has historical limits, but beyond this general prediction not much can be known. One of the continuous theoretical responsibilities of intellectuals on the Left is to define the system's potential breaking points. Such exercises are both necessary and highly problematic—necessary because without a transcendent vision, radicals are swept inexorably toward existing centers of power; problematic because it is like charting the map of an unknown country whose contours must be in part discovered, in part created.

It is therefore pointless to *act* as if the boundaries were firmly fixed or even clearly in sight. To focus exclusively on the undefinable limits of the system impairs the critical ability to assess its political and cultural possibilities and to play an active part in bringing them to pass. It may be that we are moving helplessly toward a kind of semimilitary authoritarianism. Still, it takes a special kind of madness to opt out of politics or, worse, to hope for a national disaster as a dialectical prelude to a cleansing revolution. Even if the apocalyptic imagination turns out to have been prophetic, the quest for utopian communism would nevertheless remain a destructive fiction in the America of the seventies and after. Considered as a whole, the present economic and social order is irrational. It may be theoretically dissected and condemned, but not changed as a whole all at once. People, after all, live and act in the parts of society, and it may be that we can change these parts—and even ourselves—significantly. This is a possibility as opposed to a series of utopian illusions. What more can we ask?

NOTES

1 Radical Paradoxes

1. The substitution of myth for clear historical analysis was a relatively slow process that did not gain full momentum until the middle sixties. It applies more fairly to what might be called the "new" new Left—Jerry Rubin, Abbie Hoffman, and rhetoricians of the apocalypse such as the Weathermen—than to the "old" new Leftists: to the early Tom Hayden and those involved in the formation of SDS and in the Mississippi summers, as well as to part of the *Studies on the Left* group. For a more extensive discussion, see Chapter 7, "The New Left."

2. See, for example, *Studies on the Left* between 1961 and 1965; and Massimo Teodori, ed., *The New Left: A Documentary History* (Indianapolis: Bobbs-Merrill, 1969).

3. Of course, not all Left intellectuals were infatuated. An informative account may be found in Daniel Aaron, *Writers on the Left* (New York: Harcourt Brace Jovanovich, 1961), Chapter 5, "Russia with (without) Rapture," pp. 119–48.

4. Examples: the expulsion of the anti-Stalinist opposition, the deportation of Trotsky, and the brutal collectivization of peasants in the late twenties; the contrived mass trials, Soviet policy toward Spain, and the pact with Hitler in the thirties; and finally the forced march to socialism in most of Eastern Europe during the first years of cold war. (These actions, of course, should not be measured against the fixed notion that the Soviet Union is either above criticism or beneath contempt. Each requires separate consideration and judgment.)

5. The most able account of the lapse of American socialism into sectarianism and political marginality is James Weinstein, *The Decline of Socialism in America: 1912–1925* (New York and London: Monthly Review Press, 1967).

6. Christopher Lasch, *The Agony of the American Left* (New York: Alfred A. Knopf, 1969), p. 40.

7. "In the conditions of the 1930s the surprising fact is that the influence of Marxism, or of any socialist ideas, was so slight, and that the radical movement had so little success either in approaching its immediate objectives or in establishing itself as a permanent force in American politics. The need for a 'third party' was often asserted, and from 1933 onwards there were many attempts to create a new radical party, inspired largely by the success of the Farmer-Labor Party in Minnesota and of the Progressive Party in Wisconsin. These efforts culminated in a Third Party Conference in Chicago in July 1935, but they proved vain." T. B. Bottomore, *Critics of Society* (New York: Pantheon Books, 1968), p. 45.

8. Ibid., p. 88.

9. Considering that Marxism is primarily a mode of interpreting historical process, the absence of a sophisticated historian among the independent old Left intellectuals is curious. It is probably due in part to the impact of the cold war on the American academy, and in part to the barely disguised anti-intellectualism of the old Left.

10. There is no sustained attempt here to undertake a thorough study of the specific *influences* of these individuals on the new Left organizations and publications. I rather intend to show how several fading stars of the old Left *illuminated* the main trajectories of the new radicalism during the 1960s.

11. American radicalism, of course, includes social designs other than socialism (anarchism, for example). In characterizing socialism as an acceptable solution to radical paradoxes, I imply no more than an indirect argument—namely, that *if* a mild form of socialism (including public ownership of the decisive means of production, a democratization of power, and a host of welfare measures) has been politically impossible, *then* more far-reaching schemes have, *ipso facto,* also lacked an effective political base.

12. For an interesting examination of the psychological implications of "paradox," see Paul Watzlawick et al., *Pragmatics of Human Communication* (New York: W. W. Norton & Co., 1967), pp. 187–256. I use "paradox" in the general sense of "a contradiction that follows correct deduction from consistent premises" (p. 188). Depending on the specific formulation and resolution in question, radical paradoxes can be seen as a series of "dilemmas." I use these terms more or less interchangeably, though Watzlawick suggests a useful distinction: "The most important distinction between contradictory

[i.e., dilemmas] and paradoxical injunctions is that in the face of a contradictory injunction, one chooses one and loses, or suffers, the other alternative. The result is not a happy one. . . . But . . . choice is logically possible. The paradoxical injunction, on the other hand, *bankrupts choice itself,* nothing is possible, and a self-perpetuating oscillating series is set in motion" (p. 217). The nature of radical paradoxes enforces a deliberate ambiguity as between "paradox" and "dilemma."

13. C. Wright Mills, *White Collar* (New York: Oxford University Press, 1951), p. 157.

14. Herbert Marcuse, *One-Dimensional Man* (Boston: Beacon Press, 1964), p. xiii.

15. For an interesting though one-sided assessment, see Gabriel Kolko, "The Decline of American Radicalism in the Twentieth Century," *Studies on the Left* 6 (September–October 1966): 9–26. See also Daniel Bell, *Marxian Socialism in the United States* (Princeton, N.J.: Princeton University Press, 1967).

16. Barrington Moore, Jr., "On Rational Inquiry in Universities Today," *New York Review* 14 (April 23, 1970): 30. I do not intend "intellectual" to apply exclusively to a tiny stratum of professional social critics. I assume, rather, that everyone on the Left is an intellectual insofar as he attempts to analyze society, define values, and suggest political means of embodying social ends in history. Used in this way, the term does not define a social role, nor does it presuppose any particular level of competence.

17. There is a growing body of literature on the rediscovery of imperialism and its redefinition in the light of the American experience. Two studies of particular importance are Harry Magdoff, *The Age of Imperialism* (New York and London: Monthly Review Press, 1969), and William A. Williams, *The Roots of Modern American Empire* (New York: Random House, 1970). For an excellent account of America's counterrevolutionary role in the postwar world, see Richard J. Barnet, *Intervention and Revolution* (Cleveland: World Publ., 1968). A contrasting perspective on the main question of whether neoimperialism is a theoretically necessary aspect of advanced capitalism or a politically reversible policy can be found in Michael Harrington, *Socialism* (New York: Saturday Review Press, 1972), pp. 312 ff.

18. Harry Ashmore, "Where Have All the Liberals Gone?" *Center Magazine* 2 (July 1969): 34.

19. "A Massive Breakdown," *Newsweek* 76 (July 6, 1970): 27.

20. Lasch, *The Agony of the American Left*, p. 209.

21. Leszek Kolakowski, "The Conspiracy of Ivory Tower Intellectuals," in Arthur P. Mendel, ed., *Essential Works of Marxism* (New York: Bantam Books, 1961), p. 356.

2 The Argument

1. I do not mean to convey a comic-strip view of the cold war, pitting a mild, altruistic Soviet bear against the vicious American eagle. Still, the main responsibility for originating and prosecuting the cold war during its exclusively anti-Soviet phase and beyond rests with the United States. See D. F. Fleming's *The Cold War and Its Origins*, 2 vols. (New York: Doubleday & Co., 1961); and Gar Alperovitz, *Atomic Diplomacy: Hiroshima and Potsdam* (New York: Simon and Schuster, 1965). For an excellent recent critical view of revisionist interpretations of the cold war period, see Richard Maddox, *The New Left and the Cold War* (Princeton: Princeton University Press, 1973).

2. This is, of course, a debatable claim. By a socialist or proto-socialist economy, I mean no more than that the principal means of production are publicly owned (i.e., by the state, producers' cooperatives, etc.), and that differential wages are paid on the basis of differences in the quantity, quality, and complexity of work performed.

3. One result of the general decline of rationality in the 1960s was a thorough, often intentional confusion of the varieties of anti-Communism, and a caricature of the motives of men who held such positions during the first decade and a half of cold war. As Lewis Coser suggests, there are at least four meanings associated with the term: (1) anti-Communism may "refer to opposition to a political philosophy and a program for action developed by Lenin and his disciples"; (2) it may refer to anti-Stalinism; (3) it may refer to the "goals and ideology of American foreign policy ever since the late 40's"; and (4) anti-Communism may also designate a "flourishing racket," a mode of personal advancement used by many second-rate (and worse) academics, intellectuals, and publicists of the cold war. Such distinctions are crucial to any serious discussion of figures in the anti-Stalinist Left. The democratic socialists were anti-Leninist and anti-Stalinist; they lent qualified support to United States foreign policy after World War II; and they acted out of decent though doubtless in some instances mixed motives. For an interesting symposium on postwar anti-Communism (which includes Coser's remarks) see "Liberal Anti-Communism," *Commentary* 44 (September 1967): 31–79.

4. Independent intellectuals obviously resist neat classification. In the absence of a Left politics, they tended to affiliate with one (or more) journals that provided symbolic (and often real) intellectual communities. In the United States, the anti-Stalinists associated with *Dissent* refer to themselves as democratic socialists. But this term also belongs to others who value democracy while adopting a range of critical attitudes toward existing socialisms not usually found among writers in *Dissent*.

There were other influential figures in the non-sectarian Left prior to 1960—William A. Williams, I. F. Stone, and Carey McWilliams, for example—as well as the group loosely associated with *Liberation,* a pacifist journal founded in 1956 by A. J. Muste. Among its principal contributors were Dave Dellinger and Paul Goodman. My division of independent radicals into two main groups—the democratic socialists and the plain Marxists—is therefore neither an exhaustive nor an exclusive classification.

5. Irving Howe, "New Styles in 'Leftism,'" *Dissent* 12 (Summer 1965) : 323.

6. Irving Howe and Lewis Coser, "Images of Socialism," in *Voices of Dissent* (New York and London: Grove Press, 1958), p. 17.

7. See also Howe's essay on the New York intellectuals in *The Decline of the New* (New York: Harcourt Brace Jovanovich, 1970), especially pp. 229–30.

8. The fullest outlines of this position may be found in Michael Harrington, *Toward a Democratic Left* (New York: Macmillan Co., 1968), and *Socialism* (New York: Saturday Review Press, 1972).

9. Howe, "New Styles in 'Leftism,'" *Dissent* 12 (Summer 1965): 302. Howe also included the later Mills and Marcuse in this broad category of authoritarian Leftists. See his "Intellectuals and Russia," *Dissent* 6 (Summer 1959): 295–301 (an exchange between Howe and Mills); and "Herbert Marcuse or Milovan Djilas?" *Harper's* 239 (July 1969) : 84–92.

10. C. Wright Mills, *The Marxists* (New York: Dell Publishing Co., 1962), p. 98. Mills's category is clearly a preliminary and open-ended one. He proposes a diverse international collection of plain Marxists: Isaac Deutscher, Antonio Gramsci, Rosa Luxemburg, G. D. H. Cole, Georg Lukacs, Christopher Caudwell, Jean-Paul Sartre, William A. Williams, Paul Sweezy, Erich Fromm.

11. Stanley Moore, "Utopian Themes in Marx and Mao," *Dissent* 17 (March–April 1970): 170. This essay was initially published in

Sweezy's *Monthly Review* 21 (June 1969): 33–44. Moore's is the only piece ever to have appeared in both journals.

12. "The concept of class in Marxian theory is inseparable from the concept of exploitation. In societies where the means of production are owned by separate individuals, it is possible for one group to exploit another. A group of individuals whose ownership of the means of production enables them to appropriate products of others' labour is an exploiting class. A group of individuals whose use of the means of production involves appropriation of their products by members of an exploiting class is an exploited class. Variations in the specific relations of these two groups to the means of production distinguish the specific classes of the slave, feudal, and capitalist economic formations. On the other hand, in societies where the means of production are owned by the community as a whole, it is impossible for one group to exploit another; and such societies Marx calls classless. If there is exploitation there are classes, and if not not." Stanley Moore, *The Critique of Capitalist Democracy* (New York: Paine-Whitman, 1957), p. 22. Whether, and to what extent, existing socialist societies are classless, and hence have abolished (or significantly reduced) exploitation, is a widely debated question that each of the figures examined in the four subsequent chapters answers in his own way. See also Oskar Lange, "Marxian Economics and Modern Economic Theory," in Irving Howe, ed., *Essential Works of Socialism* (Bantam Books, 1971), pp. 717–35, especially 725–26 n.

13. Moore, "Utopian Themes in Marx and Mao," p. 171.

14. For an illuminating discussion of Marx's several positions on reform and revolution as modes of transition and their contemporary implications, see Stanley Moore, *Three Tactics: The Background in Marx* (New York: Monthly Review Press, 1963).

15. Note that in this context Marx uses the term "communist society" to cover all the postcapitalist stages of the transition to communism, whereas contemporary Communist Parties use socialism to describe the present period in selected parts of the world.

16. Marx, *Critique of the Gotha Programme,* in *Selected Works* (New York: International Publishers, 1933), Vol. II, p. 563.

17. Ibid., pp. 563–64.

18. Ibid., p. 563.

19. On this point, see Michael Harrington, *Socialism,* especially pp. 49–52. " 'Dictatorship' . . . defined the class basis of a society, not its political forms, and it did not necessarily imply the repression of civil liberties" (p. 51).

20. Marx, *Critique of the Gotha Programme,* Vol. II, p. 564.

21. Ibid. But the *quid pro quo* principle is only the dominant principle, not the sole one. Both socialist and nonsocialist societies allocate portions of their surplus to guarantee the satisfaction of basic needs to those unable to work.

22. Ibid., p. 565.

23. Ibid., p. 566.

24. With the exception of Marcuse, none of the plain Marxists I consider examines alienation in any detail, though each uses some version of the concept. For an interesting discussion of alienation considered as an inescapable human condition arising from the fact of conscious subjects separated from each other and the world, see Walter Weisskopf, *Alienation and Economics* (New York: E. P. Dutton & Co., 1971), especially Chapter 1. In Part I, I follow (without accepting) Marx's very different notion of alienation. It is, in his view, a historical condition—or a series of conditions—that can be cured only by a communist community. According to Marx, several modalities of alienation are conditioned by various forms of class society that must cope with degrees of scarcity. Each historical constellation reveals a diminished form of human potentiality. Just as a stick appears bent in water, alienated man is mutilated by virtue of his existence in the historical media of precommunist societies. Marx infers man's true human nature—his unalienated potentiality—from a succession of historical moments. To enact his potential human nature, as a social creature with individual characteristics, man must create a communist community. Nothing less will do. Since I regard this as historically impossible, I consider alienation, even in Marx's sense, incurable.

For an illuminating study of Marx's concept of alienation, see Bertell Ollman, *Alienation: Marx's Concept of Man in Capitalist Society* (London: Cambridge University Press, 1971).

25. Moore, "Utopian Themes in Marx and Mao," p. 171 (emphases added). "Historical" and "utopian," as used in this study, are relative terms with normative connotations. "Historical" refers to past and present social structures, to various phenomena considered under one or another sociology of change. Historically possible social schemes, then, must meet two criteria: (1) they must be materially and technically possible; and (2) they must be at least politically plausible. Social visions that do not satisfy these criteria are provisionally classed as "utopian." Of course the utopian proposals of one era may become realistic in another; and historically possible visions may become obsolete, or utopian, with the passing of time. Applications of these

terms to specific cases will necessarily be controversial, though throughout the text I attempt to defend the general propositions that varieties of socialism are historically possible and that a global community of unalienated men is not.

26. Ibid., p. 175.

27. Ibid. For discussions of the concepts of *Gemeinschaft* and *Gesellschaft,* see Ferdinand Tönnies, *Community and Society,* translated by C. P. Loomis (East Lansing: Michigan State Press, 1957); and Fritz Pappenheim, *The Alienation of Modern Man* (New York: Monthly Review Press, 1959), especially pp. 61–103. Throughout this study I use the concepts of *Gesellschaft* and *Gemeinschaft* as ideal types, limiting cases.

28. See Harrington, *Socialism,* for a full exposition of this position.

29. Ibid., pp. 66–70. Harrington traces the concept of "anti-socialist socialism," or nationalization of facets of the economy within authoritarian political frameworks, to Bismarck.

30. One obvious mode of exploitation persists in the U.S.S.R.: the portion of the product consumed by the Soviet elite over and above their share of labor. Moreover, it is difficult to measure the justice of a system of rewards (wages) for work in the absence of democratic control over portions of the product used for capital investment, welfare, and military purposes. For an estimate of the degree of exploitation in the U.S.S.R., see Howard Sherman, *Radical Political Economy* (New York: Basic Books, 1972), pp. 234–41. See also Lawrence Crocker, "Marx's Concept of Exploitation," *Social Theory and Practice* 2 (Fall 1972): 201–215.

31. I use the terms "underdevelopment" and "misdevelopment" more or less interchangeably to refer to poor nations traditionally victimized by various forms of Western imperialism. They are *underdeveloped* to the extent that they have been prevented from modernizing. They are *misdeveloped* to the extent that a network of internal class alliances and external capital distorts economic growth, perpetuating grossly unfair allocations of wealth among a tiny minority of the very rich, the slightly larger middle classes, and a vast majority of urban and rural poor.

32. Isaac Deutscher, *Ironies of History: Essays on Contemporary Communism* (New York: Oxford University Press, 1966), p. 120.

33. I do not define "democracy" narrowly by equating it with specific institutional arrangements (such as "free elections"), but rather broadly, to include a variety of norms, values, and institutions through which the largest possible number of citizens may participate

in important public decisions. Democracy thus refers to a range of methods of decision-making. It is *itself* a mode of power, but usually a dependent one that operates within larger structures of power.

See Carl Cohen, *Democracy* (Athens, Ga.: University of Georgia Press, 1971). For an important discussion of rights and responsibilities, see Michael Walzer, *Obligations: Essays on Disobedience, War, and Citizenship* (Cambridge, Mass.: Harvard University Press, 1970).

34. See V. I. Lenin, *The State and Revolution, Selected Works,* Vol. VII (New York: International Publishers, 1943), pp. 3–112.

3 C. Wright Mills: The Lone Rebel

1. C. Wright Mills, *The Sociological Imagination* (New York: Grove Press, 1961), pp. 6, 8.

2. Ralph Miliband, "C. Wright Mills," in G. William Domhoff and Hoyt B. Ballard, eds., *C. Wright Mills and THE POWER ELITE* (Boston: Beacon Press, 1968), p. 11.

3. Harvey Swados, "C. Wright Mills: A Personal Memoir," *Dissent* 10 (Winter 1963): 36. I am heavily indebted to Richard Gillam for providing extensive criticisms of earlier drafts of this chapter as well as for offering valuable bibliographical suggestions. His forthcoming critical biography, *C. Wright Mills: The Lone Rebel,* should be the standard work on Mills. See his preliminary study, "The Intellectual as Rebel: C. Wright Mills, 1916–1946" (unpublished M.A. thesis, Columbia University, 1969).

4. C. Wright Mills, "Comment on Criticism," in Domhoff and Ballard, *C. Wright Mills and THE POWER ELITE,* p. 249. Mills's work, as I suggest in the last section of this chapter, is finally influenced by the conflict between the pessimistic implications of his studies, and his desire to be optimistic about the future.

5. Irving Louis Horowitz suggests the full sweep of Mills's biographical-intellectual career in his introduction to *Power, Politics and People* (New York: Ballantine Books, Inc., 1963): "First, social philosophy and a full absorption in the classics of social studies; second, an intense period of empirical research in the middle forties; and third, an effort at combining these interests into a workable style of sociological reflection," pp. 2–3. This chapter is mainly concerned with the third phase of Mills's career.

6. Mills, "Diagnosis of Our Moral Uneasiness," *Power, Politics and People,* p. 332.

7. Mills, *The Sociological Imagination,* p. 174.

8. Barrington Moore, Jr., "The Society Nobody Wants," in Kurt H. Wolff et al., eds., *The Critical Spirit* (Boston: Beacon Press, 1967), p. 402.

9. Mills, *The Sociological Imagination,* p. 182.

10. In his essay "The Unfinished Writings of C. Wright Mills: The Last Phase," Irving Louis Horowitz quotes Mills on his view of the importance of power: "It has been said in criticism that I am too much fascinated by power. This is not really true. It is intellect I have been most fascinated by, and power primarily in connection with that. It is the power in the intellect and the power of intellect that most fascinates me—as a social analyst and cultural critic." *Studies on the Left* 3 (Fall 1963): 17.

11. Mills, *The New Men of Power* (New York: Kelley Publ., 1948), p. 3. For an earlier discussion of powerlessness, see Mills, "The Social Role of the Intellectual," originally published in *Politics* 1 (April 1944), and reprinted in Horowitz, *Power, Politics and People,* pp. 292–304.

12. Mills, "The New Left," *Power, Politics and People,* p. 255.

13. Mills, *White Collar* (New York: Oxford University Press, 1951), p. xv.

14. Ibid., p. xvi.

15. Ibid.

16. Ibid., pp. 353–54.

17. Ibid., p. 157.

18. Quoted in Domhoff and Ballard, "Comment on Criticism," *C. Wright Mills,* p. 243.

19. Mills, *The Power Elite* (New York: Oxford University Press, 1956), pp. 3–4. The best collection of critiques of *The Power Elite* from several perspectives—especially pluralist and Marxist—is Domhoff and Ballard, *C. Wright Mills.*

20. Mills, *The Power Elite,* pp. 300–324. See Chapter 13, pp. 298–324, for a fuller discussion of the mass society.

21. Mills, "The Cultural Apparatus," *Power, Politics and People,* pp. 406–7.

22. Mills, *The Sociological Imagination,* p. 168. Mills borrows this distinction from Max Weber.

23. Ibid., p. 170.

24. Ibid.

25. Ibid., p. 166.

26. See Mills, *White Collar,* pp. 324 ff.

27. Mills, *The Power Elite,* p. 326.

28. See Gillam, "The Intellectual as Rebel," Chapter 1.

29. Ralph Miliband, "Mills and Politics," in Irving Louis Horowitz, ed., *The New Sociology* (New York: Oxford University Press, 1964), p. 78. Since Mills's practical outlook made him impatient with triviality and failure, he avoided the far Left sects: the Communists were "morally, intellectually, and politically impossible; the various Trotskyite sects were too disputatiously futile for a serious man to bother with; and the social democrats were, so to speak, too social democratic for his robust political tastes." Ibid.

30. See C. Wright Mills, *The Marxists*, pp. 36 ff.

31. Horowitz, "The Unfinished Writings of C. Wright Mills," p. 18. This is the only inventory and assessment of Mills's work in progress at the time of his death.

32. Quoted in Ralph Miliband, "C. Wright Mills," Domhoff and Ballard, *C. Wright Mills*, p. 6.

33. Mills, *The Sociological Imagination*, p. 183.

34. Ibid., p. 33.

35. Ibid., p. 50.

36. Mills, "The New Left," *Power, Politics and People*, p. 248.

37. Ibid.

38. Ibid., p. 249.

39. Ibid.

40. Mills, *The Sociological Imagination*, p. 176.

41. Mills, *The Causes of World War III* (London: Secker & Warburg, 1959), p. 97.

42. Ibid.

43. Ibid.

44. Ibid., pp. 97–98.

45. Ibid., p. 98.

46. Ibid.

47. Ibid.

48. Ibid.

49. Ibid.

50. Ibid., p. 143.

51. Mills did offer several general rhetorical principles for intellectuals. He suggested that they ought to address three main types: (1) those who are conscious of the power they wield; (2) those who remain unaware of the important consequences of their actions; and (3) those "who are regularly without such power and whose awareness is confined to their everyday milieux. . . ." *The Sociological Imagination*, p. 185.

52. Mills, *The Causes of World War III*, p. 144.

53. Mills, "The Decline of the Left," *Power, Politics and People*, p. 232.

54. Mills, *The Causes of World War III*, p. 131.

55. See Mills's letter and Irving Howe's reply in *Dissent* 6 (Summer 1959): 295–301.

56. Mills, "The Decline of the Left," *Power, Politics and People*, p. 232.

57. Ibid., p. 235.

58. Mills, "The New Left," *Power, Politics and People*, p. 257.

59. Ibid., pp. 257–58.

60. Ibid., p. 259.

61. Saul Landau, "C. Wright Mills: The Last Six Months," *Ramparts* 4 (August 1965): 50.

62. Mills, *The Marxists*, pp. 12–13.

63. Ibid., p. 28.

64. Ibid., p. 24.

65. Ibid., p. 36.

66. Ibid., pp. 36–37.

67. Ibid., pp. 473–74.

68. Ibid.

69. Landau, "C. Wright Mills: The Last Six Months," p. 51.

70. Ibid., p. 52.

71. Ibid., p. 51.

72. Quoted in Gillam, "The Intellectual as Rebel," p. 4.

73. Mills, "The Problem of Industrial Development," *Power, Politics and People*, p. 151; Baran's influence is evident here.

74. Mills, *Listen, Yankee!* (New York: Ballantine Books, 1960), p. 179.

75. Mills clearly outlines the preconditions to a decent society in Cuba and Latin America, and the narrow historical options these nations must confront. He suggests that without the dissolution of the alliance between U.S. corporations and local interests, "no real economic changes can reasonably be expected, certainly not at a sufficiently rapid rate. And without such structural economic changes, 'democracy' will remain what it now is in most of this continent: A farce, a fraud, a ceremony." Ibid., p. 178.

76. Landau, "C. Wright Mills: The Last Six Months," p. 49.

77. Mills, *The Marxists*, p. 474.

78. Horowitz, "The Unfinished Writings of C. Wright Mills," p. 18.

79. Mills, *The Power Elite*, p. 277 n.

80. Paul M. Sweezy, "Power Elite or Ruling Class?" in Domhoff and Ballard, *C. Wright Mills and THE POWER ELITE*, p. 127. Sweezy assumes that "The uppermost class in the United States is, and long has been, made up of the corporate rich who directly pull the economic levers."

81. Ibid.

82. Domhoff, "The Power Elite and Its Critics," in Domhoff and Ballard, *C. Wright Mills and THE POWER ELITE*, p. 276.

83. Ibid.

84. Ibid.

85. Ibid. Domhoff's compromise, it should be noted, stresses the primary importance of the concept of a ruling class without wholly discarding Mills's emphasis on elites.

86. Ibid., pp. 276–77.

87. Landau, "C. Wright Mills: The Last Six Months," p. 54.

88. Mills, *The Causes of World War III*, p. 14.

89. Ibid., pp. 85–87.

90. Ibid., p. 88.

91. Mills, *The Marxists*, p. 99.

92. Mills, *White Collar*, pp. 159–60.

93. Landau, "C. Wright Mills: The Last Six Months," p. 54.

4 Paul Baran: The Longer View

1. Paul A. Baran, "The Commitment of the Intellectual," in Leo Huberman and Paul M. Sweezy, eds., *Paul A. Baran: A Collective Portrait* (New York: Monthly Review Press, 1965), p. 10.

2. Ibid.

3. The biographical information for this chapter is drawn mainly from *Paul A. Baran: A Collective Portrait*, especially pp. 28–62.

4. Paul A. Baran, *The Political Economy of Growth*, 2nd ed. (New York and London: Monthly Review Press, 1962), p. xxv.

5. Paul A. Baran, "On the Nature of Marxism," *The Longer View* (New York and London: Monthly Review Press, 1970), p. 32.

6. Ibid., p. 33.

7. Ibid., p. 34.

8. Paul A. Baran, "On Marxism: A Discussion," *Monthly Review* 11 (September 1959): 144.

9. Baran, "On the Nature of Marxism," p. 36; see also "A Non-Communist Manifesto," *The Longer View*, pp. 59–60.

10. Ibid., p. 37.

11. Ibid., p. 41.

12. Ibid.

13. *Paul A. Baran: A Collective Portrait*, p. 58.

14. Ibid., p. 56.

15. Ibid., p. 94.

16. Ibid., pp. 87–88; see also pp. 41 ff for Sweezy's account of Baran's complex public and private attitudes toward the Soviet Union.

17. Paul A. Baran: "A Few Thoughts on the Great Debate," *The Longer View*, p. 376.

18. Paul A. Baran, "On Soviet Themes," *The Longer View*, p. 373.

19. Baran, "A Few Thoughts on the Great Debate," pp. 380–81. See also "National Economic Planning," pp. 115–181; and Anthony E. Scaperlanda, "The Political Economy of Liberman-Type Reforms," *Journal of Economic Issues* 5 (March 1971): 77–85.

20. An interesting series of discussions of the prospects for change in the advanced socialist nations may be found in Chalmers Johnson, ed., *Change in Communist Systems* (Stanford: Stanford University Press, 1970).

21. In his excellent analysis of the history, problems, and prospects of the Soviet economy, Howard Sherman remarks that "the undoubted difficulties" in the post-1965 reforms "will be resolved eventually either by retrogression [to tight central planning] or by further reform." Arguing that the advanced socialist countries can resolve tensions between the plan and the market in the coming decades, he foresees a "mixed system wherein the enterprise managers would make all of the current and short-run decisions concerning the use of available labor, raw materials, and capacity; while the central planners would be free of this detail, so that they could concentrate on long-run macro-economic investment planning for the expansion of capacity and the introduction of new technology," But it is impossible, according to Sherman, to predict the precise balance of planned and market socialism that each country will strike: "While some such converging trend between central planning and market socialism may be discerned in the Soviet Union and Eastern Europe, it is still not clear where on the spectrum these countries will finally be found." Howard Sherman, *The Soviet Economy* (Boston: Little, Brown and Company, 1969), pp. 317, 364. Throughout this section, I am heavily indebted to Professor Sherman's lucid and balanced treatment of the complex issues of Soviet political economy.

22. See Béla Csikós-Nagy, "Socialist Economic Theory and the New Mechanism," *New Hungarian Quarterly* 8 (Winter 1967): 37–52.

23. Baran, *The Political Economy of Growth*, p. xxii.

24. See Barrington Moore, Jr., *Soviet Politics—The Dilemma of Power* (New York: Harper & Row, 1965), pp. 339–40.

25. Barrington Moore, Jr., *Social Origins of Dictatorship and Democracy* (Boston: Beacon Press, 1966), p. 506.

26. Moore, *Soviet Politics*, p. 406.

27. Harry Braverman, "Controls and Socialism," *Monthly Review* 18 (January 1967): 38; emphasis added. For a fuller discussion of the problems of incentives in relation to socialist development, see Peter Clecak, "Moral and Material Incentives," *The Socialist Register: 1969*, Ralph Miliband and John Saville, eds. (New York and London: Monthly Review Press, 1969), pp. 101–35. See also Chapter Five, "Paul Sweezy: The Pursuit of Communism," pp. 208 ff.

28. Stanley Moore, "Utopian Themes in Marx and Mao," *Dissent* 17 (March–April 1970): 173.

29. Baran's concept of economic surplus has been the subject of considerable confusion and dispute. The later versions of surplus are discussed in the section on "Monopoly Capital," pp. 139 ff. See also *The Political Economy of Growth*, "Foreword to the Second Edition," especially pp. xvii–xxv; and pp. 22–43.

30. Paul A. Baran, "Economic Progress and Economic Surplus," *The Longer View*, p. 273; for a discussion of the third variant of surplus—"*planned* economic surplus"—see pp. 279 ff.

31. In order to contrast actual and possible states of affairs, Baran insists on the importance of viewing any social system from a point external to its dominant assumptions: "from a standpoint located outside and beyond the capitalist frame of reference, from the standpoint of a socialist society, much of what appears to be essential, productive, rational to bourgeois economic and social thought turns out to be nonessential, unproductive, and wasteful. It may be said in general that it is only the standpoint that is intellectually *outside* the prevailing social order, that is unencumbered by its values, its superstitions, and its 'self-evident truths,' that permits critical insight into that social order's contradictions and hidden potentialities. The exercise of self-critique is just as onerous to a ruling class as it is to a single individual." *The Longer View*, p. 275.

32. Baran, *The Political Economy of Growth*, p. viii.

33. Ibid., p. xxx.

34. Ibid., p. xxxii.

35. Paul A. Baran and Paul M. Sweezy, "A Rejoinder," *Monthly Review* 14 (April 1963): 674.

36. Ibid.

37. *Paul A. Baran: A Collective Portrait,* p. 47.

38. Ibid.

39. Paul A. Baran, "Reflections on the Cuban Revolution," *The Longer View,* p. 409.

40. Ibid., p. 411.

41. Ibid., p. 412.

42. Ibid., p. 416.

43. See René Dumont, "The Militarization of Fidelismo," *Dissent* 17 (September–October 1970): 428.

44. Baran: "Reflections on the Cuban Revolution," p. 409.

45. Baran, "A Few Thoughts on the Great Debate," pp. 377–78.

46. Ibid., p. 378.

47. Ibid., p. 384.

48. Ibid.

49. Baran, *The Longer View,* p. 209; see also Leo Huberman and Paul M. Sweezy, "Cooperation on the Left," *Monthly Review* 1 (March 1950): 334–44.

50. Ibid., p. 204.

51. Ibid., p. 206; for Baran's lurid intimation of American fascism in the early 1950s, see Historicus [Paul A. Baran], "Fascism in America," *Monthly Review* 4 (October 1952): 181–89.

52. Ibid.

53. Ibid., p. 208.

54. Ibid.

55. Ibid., p. 209.

56. Ibid.

57. Historicus [Paul A. Baran], "How Shall We Vote?" *Monthly Review* 4 (November 1952): 226.

58. Ibid., p. 227.

59. Baran, "Reflections on the Cuban Revolution," p. 392.

60. Ibid., p. 394.

61. *Paul A. Baran: A Collective Portrait,* p. 60.

62. Paul A. Baran, "A Letter to W. H. Ferry," *Monthly Review* 15 (June 1963): 103, 107.

63. See Paul A. Baran and Paul M. Sweezy, *Monopoly Capital* (New York and London: Monthly Review Press, 1966), pp. 363–67.

64. Ibid., p. 367.

65. Ibid., pp. 9, 10. In *Monopoly Capital,* Baran and Sweezy never fully clarify the concept of surplus. They use an amalgam of Baran's earlier formulations of the actual, potential, and planned surpluses,

without stipulating the variants in the several contexts of the book. They intend to use the surplus as a theoretical concept which includes the traditional Marxian notion of surplus value (profits + interest + rent), as well as other components of crucial importance in monopoly capitalist society: the sales effort, militarism, and other forms of waste. The surplus thus assumes "many forms and guises." The main body of the book is concerned with a theoretical elucidation of the concept of surplus and its components; the appendix, written by Joseph Phillips, attempts to estimate the magnitude of surplus for the years 1929–63 (see pp. 369–92).

66. Ibid., p. 8.

67. Ibid.

68. Ibid.

69. Ibid., p. 14.

70. Ibid., p. 7.

71. Ibid., p. viii (emphasis added).

72. See Paul M. Sweezy, "Keynesian Economics: The First Quarter Century," in Paul M. Sweezy, *Modern Capitalism and Other Essays* (New York and London: Monthly Review Press, 1972), pp. 79–91.

73. Baran and Sweezy, *Monopoly Capital,* p. 108.

74. Ibid., p. 52; see also pp. 6 n, 44, 47.

75. Ibid. p. 53.

76. Ibid., p. 60. Baran and Sweezy note several exceptions: "natural" monopolies such as telephone and electric power, because of their importance to the entire corporate class, must be regulated to keep costs reasonable; so also must the extractive industries, whose profits, in contrast, tend to be narrow, unless widened by government grants, tax breaks, and the like. But these exceptions, according to the authors, make the whole system conform all the more closely to their model. See pp. 64–66.

77. See ibid., pp. 68, 71.

78. Ibid., p. 72. The authors suggest that their law of rising surplus "immediately invites comparison . . . with the classical-Marxian law of the falling tendency of the rate of profit." But they do not go on to make a clear comparison. This is but one of the many instances of faulty and incomplete scholarship that critics have pointed out. See, for example, the symposium on "Marxism and *Monopoly Capital,*" *Science & Society* 30 (Fall 1966): 461–96.

79. See Baran and Sweezy, *Monopoly Capital,* pp. 80–81.

80. Ibid., p. 89.

81. Ibid., p. 108.

82. See ibid., pp. 219–22.

83. The argument for rising surplus also depends on the validity of the monopoly theory of pricing. Otto Nathan casts doubt on this assumption: "It seems very unrealistic to apply a generalized monopoly pricing theory to a market structure which, as was set forth earlier, is far from being a monopolistic organism and defies generalization. . . . There can be no general application of either a competitive or monopolistic price theory . . ." given the complex realities of the American economy. "Marxism and *Monopoly Capital,*" pp. 493–94.

Robert Heilbroner suggests another source of exaggeration: "I am not convinced of their argument that corporate profits tend to grow within the economy, since I believe they overlook the prevailing permissive corporate attitude toward wage raises, and ignore the possibility . . . that corporate output is a declining proportion of total national output." "A Marxist America," in Robert L. Heilbroner, *Between Capitalism and Socialism* (New York: Random House, 1970), p. 243. See also Victor Fuchs, *The Service Economy* (New York: National Bureau of Economic Research; distributed by Columbia University Press, 1968).

And George Shaw Wheeler argues that the authors seriously underrate the absorbent power of "routine" innovation—that is, of exogenous investment: "A Book of Questionable Scientific Merit," *Political Affairs* 46 (February 1967): 30.

84. On this point, see Myron Sharpe in "Marxism and *Monopoly Capital:* A Symposium," *Science & Society* 30 (Fall 1966): 468.

85. Maurice Dobb, "Marxism and *Monopoly Capital:* A Symposium," *Science & Society* 30 (Fall 1966): 474.

86. Baran and Sweezy, *Monopoly Capital,* p. 64. (The reference is to *The Communist Manifesto.*)

I borrow the term "state system" from Ralph Miliband: " 'the state' is not a thing . . . it does not, as such, exist. What 'the state' stands for is a number of particular institutions. . . ." Miliband includes the national government, the administration, the military and the police, the judicial branch, and subcentral government and parliamentary assemblies. These, "together, constitute its reality, and . . . interact as parts of what may be called the state-system." *The State in Capitalist Society* (New York: Basic Books, 1969), p. 49.

87. Baran and Sweezy, *Monopoly Capital,* p. 157.

88. Ibid., p. 143; for Baran and Sweezy's discussion of the effects of government spending on the surplus, see pp. 143 ff. For a critique, see George Shaw Wheeler, "A Book of Questionable Scientific Merit."

89. Ibid., p. 151.

90. Ibid. The authors do not consider state and local expenditures because there has been little *relative* change in them between 1929 and 1957, the last year for which they present data. See pp. 161 ff.

91. Ibid., p. 164.

92. Ibid., p. 173.

93. Ibid., p. 176; see also pp. 175 ff. Note again the loose style of argument. The authors might have been able to sustain this point had they argued—or even explicitly assumed—that no other "outside" forces or internal measures would have intervened in the absence of the Second World War.

94. Ibid., p. 209.

95. Ibid., p. 210.

96. Ibid., p. 213.

97. Ibid., p. 216.

98. Ibid., p. 217.

99. For a more complete explication of this notion, see Peter Clecak, "Social Criticism and Illusions of the Open Society," *Massachusetts Review* 10 (Spring 1969), especially pp. 256 ff.

100. *Monopoly Capital*, pp. 8–9.

101. David Horowitz, "Analyzing the Surplus," *Monthly Review* 18 (January 1967): 55.

102. Baran and Sweezy, *Monopoly Capital*, p. 177 n.

103. Ibid., p. 338.

104. Ibid., p. 338 n.

105. Ibid., p. 364.

106. Ibid., p. 342.

107. Ibid., p. 343.

108. Ibid., p. 345.

109. Ibid., p. 346. Here as elsewhere, the basic pattern of negation suggests Baran's experience at the Frankfurt School for Social Research. The implications of these assumptions and habits of mind are explored further in Chapter Six, "Herbert Marcuse: From History to Utopia."

110. Ibid., p. 344.

111. Hyman Lumer, "Monopoly Capital: The Baran-Sweezy Model," *Political Affairs* 46 (February 1967): 17.

112. Heilbroner, "A Marxist America," p. 245.

113. Ibid., pp. 245–46.

114. Baran and Sweezy, *Monopoly Capital*, p. 109; see also p. 268 n.

115. Baran, "Reflections on the Cuban Revolution," *The Longer View*, p. 436.

116. *Paul A. Baran: A Collective Portrait*, p. 62.

5 Paul Sweezy: The Pursuit of Communism

1. "Foreword," in Leo Huberman and Paul M. Sweezy, eds., *Paul A. Baran: A Collective Portrait* (New York: Monthly Review Press, 1965), p. viii. Many of the references in this chapter are to editorials jointly signed by Sweezy and Leo Huberman, who coedited *Monthly Review* from 1949 until Huberman's death in 1968. I have assumed throughout that the works quoted were conceived and drafted by Sweezy. In one obvious sense, this procedure is unwarranted, for during the first two decades of *Monthly Review*, Sweezy and Huberman worked closely together on all aspects of the magazine (and on Monthly Review Press as well), disagreeing in print on no more than three occasions. After making full allowance for the collaborative nature of their venture, however, I think it proper to attribute the main responsibility to Sweezy for two reasons. First, Sweezy's other works— *The Theory of Capitalist Development, Monopoly Capital,* and his many essays in *Monthly Review*—express themes developed in the editorials; for example, the editorials on transitional social systems in the sixties are quite plainly part of Sweezy's developing views on the nature and fate of socialism in history. (As a corollary, Huberman's separately written essays do not bear the same relation to most of the jointly written pieces referred to in this chapter.) Second, Sweezy's own account of the division of responsibilities corroborates my assumption: "Often when the time came to write the 'Review of the Month' for the next issue of the magazine, Leo was tied up with other matters and could not find the time for actual writing. We would decide on a subject and discuss in detail what we wanted to say. And then I would stay away from the office for several days, or even a week or two, and produce a draft." Then Huberman "went over everything with the greatest care and hardly ever failed to come up with many questions and suggestions for improvement." Paul Sweezy, *Leo Huberman* (New York: Monthly Review Press, 1968), pp. 49–50.

2. Huberman and Sweezy, "Where We Stand," *Monthly Review* 1 (May 1949): 1 (and reprinted in May issues until 1967). In subsequent references, *Monthly Review* is abbreviated as *MR*.

3. Like Baran, Sweezy is an international figure, though he has been neglected in the United States by the academic community and by

fashionable intellectuals. As an economist, he has been patronizingly regarded as the leading American exponent of a moribund tradition. Lewis Coser, a member of the *Dissent* group, commented that Sweezy is "a highly competent economist . . . whose *Theory of Capitalist Development* (1942) is one of the most lucid expositions of Marxist economics in any language. . . ." "USA: Marxists at Bay," in Leopold Labedz, ed., *Revisionism: Essays on the History of Marxist Ideas* (New York: Frederick A. Praeger, 1962), p. 354.

Elsewhere in the West, he is considered a major economist and social critic. In 1969, as an example, he was invited to deliver the annual Alfred Marshall lectures at Cambridge, England. Throughout Latin America and in parts of Asia, Sweezy is probably as well known and respected in intellectual circles as any contemporary American social critic. That he has been eclipsed in his native country by legions of less important social critics is but one sign of intellectual hard times. In the middle and late sixties, however, Sweezy exerted considerable influence on the Marxist sectors of the new Left: *Monopoly Capital* is widely read; many of his essays have been reprinted in anthologies used as college texts; and along with Marcuse, he was (alone among his generation) invited to address students during the rebellion at Columbia in 1968.

4. Irving Howe, "New Styles in 'Leftism,' " *Dissent* 12 (Summer 1965): 303. In addition to Howe's brief critique, see Coser, "USA: Marxists at Bay," pp. 351–56; also Peter Clecak, "Introduction" to the Greenwood Publishers reissue of *MR*, Vols. 1–12 (1949–60), pp. i–xii. Other "critiques" of *MR* that have appeared from time to time in publications of Left sects generally fail to reach even minimal standards of civilized discourse. See, as an example, Eric Jacobson, "A Comment on *Monthly Review:* Imperialism's War and 'Peace' Both Offensive," *Progressive Labor* 5 (May–June 1966): 69–76.

5. Paul M. Sweezy, "Marxism: A Talk to Students," *MR* 10 (October 1958): 223.

6. Huberman and Sweezy, "Where We Stand," p. 1; see Paul M. Sweezy, *Socialism* (New York: McGraw-Hill, 1949), pp. 22 ff.; also Paul M. Sweezy, "Marxian Socialism," *MR* 8 (November 1956): 225–41; and Paul M. Sweezy, *The Theory of Capitalist Development* (New York: Monthly Review Press, 1956), p. 54. This is Sweezy's first major book, written in 1942. I have not commented on it extensively in this assessment of his work, which focuses on the postwar years. Moreover, I believe that his most important contributions to

radical social thought are scattered throughout the more than twenty volumes of *MR*.

7. Huberman and Sweezy, "China and Socialism," *MR* 1 (May 1949): 6.

8. Sweezy, *Socialism*, p. 10.

9. Ibid.

10. Sweezy, "Marxian Socialism," p. 233.

11. Ibid.

12. Huberman and Sweezy, " 'The Communist Manifesto' After 100 Years," *MR* 1 (August 1949): 113.

13. Ibid., pp. 119–20.

14. Sweezy, "Marxian Socialism," p. 234.

15. Huberman and Sweezy, " 'The Communist Manifesto' After 100 Years," p. 120.

16. Sweezy, "Marxian Socialism," p. 235.

17. Huberman and Sweezy, " 'The Communist Manifesto' After 100 Years," p. 120.

18. Huberman and Sweezy, "Stalin and the Future," *MR* 4 (April 1953): 449.

19. Ibid., p. 450.

20. Ibid., p. 451; see also Huberman and Sweezy, "Forty Years Later," *MR* 9 (November 1957): 209–215; and Huberman and Sweezy, "On Trials and Purges," *MR* 4 (March 1953): 385–97. In Sweezy's estimation, Trotsky misplaced his faith in the world revolution as a way of ending Russia's isolation; Kamenov, Zinoviev, and Bukharin favored a policy of "anti-socialist" concessions, especially to various echelons of the Russian peasantry, that would have slowed down economic development, probably ensuring military defeat in World War II.

21. Huberman and Sweezy, "The Fall of Malenkov," *MR* 6 (March 1955): 403.

22. Huberman and Sweezy, "After the Twentieth Congress," *MR* 8 (July–August 1956): 70.

23. Ibid., p. 71: "Stalinism is not a social system but rather a sociopolitical superstructure which arose in a backward mixed society which had to choose between going forward to socialism or backward to capitalism." This formulation separates the "socialist" base from the repressive superstructure, but not convincingly.

24. Ibid., pp. 72–73.

25. Ibid., p. 72.

26. Ibid., p. 73.

27. Ibid.
28. Ibid., p. 74.
29. Ibid., pp. 74-75.
30. Ibid.
31. Huberman and Sweezy, "China and Socialism," p. 5.
32. Ibid., p. 7.
33. Ibid., p. 8.
34. See Paul M. Sweezy, "A Marxist View of Imperialism," in Paul M. Sweezy, *The Present as History* (New York: Monthly Review Press, 1953), p. 85; and Huberman and Sweezy, "Point Four vs. Social Revolution," *MR* 2 (June 1950): 36.
35. See Huberman and Sweezy, "The United States and Latin America," *MR* 6 (July 1954): 97-101. Sweezy used the notion of "historical borrowing" to account for disparities between the actual course of socialist revolutions and his first version of Marxist theory: "there is no contradiction between Marxian theory and the fact that the socialist revolution, having once taken place in Russia, spread first to relatively backward countries. For Marx and Engels fully recognized what might be called the possibility of historical borrowing. One consequence of the triumph of socialism anywhere would be the opening up of new paths to socialism elsewhere. Or, to put the matter differently, not all countries need go through the same stages of development; once one country has achieved socialism, other countries will have the possibility of abbreviating or skipping certain stages which the pioneer country had to pass through." Huberman and Sweezy, " 'The Communist Manifesto' After 100 Years," p. 115.
36. Huberman and Sweezy, "After the Twentieth Congress," p. 77. For an earlier anticipation of the possibilities of peaceful transition, see Sweezy, *The Theory of Capitalist Development*, pp. 348-63.
37. Huberman and Sweezy, " 'The Communist Manifesto' After 100 Years," p. 117.
38. Ibid., p. 118.
39. Ibid., p. 119.
40. Paul M. Sweezy, "Recent Developments in American Capitalism," *MR* 1 (May 1949): 21; see also Huberman and Sweezy, "Economic Retrospect and Prospect," *MR* 1 (January 1950): 261; Huberman and Sweezy, "The Threat of Depression," *MR* 4 (June 1952): 38; Huberman and Sweezy, "What Happened to the Economic Crisis," *MR* 4 (October 1952): 177-80; and Huberman and Sweezy, "Slump and Cold War," *MR* 9 (February 1958): 321-28.

41. Paul M. Sweezy, "Certain Aspects of American Capitalism," *MR* 3 (November 1951): 221. Throughout the fifties the editors conducted a continuous critique of Left-liberal schemes of reform. See, as an example, their devastating review of J. K. Galbraith's *American Capitalism:* "The Sixty-Four Dollar Question," *MR* 4 (August 1952): 97–106.

42. Huberman and Sweezy, "Fascism and the United States," *MR* 4 (July 1952): 70.

43. Huberman and Sweezy, "The Crisis of McCarthyism," *MR* 6 (January 1955): 311. See also their "The Roots and Prospects of McCarthyism," *MR* 5 (January 1954): 417–34.

44. Sweezy was also personally affected by the eclipse of civil liberties during the McCarthy period. His contempt-of-court case, beginning in New Hampshire in 1954, reached the U.S. Supreme Court, which reversed the ruling of the state courts several years later. See "Opinions in the Sweezy Case," *MR* 9 (September 1957): 137–50.

45. See Huberman and Sweezy, "The Outlook for American Socialists," *MR* 4 (May 1952): 1–11.

46. Ibid., p. 4.

47. Ibid., p. 5.

48. Ibid.

49. Paul M. Sweezy, "Peace and Prosperity," in *The Present as History,* p. 369.

50. Huberman and Sweezy, "Sound the Alarm!" *MR* 2 (September 1950): 139. This is a typical summary of Sweezy's analysis of U.S. foreign policy in the early fifties. In a prescient analysis of the Indo-Chinese situation after Dien Bien Phu, the editors posed the crucial question: "Are we going to take the position that anti-Communism justifies anything, including colonialism, interference in the affairs of other countries, and aggression? That way . . . lies war and more war leading ultimately to full-scale national disaster." Huberman and Sweezy, "What Every American Should Know About Indo-China," *MR* 6 (June 1954): 70–71.

Throughout this chapter, I use the term "American ruling class" neutrally, following Sweezy's Marxian definition. See his important two-part essay, "The American Ruling Class," *MR* 3 (May and June 1951): 10–17; 58–64.

51. Huberman and Sweezy, "The Consequences of Geneva," *MR* 6 (September 1954): 167. In 1951, for example, the war faction seemed momentarily in ascendancy, until Truman recalled MacArthur from Korea. Again in 1954, "the Dulles-Nixon-Radford-Knowland effort to

get the United States involved in Indo-China" constituted another attempt to launch a war with China. Ibid., p. 166. By 1956, the party of war appeared to be in decline, though for Sweezy it posed a continuing if frequently latent threat.

52. Huberman and Sweezy, "Problems of American Socialism," *MR* 6 (June 1954): 86.

53. Huberman and Sweezy, "The Hungarian Tragedy," *MR* 8 (December 1956): 259.

54. Of course Sweezy did not have the kind of personal investment in a political organization that Communist Party intellectuals and functionaries did. For them, personal commitment, ideology, and the organization were intricately bound together; hence the consequences of adopting new perspectives at odds with the prevailing orthodoxy were profound. But Sweezy was not merely an itinerant intellectual either; his first paradigm formed the basis of *MR*'s editorial policies during its first decade. The gradual abandonment of this paradigm required, in effect, an elaborate public apology to a loyal readership.

55. Huberman and Sweezy, "Which Way for the Soviet Union?" *MR* 9 (October 1957): 177–84; "Forty Years Later," *MR* 9 (November 1957): 209–215.

56. Huberman and Sweezy, "Forty Years Later," p. 212.

57. Ibid.

58. Huberman and Sweezy, "Which Way for the Soviet Union?," p. 182.

59. Huberman and Sweezy, "Forty Years Later," pp. 213–14.

60. Ibid., pp. 210–11.

61. Paul M. Sweezy, "Socialism in Europe, East and West," *MR* 9 (February 1958): 329, 330, 331.

62. Ibid., pp. 333, 334, 335.

63. Paul M. Sweezy, "The Yugoslav Experiment," *MR* 9 (March 1958): 364.

64. During the middle fifties, the number of favorable articles on China in *MR* increased. By the early sixties, the main focus of the magazine was on developments in the socialist and capitalist parts of the third world.

65. Huberman and Sweezy, "The Chinese Communes," *MR* 10 (February 1959): 375.

66. Ibid., p. 373 n.

67. Ibid., p. 378.

68. Huberman and Sweezy, "The Steel Strike in Perspective," *MR* 11 (February 1960): 362.

69. Huberman and Sweezy, "The Theory of U.S. Foreign Policy," *MR* 12 (September 1960): 277.

70. Sweezy and Huberman, eds., *Paul A. Baran: A Collective Portrait*, p. 47.

71. Huberman and Sweezy, *Cuba: Anatomy of a Revolution* (New York: Monthly Review Press, 1960), p. 89.

72. During the sixties, as Sweezy became increasingly interested in the modes of qualitative change in history, he frequently invoked Thomas S. Kuhn's *The Structure of Scientific Revolutions* (Chicago: University of Chicago Press, 1962), especially his theory of paradigms.

73. Paul M. Sweezy, "The Future of Capitalism," in David Cooper, ed., *To Free a Generation* (New York: Macmillan Co., 1968), p. 99.

74. See Paul M. Sweezy, "Karl Marx and the Industrial Revolution," in *Modern Capitalism and Other Essays* (New York and London: Monthly Review Press, 1972), pp. 127–46.

75. Huberman and Sweezy, "The U.S. in Vietnam: The Road to Ruin," *MR* 16 (April 1965): 801. The major essays on the war in Southeast Asia are collected in Paul M. Sweezy, Leo Huberman, and Harry Magdoff, *Vietnam: The Endless War* (New York and London: Monthly Review Press, 1970).

76. Huberman and Sweezy, "The Sino-Soviet Dispute," *MR* 13 (December 1961): 338, 344.

77. Huberman and Sweezy, "The Split in the Socialist World," *MR* 15 (June 1963): 16.

78. Huberman and Sweezy, "The Strategy of Armed Struggle," *MR* 18 (September 1966): 15. Here Sweezy relies on Latin-American experiences, taking the cautious view that the Chinese paradigm of revolution—beginning in the countryside and moving to the cities— ought not be mechanically imposed on other continents. But like many Marxists, he was unable to follow his own general advice. A year earlier, on the strength of eyewitness accounts by a Latin-American journalist, the editors of *Monthly Review* proclaimed a theoretical and strategic "breakthrough" of continental significance. The Guatemalan guerrillas, they pretentiously announced, had exploded the old myth that revolution in backward countries requires "a coalition of class forces including the petty-bourgeois and the so-called national bourgeoisie," replacing it with a global view: the international imperialist enemy demanded an international revolutionary opposition. Under the leadership of Yon Sosa, the guerrilla group MR-13 had adopted a "straightforward socialist program"; declared that the "means to its realization must be a workers' and peasants' state"; and proved that

this "strategy, rather than isolating the masses," can meet "with resounding and cumulative political success." The strategy of the Guatemalan revolutionaries, Sweezy argued, went beyond Che Guevara's "essentially paternalistic" conception of a revolution "conducted by a guerrilla army with the aid of peasants." The guerrillas of MR-13, on the contrary, organize the peasants in order to become "their revolutionary instrument." The strategy flowing from this "dialectical" premise "puts more emphasis on the political—on breaking up the existing state power—than on the military. The climax of the revolution is seen not as a series of pitched battles but rather as an armed insurrection, with the action of the guerrillas in the countryside being closely coordinated with that of the workers and students in the cities and towns. Out of this would emerge *from the outset* a workers' and peasants' state." "The Breakthrough in Guatemala," *MR* 17 (May 1965): 2, 6, 7.

After 1965, Sweezy periodically entered other debates over the strategy and tactics of armed revolution in Latin America, defending the romantic views of MR-13 against attacks from Fidel (at least until the guerrillas lost out), and participating in the controversy over the French Marxist Jules Régis Debray's theory of military foci. The intricate polemics need not be reviewed here, for Sweezy's revolutionary lyrics were usually off key. His main argument for armed revolution as the only road to socialism depended on the elimination of alternative routes. Actual failures of small revolutionary bands could therefore not be adduced as evidence against the basic indirect argument; such defeats were, rather, lamentable preludes to later successes. Unable to offer remedies for faulty strategies and tactics (beyond the usual Marxist bromides), he wisely withdrew from such debates toward the end of the sixties. See Huberman and Sweezy, "The Tri-Continental and After," *MR* 17 (April 1966): 1–34; Huberman and Sweezy, "Debray: The Strength and the Weakness," *MR* 20 (July–August 1968): 1–11; and "Régis Debray Replies," *MR* 20 (February 1969): 14–22.

79. Paul M. Sweezy, "The 22nd Congress and International Socialism," *MR* 14 (May 1962): 52–53.

80. Paul M. Sweezy, "Czechoslovakia, Capitalism and Socialism," *MR* 20 (October 1968): 6, 7, 11.

81. Paul M. Sweezy, reply to Charles Bettelheim, "On the Transition Between Capitalism and Socialism," *MR* 20 (March 1969): 14–15; several essays on problems of transition are collected in Paul M.

Sweezy and Charles Bettelheim, *On the Transition to Socialism* (New York and London: Monthly Review Press, 1971).

82. Huberman and Sweezy, "Lessons of Soviet Experience," *MR* 19 (November 1967): 14.

83. Paul M. Sweezy, "The Future of Socialism," *MR* 22 (March 1971): 14-15.

84. Huberman and Sweezy, "Lessons of Soviet Experience," pp. 18, 19.

85. Ibid., pp. 20, 21.

86. Ibid., p. 14.

87. Sweezy, "Czechoslovakia, Capitalism and Socialism," p. 11.

88. Huberman and Sweezy, "The Cultural Revolution in China," *MR* 18 (January 1967): 11, 12.

89. Ibid., p. 13.

90. Ibid., pp. 14, 15, 15-16.

91. Huberman and Sweezy, "Understanding the Cultural Revolution," *MR* 19 (May 1967): 11.

92. Paul M. Sweezy, "The Transition to Socialism," *MR* 23 (May 1971): 3.

93. Ibid., pp. 5, 8, 16.

94. Huberman and Sweezy, "The Fall of McNamara," *MR* 19 (January 1968): 11. This is also the mood that informs the coda to Baran's *Monopoly Capital;* see Chapter 4 of this book.

95. Huberman and Sweezy, "Vietnam and the 1968 Election," *MR* 19 (June 1967): 11, 12.

96. Huberman and Sweezy, "Socialism and the Negro Movement," *MR* 15 (September 1963): 231.

97. Huberman and Sweezy, "Reform and Revolution," *MR* 20 (June 1968): pp. 2, 9, 10.

98. Harry Magdoff and Paul M. Sweezy, "The Old Left and the New," *MR* 21 (May 1969): 8-9, 10. (Magdoff replaced Huberman as coeditor of *MR* early in 1969.)

99. Ibid.

100. For an earlier example of facile comparisons between capitalist and socialist nations, see Sweezy and Huberman, "Trained Manpower: U.S.A. versus USSR," *MR* 8 (April 1957): 417-26.

101. Robert L. Heilbroner, "Reflections on the Future of Socialism," in Robert L. Heilbroner, *Between Capitalism and Socialism,* p. 87.

102. Huberman and Sweezy, *Socialism in Cuba* (New York and London: Monthly Review Press, 1969), pp. 146, 148.
103. Heilbroner, p. 109.
104. Huberman and Sweezy, *Socialism in Cuba,* p. 218.
105. Ibid., p. 219.
106. Ibid., p. 221.

6 Herbert Marcuse: From History to Myth

1. While at Freiburg, Marcuse studied with Martin Heidegger. During this period he sought to reconcile Marxism with Heidegger's phenomenology. See, for example, his "Contributions to a Phenomenology of Historical Materialism" (1928), reprinted in English in *Telos* 4 (Fall 1969): 3–34. Heidegger's influence on Marcuse's conception of authentic existence as the mode of man who makes himself free through radical praxis persists throughout his critical odyssey. Along with conceptions of man in Marx's early writings, it is at the philosophical core of the various mythic figures that Marcuse creates, especially transitional man who is part Promethean. See also Martin Jay, "How Utopian Is Marcuse?" in George Fisher, ed., *The Revival of American Socialism* (New York: Oxford University Press, 1971), especially pp. 246–47.
There is very little published biographical material on Marcuse. For this sketch I have used data provided in Richard Goodwin, "The Social Theory of Herbert Marcuse," *Atlantic Monthly* 227 (June 1971): 68–85, and Paul A. Robinson, *The Freudian Left* (New York: Harper & Row, 1969), pp. 147–244.
2. Marcuse's first book, *Hegels Ontologie und die Grundlegung einer Theorie der Geschichtlichkeit* (Frankfurt am Main, 1932), "exhibited great technical expertise," according to Robinson, but "it gave no promise of the originality or forcefulness of Marcuse's major contribution to Hegel scholarship in *Reason and Revolution." The Freudian Left,* p. 155.
3. In this study I have chosen to concentrate primarily on these representative works, along with selected parts of *Reason and Revolution* (Boston: Beacon Press, 1960), and *Negations* (Boston: Beacon Press, 1968), a collection of Marcuse's essays, mainly from the thirties. There are, of course, other important pieces which I have consulted, notably "Repressive Tolerance," in Robert Paul Wolff, Barrington Moore, Jr., and Herbert Marcuse, *A Critique of Pure Tolerance* (Boston: Beacon Press, 1965), pp. 81–117, as well as a rich

collection of lectures from the fifties and sixties, *Five Lectures* (Boston: Beacon Press, 1970). A comprehensive list of Marcuse's writings through 1966 is found in Kurt H. Wolff and Barrington Moore, Jr., eds., *The Critical Spirit: Essays in Honor of Herbert Marcuse* (Boston: Beacon Press, 1967), pp. 427–33.

In the late sixties there was an explosion of criticism of Marcuse's thought, ranging from diluted and distorted versions in the popular and sectarian Left press to serious efforts at analysis, interpretation, and evaluation. Marcuse was viciously and ignorantly attacked from every point on the contemporary ideological spectrum. Echoing denunciations in *Pravda* (by Yury Zhukov), Joseph Reynolds writes in the American Communist Party journal that "a Marxist-Leninist can only cry out at this quarrel between Marcuse and Reich: 'A plague on both their sexual houses' "! (Joseph Reynolds, "Neo-Freudianism," *Political Affairs* 50 [October 1971]: 26). But the Maoist organ of the Progressive Labor Party reached the lowest level of "criticism," charging Marcuse with, among other things, being an agent of the CIA (*Progressive Labor* [February 1969]: 61–66). In a considerably more sophisticated attack from the Right, a *National Review* critic, borrowing from Yeats, describes Marcuse as "an old bellows full of angry wind" (John Sparrow, "Marcuse: The Gospel of Hate," *National Review* 21 [October 1969]: 1068–69). See also Eliseo Vivas, *Contra Marcuse* (New Rochelle, New York: Arlington House, 1971). Judging from his essay, Vivas, like his polemical counterparts on the Left, tells us more about himself than about his subject.

Without attempting to cite all the serious studies of various aspects of Marcuse's thought, I suggest the following sources in English as most helpful. On Marcuse's early work and his revaluation of Freud: Erich Fromm, "The Human Implications of Instinctivistic 'Radicalism,'" in Irving Howe, ed., *Voices of Dissent* (New York: Grove Press, 1958), pp. 313–20. See also the piece by Marcuse that occasioned Fromm's essay, "The Social Implications of Freudian 'Revisionism,'" *Voices of Dissent,* pp. 293–312. Peter Sedgwick, "Natural Science and Human Theory: A Critique of Herbert Marcuse," in Ralph Miliband and John Saville, eds., *The Socialist Register: 1966* (New York: Monthly Review Press, 1966), pp. 163–92; Paul Robinson, *The Freudian Left;* Anthony Wilden, "Marcuse and the Freudian Model: Energy, Information, and *Phantasie,*" *Salmagundi* 10–11 (Fall 1969, Winter 1970): 196–245. On Marcuse's social theory and political analyses: Maurice Cranston, "Herbert Marcuse," *Encounter* 32 (March 1969): 38–50; Alan Graubard, "One-Dimensional Pessimism:

A Critique of Herbert Marcuse," *Dissent* 15 (May–June 1968): 216–28; George Kateb, "The Political Thought of Herbert Marcuse," *Commentary* 49 (January 1970): 48–63; David Spitz, "Pure Tolerance," *Dissent* 13 (September–October 1966): 510–25. And on Marcuse's utopianism: Martin Jay, "How Utopian Is Marcuse?"; Theodore Roszak, *The Making of a Counter Culture* (New York: Doubleday & Co., 1969), pp. 84–123.

4. Wolff and Moore, Jr., eds., *The Critical Spirit: Essays in Honor of Herbert Marcuse,* p. xi.

5. Marcuse, "Foreword," *Negations,* p. xv.

6. See especially *Reason and Revolution,* pp. 273–322, for Marcuse's early reading of Marx. The question of Marcuse's intellectual indebtedness to Hegel and Marx has occasioned considerable discussion. In a harsh attack—*Herbert Marcuse: An Exposition and a Polemic* (New York: Viking Press, 1970)—Alasdair MacIntyre insists that Marcuse is really a Left Hegelian, not a Marxist. The resolution of this matter depends, among other things, on whether Marx's thought is taken as a mere excrescence of Hegel's. I prefer to leave the question of influences deliberately vague: Marcuse is obviously indebted both to Hegel and Marx. (His own account of the similarities and differences is instructive. See Marcuse, *Reason and Revolution,* pp. 312 ff. This should be read cautiously, however, for as several critics have noted, it is frequently difficult to distinguish between Marcuse's exposition and his endorsement of the ideas of others.) Robinson's formulation (*The Freudian Left,* p. 162) strikes me as the fairest scholarly assessment of the problem: Marcuse's "analysis of Hegel as revolutionary social critic was an analogue to his analysis of Marx as philosopher. The composite result of these parallel endeavors was to reduce substantially the ideological distance between the two thinkers." My intention throughout this chapter is to demonstrate Marcuse's continuing dependence on fundamentally Marxian categories of thought: he is essentially a utopian Marxist committed to developing his own dialectic of liberation.

7. Marcuse's reading of Marx in *Reason and Revolution* is one of the first attempts to integrate the early and late Marx in the light of the *Economic and Philosophical Manuscripts of 1844.* Marcuse uses the *EPM* to emphasize the dialectic of liberation as central to classical Marxism, as well as to his own developing outlook: "We have dwelt rather extensively upon Marx's early writings because they emphasize tendencies that have been attenuated in the post-Marxian development of his critique of society, namely, the elements of communistic indi-

vidualism, the repudiation of any fetishism concerning the socialization of the means of production or the growth of the productive forces, the subordination of all these factors to the idea of the free realization of the individual. *Under all aspects, however, Marx's early writings are mere preliminary stages to his mature theory, stages that should not be overemphasized"* (emphasis added). Marcuse, *Reason and Revolution,* pp. 294–95.

8. Ibid., pp. 274–78.

9. Marcuse assumes that "the subsumption of individuals under classes is the same phenomenon as their subjection to the *division of labor."* Ibid., p. 290.

10. Ibid., p. 282. Marcuse carefully distinguishes between "labor" and "work," suggesting that the abolition of labor, according to Marx, means "in the last analysis" the elimination of "that activity which creates surplus value in commodity production, or which 'produces capital.' " Ibid., p. 293. But work, considered as the *free* expression of man's creative powers, will be a central feature of communist society. Marcuse generally retains and elaborates this distinction in later works. See Notes 51 and 134.

11. Ibid., p. 283.

12. Ibid., p. 295. Marcuse assumes that "all the Marxian concepts extend, as it were, in these two dimensions, the first of which is the complex of given social relationships, and the second, the complex of elements inherent in the social reality that make for its transformation into a free social order. This twofold content determines Marx's entire analysis of the labor process." Ibid., pp. 295–96. For a fuller treatment of the conceptual scheme underlying this use of terms, see Bertell Ollman, *Alienation: Marx's Conception of Man in Capitalist Society* (London: Cambridge University Press, 1971), especially Chapters 2 and 3, pp. 12–42.

13. Marcuse, *Reason and Revolution,* p. 251.

14. Ibid., p. 318. "it would be a distortion of the entire significance of Marxian theory to argue from the inexorable necessity that governs the development of capitalism to a similar necessity in the matter of transformation to socialism," p. 317. Compare this with Sweezy's discussion of the voluntarist dimensions of Marxian theory and his tardy recognition of the indeterminate character of postcapitalist transitions, summarized in Chapter 5 of this book, pp. 132 ff.

15. Marcuse, *Reason and Revolution,* p. 398.

16. This general perspective on bourgeois democracy runs through all of Marcuse's work. For an early example, see Herbert Marcuse

"The Struggle Against Liberalism in the Totalitarian View of the State" (1934), Marcuse, *Negations,* pp. 3–42.

17. Marcuse, *Reason and Revolution,* pp. 282–83. But Marcuse's attitude toward the Soviet experience has been consistently ambivalent. See pp. 206–09 below for a further discussion.

18. An early articulation of the principles of critical theory, which Marcuse later calls dialectical theory, is found in "Philosophy and Critical Theory" (1937), Marcuse, *Negations,* pp. 134–58. Compare this with Herbert Marcuse, *One-Dimensional Man* (Boston: Beacon Press, 1964), pp. ix–xvii, and Chapter 8, "The Historical Commitment of Philosophy," pp. 203–24. In my analysis of Marcuse's critical theory, I do not pretend to assess the work of other members of the Frankfurt school.

19. In "The Struggle Against Liberalism in the Totalitarian View of the State," Marcuse describes the twentieth-century descent into varieties of totalitarianism as a direct fulfillment of Marx's tendential laws of political economy: "The turn from the liberalist to the total-authoritarian state occurs within the framework of a single social order. With regard to the unity of this economic base, we can say that it is liberalism that 'produces' the total-authoritarian state out of itself, as its own consummation at a more advanced stage of development. The total-authoritarian state brings with it the organization and theory of society that correspond to the monopolistic stage of capitalism." Marcuse, *Negations,* p. 19.

20. See Marcuse, *One-Dimensional Man,* especially Chapters 5–7, pp. 123–99.

21. See Chapter 2, "The Argument," pp. 26 ff.

22. See Marcuse, *Negations,* "Philosophy and Critical Theory," p. 145.

23. According to Marcuse, then, the values of reason, freedom, and happiness are not merely "subjective" personal notions, but rather "objective" public values discovered, modified, and preserved in successive versions of "critical theory." It is in this historical tradition of philosophy that he finds the origins of his utopian values and visions. Marcuse's primary interest in any philosopher does not center on his politics, nor even on the consistency of his thought, but rather on the "progressive" elements and "revolutionary" implications in his work as well as in the tradition as a whole. Hence it is both accurate and necessary to speak of Marcuse's Hegel, Marcuse's Marx, and Marcuse's Freud.

Though Marcuse provides adumbrated versions of his barnstorming tours through the history of Western philosophy and culture in his later works, the early discussions, though fragmentary, are the best. See especially the following essays in *Negations:* "The Concept of Essence," pp. 43–87; "The Affirmative Character of Culture," pp. 88–133; "Philosophy and Critical Theory," pp. 134–58; and "On Hedonism," pp. 159–200.

24. See Marcuse, *Negations,* "Philosophy and Critical Theory," p. 136; in Marcuse's postwar work, "happiness"—life without needless pain or labor—takes on added psychological meanings. But he assumes the centrality of the concept in his early writings: "the Marxian theory has developed a full contradiction to the basic conception of idealist philosophy. The idea of reason has been superseded by the idea of happiness." Reason, in this view, is the instrument for discovering happiness as an historical possibility at certain stages of social development. Marcuse, *Reason and Revolution,* p. 293.

25. Marcuse, *Negations,* "Philosophy and Critical Theory," pp. 154–55.

26. Robinson, *The Freudian Left,* pp. 150–51; Wolff and Moore, Jr., *The Critical Spirit: Essays in Honor of Herbert Marcuse,* p. 430.

27. Marcuse, *Negations,* p. xv.

28. Marcuse's sketchy theoretical account of the genesis and development of fascism was both unoriginal and highly controversial. It closely follows Franz Neumann's fuller analysis. See Marcuse's preface to Neumann's *The Democratic and Authoritarian State* (Glencoe, Ill.: The Free Press, 1957), pp. vii–x. For an alternative view, see Barrington Moore, Jr., *Social Origins of Dictatorship and Democracy* (Boston: Beacon Press, 1966), Chapter 8, pp. 433–52.

29. Marcuse uses the term "workers' movement" ambiguously in the thirties, to designate the proletariat of classical Marxian theory and to refer to those political organizations within the working class that he considers genuinely revolutionary *and* socialist.

30. From the beginning, Marcuse avoided concrete levels of political and intellectual discourse. Though he participated in a collaborative work on the political functions of the European family while associated with the Frankfurt group (a study that prefigured T. W. Adorno et al., *The Authoritarian Personality*), Marcuse "took no part in the actual empirical research, thus setting a kind of negative precedent for all of his subsequent social criticism." Robinson, *The Freudian Left,* p. 153.

31. Ibid., p. 192.

32. The ambiguous "progress" of postwar capitalism reinforced Marcuse's conviction that previous socialist goals and visions "were not radical enough . . . they rejected too little and held too little to be possible. . . ." Marcuse, *Negations,* p. xvii. This is a curious retrospective judgment of his own prewar utopian vision, which clearly overshot historical—or at least political—possibilities. Nor does Marcuse show how a more ambitious vision would have helped radical movements anywhere.

33. Marcuse was also associated with the Russian Institute at Columbia during this period, presumably shaping the theses of *Soviet Marxism* (1958) (New York: Random House, 1961). See, in addition, Marcuse, "Recent Literature on Communism," *World Politics* 6 (July 1954): 515–25.

34. See Marcuse, *Eros and Civilization* (New York: Random House, 1962), p. 11: "Civilization begins when the primary objective—namely, integral satisfaction of needs—is effectively renounced."

35. Ibid., pp. 11–12. Throughout this section, I make no attempt to estimate the ontological status or therapeutic usefulness of the Freudian concepts employed by Marcuse. But the metapsychology of Freud, especially in Marcuse's hands, does seem fanciful; see Peter Sedgwick, "Natural Science and Human Theory," pp. 172–73: "We shall . . . lay no special emphasis on the fact that there is rather more evidence for the existence of leprechauns than there is for the reality of an energizing libido, or for Eros and Thanatos as fundamental drives of organic life."

36. Marcuse, *Eros and Civilization,* pp. 13–14; see also p. 224.

37. Ibid., pp. 15–16; see also pp. 52 ff.

38. Ibid., pp. 82–83.

39. On this point, see the revisionist controversy between Erich Fromm and Marcuse, in Howe, ed., *Voices of Dissent,* pp. 293–320.

40. Marcuse, *Eros and Civilization,* p. 33.

41. See ibid., pp. 113–14; 138 ff.

42. Ibid., pp. 32 ff.

43. Ibid. Note also the similarity between "surplus repression" and Baran's concept of "surplus."

44. Ibid., p. 203. Note that Marcuse never advocated a crude political version of "the worse, the better" hypothesis. Unlike many young Leftists of the sixties, he has a sense of twentieth-century history and understands that socialism is not the "determinate negation" of fascism in history.

45. This is especially the case in the essays written after 1936, a watershed year because of the Moscow purges and the checkmating of revolutionary forces in Spain.

46. Marcuse, *Eros and Civilization*, p. 129.

47. Ibid., pp. 130, 150–51, 156. See also pp. 189 ff.

48. Ibid., pp. 168, 174–75.

49. Ibid., pp. 170, 171. See also p. 5. Marcuse claims that Schiller's aesthetic analysis, properly understood, implies an approach to the political problem of "the liberation of man from inhuman existential conditions. Schiller states that, in order to solve the political problem, 'one must pass through the aesthetic, since it is beauty that leads to freedom.' " Ibid., p. 171. In my view, this conflation of aesthetic and historical/political categories mars all of Marcuse's postwar work.

50. Ibid., p. 181. Note that throughout this section, Marcuse hedges his speculative arguments, using the subjunctive mood very frequently. The logic of his arguments in favor of a nonrepressive civilization seems largely determined by the main hypothesis, not by any hard evidence. In fact, he cites only a handful of sources beyond Freud.

51. Ibid., p. 185. Marcuse retains and amplifies the earlier distinction between labor and work, pp. 199 ff. See Notes 10 and 134.

52. Ibid., p. 207. This notion parallels the two trends of hedonism—Cyrenaic and Epicurean—which Marcuse discusses in "On Hedonism," *Negations,* pp. 159–200.

53. Marcuse, *Eros and Civilization*, pp. 191, 205. Marcuse qualifies this notion: "instinct itself is beyond good and evil, and no free civilization can dispense with this distinction." He suggests that under nonrepressive conditions, natural self-restraint will become the instinctual basis of a new morality. Ibid., p. 206. (As in so many other instances, Marcuse sees the devastating qualification, which makes it all the more difficult to understand why he maintains the central point.)

54. The notion of abundance is carried over from Marcuse's early utopian Marxism. In his postwar writings, however, he vacillates between maximum and minimum definitions of abundance. Compare the following passages from *Eros and Civilization*: "The reconciliation between pleasure and reality principle does not depend on the existence of abundance for all. The only pertinent question is whether a state of civilization can be reasonably envisaged in which human needs are fulfilled in such a manner and to such an extent that surplus-repression can be eliminated" (p. 137). And: "Non-repressive order is essentially an order of *abundance:* the necessary constraint is brought about by

'superfluity' rather than need" (p. 177). Marcuse generally recognizes that unlimited abundance is impossible, but he clings to the debatable minimum definition. See the discussion of *One-Dimensional Man*, below, pp. 204 ff.

55. See Marcuse, *Eros and Civilizaton*, pp. 170–71, 175–76.

56. Ibid., p. 205. See, for example, Marcuse, *One-Dimensional Man*, pp. 39–41; Marcuse, "Repressive Tolerance"; and Marcuse, *An Essay on Liberation* (Boston: Beacon Press, 1969), pp. 65 ff.

57. Marcuse, *Eros and Civilization*, p. 206 (emphasis added).

58. Marcuse, *One-Dimensional Man*, p. ix.

59. "Advanced industrial society" is Marcuse's term for late capitalist societies. It refers *generally* to nations of the West and *specifically* to the United States, the most developed capitalist society. Marcuse thus follows Marx, who grounded his analysis of the capitalist mode of production in the case of England but suggested its potential relevance to other nations: "If, however, the German reader shrugs his shoulders at the condition of the English industrial and agricultural labourers, or in optimist fashion comforts himself with the thought that in Germany things are not really so bad; I must plainly tell him, *'De te fabula narratur!'* " Karl Marx, *Capital I*, "Preface to the First German Edition." Translated from the third German edition by Samuel Moore and Edward Aveling (New York: International Publishers, 1967), p. 8.

Baran and Sweezy also follow this procedure. See *Monopoly Capital* (New York and London: Monthly Review Press, 1966), p. 11. But in the postwar period, Marcuse prefers the more general term "advanced industrial society" to monopoly capitalism (which he used in the thirties)—for two apparent reasons: "advanced industrial society" *includes* the meanings of monopoly capitalism but goes beyond them (see *One-Dimensional Man*, p. xv, 53); between 1946 and the middle sixties, academics and social critics who used explicitly Marxian terminology and concepts to examine U.S. society were generally ignored. In 1967, when the parameters of debate among intellectuals had widened considerably, Marcuse made good the default, stating that "advanced industrial society" refers to "advanced capitalism" and that the technological " 'apparatus' " is an "instrument of domination in the hands of the ruling classes. . . ." Marcuse, "On Changing the World: A Reply to Karl Miller," *Monthly Review* 19 (October 1967): 44. Thereafter he uses "monopoly capitalism" more explicitly. See Marcuse, *An Essay on Liberation*.

60. Marcuse, *One-Dimensional Man*, pp. ix–x.

61. For a brief history of the *Grundrisse,* see Eric Hobsbawm's introduction to Karl Marx, *Pre-Capitalist Economic Formations* (New York: International Publishers, 1965), pp. 8 ff: "The time and place of publication caused the work to be virtually unknown until 1952 when the present section of it was published as a pamphlet in Berlin, and 1953, when the entire *Grundrisse* were republished in the same city. This 1953 German edition remains the only accessible one." See also Martin Nicolaus, "The Unknown Marx," an essay that brought this facet of Marx to the attention of a somewhat wider audience in the West (*New Left Review* 48 [March–April 1968]: 41–61).

I don't mean to imply, of course, that Marcuse relies solely on the Marx of the *Grundrisse.* He uses other sources to characterize the absorption of previously antagonistic classes into one-dimensional society, especially C. Wright Mills, Daniel Bell, and parts of Serge Mallet's analyses of the new working class, without endorsing Mallet's conclusions. (These appeared first in *Les Temps Modernes* and *La Nef* in the late fifties.) See Marcuse, *One-Dimensional Man,* pp. 22–34.

62. Marcuse, *One-Dimensional Man,* pp. 36, 37.

63. See ibid., pp. 35–38. Marcuse uses "qualitative change" to designate a social transformation that (a) brings about *genuine* (i.e., *utopian*) socialism and (b) is effected by revolutionary means. "Quantitative" changes occur *within* a social system.

64. See Chapter 4, "Paul Baran: The Longer View."

65. See Marcuse, *One-Dimensional Man,* p. 52. Marcuse's vision of "genuine" or "real" socialism includes *both* the socialization of the productive apparatus *and* the liberation of consciousness prior to the revolution against capitalism, at least on the part of the minority that effects the transition.

66. Marcuse recognizes that the proletariat of classical Marxism (the factory workers whose class consciousness was to have been fashioned by the conditions of their work and created through political education and organization) represents a declining proportion of the total workforce. And, following Mills in *White Collar,* he offers this negative assessment of the "new working class": "The stepped-up drive to organize the growing white-collar element in the industrial unions, if successful at all, may result in a growth of trade union consciousness of these groups, but hardly in their political radicalization." Marcuse, *One-Dimensional Man,* p. 38; see also *An Essay on Liberation,* pp. 16, 54–57.

67. Marcuse, *One-Dimensional Man,* p. xvi.

68. See Marcuse, "On Changing the World: A Reply to Karl Miller."

69. Marcuse, *One-Dimensional Man,* p. 7. For Marcuse's discussion of autonomous and heteronomous, true and false needs, see pp. 4–8.

70. Ibid., p. 9.

71. See, especially, Allen Graubard, "Herbert Marcuse: One-Dimensional Pessimism," *Dissent* 15 (May–June 1968): 216–28.

72. Marcuse, *One-Dimensional Man,* p. 9.

73. Ibid., p. xv. On this point, see George Kateb, "The Political Thought of Herbert Marcuse," p. 53.

74. Marcuse, *One-Dimensional Man,* pp. 12, 73.

75. For a more skillful discussion, see Herbert Marcuse, "Freedom and Freud's Theory of Instincts," and "The Obsolescence of the Freudian Concept of Man," in Marcuse, *Five Lectures,* pp. 1–27, 44–61.

76. Marcuse, *One-Dimensional Man,* pp. 50–51, 51, 7–8.

77. Critics, for example, associated with the journal *Dissent*—Irving Howe, Michael Harrington, et al.

78. See, for example, David Horowitz's intelligent critique, "One-Dimensional Society?" *International Socialist Journal* 4 (December 1967): 811–30; and a less subtle examination by Karl Miller, "The Point Is Still to Change It," *Monthly Review* 19 (June 1967): 49–57.

79. Like *Monopoly Capital, One-Dimensional Man* suffers from a long hiatus between the time of conception and the date of publication. Marcuse articulated parts of his thesis as early as the 1930s. An early version of Chapter 4 appeared in *Dissent* under the title "Language and Technological Society," *Dissent* 8 (Winter 1961): 66–74.

80. Marcuse, *One-Dimensional Man,* pp. 256–57.

81. The thesis of one-dimensionality that Marcuse elucidates is a *possible* account of the present in the sense of a Kantian "deduction"—an internally coherent argument with a theoretically possible application.

82. See also *The Communist Manifesto* for an early example of a proposed mediation between immediate and long-range aims: "The Communists fight for the attainment of the immediate aims, for the enforcement of the momentary interests of the working class; but in the movement of the present, they also represent and take care of the future of that movement." Marx-Engels, *Selected Works,* p. 62.

83. Marcuse, *One-Dimensional Man,* pp. 256, xiii (emphasis added).

84. Ibid., p. 232.

85. *And* a reduction in living standards in the advanced countries. See ibid., p. 242, and Note 54.

86. Kateb, "The Political Thought of Herbert Marcuse," p. 57.

87. Marcuse, *One-Dimensional Man*, p. 14.

88. See Marcuse, "Repressive Tolerance," p. 99. Despite (perhaps because of) his utopian Marxism, Marcuse remained within the acceptable practical limits of social commentary during the exclusively anti-Soviet phase of the cold war.

89. Marcuse depends heavily on an independent Marxist position concerning prospects for change in the post-Stalin era articulated by, among others, Isaac Deutscher. See Deutscher, *Russia, What Next?* (New York: Oxford University Press, 1953). Curiously, Deutscher is not cited in either *Soviet Marxism* or *One-Dimensional Man*.

90. Marcuse, *One-Dimensional Man*, pp. 39, 41, 42.

91. Ibid., p. 42. Political liberalization thus becomes an analogue to democracy in competitive capitalist societies, a potentially free mental space that might permit the growth of a genuine socialist opposition.

92. Ibid., p. 43.

93. This is, of course, a complicated—and doubtless unresolvable—theoretical/historical problem. For two interesting anti-Stalinist views, see Ernest Mandel, *Marxist Economic Theory* (New York and London: Monthly Review Press, 1969), Vol. 2, pp. 548–604; and Roy A. Medvedev, *Let History Judge: The Origins and Consequences of Stalinism* (New York: Alfred A. Knopf, 1971).

94. Marcuse, *One-Dimensional Man*, pp. 43, 44.

95. Ibid., pp. 43, 45.

96. Ibid., pp. 47, 46. Marcuse, of course, explicitly acknowledges the use of myth as a mode of understanding the contemporary world: "Today, the rational and realistic notions of yesterday again appear to be mythological when confronted with the actual conditions. The reality of the laboring classes in advanced industrial society makes the Marxian 'proletariat' a mythological concept; the reality of present-day socialism makes the Marxian idea a dream. The reversal is caused by the contradiction between theory and facts—a contradiction which, by itself, does not yet falsify the former. The unscientific, speculative character of critical theory derives from the specific character of its concepts, which designate and define the irrational in the rational, the mystification in the reality. Their mythological quality reflects the mystifying quality of the given facts—the deceptive harmonization of the societal contradictions" (pp. 188–89).

97. Since critical (or dialectical) theory is an instrument for pro-

jecting *tendencies*, the "resolutions" that Marcuse sought were theoretical in nature though they also amounted to anticipations of changes within history. See Marcuse, *One-Dimensional Man*, p. 253.

98. For an interesting though rather tasteless interpretation of Marcuse's appeal to young Leftists, see Ronald Aronson, "Dear Herbert," in *The Revival of American Socialism*, pp. 257–80. This long letter, ironically, represents Aronson's own attempt to come to terms with Marcuse, his teacher and partial father figure.

99. See Paul Breines, "From Guru to Spectre: Marcuse and the Implosion of the Movement," in Paul Breines, ed., *Critical Interruptions* (New York: Herder and Herder, 1970), pp. 1–21.

100. Marcuse himself was careful to distinguish his own status as an intellectual from that of active revolutionaries: "I particularly object to the juxtaposition of my name and photograph with those of Che Guevara, Debray, Rudi Dutschke, etc., because these men have truly risked and are still risking their lives in the battle for a more human society, whereas I participate in this battle only through my words and my ideas. It is a fundamental difference." "Marcuse Defines His New Left Line," *New York Times Magazine*, October 27, 1968, p. 29.

101. Since many of Marcuse's most "provocative" formulas were cast in the language of advertising (e.g., "Free election of masters does not abolish the masters or the slaves"), he was easily packaged for mass consumption. And there was, of course, a grain of truth in the characterization of Marcuse as a surrogate father. See, for example, Irving Kristol, "The Improbable Guru of Surrealistic Politics," *Fortune* 80 (July 1969), pp. 191, 194.

102. Marcuse's contract, which because of his age had to be renegotiated each academic year, was not renewed for 1970–71.

103. See Breines, *Critical Interruptions;* and Marcuse, "Democracy Has/Hasn't a Future . . . A Present" (a symposium), *New York Times Magazine*, May 26, 1968, p. 104.

104. Marcuse, "Varieties of Humanism," *Center Magazine* 1 (July 1968): 14.

105. Marcuse, "On the New Left," in Massimo Teodori, ed., *The New Left: A Documentary History* (Indianapolis: Bobbs-Merrill, 1969), p. 469.

106. Marcuse, "A Note on Dialectic," preface to the 1960 edition of *Reason and Revolution*, p. xi.

107. Kateb, "The Political Thought of Herbert Marcuse," p. 48.

108. Transitional man brings together—and partially resolves in theory—"the two strains in Marcuse's vision of the liberated society: first, the stress on radical action, on the deed, on self-creation as the only mode of authentic being; and second, the unity of opposites, the true harmony of pacified existence, the end of conflict and contradiction." Martin Jay, "How Utopian Is Marcuse?" p. 251.

109. Marcuse, *An Essay on Liberation,* pp. 9–10, 26.

110. Marcuse, like others in the Marxian tradition, respects the tension between determinism and voluntarism, maintaining that their specifications change with changing historical conditions. In his later essays, he searches for an historical agent of change who is uncorrupted and uncorruptible, whether voluntarily (by his own will) or involuntarily (by virtue of his place in the social order).

111. Marcuse, *An Essay on Liberation,* pp. 16–17. Marcuse explicitly notes that his use of biological terms does not "imply or assume anything as to the way in which needs are physiologically expressed and transmitted" (p. 10 n). But he does not intend to use this terminology simply as metaphor, either. These terms "designate the process and the dimension in which inclinations, behavior patterns, and aspirations become vital needs which, if not satisfied, would cause dysfunction of the organism" (p. 10 n).

112. See ibid., Chapter 2, "The New Sensibility," pp. 23–48.

113. Ibid., p. 10 (emphasis added).

114. Ibid., pp. 7, 60 (emphasis added).

115. See "The Port Huron Statement," in Paul Jacobs and Saul Landau, *The New Radicals* (New York: Random House, 1966), p. 151, for a similarly grandiose characterization of the early new Left's mission.

116. Marcuse, *An Essay on Liberation,* p. 63.

117. Ibid., p. 79.

118. Ibid., p. 71. Here again Marcuse mythicizes Marx. Compare the use of biological metaphors in *An Essay on Liberation* with the leading social metaphor in the "Preface to a Contribution to the Critique of Political Economy," *MESW,* pp. 181–85: "the productive forces developing in the womb of bourgeois society create the material conditions for the solution of that antagonism" (i.e., between the social character of production and the private appropriation of profit), p. 183.

119. Marcuse, *An Essay on Liberation,* pp. 51, 53.

120. Ibid., p. 63.

121. See Marcuse, *Five Lectures,* pp. 87 ff.

122. Marcuse, *An Essay on Liberation,* pp. 65, 63. See also Irving Howe, "Herbert Marcuse or Milovan Djilas? The Inescapable Choice of the Next Decade," *Harper's* 239 (July 1969): 84–92.

123. Marcuse, *An Essay on Liberation,* p. 65; see also p. 68.

124. "Ultra-Left" is, of course, a vague and highly charged term. I use it in this context to refer to antireformist political strategies and tactics defined by Marxists (and small Marxist groups) in the Western countries.

125. Marcuse, *An Essay on Liberation,* pp. vii ff. Compare this version of the Great Refusal with the one in *Eros and Civilization,* pp. 136, 154: "This Great Refusal is the protest against unnecessary repression. . . ." It is a refusal to "accept separation from the libidinous object (or subject)."

126. Marcuse, *An Essay on Liberation,* p. viii. Marcuse also adds students and intellectuals in the Communist nations of Europe. See ibid., pp. 22, 25–26. Following Sweezy and others, he went so far as to cast the masses of the third world as "heirs of the Marxian proletariat," declaring that "corporate capitalism is now a global system, and what may appear today as an external proletariat is actually an internal proletariat in terms of the world. . . ." Marcuse, "Varieties of Humanism," p. 14.

127. Marcuse, *An Essay on Liberation,* pp. 82, 84.

128. Marcuse, "Varieties of Humanism," p. 14.

129. Marcuse, *An Essay on Liberation,* p. 52.

130. That is, Marcuse, unlike Sweezy, can accommodate a reasonably broad range of particular analyses without losing his own sense of theoretical continuity: every new position he takes is represented as yet another confirmation of critical (or dialectical) theory.

131. Marcuse, *An Essay on Liberation,* pp. viii (second phrase with my emphasis), x, 57.

132. For an interesting discussion of mythic elements in Marx, see Robert Tucker, *Philosophy and Myth in Karl Marx* (London: Cambridge University Press, 1961), especially pp. 218–32. The crucial characteristic of mythic thought, according to Tucker, is "that something by nature interior is apprehended as exterior, that a drama of the inner life of man is experienced and depicted as taking place in the outer world" (p. 219). Although Marcuse takes a more dialectical view of the relationship between men and their historical and cultural contexts than Tucker's perspective allows, he does interiorize his mythic view of a future society, locating the vision in transitional man and imagining that this figure, once in control of the working class,

will re-create the world after his own image, and according to his own needs.

133. Marcuse, *An Essay on Liberation,* p. 20.

134. See *Capital III* (New York: International Publishers, 1967), p. 820: "the realm of freedom actually begins only where labour which is determined by necessity and mundane considerations ceases; thus in the very nature of things it lies beyond the sphere of actual material production. . . . Freedom in this field can only consist in socialized man, the associated producers, rationally regulating their interchange with Nature, bringing it under their common control, instead of being ruled by it as by the blind forces of Nature; and achieving this with the least expenditure of energy and under conditions most favourable to, and worthy of, their human nature. But it nonetheless still remains a realm of necessity. Beyond it begins that development of human energy which is an end in itself, the true realm of freedom, which, however, can blossom forth only with this realm of necessity as its basis. The shortening of the working-day is its basic prerequisite."

135. Marcuse, *An Essay on Liberation,* pp. 21–22.

136. On this point, see Shlomo Avineri, *The Social and Political Thought of Karl Marx* (London: Cambridge University Press, 1968), pp. 162–74.

137. See, for example, "Marcuse Defines His New Left Line," p. 30.

138. "Democracy Has/Hasn't a Future," p. 104. Marcuse takes a slightly different view in "The Problem of Violence and the Radical Opposition" (1967), Marcuse, *Five Lectures,* p. 88. But note also *Professor* Marcuse's dubious ethical appeal in this context.

139. If Marcuse is baroque, his followers tend to be rococo. See, for example, the essays in *Critical Interruptions.* In a long piece on "One-Dimensionality: The Universal Semiotic of Technological Experience" (pp. 136–86), Jeremy Shapiro finally comes down to the political question of extending "the community's realm of choice and decision over the entirety of social life in the interest of needs that do not require domination." He offers a "dialectical process of communication" with four central features as the opening onto a viable politics. Here is the first point: "in seeking to reverse the imperatives of the system and let subjectivity predominate over, although remaining within objectivity, it must begin with those areas of choice, decision, and freedom which individuals experience as such, heighten experience of the difference between these areas and those in which there is no choice, show that areas of life that are accepted as pre-given represent

choices among alternatives, and use imagination and education to project means of opening these self-regulating areas to choice." *Etc.,* pp. 181–82.

140. The character of Marcuse's work, suggestive as much of it is, virtually blocks further dialogue, and renders a good deal of the criticism either repetitious or irrelevant. Those who do not accept Marcuse's version of critical theory find it easy to demonstrate the compendium of his flaws. However accurate, such exercises often seem beside the point precisely because of the *obviously* slippery and frequently shoddy texture of Marcuse's thought. As many critics have shown, his readings of major philosophers often ignore the context and intent of their ideas. But this line of investigation quickly degenerates into a game of mirrors; for if the critic allows himself to be caught up in endless comparisons, while refusing to deal with *Marcuse's* Hegel, *Marcuse's* Marx, or *Marcuse's* Freud, he inevitably takes the social theory too seriously—or too lightly—and slights its aesthetic structure and dynamic.

For a good discussion of these difficulties, see Alasdair MacIntyre, *Herbert Marcuse: An Exposition and a Polemic,* p. 141. Unfortunately, MacIntyre is generally better at identifying the critical problems than at unraveling them.

141. With some qualifications, Marx's comment on Proudhon might be applied to Marcuse's utopian position: "He makes a gratuitous assumption and then, as the actual development contradicts his fiction at every step, he concludes that there is a contradiction. He conceals from you the fact that the contradiction exists solely between his fixed ideas and the real movement." *MESW,* p. 674.

142. This assessment, it should be noted, does not include a negative judgment of Marcuse's moral character. He is, to judge from the body of his work, a deeply moral man.

143. Not always, of course. Marcuse is a sophisticated man, capable of comparative assessments. Though he *stresses* comparisons between what is and what (he thinks) could be, he often acknowledges other frames of reference: what is/what was, etc. For two examples of the moderate Marcuse, see Marcuse, "Ethics and Revolution," in Richard T. DeGeorge, *Ethics and Society* (New York: Doubleday & Co., 1966), pp. 133–47 (a lecture, interestingly enough, delivered at the University of Kansas); and Marcuse, "Love Mystified: A Critique of Norman O. Brown," in *Negations,* pp. 227–43.

144. Within the inevitably compromising context of ethical judgment, however, the problem of degree becomes crucially important.

145. See Roszak, *The Making of a Counter Culture*, pp. 92 ff.

146. Breines, ed., *Critical Interruptions*, p. 137.

147. See Marcuse, *An Essay on Liberation*, pp. 3 ff; and *Reason and Revolution*, p. 93: "The world in reality is not as it appears, but as it is comprehended by philosophy." This formulation suggests the ambiguous status of Marcuse's own social theory—part philosophy, part myth—which becomes a kind of fiction.

7 The New Left

1. C. Wright Mills, "The New Left," in Irving Louis Horowitz, ed., *Power, Politics and People* (New York: Ballantine Books, Inc., 1963), p. 259. There is, of course, a vast body of primary and secondary literature on the new Left of the sixties, much of it scattered in small journals and "underground" papers. The best collections of primary materials are found in Massimo Teodori, ed., *The New Left: A Documentary History* (Indianapolis: The Bobbs-Merrill Company, 1969); Paul Jacobs and Saul Landau, *The New Radicals* (New York: Random House, 1966); Mitchell Cohen and Dennis Hale, eds., *The New Student Left* (Boston: Beacon Press, 1966); and Priscilla Long, ed., *The New Left* (Boston: Porter Sargent Publishing, 1969). Among the most interesting interpretations are Ronald Aronson, "The Movement and Its Critics," *Studies on the Left* 6 (January–February 1966): 3–19; Irving Howe, ed., *Beyond the New Left* (New York: McCall Publishing Company, 1970); James Weinstein, "The Left, Old and New," *Socialist Revolution* 10 (July–August 1972): 7–60. Michael P. Lerner, *The New Socialist Revolution* (New York: Dell Publishing Company, 1973). For a Communist point of view, see Gil Green, *The New Radicalism: Anarchist or Marxist* (New York: International Publishers, 1971).

2. Diana Trilling, "On the Steps of Low Library," *Commentary* 46 (November 1968): 55.

3. Barrington Moore, Jr., "Revolution in America?" *New York Review of Books* 12 (January 1969): 10.

4. Greg Calvert and Carol Neiman, *A Disrupted History: The New Left and the New Capitalism* (New York: Random House, 1971), p. 10.

5. Lasch, *The Agony of the American Left* (New York: Alfred A. Knopf, 1969), pp. 180, 182.

6. Elements of the new Left rejected Bell's conservative theory of

historical stasis only to accept Marcuse's radical version a few years later.

7. References to "The Port Huron Statement" are from Paul Jacobs and Saul Landau, *The New Radicals*, pp. 150–62.

8. Tom Hayden, *Rebellion and Repression* (New York and Cleveland: World Publishing Company, 1969), p. 23.

9. Of course, throughout the 1960s, both the black and the white radical movements reacted against the larger forces of American society and culture. The parallel changes in their conceptions of society and politics are, as James O'Brien puts it, "variations on a theme: the recognition that American liberalism was not enough, that the good society was one in which people shaped their own institutions to meet their own needs." "A History of the New Left" (Boston, 1968), p. 1 (pamphlet). For excellent interpretations of the black movement in the sixties, see Harold Cruse, *The Crisis of the Negro Intellectual* (New York: William Morrow and Company, Inc., 1967); *Revolution or Rebellion?* (New York: William Morrow and Company, Inc., 1970); and Lasch, *The Agony of the American Left,* pp. 117–68.

10. Hayden, *Rebellion and Repression,* pp. 23, 24.

11. Ibid., p. 24.

12. Ibid., p. 25.

13. Nathan Glazer, "The New Left and Its Limitations," *Commentary* 46 (July 1968): 39.

14. Several organized efforts to evolve a theory were associated with the movement in the 1960s: SDS's Economic Research and Action Project (ERAP) in 1963; later, the Radical Education Project (REP), which stressed social theory but managed to do little more than reprint the work of older Leftists, foreign and domestic (the writings of plain Marxists, especially Sweezy, were frequently reprinted in this series). A few individuals in the movement—Carl Oglesby, Tom Hayden, Martin Nicolaus, among others—did produce a slim body of proficient social criticism. Moreover, the revival of radicalism stimulated the beginnings of a large body of literature by and about radicals in the universities, some of it good. Some of the most interesting work has been produced by such revisionist historians as Christopher Lasch, Eugene Genovese, and Jesse Lemisch. See Barton J. Bernstein, ed., *Towards a New Past: Dissenting Essays in American History* (New York: Pantheon Books, 1967).

15. Carl Oglesby, "Liberalism and the Corporate State," reprinted in *Monthly Review* 17 (January 1966): 27.

16. For an interesting account of the ideological differences among

the various revolutionary sects—RYM I (Weathermen); RYM II (the SDS national office franchise); the Worker-Student Alliance (a Progressive Labor Party front); and independent revolutionary groups, see Jack Weinberg and Jack Gerson, "The Split in SDS" (New York: International Socialist Pamphlet), 1969.

17. Hayden, *Rebellion and Repression*, p. 17.

18. Quoted in Weinberg and Gerson, "The Split in SDS," p. 5.

19. "Weatherman Conducts a 'War Council,'" *The Guardian* (January 10, 1970): 14. Subsequently, Dohrn repudiated terrorist activity without a "mass base." For a moving portrait of a bright student caught up in the Weathermen's pathology of violence and accidentally killed while working with homemade bombs, see J. Kirk Sale, "Ted Gold: Education for Violence," *Nation* 210 (April 1970): 423–29.

20. For an example of the generally shallow contributions of literary critics to the radicalism of the sixties, see Louis Kampf and Paul Lauter, eds., *Politics of Literature* (New York: Pantheon Books, 1972).

21. Mark Rudd, "Columbia: Notes on the Spring Rebellion," in Carl Oglesby, ed., *The New Left Reader* (New York: Grove Press, 1969), p. 300 (emphasis added).

22. In popular new Left literature, the discussion of socialist countries rarely rises above the level of slogans and clichés. See, for example, back issues of *New Left Notes,* the official SDS publication.

23. Shin'ya Ono, "A Weatherman: You Do Need a Weatherman to Know Which Way the Wind Blows," *Leviathan* 1 (December 1969): 15.

24. Two important studies of student radicals (not confined to the revolutionaries) are Kenneth Keniston, *Young Radicals* (New York: Harcourt Brace Jovanovich, 1968); and Charles Hampden-Turner, *Radical Man* (Cambridge, Mass.: Schenkman Publishing Company, 1970), especially Chapter XII, pp. 349–95. A less enchanted observer of the young radicals than Keniston, Norman Cantor takes the view that "if there was a class basis to the student revolt, it lay in the peculiar character of the suburban middle class, who could offer their children security without power." *The Age of Protest* (San Francisco: Leswing Press, 1969), p. 307.

25. Jerry Rubin, *Do It!* (New York: Simon and Schuster, 1970), p. 116.

26. Ibid., pp. 249, 256.

27. Ibid., p. 256.

28. Abbie Hoffman, *Woodstock Nation: A Talk-Rock Album* (New York: Random House, 1969), p. 8.

29. Ibid., p. 133.

30. Quoted in Sandy Darlington, "Gimme Shelter," *Hard Times* 15 (December 1969): 3.

31. Hoffman, *Woodstock Nation,* p. 10.

32. Ibid., pp. 11–12.

33. Ibid., p. 11.

34. For an interesting biographical sketch of Jerry Rubin, see J. Anthony Lukas, "The Making of a Yippie," *Esquire* 72 (November 1969): 126 ff.

35. Quoted in Gary Wills, "The Making of the Yippie Culture," *Esquire* 72 (November 1969): 135.

8 The Future of Socialism

1. Bernard Rosenberg, "Marxism: Criticism and/or Action," in Irving Howe, ed., *Voices of Dissent* (New York and London: Grove Press, 1958), p. 55.

2. Robert L. Heilbroner, "Roots of the Socialist Dilemma," *Dissent* 19 (Summer 1972): 463–70. See also Svetozar Stojanović, *Between Ideals and Reality: A Critique of Socialism and Its Future* (New York: Oxford University Press, 1973).

3. For an interesting discussion of the elusive concept of exploitation, see Barrington Moore, Jr., *Reflections on the Causes of Human Misery* (Boston: Beacon Press, 1972), pp. 53 ff.

4. In this context, I use the concepts of liberty, equality, and fraternity generally, to include a variety of notions discussed in earlier chapters.

Liberty refers to modes of personal freedom, legal protection of individual rights and various forms of political democracy, all of whose meanings change somewhat within and across social systems.

Equality refers to political, social, and legal mechanisms that help to ensure similar opportunities for every citizen. It also takes on another socioeconomic meaning as distinguished from absolute egalitarianism, which entails equal rewards and the abolition of all social hierarchies. By equality I mean in fact a tendency toward the reduction of inequality (a tendency that should never be fully realized in society). Socialist "equality" is in large measure achieved by the elimination of vast concentrations of private wealth, tolerable income differentials, and a sharply graduated income tax.

Fraternity refers broadly to the range of principles and institutional mechanisms associated with the quest for social ties among people. In the broadest sense, it includes the goal of ending alienation, the idea of community, and the notion of happiness.

5. The metaphor of the social whole is more than ever a fiction. The complexity of modern social organization renders attempts to understand the parts in relation to a dynamic whole highly problematic.

6. Howard Sherman offers a theoretically plausible version of the orthodox argument concerning the gradual transition from socialism to communism, by which he means "an economy of 70 or 80 per cent free consumer goods. . . ." In his view, this ratio would permit the development of certain characteristics of communist man—a less competitive, more social creature. But Sherman does not suggest a plausible politics of transition. See Howard Sherman, *Radical Political Economy* (New York & London: Basic Books, 1972), pp. 334–58.

7. Barrington Moore, Jr., "The Society Nobody Wants," in Kurt H. Wolff and Barrington Moore, Jr., eds., *The Critical Spirit* (Boston: Beacon Press, 1967), p. 402.

8. Leon Trotsky, *Literature and Revolution* (New York: Russell and Russell, 1957), p. 256.

9. Heilbroner, "Roots of the Socialist Dilemma," p. 470.

Index

73 74 75 76 77 10 9 8 7 6 5 4 3 2 1